ROUTLEDGE
COLONIALISM

Volume 18

COLONIAL SEQUENCE
1930 TO 1949

COLONIAL SEQUENCE
1930 TO 1949

A Chronological Commentary upon British Colonial Policy Especially in Africa

MARGERY PERHAM

Routledge
Taylor & Francis Group

LONDON AND NEW YORK

First published in 1967 by Methuen & Co Ltd

This edition first published in 2023
by Routledge
4 Park Square, Milton Park, Abingdon, Oxon OX14 4RN

and by Routledge
605 Third Avenue, New York, NY 10158

Routledge is an imprint of the Taylor & Francis Group, an informa business

British Library Cataloguing in Publication Data
A catalogue record for this book is available from the British Library

ISBN: 978-1-032-41054-8 (Set)
ISBN: 978-1-032-44578-6 (Volume 18) (hbk)
ISBN: 978-1-032-44579-3 (Volume 18) (pbk)
ISBN: 978-1-003-37287-5 (Volume 18) (ebk)

DOI: 10.4324/9781003372875

Publisher's Note
The publisher has gone to great lengths to ensure the quality of this reprint but points out that some imperfections in the original copies may be apparent.

Disclaimer
The publisher has made every effort to trace copyright holders and would welcome correspondence from those they have been unable to trace.

MARGERY PERHAM

Colonial Sequence

1930 to 1949

A CHRONOLOGICAL COMMENTARY UPON
BRITISH COLONIAL POLICY
ESPECIALLY IN AFRICA

METHUEN & CO LTD
11 NEW FETTER LANE LONDON EC4

Distribution in the U.S.A.
by Barnes & Noble, Inc.

Contents

INDEX

Introduction

The publication of these occasional writings needs explanation and, I think, apology. The proposal came from a firm of publishers. I received it with surprise and some hesitation. It was only when I looked through the list of what I had published over thirty-five years that I realized that the collection might have an interest in addition to, or even apart from, any great intrinsic merit in the writings themselves. This interest could be in the serial impression made upon a single mind by the evolution of Britain's colonial policy and government over a long series of years, and these among the most important in our imperial record when the colonial empire at once reached its greatest extent and moved to its end with unforeseen rapidity and completeness. The main concentration in what follows is upon Britain's changing relations with Africa where our power has been at once so extensive, so complete and so brief.

The collection which follows, covering the years 1930 to 1949, has another adventitious merit beside that of continuity. I was fortunate enough, through the generous provision of the Rhodes Trust, the Rockefeller Foundation and, later, of my own College, Nuffield, to alternate study in Britain with frequent travels abroad. These travels enabled me to check what I could learn from books, lectures and periodicals with the actualities of administration in the field. This kind of alternation later became the usual routine for students of African affairs, especially for our rich American cousins, but in the thirties and forties it was a more unusual privilege. While I like to think that the writings that follow are in the main autonomous they must in some measure reflect the current ideas of the officials of the Colonial Service whose work, from that of governors down to that of assistant district commissioners, I was enabled to study. These men, with very rare exceptions, met even my earliest and most inexpert investigations with frankness and the practical help I needed. They provided hospitality from that of Government House to the mud and thatch rest-house or the tent and porterage of the *safari* through the bush. It may be that, in earlier days, when communications were bad and there was, relatively to more recent years, less interest and understanding directed to their work, these officials welcomed an inquiring visitor. My debt towards those who educated me extends to missionaries and, of course, to Africans, though in the earlier years covered by this volume few of these outside the West Coast towns were yet ready to define and discuss the problems of their colonial status.

The colonial record has to be read in the light of the total situation of the ruling power which in turn must be seen in its world context. It is a truism that the years since the first World War have seen more fundamental changes in the affairs of men than any other period of the same length, and that the velocity of change has been rising. A major reason for this acceleration has been the growth of communications. Men no longer remain enclosed within their own country or even their own continent; they have become increasingly sentient members of a world in which any major change directly affects and, too often, endangers them. The most prosperous and highly organized nations are the most conscious of both the new opportunities and the new dangers of the world. When they extended their spheres of power and influences over the isolated and tribal peoples, they brought with them the fruit from the tree of knowledge of the world which they could not long withhold from their new subjects even if they had wished to do so. But the colonial peoples could only attain knowledge of the good and evil of their colonial status and of the world of which it formed a part when a sufficient number of them had mastered the language of their rulers and some of the knowledge to which it was the key. The peoples of the Asian and American continents fell under Western domination or influence before the period of accelerating change. But for most of tropical Africa the really effective penetration, with the full development of administrative and economic power and of Western education, began only during the post-1918 period and did not reach full intensity, outside limited areas, until the second World War. The influence of the West was at its strongest when it was on the edge of losing its near monopoly of power. Increasingly in the forties and fifties, the major colonial nations and the world in general began to realize the great relative reduction in their power which had resulted from the second World War.

I have recalled these well-known facts so that we may characterize the period covered by these collected articles. During most of the thirties and for most of Africa, coming events cast only a faint shadow over Britain's work in the continent. In the twenties, and even in most of the thirties, the government of Africa was carried on as a leisurely, distant and specialized operation. The affairs of the colonies, and especially of Africa, always excepting contentious Kenya, could be regarded as a very subsidiary theme in the main plot of Britain's external activities. It is an enlightening test to look up 'Africa' or the colonies, individually or generally, in the indexes of such serious textbooks as Professor Mowat's *Britain between the Wars, 1918–1940* or Mr A. J. P. Taylor's *English History, 1914–1945*. Much of tropical Africa, always excepting Kenya, was largely quiescent during the inter-war years and even for a time after the second war. It was the sudden and rapidly accelerating demand of African leaders for independence during the fifties, followed by the clamant international assertions and economic demands of the new ex-colonial nations, which have concentrated British and, indeed, much of world attention upon this so-called third world and especially upon Africa. Since then this continent has demanded attention upon an increasingly deep and universal level as the separate areas of social tension and conflict in the world between the white and the dark peoples have spread and mingled until they have become one many-sided racial issue, with the new African nations leading in protest and assertion.

The main thrust of the African colonies towards independence came after the second World War but it did not gain effective strength until the fifties. The years of peace and of war covered in this volume were, though this was not realized, the seminal period for the later exuberant growth of nationalism or, less inaccurately, Africanism. This growth has been rapid and clamorous, expressed in a denunciation of the colonial régime which was essential to Africans both as a political springboard and as a racial assertion. There were many other nations, some with an ex-colonial background, some committed to Communism, who had an interest in supporting and indeed intensifying the anti-colonial case. The preceding colonial period has therefore been flooded with a harsh retrospective light. In this light the African tribes are seen as nations held down by an oppressive colonialism, and the victims of selfish economic exploitation. It is not easy to correct this politically useful image. The menacing pressures of international problems upon the active generation today are so heavy that few have leisure to consider the genesis of the situations with which they have to deal. Yesterday is often the most obscure period of history. Yet the colonial episode, especially in equatorial Africa, has been so brief that its total survey would not seem to demand too much time or trouble. The earlier quiescence of the colonies, and the policies which this quiescence and the sense of a very long time for the colonial task induced, are subjects vital to an understanding of their sudden and increasingly clamant assertion during the last ten years. This earlier political somnolence of most of the

African peoples under British rule was reflected in the complementary conviction of the ruler that 'self-government' – 'independence' in the present sense being then unimaginable – was so far away that its prospect could have little or no influence upon current administrative plans. I have found it difficult in recent lecturing and writing to bring home to those, whether African, British or American, who have been concerned with the affairs of the continent in the last ten or fifteen years, the governing importance of this time factor.

The policy of gradualism reflected the realities of Africa as the British saw them during the process of acquisition in the closing years of the last century and in the earlier decades of this one. The passivity upon our side was a reflection of the inability of all but a few score of Africans to understand the full significance of their having become part not only of an empire but of a world which, at a much later date, was to show itself increasingly full of meaning for them. The Colonial Service, exiles from their own country, very thin upon the ground, and chosen rather more for character than intellect, had to carry on their many-sided work with little stimulus either of metropolitan interest from above or of effective pressure from below. Men, that is groups of men, do not act without some external stimulus: they do not make plans for the unimaginable. The Colonial Service was, moreover, dealing with societies which were numerous, heterogeneous and incommensurable with anything in their own national experience. I must have met hundreds of these men, some of them working alone in remote, backward and unhealthy districts, and the great majority of them struck me as hardworking, keen, humane and, perhaps I need hardly say, uncorrupt. But few had any urgent sense of working against time. I hope that my close nexus in this period with the ideas of the Colonial Service, either by studying their actions or their writings, or by dealing at Oxford with the officials sent there for special courses after a few years' service, has not given too official a colour to my views. My base was in this country and if I can claim any continuous theme running through these articles, it is their reflection of Britain's changing conception of the colonial task, a slow development at first, the pace increasing with the second war. Its aftermath, culminating in the recent almost convulsive adjustment to African demands for complete independence, lies beyond the date with which this collection ends.

It may be objected that even in the first quarter of this century there were seers and prophets to whom British opinion should have been more responsive, among them A. J. Hobson, E. D. Morel, Leonard

Woolf – still with us – and others. But in this period the condemnations of imperialism were often theoretical, reflecting or adapting Marxist principles, negative in their teaching, sometimes faulty even in their economics. Such views were regarded as utterly inapplicable by those most concerned at home and abroad with the struggle to bring the beginnings of Western law, order, education and economic development to what seemed to them the gross poverty and disorder of tribal Africa. It was only as the left-wing critics, with the Labour Party's growing hopes of exercising power, became more knowledgeable and reformist, and as an increasing number of educated Africans entered into a dialogue with them, that the possibilities of advance by stages towards self-government took practical shape. It was then overwhelmed by a new wave of impulsion towards immediate and complete independence. It should be remembered that although Liberal and Socialist politicians and writers played a major part in the forward movement of thought it was never their monopoly. There was liberalism of this kind on the Conservative side and among persons of thought and action with little political affiliation, including some men of high authority in the Colonial Service.

To make the collected articles which follow more intelligible and to show where I stood, or rather, I hope, moved, in this progression of thought, I must supply a minimum of biographical background. I had been romantically drawn to Africa as a child by early reading of hunting stories and of Rider Haggard's novels. The interest became more substantial when my elder sister went to East Africa and, in 1911, married a man who, going north after fighting in the South African War, had enjoyed an adventurous career exploring, fighting and hunting with the famous 'Karamoja Bell' in the then almost undemarcated and unadministered wilds of the regions of the Upper Nile. Major Rayne, deciding to settle down, took his wife to live in one of Africa's wildest regions, the lion-infested banks of the Juba River, then the northern frontier of the Protectorate of East Africa. He experimented with cotton cultivation until the 1914–18 war recalled him to fight in East Africa, after which he joined the Colonial Service and was posted to administer in the same part of Jubaland. Here my sister and her first two infants were cut off by the rebellious local Somali tribe and her husband's assistant district officer was speared to death by them. After this Major Rayne returned for a time to the army to fight in the final and victorious campaign against the Mad Mullah in British Somaliland and stayed on in that arid dependency in the Colonial Service. Thus it was that soon after I left Oxford I went out with my sister to British Somaliland, only to be met on landing with the news that the tribes were 'up' in the hinterland to which we were bound and that her husband had only just escaped with his life as he ran down a dry watercourse with a fellow commissioner who was killed beside him. A little later the governor, rather hesitantly, allowed us to go up-country – the first white women to live on this Ethiopian border where we occupied the first European-style house built at Hargeisa, close to the camp of the Camel Corps. I was able to trek on camel and mule with my brother-in-law along the frontier in a region still, to my great joy, marked 'unexplored' on the map, meeting trekking Somalis who had never seen a white person, and with our camps at night endangered by lions. As a further excitement, the struggle of the Muslim Lij Yasu for the Ethiopian throne of the King of Kings, spilled over on to our side with his attempt to incite the Somalis of the Camel Corps to mutiny and kill their officers, and, of course, ourselves. Runaway slaves from Ethiopia flung themselves at our feet imploring us to let them stay and work with us for a minimum of food in order to save themselves from mutilation or worse if they should be sent back. To add to the dangers of wild men and wild beasts, a killing drought struck the already arid region. I have recalled these biographical facts to show that my first knowledge and experience of Africa was of the continent at its wildest and most dangerous, the Africa which dictated the character of much of Britain's earlier administration.

I did not get back to Africa for a few years as I was earning my living as a university teacher at Sheffield and Oxford. But when I did I could still find some of the old harsh, almost unchanged Africa in north-eastern Nigeria, round Lake Chad. On the hills of that region and in the southern Sudan I saw the still-naked pagans who had been driven to live on their terraced rocks to escape the centuries' old slave-raiding of their Muslim neighbours: they either fled at my approach or flung themselves at my feet pouring earth on their heads. Over the remoter parts of this tropical Africa of the early thirties European rule had still done little more than stop slave-raiding and inter-tribal war; it had checked ritual murder or the killing of witches and twins, and alleviated famine, sleeping sickness, rinderpest and other dramatic scourges. But even in south-eastern Nigeria I read court records of cannibalism, sometimes carried out for magical purposes upon a commercial scale.

It was not only the Africa of the twenties and thirties which stamped some of its grim realities upon my mind. I was also made very much aware of the still earlier Africa reaching back to the nineties. This was because in 1929 I made a contact, which was to have important results for me, with Lord Lugard. In talking with him and reading his writings I was able to visualize the ravages of inter-tribal wars and of Arab and African slave-raiding in an Africa which was, after all, only a few decades earlier than the one I knew.

These early and deep impressions may explain not only my own first attitude to Africa, and especially to its problems of government, but also those which were widely held by many concerned with the continent and which are reflected in the earlier writings collected in this book. Today the tendency is to forget the Africa of yesterday or, learning from the new generation of archaeologists allied with historians and ethnologists – some of them African – to trace, behind the superficial crudities of black and pagan Africa, the lineaments here and there of civilizations, ancient, varied, shifting, obscure, isolated, but claiming our respect now that we have at last the key to their value.

It follows that as one of the earlier generation of students of African government I know that I am open to the rebukes of many people, including not only this new school of scholarly interpreters of the past, but also of the new African leaders and writers. For these last their individual self-respect and their necessary cult of a new pride and self-confidence, both regional and continental, political and racial, alike demand the support of a high concept of the African civilization which, they claim, colonial nations have both injured and defamed. What the politician believes, still more what he makes his people believe, is of the highest importance; it supplies the motive power by which he evokes and directs political action. As students, seeking the truth as far as our own knowledge and prejudices allow, we must I think admit that exaggeration and misunderstanding were not only upon one side but that in the earlier years of acquisition and administration in Africa Western pioneers and officials were often inclined to interpret African culture in the light of their interest in imposing and retaining power. They failed to see that naked tribes, ruled by chiefs dressed in skins, could reflect, for all their small scale and their material poverty, the essential realities of politics and breed characters with a full equipment of the virtues, and of course, the vices, of the human potential.

This recognition of African humanity and so of its rights might have checked the harshness of some of the earlier contacts between tribes and British agents but it could hardly have led to a full understanding of the hundreds of African societies, many of which still await the interpretation of skilled research. And it is surely not historically valid, however politically useful, to condemn an earlier generation for not acting upon knowledge which they could not have possessed. African ethno-history is still being published in its first instalments. Yet many early administrators did try to respect societies of which they could understand little below the external manifestations evoked by their mutual contact. This led them, in various places and in many different ways, and not only in Africa, to try to study these societies and to preserve them in a subsidiary working alliance with their own new foreign and overriding control. This policy, in which economy often reinforced humanity, has been called that of protectorate or over-rule. It was most successful in action and most fully developed in practice, legal definition and theory by Lord Lugard in Northern Nigeria. Here, as the tide of colonial power recedes, the historic Muslim emirates emerge from the flood changed – not only developed but in some measure reformed – and yet substantially the same in their various sizes and structures, their religion, disciplines and loyalties, as when they submitted so easily to the quick and sudden stroke of British power less then seventy years ago.

A substantial literature has developed about indirect rule in its original locus, its extension elsewhere and its relationship with similar but not identical administrative expedients. The indirect method certainly suited the colonial rulers, short as they were of staff and money as well as knowledge. But they also found it impressively viable in earlier relationships and in favourable contexts where African societies still retained not only their outward form but some of their original vitality. Wide generalizations, whether of praise or condemnation, are not appropriate in a continent embracing political units of such immense variety in size and character and to one passing through such rapid changes in its brief tenure by colonial power. I have said this much because a number of the earlier articles collected in this book deal with this subject of indirect administration, or reflect what may be called that indirect approach, which later seemed to Western-educated Africans to bar their direct approach to national self-government. It seemed to me important, even at the cost of some repetition, to recall the ideas dominating African administration in the thirties which reflect the optimism, indeed enthusiasm of these years, about the indirect principle.

When reading these earlier articles the background of time and place should be remembered. I reached Tanganyika by way of several regions where I had been deeply depressed to find that little or no principle governed native administration. In the Union and in Southern Rhodesia

B

Africans were regarded mainly as labour. I met some humane and well-informed officials but on the whole there was little attempt on the part of the authorities to see Africans either as individual persons or as members of tribal societies not yet wholly destroyed. In the High Commission Territories, in spite of the greater liberalism and respect for African societies, there was little or no constructive policy to adapt them to changing trends and it was tragic to see a chief of the character and ability of Tshekedi Khama being embittered by prejudice and neglect. It will therefore be understood that on arrival in Tanganyika the contrast in the administrative situation was exhilarating. Here was something quite new to me, a set of constructive, forward-looking principles, drawn very largely from the work and teaching of Lord Lugard, and intelligently based not only upon a respect for Africans and their societies as they were, but as they could be helped to become. The Governor, Sir Donald Cameron, who was my host, and his Secretary for Native Affairs, Sir Philip Mitchell, whom I accompanied upon some of his official travels, both men of strong character and great intelligence, were enthusiastic practitioners of the indirect rule principle. I make no apology for my having been deeply impressed by their policy or for my attempts then and for some years afterwards to interpret indirect rule in my writings. I thought it would be of interest to include the talk I gave on the subject at the Royal Society of Arts along with the discussion in which several people then prominent in African affairs, including Lord Lugard himself, and some critical Africans, made contributions.

The thirties may be regarded as the great decade of indirect rule over much of British Africa and, indeed, beyond. Of course no one principle could embrace a continent containing not only such an immense variety of groups but also subject to such strong and variable new influences falling unevenly upon regions, tribes and even generations within tribes. Yet administrative officers, with ever-growing duties, and constant changes of posting, had to work to some accepted pattern and most African societies were misleadingly malleable on the surface while remaining obscure in their deeper levels. Increasingly during the forties, however, it was realized that the new Africa was bursting out of the old administrative shell and that 'the educated African' was not a disruptive exception but a representative portent, one already capable in some places of undermining a system which excluded him. Because 'indirect rule' had been so dominant and had too long outlived its usefulness, the tendency among converts to new methods was to denounce it with the peculiar energy applied to heresies by the converted and to forget the measure of practical success it had achieved at a certain stage in certain places. Perhaps we can see now that in the unprecedented conditions created by Europe's penetration of Africa no wholly successful method of government could have been devised either by Europeans or Africans, if indeed either side could have given any continuous content to the word 'success'.

Readers may be inclined to smile at what may seem to them in places the uncritical, unforeseeing commendation with which, in the thirties, I reported upon indirect rule. But what I said may be a useful reminder to us in these days of much more uncritical and inclusive condemnation of Britain's administration, in spite of its wide variations in time and place, under the blanket terms of colonialism and imperialism. The earlier articles in this collection will at best bear witness to the sympathy and respect with which our officials approached African society, and therefore its members. Critics should be asked what better method should have been applied at a time when the great majority of African tribes still maintained much of their vitality and separatism. I think I can claim to have recognized that the indirect principle was not universally applicable. To the surprise both of the Colonial Service and of the majority of the Africans themselves the outer world, with its powerful economic forces and political ideas, broke in upon Africa's long isolated world, so that rapid adjustments were needed. These the colonial governments were not always quick enough to make. It was of course easier for the travelling critic to recognize these forces than it was for a service, scattered about Africa, more of its members in the bush than in the few towns or among the tribes most exposed to the new forces. It may well be that from the vantage point of the latest evidence about Africa, we may judge that tribalism was ˊnot a force that should have been ignored, still less repressed, especially by a service in which European officials, who were to be counted at first in scores and later in hundreds and often inevitably ignorant of the many tribal languages, were in charge of Africans numbering millions.

The other main theme covered in the collection of writings in this book is, of course, supplied by the second World War. As far as the British Empire was concerned the stroke of conflict fell upon south-east Asia and north-east Africa. The German occupation of France and the fluctuating campaigns on the Mediterranean coast had effects which ran deeply into the tropical African hinterland. Most of French tropical Africa was held by the captive French government: only the poorer equatorial group remained, like the Belgian Congo, with the Allies, though shorn of metropolitan government. Egypt, for the second time, became an unwilling Allied base. The Western powers, and especially Britain, now suffered for their acquiescence in Italy's rape of Ethiopia. The Sudan was in peril. British Somaliland was overrun. An arduous reconquest had to be undertaken by Britain with forces which included troops and labour units from many parts of tropical Africa. African troops went on to play their part in driving the Japanese out of south-east Asia.

The military operations could be followed on the maps of the three continents involved. The economic strains, still more the immediate political effects of division and defeat upon the colonial powers, were rather harder to assess. Deeper still, as we have seen, and only coming to the surface in Africa during the next ten years, were the effects of these conflicts and losses upon the minds of men, both rulers and ruled. But that is a sequel which is only just becoming apparent in the last years covered by this political anthology.

The war confined me to Britain. Here there were many tasks to be done, more or less related to the war. Among them, at the instance of the Foreign Office, was a historical and political study of Ethiopia, carried out in co-operation with writers dealing with other aspects. This country had suddenly become of major importance to Britain and background information about it was found to be inadequate. The war was, indeed, a stimulus to research in a number of directions. It was realized that its stresses and losses would need the remedy of new constitutional policies for which preparation must be made before peace should break out. Nuffield College, founded in 1939 though still not physically erected, gave the opportunity and the resources to direct a series of studies of colonial constitutions. Another field which had to be prepared for post-war growth – indeed in many regions for a first planting – was that of higher education. In Africa this was almost a virgin field. So the work of successive bodies was begun – Colonial Office Advisory Committee, its higher education sub-committee, Asquith Commission, travelling committees to West Africa and the West Indies, Inter-University Council. As a member of these bodies, except for West Africa, I was able to take part in this new and exciting programme. With the Vice-Chancellors of St. Andrews and Birmingham Universities, I flew out to the West Indies through the military sphere, following a roundabout route via Portugal, Dakar, Brazil, Venezuela and so to Trinidad and the other islands. With help from West Indians we recommended the foundation of a University of the West Indies in

Jamaica. This was followed for me by an attempt under the British Information Service to lecture Americans, now in the war and already thinking of terms for peace, out of their dark suspicions of British imperialism, past and prospective.

The collection ends with the Anglo-Egyptian Sudan, the first British Colonial territory – for such in fact it was – reaching out towards independence and with a general survey of the coming problems of Colonial emancipation as they appeared to me in 1949.

Oxford, April 1967   MARGERY PERHAM

Notes and Acknowledgements

With this much explanation these occasional writings must speak for themselves in the political and administrative contexts of their dates. Some editorial comments are needed. The items are printed without correction except for that of some very minor errors of fact or of grammar arising from the haste and compression of their writing. I have refrained from all but the most essential introductory explanations while footnotes are at a minimum. For articles from *The Times* sub-headings have been removed. Some leading articles which provide background or illuminating comment have, with the permission of *The Times*, been included. Some letters to *The Times* have been printed as brief evidence upon current controversies but they, too, have been left to speak for themselves with little or no background. I have added a brief chronology of the main events in the colonial and especially the African sphere.

Acknowledgements must be made to *The Times* for permission to reproduce not only my own letters and articles but six of their own leading articles commenting upon these. Acknowledgements for permission to reprint material are also due to *The Listener*, *The Spectator*, *Foreign Affairs*, Faber & Faber Ltd., the Oxford University Press, the Royal Society of Arts and *Africa*.

Chronological Table

Year	Colonial Secretary	General Events	African Events
1930	Lord Passfield [*June* Dominion affairs separated from Colonial under J. H. Thomas]	World Economic Depression 1930–31	*June* White Papers on Closer Union in East Africa and on Native Policy in East Africa
1931	*August* J. H. Thomas [*August* Statute of Westminster] *Nov.* Sir Philip Cunliffe-Lister		*Nov.* Report of Joint Select Committee on Closer Union in East Africa defines 'paramountcy of native interests'
1932			*June* Moyne Financial Report on Kenya *Dec.* Discovery of gold in Kakamega in Kenya
1934			*May* Morris Carter Land Commission Report on Kenya
1935	*June* Malcolm MacDonald *Nov.* J. H. Thomas		*May* Copperbelt riots in N. Rhodesia *Oct.* Italy invades Ethiopia
1936	*May* W. Ormsby-Gore		*August* Anglo-Egyptian Treaty of Friendship *Sept.* Pim Report on Finance in Kenya
1937			*Sept.* Report of Commission on Higher Education in E.A.
1938	*April* Malcolm MacDonald		Publication of Lord Hailey's *An African Survey*

Year	Colonial Secretary	General Events	African Events
1939		*Sept.* World War	*March* Bledisloe Report on Federation in Central Africa
1940	*May* Lord Lloyd	Capitulation of France	*April* Copperbelt riots *June* Italy invades Somaliland *August* Proclamation of Free France in Equatorial Africa
1941	*Jan.* Lord Moyne	*Dec.* U.S.A. enters war	Ethiopia and British Somaliland recovered from Italians
1942	*Feb.* Viscount Cranborne *Nov.* Col. Oliver Stanley		
1944			*May* Advisory Committee for N. Sudan established
1945	*July* G. H. Hall	World War ends	Report of Asquith Commission on Higher Education in Colonies
1946	*Oct.* A. Creech-Jones		Tanganyika and Cameroons placed under United Nations Trusteeship Anglo-Egyptian Treaty over Sudan fails
1948			East Africa High Commission begins to operate. Executive Council and Leg. Assembly set up in Sudan *May* Dr Malan into power in S. Africa

Bibliography of works by Margery Perham
1935-66

1935 With Lionel Curtis, *The Protectorates of South Africa*, London, pp. 119.

1936 *Ten Africans*, London, pp. 356. Editor. Reprinted 1963

1937 *Native Administration in Nigeria*, London, pp. 404. Reprinted 1962.

1941 *Africans and British Rule*, London, pp. 98.

1942 *The Colonies*, Reprinted from *The Times*, London, pp. 24.

1942 With Jack Simmons, pp. 247 *African Discovery*. Reprinted 1963.

1944 With Elspeth Huxley, *Race and Politics in Kenya*. A correspondence between E. Huxley and M. Perham, London, pp. 247, rev. edition 1956, pp. 302.

1948 *The Government of Ethiopia*, London, pp. 481. New Edition forthcoming.

1956 *Lugard: The Years of Adventure 1858–1898*. The First Part of the Life of Frederick Dealtry Lugard, later Lord Lugard of Abinger, London, pp. 750.

1959 With Mary Bull, Editors, *The Diaries of Lord Lugard*, Vols. 1–3 East Africa 1889–1892, London, pp. 432; 481; 454.

1960 *Lugard: The Years of Authority 1898–1945*. The Second Part of the Life of Frederick Dealtry Lugard, later Lord Lugard of Abinger, London, pp. 748.

1961 *The Colonial Reckoning* (An Expanded Version of the Reith Lectures), London, pp. 160.

1963 With Mary Bull, Editors, *The Diaries of Lord Lugard*, Vol. 4. 444 pp.

1966 *African Outline* (An Expanded version of 4 Talks given on the B.B.C. Third Programme 1965) London.

White Rule in Samoa

In the late summer of 1929 I visited the Samoan islands. Tutuila and three small islands had been ruled by America since 1889; Upolu and Savai'i were allotted under mandate to New Zealand after the 1914-18 war during which they were taken from the Germans. I went there, after visiting Hawaii and Fiji, largely because I thought it would be interesting to investigate the troubles reported in both the Samoan groups. I was able to begin inquiries into America's problems in Washington and San Francisco, where I met some of the Samoan dissidents. I had some difficulty in disembarking at the American naval base of Pango Pango and lived for a time in a hut with the Samoans. I had difficulties also in and around Apia, where the 'rebels' appeared to range close to this town which was the administrative head-quarters. Upon reaching Africa I wrote two articles upon Samoa, the first of my writings to be published in The Times. *They appeared on April 10 and 11 and were accompanied by the following leading article which gives some of the background.*

The Times Leader 11 April 1930

THE ART OF GOVERNING SAMOANS

The difficulties of the New Zealand Government in Samoa have grown markedly less in the last few weeks. In December there was a serious riot, in which one policeman and nine Samoans lost their lives, on the occasion of the return from deportation of one of the white leaders of the Mau who had been involved in the first outbreak in 1927. After the riot the New Zealand Government acted with decision; a cruiser was sent; the training of a special military police force was put in hand; and the Mau was proclaimed a seditious organization and driven to surrender after some weeks of wandering in the bush. But these measures were followed by gentle words and an invitation to the Samoan chiefs to confer, and during March a good deal of progress was made towards re-establishing good relations. As the impressions published yesterday from the pen of a Rhodes Travelling Fellow suggest, there has always been a lighter, often a fantastic, side to the campaign against the New

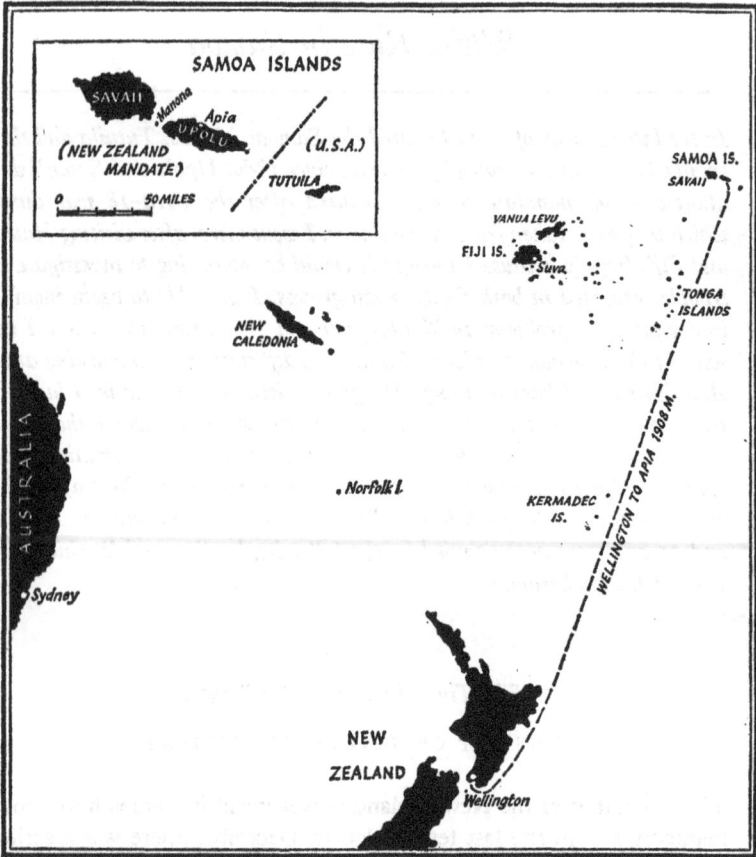

SAMOA ISLANDS

SAVAII

Manona

Apia

UPOLU

(NEW ZEALAND MANDATE)

(U.S.A.)

0   50 MILES

TUTUILA

SAMOA IS.

SAVAII

VANUA LEVU

FIJI IS.

Suva

TONGA ISLANDS

NEW CALEDONIA

Norfolk I.

KERMADEC IS.

WELLINGTON TO APIA 1906 M.

AUSTRALIA

Sydney

NEW ZEALAND

Wellington

1 *Samoa*

Zealand administration, which has redeemed episodes that read over-heavily in print. The administrator and the Samoans are now pledged to make a new start together, frankly changing those arrangements – in particular the constitution of the advisory Parliament, or Fono of Faipules – which have worked badly in the past. The trouble has been primarily a conflict of temperaments. In the early days of the Mandate the New Zealand administration made powerful enemies among the copra merchants by raising the price paid to the native producers. But those enemies would not have achieved their success if there had not been a good deal that was uncongenial to the Samoans in the methods and

manners of their new rulers. A recent commission from New Zealand
has criticized in outspoken terms the manner in which government
appointments in Samoa were filled in the early days of the Mandate. The
concrete results – in the way of health improvement, for instance – that
won for New Zealand special compliments from the Mandates Commission, had their unfortunate side when zeal for measurable triumphs
led to haste and impatience with cherished and traditional Samoan ways.
Samoans are not alone in being temperamental in the presence of social
reformers bent on their improvement, but their recalcitrance has been
an irritating mystery to many New Zealanders conscious that their
country is endeavouring, at considerable expense, to establish a high
tradition of disinterested rule. There is special significance in the
expressed opinion of Sir Apirana Ngata, the Maori statesman, that, if
only the dignity of both parties can be saved, all should yet be well. It
was probably the successful avoidance of any Maori problem in New
Zealand that made the administration over-confident about Samoa, and
certainly too little attention seems to have been paid to the punctilios
which the Samoans, separated from the Maoris for a thousand years,
have developed and cherish, for their sunny good nature is combined
with a deep pride. In short, successful rule in Samoa is chiefly a matter
of touch. Nature has done so much for the Samoans that there is no
need of the regimentation that less fortunate peoples must endure, and
the martinet is as much out of place as the central heater.

If lovers of round statements can say that the rule of New Zealand
has been the right thing being done in the wrong way, they can also say
that American Samoa shows the wrong thing being done in the right
way. Theoretically direct rule by the American Navy sounds unpromis-
ing. It might have been expected to lead to all sorts of trouble analogous
to the troubles that have so commonly followed the appearance of
American marines as the government in various parts of the Caribbean.
As a matter of fact, as this morning's article bears further witness, things
have gone remarkably well in American Samoa, and it is probable that
more elaborate and orthodox constitutional arrangements would have
produced less happy results by creating a number of new relationships
each with its possibilities for the taking of umbrage and the giving of
offence. If New Zealand may hope to be emerging from her troubles in
Samoa, America has still to steer clear of the danger of creating gratui-
tous troubles for herself. The tide is set strongly in the United States
today in the direction of organizing everything as thoroughly and scien-
tifically as possible, and Samoa could not expect to escape indefinitely.

The fields of political theory and of applied sociology have been cultivated of recent years, eagerly and laboriously, by innumerable American Professors with a deferred taste for public life and recollections of
the career of Woodrow Wilson; and the range and number of what are
called government sciences have been eagerly extended by many zealous
pioneers and by not a few pretenders and charlatans. There are plenty
of theorists, longing to play with Samoa, from whom the strong arm of
the United States Navy has so far protected the islanders. Congress has
now appointed a Committee, headed by two distinguished Senators, to
look into the constitutional anomaly of Samoa and to strive to better
what is already well. But common sense is not likely drastically to alter,
for no compelling reason, arrangements which seem to suit a people at
once so delightful and so incalculable.

The Times 10 and 11 April 1930

1. Difficulties of the Mandate

It is not easy to understand why the Samoans seem unable to reconcile
themselves to the Mandatory government of New Zealand. The territory
is small; the natives have the reputation of being the most amiable in the
world; no one questions that New Zealand has conceived her obligation
in humane and liberal terms. Yet the history of the last three and a half
years has been one of sullen passive resistance culminating in January
in serious disorders. Even those who have studied the literature of the
controversy may wonder whether, behind the multitude of causes,
occasions and personalities there put forward, some single all-explaining
factor is not being obscured. The suspicion is reinforced when it is
remembered that, a few miles away, those islands of the group that are
under the American flag live in comparative loyalty and order.

  I recently visited the islands and New Zealand and met many of those
most closely concerned with the administration of the islands and some
of the leading members of the Mau, or opposition party. In Western
Samoa I found a situation that must be unique in the history of native
government. It was difficult to know which to admire more, the restraint
of the administration or the moderation of its opponents.

  The Mau had gained the allegiance of two-thirds of the inhabitants,
its directing committee was gathering taxes, exercising jurisdiction, and
refusing the invitations of the government to meet and discuss grievances.
A body of specially imported police, scattered in twos and threes through

the islands, was being resisted in the duty of making arrests by crowds of armed villagers and largely reduced to helplessness. The government has been forced to abandon direct taxation, a significant surrender with a primitive people. Until January the tension had not issued in bloodshed; on the contrary, certain rules had been tacitly agreed upon which allowed the life of the community to proceed almost on normal lines.

There was even an element of farce in the situation that will be familiar to readers of the 'Vailima Letters' and the 'Footnote to History'. The police, having abandoned an arrest in the face of crowds of apparently infuriated villagers, might be entertained to chicken and the national drink of kava. A visitor like myself could wander where the King's writ no longer ran, sure of courtesy and hospitality. The story is told of the first visit of warships when a large number of members of the Mau were rounded up upon a point of land near Apia and held there by means of wire and sentries. The barrier was clearly inadequate, and, when heads were counted in the morning, it was found that there was a difference of about a hundred. But it was not, as it would have been in any other country in the world, a hundred less, but a hundred more.

This atmosphere of comedy suggests the first of the special difficulties that have faced the Mandatory government. The Samoans, with all their charm, are not easy to rule. Few peoples in the world can be so enriched by nature, which supplies fish, bread-fruit and coconuts at their very doors and they have the wilfulness and independence of the rich. They have leisure, too, in which to dance, to sing and weave garlands, to go on visits, one whole village to another, to play brighter cricket than our reformers ever imagined, and, above all, to talk politics and organize parties. The complacency of the insular is theirs, enhanced by remoteness and ignorance. When a Samoan was shown a map of the world, with his islands a few pricks on the expanse of the Pacific, he remarked, with a look of incredulity and scorn, that he would like to know who made that map.

His contacts with the white man have hardly been of a kind to correct these tendencies. The islands are supremely beautiful; story-writers have exhausted their vocabularies without doing them justice; but they seem to have a magic which makes the white man look always slightly ridiculous, like a clown in fairyland. It is impossible not to smile with Stevenson at the scuffles of the consuls. The white man has too often shown his greed and folly, rather than his strength and wisdom. The Samoan has seen several changes of government; he has watched a punitive international Armada pounded to scrap-iron against his reefs, while he magnanimously fished out the survivors; he has been taught to regard himself complacently as a centre of European diplomacy.

All this was no healthy apprenticeship to subjection, as Germany soon learned. Fourteen years was all she had in which to establish her rule, which, excellent in parts, was yet marked with recurrent feverish symptoms – native opposition, banishments of chiefs, visits of warships, appeals over the head of the Governor to the Parliament in Berlin. It is, perhaps, small wonder that the Samoan saw no reason to re-write his decision: 'God made the Samoans first, then the Tongans, then white men and pigs.'

Another difficulty inherent in the situation was the position of the half-caste, who retains his links with both races. He is peculiar to the Pacific and embarrassing to the government. It was this that enabled the rich half-caste trader, Mr Nelson, to combine in his own person the leadership of three communities.

Such have been New Zealand's difficulties. But native government all over the world presents its local problems: is New Zealand to be acquitted of all fault on the ground that hers were peculiarly insoluble? It seemed impossible, when studying the situation on the spot, to come to any other conclusion than that New Zealand had committed one fault, that of being inexperienced. To put this forward as the underlying reason may appear, at first sight, to state the obvious and to be a most unhelpful suggestion. Yet, if lessons are to be learned from past failure, it is important to analyse the results of inexperience.

It is better, perhaps, to pass over quickly these results so far as they were shown in New Zealand itself by those directly responsible for the administration, by Parliament and the people generally. It has been said that a democracy cannot govern an empire. Certainly it is hard for a small democracy to govern a small empire, and it seems an excess of zeal to list the inevitable mistakes. It is enough to say that they led to hesitation and inconsistency; Samoa became all too much a party matter; every event in the islands found immediate echo in New Zealand, and New Zealand's response re-echoed back in the islands.

There is, however, one result of inexperience upon which it is important to dwell. It is a characteristic of colonial society to undervalue the expert in government, and there is no more expert branch than the administration of a native community, especially one so complex, aristocratic, and sensitive as the Samoans. To succeed it was necessary to attract the pick of the character and brains of the country, and then to hold back constructive schemes until they had served their apprenticeship. New Zealand in the flush of good intentions, conscious that under the mandate system the eyes of the world were upon her, confident that her success with one Polynesian race was pledge of her success with another (an assumption which ignored radical differences in their position), seems to have overlooked the fact that she had not that trained colonial service that must be hands and eyes in such a venture.

That there was no proper system of recruiting for the service, that the general standard was low, even discreditable to the Mother Country, that certain departments were guilty of serious inefficiency – all this is admitted, even strongly asserted, in a report on the service laid before Parliament early last year. The wording is severe, and justice is hardly done to those individuals who, in spite of all difficulties, have risen above conditions and served the Samoans and their country well. Some of the results are obvious: the extensive nature of a programme of reform calculated entirely in the supposed interests of the natives; the haste with which these reforms were set in motion, and, once opposition had developed, the failure to apply fairness and sympathy at the right moments and in the right proportions, an art that comes either by genius or long experience and then needs, for its success, loyal and intelligent support from home. What was a less obvious process, but no less unfortunate, as all those experienced in native affairs know, was the day-to-day accumulation of little mistakes and misunderstandings – the giving of offence, the invisible wastage of prestige.

I did not find that in New Zealand this conclusion was being drawn from the facts. Opinion there was disillusioned, if not bewildered. Had not New Zealand taken up her Mandate with the most altruistic resolutions? Had she not lavished benefits upon the Samoans, spent more than £250,000 upon them without hope of return? Had she not met their prolonged ingratitude and defiance with unparalleled humanity and restraint?

All this was true, and convincing proof that good will is not enough. Even the committee which so drastically criticized the service did so purely on grounds of departmental efficiency, and recommended the seconding for short periods of civil servants from Wellington. It is true that the Native Department, in a scant paragraph, is excepted, but no realization is shown of its paramount importance, or of the complete lack of any oncoming sequence of men who know the language and understand the social system and psychology of the islanders, or, equally important, have earned their liking and respect. For a small country, and that an agricultural one, to build up a Civil Service presents many

C

difficulties, but now that an arrangement has been made for New Zealand to present candidates for the Imperial Colonial Service, it should not be impossible for her, by way of exchange, to draw upon that service to bridge the gap while these young men are training.

Criticism is easy, and nowhere more so than in the sphere of native government. Criticism of New Zealand should never be separated from appreciation, because she has, to her great honour, set a new standard to the world in the idealism, the generosity, and humanity with which she has endeavoured to live up to the lofty obligations of Article 22 of the League Covenant. If this idealism at home could be expressed in skilled and patient administration in the islands, then Western Samoa might become a model to the world.

II. *The American Method*

The western islands of Samoa, under the Mandatory government of New Zealand, have for some years caught the light of public attention. The smaller American islands to the east have, since the partition of 1900, lain in the shadow, though America has recently been reminded of these fragments of imperial responsibility.

In 1900 Germany obtained the lion's share of the Samoan Islands, but one of America's little group to the eastward hid a treasure which the western islands could not match. It is certainly well hidden, for it was not until our ship, creeping slowly alongside the sylvan sea-mountain of Tutuila, was right opposite the gap that it was revealed that the narrow island is cut almost in half by a harbour shaped like the hind leg of a dog.

The traveller round the world is asked, by possessive nationalists, to give the palm to many harbours, but mine should go to Pago Pago (or Pango) as I first saw it, with the breakers piling on the reef outside, the sheer volcanic walls, shaggy to the summit with trees, with the mists on their shoulders catching fire at the first touch of the rising sun. A file of palms runs round the harbour and leans over the water as if to watch the little lemon and electric-blue fishes threading the coral. It was not, however, for its beauty that America coveted it. Pago Pago is one of the best harbours in the Pacific – or rather was, for modern fleets have reached a number and size that make its accommodation seem modest.

From 1900 until recently America ruled this island paradise by means of one of the most complete despotisms in the world. The commandant of the naval station is also, by appointment from the President, Governor of American Samoa, with its 9,000 native inhabitants. With astonishing disregard of American constitutional principles he combines in his own person executive, legislative, and judicial authority. Nor is this the symbolic concentration of a shadowy chief person. The Governor is a working Governor, and he may find, and has found, himself in the position of giving or withholding pardon from his own sentence in the High Court inflicted for a breach of a law proclaimed and executed by himself.

This form of native government is one which we must condemn on principle, but which, perhaps, many English colonial officials may envy. Admirable it has certainly been in its results, in spite of a few, a very few, scandals. The legislation has been that of men of common sense and complete disinterestedness. The vital land question was solved at once by a regulation which prevents any but a Samoan native from owning land. Thus even the half-castes are excluded. Native customs have been recognized; native institutions retained in active co-operation with the naval government. The highest chiefs are district governors with important functions to perform. Native judges sit even in the High Court. They form the district courts, sitting with an American judge, who is the only civilian in the administration, and native magistrates hold village courts. The disposal of the copra crop, which has been a subject of controversy in the Western Islands, was settled by the government buying the whole of it and putting it up to public auction. A monthly paper in English and Samoan, and containing news, regulations, statistics of health and trade and a full monthly statement of revenue and expenditure, is distributed free to every household in the islands. An annual *fono* (meeting) is held of delegates from all parts of the islands and these have already discussed the agenda with district councils.

Thus the despotic naval Governors have chosen to work with and for the islanders in a most democratic spirit. By so doing the government – with an exception that must be made later – has been successful and popular and has won the loyalty of the charming but capricious islanders. I had the privilege of being the guest of one of the native chiefs, and it is impossible to be among them without realizing that they are not only happy but that contact with a white government has not despoiled them of their pride and self-respect.

Naval government has another great advantage to recommend it. It is an easy solution of the problem of staffing, which has been the great cause of the trouble in Western Samoa. The United States has, like the Mandatory government, no colonial service upon which to draw; the next best thing was to appoint men from a service where there would be reasonable ability, the maximum amount of honesty and detachment, much common sense and capacity to handle men, and that dignity which the hierarchy and discipline of a fighting service can maintain. The Governor, first and last a naval officer, spending two years on the island, has naturally been disposed to offer the minimum amount of interference. Moreover, the islands, small and poor, had the services of a complete and efficient staff, administrative, medical and public works, paid on the Navy register.

The system is not ideal; the lack of special training and the short terms of service stand in the way of that; but, in all the circumstances, it has not fallen far short. It has two valuable testimonies – that of increasing population and of strong approval from a quarter where standards are, and should be, exacting almost beyond achievement, that of the anthropologists as represented by Dr Mead, who has conducted research work in the islands.

The outside world has broken in upon this Pacific idyll. A sudden searchlight has been turned upon the little islands from America, and the edifice of government, so excellent in practice, has been revealed in all its theoretical iniquity. Not only that, its constitutional foundations have been shown up as faulty, almost non-existent. It has been discovered that though in 1900 and 1904 the chiefs offered to cede their islands, the offer has never been acknowledged, far less accepted. Indeed, the little territory has been living for 30 years in a state of constitutional sin which would make an international lawyer hide his face. On two occasions, when the chiefs requested an answer, President Roosevelt sent a soothing letter and 'a silver watch and chain (with case), a silver medal (with case)', and a diploma to those who had signed the offer. It may be surmised that, as in the United States it was still supposed to be the close season for annexations, the President preferred not to advertise his recent 'bag'.

Honolulu claims the credit, if credit it be, of having invented the Samoan question in America. Honolulu is half-way house between Samoa and San Francisco, very proud of her modernity, inclined to gossip, and rather sorry for her quiet, old-fashioned little cousin-islands. A Mau movement in Tutuila found sympathy and publicity in Honolulu. The Mau of Eastern Samoa is, however, very different from that in Western Samoa. The half-castes are discontented owing to their exclusion from land ownership, and some of the natives, led by them, have become vaguely suspicious that not enough is being done for them by way of education, and that the despotic naval government is something of an insult and, if it is not tyrannous, it ought to be. Their desires for change crystallize into the form of a demand for civil government. I talked to leaders of both the American and New Zealand Mau movements, and the former distinguished themselves by their assertions of loyalty towards America and their personal affection and respect for the naval Governor.

This was Governor Graham, then in the act of retirement after handling most ably this mild opposition. To give one example of his tact: The Mau built a clubhouse for their meetings and must needs fly the Stars and Stripes above it. They asked the Governor to sell them a flag. He refused. The American flag could not be sold, but it could be given, and give it he did, and went down in person to do so and to open their club for them and congratulate them upon their constitutional behaviour and political education.

Meanwhile Congress, to clear the little islands from sin and itself from a long reproach, passed in the spring of 1929 a joint resolution accepting the offer made 30 years ago by the chiefs. It did more; as a result of representations from the Governor, who decided that the time had come to doff the cloak of despotism, it appointed a committee of two Senators, two Congressmen, and two Samoan chiefs. These will conduct their inquiries in the islands this summer, and it will lie with them to recommend what changes, if any, are necessary in the constitution.

Those who know and love these graceful and happy people can only hope that the naval government, defined and improved, will be allowed to continue its unostentatious rule. One cannot contemplate with any pleasure the substitution of a civilian government, affected as it must be by political changes and interests, and letting loose upon those gentle people the full force of American efficiency and idealism.

The naval government has had many advantages that the New Zealand mandatory has not – continuity; detachment from politics; from some aspects a better 'colonial' service; a much smaller population and islands that stood a little out of the diplomatic eddies that washed round Upolu. New Zealand is small; America is vast, and she was represented to Samoa in the aspect of naval power. Contrast and comparison should be interesting during the next few years. The islands may seem insignificant, but the smallest problem of native government is big enough to test the heart and head of a whole country. And one who has been to Samoa may, perhaps, be allowed to believe that the supreme beauty of the islands and the islanders give them a special claim upon the interest of the world.

Tribal Rule in Africa

The Times 26 and 27 November 1930

1. The Indirect Principle in Tanganyika

Indirect rule for Africa is a fashionable conception today, but is very widely misunderstood. This is perhaps to be expected. African problems, fascinating and urgent, invite generalizations which are hard to check when their subject is so vast, so inaccessible and, in some ways, so inscrutable. It is the variety of forms and policies that strikes the student of native administration, and makes him abandon, one by one, the equipment of ideas with which he left England.

Putting on one side Northern Nigeria, where indirect rule, a necessity of the situation, was first consciously developed into a system, its principles are applied in southern and eastern Africa in all degrees, from their completest form in Buganda to the tentative courts and councils in Southern Rhodesia and the Union, which, if not properly speaking indirect rule at all, are at least a belated compliment to the idea. A clear dividing line is made by the facts of origin: indirect rule is either historical – our recognition of what we found in existence, as in Basutoland, Barotseland, Buganda and elsewhere – or it is a deliberate attempt to regularize, even to reconstruct, a measure of native self-government. These two kinds fall in turn into divisions according to the policy of those in control. Thus while in Basutoland the paramountcy of Moshesh, sheltered by vague agreements, was long allowed to crumble quietly into ruin, that of the Kabaka in Buganda was repaired and extended until it is the model native government between Capetown and Khartoum. In the other class there is a world of difference between the policies of Kenya and Tanganyika; still more between those of Tanganyika and South Africa, to which latter country the policy followed in the mandated territory appears absurd, if, indeed, as witness the last Union election, it does not appear dangerous.

In eastern Africa indirect rule is expressed in different ways in Tanganyika, Kenya and Uganda. I have chosen to write of Tanganyika because there it is being applied on so large a scale, and directed by such clear and far-reaching principles, while it is yet so new that its significance is hardly realized, and its results are only just beginning to show.

Let us remind ourselves that Tanganyika has nearly 5,000,000 natives, and that, although there are three provinces where a few thousand Europeans are intermixed with them, the vast majority live in purely native areas, while the west and north-west form a solid block of purely native territory, containing nearly 3,000,000 people, a territory as large, and nearly as populous, as its neighbour Uganda.

Direct government of such a territory is impossible, though it is always possible to make a pretence of it, to ignore and to weaken, if you cannot destroy, the organization of native society, which then continues a submerged and enfeebled life, regulating those multifarious and mysterious concerns of marriage, land and inheritance which, if brought to the district officer, would overwhelm him. In Tanganyika, where the native authorities record as well as try these cases, they numbered in 1929 no fewer than 64,000. Nor is the problem only one of numbers: it is one thing to check records and prevent injustice; it is another to find time to unravel all the coils of civil litigation in accordance with native law and custom. To take a judgement at random as an example:

The Court has now divided the cattle as follows: The Defendant will take one big cow as his property and one leg of the calf, and the Complainant will take three legs of the calf. From the other five legs the Defendant will take three legs, and the Complainant two legs, because the Defendant took care of all the properties before the Complainant was born: also, he is the elder brother. It by no means followed, let me add, that the judgement meant the immediate dissevering of the animals at issue.

In matters other than judicial all the forces that go to make for tribal solidarity and loyalty to chiefs and sub-chiefs, instead of being neglected or turned back upon themselves to make morbid growths, are directed into social activities. These are no feeble forces that we, out of an anthropological romanticism, are keeping alive. Even in South Africa, where they have been subjected to attack, conscious and unconscious, for a hundred years and more, they still survive. In the mines of Johannesburg the visiting chief is offered tribute by his tribesmen. Among the Zulus the old sense of pride and cohesion struggles to express itself in the only legitimate form of a Zulu society, with an executive committee, an annual general meeting, and a guinea subscription, while the descendant of Chaka and Cetewayo acts as patron.

In Tanganyika these forces are enormously stronger. To believe, as so many people do, that to recognize and employ them is merely to crystallize the obsolete is a misconception based on the evidence of past

2   *Eastern Africa, inter-war period*

mistakes, and one which it is of the highest importance to correct. As electric current, an element as old as creation, can be switched to a hundred modern uses, so this strong primitive force can be connected directly with all those twentieth-century activities that may be summarized as welfare work. The organized vitality of the tribe, of which the highest concentration was once expressed in war, can now be harnessed to economic production, to education, hygiene and a dozen other constructive activities, with results which, if only the process is allowed to continue on its present lines, may astonish the world in another 50 years.

How, in detail, are these principles applied? The native courts, immemorial as they are, are recognized and divided into categories according to their powers. They deal with practically the whole of the civil litigation between natives; in criminal matters their powers are limited by some special exceptions and by the definition of maximum penal penalties – ten-pound fines, six months' imprisonment, and eight strokes with the cane. Each case is briefly recorded in Swahili by clerks in special registers, which are checked and re-checked by the administrative officers at frequent intervals. Procedure is left to the presiding chiefs and elders; it may safely be so left, as all can testify who have witnessed the dignity and publicity of their courts and the deep Bantu sense of justice there shown. Since it is one of our constitutional commandments that true responsibility comes only with the raising and spending of revenue, we find native treasuries, into which is paid a rebate of the direct tax collected by the native authorities themselves, and court and licence fees. The money is spent, with the advice of the district officer, upon the salaries of the native administrative staff, who range from chiefs to messengers, and upon social services.

Executive power is wielded by chiefs or councils, officially gazetted as Native Authorities. It is difficult to generalize about them. In Tanganyika white interpretation of tribal government has not been standardized at headquarters and imposed as a rigid pattern upon the districts. No effort has been spared, especially since the advent of the present Governor, Sir Donald Cameron, to discover the true form of each group, even where fuller knowledge has demanded successive and inconvenient adjustments. Within the legal outlines of treasuries, courts and authorities there is room for a rich variety of forms. The units are large or small; their populations vary between 5,000 and 350,000; there are paramount chiefs, councils of chiefs, and, in less consolidated groups, councils of elders. But the government, believing that the beginning must be the discovery of the natural native grouping, does not believe that this is also the end, and so, while careful neither to distort nor to press development, its experience leads it to favour federations of chiefs of the same or similar tribes, who, independent as executive authorities, together form a Federal Council, a Court of Appeal from their own subordinate courts, and a joint Native Treasury.

Upon this complete form of indirect rule fire has been directed from three different camps. First there are those who, judging by the standards of public honesty and efficiency in England, dwell upon the abuses and the peculation that may obtain under indirect rule. Occasional abuses do occur; there are fairly frequent cases of peculation, mostly on a small scale. What is surprising is that when the searchlight of modern inspection and audit is turned upon a primitive people, many of whom hardly understand the meaning of money, more errors are not revealed. Moreover, the critics sometimes forget that the alternative of direct rule is to impose our standards ready-made, to treat natives like marionettes, to make a good show by manipulating them so that they appear to act like their masters while they remain inert and uncomprehending.

Then there is what may be called the 'own lines' school, who draw inspiration from a dwindling group of anthropologists, and criticize on the grounds that tribal institutions are being prostituted in the service of a rapid Westernization. The Tanganyika Government would probably plead guilty to this, for, as I have already suggested, it is believed here that native institutions are not static but dynamic, and that, since Westernization must come, it is better to Westernize people in communities than as detached units. As to whether the pace is too fast, opinions are again divided, but in an experiment so new and vast human wisdom falls short, and the issue can only be left to trial, and even error, at the hands of the experts in charge.

Criticism comes also from those who might call themselves the progressives, or the realists. Among them are most American Africans, and many educated South African natives. They would argue that the chief is an anachronism in the twentieth century, and that to support tribal institutions is an attempt to side-track the African, perhaps a deliberate attempt, lest, in his overwhelming numbers, he should overtake us along the high road of civilization. In so far as it comes from Africans, this is the view of those who have lost or are losing their own past, fragments of shattered communities whose very necessary ambition it is to enter into the European society that surrounds them, and who, like the *nouveaux riches*, look with shame at their own poor relations. When held by European well-wishers this view results from their observation of the response of detribalized natives to the stimulus of the white community around or beside them. We can leave on one side the question whether such development is the best. It is one that has no relevance to East Africa, certainly not to Tanganyika, where there are large populations that have no contact, and almost certainly never will have any contact, with European communities able to disintegrate and influence them.

Moreover, the depreciation of the tribal system is based either upon the experience of South Africa, with its atrophied chiefs drinking themselves to death in reserves from which the vital manhood is drained away, or upon a misconception of the nature of the system. Bantu chieftainship must be translated into English in terms of democracy rather than of aristocracy, still less of monarchy. True Bantu society is not so very different from that which was once our own, as pictured by Tacitus in his *Germania*. There is a fundamental Bantu conception we can hardly understand: that the tribe, living and dead, is an organic unit, whose life is embodied in the life of the chief. He is guided by his elders, and precedence in court and counsel is sometimes in inverse ratio to importance. His power and wealth, manifested in land and cattle, must, under primitive conditions, work to the benefit of all his people. Under the chief and sub-chief is the close-knit Bantu society, where exists an equality of wealth and status that the Socialist might envy, and which is regulated in detail by the authority of patriarchs of families and groups of families.

In Europe we did not know how to progress without destroying the whole system, the good with the bad, and acquiring peace and efficiency at the price of equality. In South Africa we have injured it; perhaps fatally. Is it too much to hope that, where such societies have existed into the twentieth century, instead of destroying we may, with the knowledge and sympathy now available, develop them into something happier and healthier than South Africa can ever hope to show?

II. *The Native Courts*

The first article aimed at interpreting the general principles upon which the Native Administration of Tanganyika is based. In this second will be given some pictures of the achievements of the Administration as they appear to the traveller. They are chosen from the great block of purely native territory in the west, because in the areas where white settlement has taken place tribal institutions cannot function with the same fullness and freedom. It must be remembered that indirect rule in its present complete form has developed only since 1925, and in some parts, as it is a development in which haste is generally disastrous, it is only now assuming definite shape. Ask the age of this school or that clinic, and the answer is nearly always one or two, seldom three or four, years. The point is worth emphasizing, for all calculations about Tanganyika, political or economic, should be based on the expectancy of a bountiful harvest of results in 20 or 30 years' time.

Let us visit first the Province of Mwanza, mainly inhabited by those cheerful and industrious people, the Wasukuma. From an aeroplane their lands would be seen lying in swelling plains, running for 200 miles southwards from the shores of Lake Victoria, patched with fields of millet, ripening a red bronze, and with smaller dark green squares that are cotton, ground-nuts and sweet potatoes. There was maize, but that has mostly been gathered into the woven bins whose giant shapes loom through the darkness of the huts. These huts, little circles of grey thatch from the air, are plentifully sprinkled about the open land, wreathed in groups of twos and threes by olive-green euphorbia hedges. All this is picked out on a background of grassland, already, in a month of dry weather, burnt golden by the sun, and worn into patches by erosion. In this densely populated, highly cultivated country are islands of dense green, exhausted and abandoned lands upon which bush has encroached, and from which the tsetse fly now exiles man and beast.

A collection of white buildings marks the headquarters of the Sukuma Federation, a group of independent chiefs, who, each retaining executive authority in his own chiefdom, have combined to form a joint treasury and court of appeal.

Each chief, when he comes to headquarters, uses one of the row of little two-roomed houses. Beside these is the court house, reached from the road by a drive flanked with flower-beds. In front flies the flag of the Federation, the black bull of Sukuma traditions on a golden ground. The court house is open to the winds and the public. On the platform, each in his own carved chair, sit the ten chiefs. They present a contrast significant in this stage of African development. Four young men on one side are dressed in European or semi-European fashion: one, who speaks English, is of the first generation to be educated at the Tabora school for sons of chiefs. On the other side sits Wamba, a handsome man and barbaric by comparison, wearing a blue and purple cloth in casual toga fashion, with the sandals of lion-skin and the anklets and bracelets of shells that are the appurtenances of a chief. He has claims to be para-mount chief, but the system of having an elected chairman allows the stout, powerful old man in the middle to exercise his natural powers of leadership. No chief justice ever looked his part more than this Mak-waia, one of those men who speak quietly and are always heard. He is dressed in a royal blue robe, heavily embroidered with gold; the King's

Medal for African Chiefs hangs round his neck; and his head is bound in a turban of multi-coloured silk. Beside him sits a chieftainess, Nzile of Saluwe, in a toga of striped silk and an orange turban. She has the royal shell on her neck, but on her feet she wears, not lion-skin sandals, but men's golfing brogues and socks. Though not beautiful, she is masterful (four consorts are said to have escaped from her kraal); she has a sense of humour, and plays her part effectively.

Facing the platform stand the litigants, a woman, her husband, and the man he is accusing of rape. These are Swahili loafers who consider themselves superior to the up-country natives before whose court they have come. Their judges soon turn the case to one of adultery, and then, suspecting that the husband has in fact been commercializing his wife's honour, adjourn it to the next session.

The next defendant claims to be an Arab, but is clearly another Swahili. He is a lorry-driver, and was so foolish as not only to drive his lorry along one of the roads maintained by the Federation, and closed on account of the rains, but also to run out of petrol outside Makwaia's country house, and to borrow a tin from that magnate. Makwaia lent him the petrol, and ran him in before the court. He is one of a class of trader who often exploits the native, and as such has no friend on the Bench. Yet his judges take much time and trouble in estimating the degree of wilfulness in his offence. He says he could not read the notice. 'Is it the custom in this country,' asks Wamba, 'to put notice-boards across roads for no reason?' Nzile suggests a hundred shillings or one month. 'Ought to be six,' growls another chief, like any old J.P. in England; 'these lorry-drivers need teaching a lesson.' But leniency prevails. Makwaia pronounces judgement, and adds very gravely, amid shouts of laughter, 'And don't you forget my tin of petrol!'

This federal appeal court is more formal and less democratic than those of the individual chiefs. I called at Nzile's court a few days later. My visit interrupted the proceedings a little as the whole court, elders, audience and prisoners, turned out with the chieftainess to greet me with songs and beating of drums. The court house was a simple, round structure of mud and thatch: every inch of floor was covered by squatting natives, and the six wide windows were blocked by the heads and shoulders of their women. I sat on the platform with Nzile and a dozen elders. An old man, in burning out his bees, had set fire to the grass. The seniors in the audience freely offered their opinion; Nzile called upon each of the elders by name; and, after engaging in an amicable discussion with the prisoner, pronounced a sentence of fifty shillings or

one month. Then, turning to the court, she asked, 'Are there any protests?' Silence. 'Do you all agree?' A forest of hands. It is difficult to
believe that where justice is administered under such conditions there is
much scope for miscarriage, still less for abuse or corruption. I have
corrected the impression by studying cases in the court-books of a
dozen or more districts, and they bear witness to the African's sense not
only, or so much, of justice in our conception, but also of something for
which it is difficult to find a name – of fairness, of equality, of a capacity
to balance up the claims of individuals in relation to those of the group,
and to come to a decision that satisfies even, it would seem, the party
penalized.

To return to the Sukuma Federation. Leaving the court, you find in
front of you another of the institutions made possible by concentration
of revenues, the school, where the sons of chiefs and headmen spend
four years, of which period perhaps the less important part is devoted
to acquiring the elements of education. The boys live, under the simplest
conditions, in four 'villages', each under an elected headman. Discipline
is carried out in their own court, with its official court-book, while the
resident chief often comes across the road to attend its sessions. There
are also the school plantation, carpentry and tailoring shops, and the
school band in which they express their joy in music.

Close by is the Native Administration Farm, with seed-beds, experimental plots, ploughing demonstrations, and stud bulls for the grading
up of native stock. On a neighbouring hill stands the leper settlement,
and also the maternity home and clinic in which last year nearly a thousand babies were born. Many more were reached by out-patient work.
Native women are being trained who, it is hoped, will go out into the
villages, advance-guards in the battle against the appalling loss of infant
life. There is no space, however, to record all the work that figures on
the Federation balance-sheet with its £9,000 revenue; the tribal dispensaries, the roads, dairies, anti-locust operations and the rest. Nor does
this unit stand alone.

There is, however, one piece of work that demands special attention –
namely, clearing the fly bush. To see this in its most striking form one
must go north to another province. Not that the Sukuma Federation
does not do its part, but its efforts are distributed over a number of areas.
In the Kwimba district of Mwanza province I was privileged to see
reclamation work on a grand scale. Fifteen thousand men let loose upon
the bush at the same moment on a front eight miles long is a sight not
easily forgotten. Armed with axes and knives they fell upon the thick

scrub as if it were an enemy, hacking and slashing in time to their songs, while here and there in the line a great shout would go up as a big tree crashed to the ground, and the group would run together and fall upon the next one. Each of the four tribal divisions was commanded by its chief; each company was under its headman.

The men walk in to this work any distance from 10 to 40 miles. They provide their own tools and bring their own food for ten days, with cooking pots and a couple of skins for cloak and ground-sheet. They arrive on a special day, set to work to build themselves grass huts in five camps, 3,000 men in each, and are ready to work at six o'clock the next morning. The arrangements, carried out through the tribal authorities, work without a hitch. There is no payment except a feast of meat three times a week; very few of the workers will gain directly from the clearing, yet they turn out gladly at the wish of their chiefs.

And what are the results? The people, hemmed in by fly bush, take new heart and win back their country. In three years they have cleared about 60 square miles, which is already filling up with an industrious black peasantry. It made the heart glad to see the shape of a rich river valley appearing from under a smother of fly-ridden bush. But the huge machine can only be made to work by touching the right lever, and it takes a great deal of patience and sympathy to find it.

It is Empire Day at Bukoba in the province that adjoins Uganda and closely resembles it; the brightest and almost the hottest day possible in this world. Lake Victoria is a triumphant blue, dotted with green islands and cut into by promontories of tumbled grey granite. On the flat land behind the shire 20,000 people form a huge oval. They are a gay but orderly crowd, and dressed in a way that speaks prosperity; the men in European suits or long white *kansus*, the women in flowing silks. Incidentally it is a prosperity founded on coffee; in Bukoba district alone there are 60,000 coffee growers, who in 1928 produced about 7,000 tons of coffee.

On to the ground marches a sequence of eight processions, each headed by a flag and a smart band, while at the rear the primitive is represented in the tribal dancers and mummers, grotesque in dress and action. Well in front of each procession strides one man. Seven wear tropical suits and sun-helmets; the eighth, a very fat man, has a German hussar uniform, his brazen helmet drawing all the rays of the sun upon his unfortunate head. These are the big chiefs of Bukoba, members of a federal council like that of the Sukuma, now leading their tribes to the great event of the year, the intertribal sports.

They have behind them a record of fighting stretching back to the dim days when the fathers of their dynasties first came south from Bunyoro. A few years ago they could not cross each other's dominions, still less would they enter the same room. Now they foregather in the chiefs' pavilion and strain their eyes to follow the fortunes of their champions as they compete in archery, spear-throwing, running and wrestling. The excitement is intense. One young chief, fresh from school in Uganda, competes for his tribe. Winners of events run to the chiefs' pavilion and prostrate themselves, clasping the ankles of their jubilant sovereigns. The chiefs' sons, and at last even the old chiefs themselves, break on to the ground for the final event, the tug-of-war, and urge their straining teams to victory.

At last, after four hours, it is over. Lwaijumba of Kiamtwara has won the chief trophy for the third time. His people spill on to the ground from all sides and follow the silver cup which he flashes high over his head. The cup and the sports are new, but the harsh throbbing song is as old as the tribe and its loyalty to the chief. And the sports may be regarded as a striking symbol of how, under the native policy of the Tanganyika Government, the best of the old and the best of the new may be brought together.

The Times Leader 27 November

INDIRECT RULE IN AFRICA

The two articles on the system of government in Tanganyika, of which the second appears on this page today, are the fruit of the itinerant studies of a Rhodes Travelling Fellow, whose impressions of Samoa were printed in *The Times* in April of this year. The subject with which they deal, the preservation and adaptation of tribal institutions, is of the first importance in Africa at the present moment, and the Tanganyikan experiment has a special interest of its own. To conserve the authority of traditional and established rulers wherever possible has been one of the principal axioms of British policy in Asia and Africa alike, and indirect rule, as practised in the Sudan and Nigeria, has now won general recognition. But it is also recognized that its success is directly in proportion to the strength and worth of the local institutions already in existence. The strong Mohammedan emirates of Northern Nigeria provided Lord Lugard with the right material for the achievements which have made Northern Nigeria the classical instance of the system. The natives of Tanganyika, and of East Africa generally, have offered a much less promising field. The extreme disorganization of tribal life and disintegration of tribal authority which the East African campaign brought in its train added enormously to the difficulty of the task. Today, after more than ten years of Mandatory status, the after-effects of the earlier history of the Territory are still being experienced. It has been found in Nigeria, in the Southern Province, that the system of indirect rule is least happy in its results when from one cause or another a native is invested with authority for some other reason than that the natives of the tribe regard him as the rightful chief. Tanganyika has had its full share of the difficulties that arise both through confusion of claims to tribal authority and through the frailties of rightful chiefs; but the present Governor, Sir Donald Cameron, whose term of office expires in a few months, can look back on a period in which confusion has been steadily cleared up, while the standards that can be set before native chiefs have risen, and the system of tribal authority has taken firm root as the main instrument for carrying out the Mandate.

D

Native Administration in Tanganyika

[Reprinted for *Africa, Journal of the International Institute of African Languages and Cultures* Vol. IV No. 3. July 1931]

This talk was given soon after my return from my two and a half years of study and travel as a Rhodes Travelling Fellow. I spent eighteen months in East Africa, much of it in Tanganyika where with the help of the Governor, Sir Donald Cameron and the Secretary for Native Affairs, Sir Philip Mitchell I was able to visit every province but one. This talk represents my first enthusiastic but not wholly uncritical encounter with 'indirect rule' in conditions which allowed me time to study a number of tribal units with some care, this by administrative not by anthropological standards. As mentioned in the talk, I had the somewhat formidable test of giving the talk in the presence of Lord Lugard and of the anthropologist, the Rev Edwin Smith.

The System of Native Administration in Tanganyika

The object of my visit to southern and eastern Africa was to make a comparative study, but I intend in this paper to deal with Tanganyika. This is not because I overestimate its importance or its singularity. Indirect rule in its general sense is not an invention of this age, and even in the special sense it has acquired during the last twenty years the classic example is in Nigeria. I know that you will all feel with me what a privilege it is for us to meet here at the invitation and in the presence of that administrator whose career was first bound up with the acquisition of East Africa and then with the construction of the system of government in West Africa, the influence of which now reacts upon the East. Exactly what Tanganyika owes to Nigeria could only, perhaps, be learned by 'listening in' at a conversation between Lord Lugard and Sir Donald Cameron of a kind that we may suspect has been taking place during the last few weeks. I certainly do not know myself, though I hope to go out shortly to the West Coast in order to find out, if only in part.

Nor, though I shall concentrate upon that very constructive piece of work that has been carried through during the last six years by Sir Donald Cameron, do I forget that Sir Horace Byatt had ably laid the foundations during a very difficult period; nor do I think Sir Donald's work stands in need of being exalted by a depreciation of German methods that has already gone a good deal farther than the truth.

Whether or not it is successful, the government of Tanganyika is bound to be important. Its large area lies between the northern and southern British territories, and whatever develops there will react north and south with increasing force. Tanganyika has already figured in a South African election, while the Nyasaland Government has made an official investigation of the system in force north of the border, before revising some of its own native institutions. Moreover, this advanced system of native local government is being developed in a country where there is white settlement.

The importance of the system of Native Administration in Tanganyika, however, lies mainly in its intrinsic qualities, and it is these that I want to bring out. I do not think it is necessary for me to spend very much time upon the legal framework of the system, which is made up of the ordinances providing for native courts, native authority and the rest. Their composition does not vary greatly from that of laws in force in Uganda and elsewhere, and such differences as there are would not convey any impression of the special character of the Tanganyika system. Briefly, units of Native Administration are recognized by the government and clothed with statutory powers. These units combine executive, judicial, legislative and financial powers within the limits proper to local government; not many of the affairs of an African peasantry go outside those limits. The measure of control on the part of the political officers varies in accordance with the varying development of the tribes, but is mostly confined to advice and supervision, to the checking of court records, and to very careful co-operation in all the business connected with finance.

These bare bones live only by the spirit which has been breathed into them during the last five or six years. I think the character of the administration can best be understood if we consider first the methods by which it was built up. No ready-made scheme was applied from above, but officers all over the country were set to work to study the racial composition and the institutions of the peoples under their charge, in order that the true native authorities might be found; the tribute and service due to them commuted for cash payments which should supply native treasuries; the people correctly grouped about them, and the courts extended and regularized as part of the whole system. All through 1925 there poured into Dar es Salaam bulky reports bearing witness to the research that was going on in every district in the Territory. In many, I think in most cases, the first suggestions were sent back with the advice to try again; sometimes they had to be revised many times, and it is interesting to notice the growing competence and deepening knowledge shown in these files over a period of years. The whole service, in fact, went to school during the first year or two, greatly, as they all assert now, to their benefit, and I do not think that Sir Donald Cameron would claim that he himself was only a teacher.

The first point to notice about a system thus developed is that it is based with elaborate care upon the tribal institutions. At headquarters as well as in the field the temptation towards a convenient uniformity was resisted and the plastic legal forms were moulded round the jumble of realities left by tribal history. Thus, a unit of native authority might be a chief with 2,000 or 200,000 subjects. The chief might stand alone or be a paramount chief with sub-chiefs under him. Again, a number of independent units might come together to form a common treasury and court of appeal, each retaining executive authority in its own area. This has, indeed, been a frequent development, as the almost dramatic results achieved through the pooling of financial resources have appealed to a people hungry for educational and medical services. A native authority may also be represented by an individual petty chief or head-man or by a group of such in a tribal council. Even this does not convey the richness of the variety, since the racial composition, the customs, and degree of development of the tribes present wide con-trasts, from the advanced chieftaincies of Bukoba, akin to those of western Uganda, through all stages of Bantu society down to the least coherent, and across all the degrees between the pure agriculturalist and the pure pastoralist; between Bantu and Hamite. The fidelity with which indigenous forms have been followed is, perhaps, the feature of the system which is best known; what is probably less appreciated is that the process was not only one of study on the part of the officers but also of consultation with the people. I might give as an example the method followed in setting up native authorities in one of the most difficult areas in the country, that of the disintegrated people round Dar es Salaam. It has taken years of combined study and consultation to dis-cover how to replace the direct rule which at first seemed the only pos-sible form. When, only last year, a scheme was decided upon, an officer was sent round on tour through the 130 village centres to explain the plan and discuss it with the people. They were then left for a period of a month or two to talk it all out among themselves, after which a second tour was made to collect their decisions and accept the *wadewa* or headmen of their selection. The officer was not present at these elections, which, to be valid, had to be attended by 70 per cent. of the adult males, and in which the choices were made in that happy and mysterious manner which is the secret of the Bantu, by which, without recourse to voting, unanimity is obtained.

The second characteristic to notice in the Tanganyika system is the thoroughness with which the whole service was instructed in the new policy. Drawing upon his experience in Nigeria, the Governor issued a series of Native Administration Memoranda in which he communicated not only orders but ideas. These memoranda, which have lately been revised in the light of five years' experience, contain instructions about the supervision of native courts and the issue of poll-tax receipts, but they also contain the principles upon which the system is based and discuss the ultimate objective. It is difficult to exaggerate the contrast between an administration which is working simply with the help of *ad hoc* instructions and by the light of a tradition which tends at times to grow a little dim, and one in which every member knows, not only what he does, but also why he does it. When we remember how many young men, going from the universities to Tanganyika, are being trained from the start in such a combination of theory and practice, it seems that we may count upon a school of native administration being built up whose members Lord Lugard may look upon as his spiritual grandsons.

The third feature of the system which naturally arises out of the others is its evolutionary character. Since the besetting disease of every administration is an ossification arising out of complacency, it is instructive to study one in the rare phase of vigorous growth. I can best do this by means of three examples which will serve to show that the administration did not sink into repose after the first two years of constructive effort, but has carried on a continuous process of study and development.

Let us consider first the change in the conception of the chief. There is no doubt that in the earlier part of their inquiries the officers were in full cry after the chief. Find that potentate, verify his dynastic credentials, list his powers, and the main work was done. The chief was in some cases quite ready to help, though in most instances he had too much good sense to exercise outside their constitutional limits the powers we had recognized. With each succeeding year administrative officers have understood these limits better and have found that they make the Bantu chief something rather different from the chief of their preconceptions. There is a growing emphasis in their reports upon the constitutional

checks that surround him which is reflected in the instructions sent out
from headquarters. In nearly every tribe the authority is exercised
through groups of counsellors, often hereditary and sometimes elaborately ordered. And now a further stage of knowledge is being reached
in that in many chieftaincies something behind the counsellors is appearing, the original, basic organization of all tribal society, that of the
family, and the extended family, in which there is a clear distribution of
social functions. It was, rather strangely and very creditably, some notes
supplied to me by the *Mukama* of Bunyoro that brought home to me
how the simpler and earlier organization of the Bantu tribe, upon which
the *Mukama's* dynasty, with its developed centralization and appointed
civil service, had imposed itself, still lived on in spite of the failure of the
British administration to recognize it. Later, I encountered an officer
in north-west Tanganyika, engaged upon researches along the same line,
though in his case the Hamitic dynasty was less advanced and the survival
of the basic organization probably more vigorous. He admirably
described the system as one of indirect rule by the chiefs through the
sub-chiefs, who are little more than liaison officers between himself and
this still vital village organization. Here both the men and the women
are divided into two groups, the elders, *ba-zikulu* and *ba-shika*, and the
younger who carry out their orders, *ba-sumba batale* and *ba-shika batale*.
I hope, however, that he will himself publish the results of his investigations. The more Bantu society is studied, the more does it seem to contain the element of true democracy, and there is a fair hope that the
Tanganyika administration will study and utilize this element to the
full.

It is because the administration is still at school that some of the worst
blunders that we can make in Africa – though half the time we never
know that we are making them – have been avoided. This brings me to
my second illustration. I expect most people here have read *The Golden
Stool*. I think part of the equipment served out by the Public Works
Department to administrative officers should be a miniature golden
stool to keep upon their office desks, or, perhaps, to set as a mascot
upon the motor-cars from which so much of their work is now done.
Yet I am sure that Mr Edwin Smith, whom we have with us here, will
be glad to hear the story of the mistake that was *not* made, of the golden
stool that was *not* stolen, a story that ends happily largely owing to the
growth of that better conception of our responsibilities to which he has
contributed so much.

In a certain part of Tanganyika it was proposed at the same time to raise the tax and to insist upon the full payment of tax for plural wives. It happened to be a tribe full of much-married men, double figures being fairly common. The increase in their obligations was large and sudden. The people murmured. They moved in a way that struck the local officials as peculiarly disorderly, since the paramount chief and sub-chiefs seemed to be thrust aside, while the crowd advanced to a meeting with their district commissioner led, it seemed, by unknown agitators, who usurped the part of the chiefs in speaking for the people. It was this anarchic character of the movement that seemed specially alarming, and measures to restore discipline were suggested. One was that a company of the King's African Rifles might happen to choose this time and this district for a patrol, and if, near the scene of the trouble, they should pause for a little machine-gun practice upon a row of cooking-pots, a useful impression might be created. There was, however, doubt at head-quarters. The Governor seems to have relied upon his instinct, which told him that when tribal Africans, who are among the most orderly people in the world, behave in such a peculiar manner there must be something wrong, but not necessarily upon their side. There was there-fore no patrol and no general punitive measures; the new taxation was modified, and shortly afterwards an officer with an anthropological turn of mind went down there, and the real explanation was soon forth-coming. It appeared firstly that the paramount chieftainship was one of those rather artificial erections which were sometimes put up in the earlier days of construction and had collapsed at the first strain, and, secondly, and more important, that in the constitution of this tribe were certain hereditary officers, called *amafumu* (singular *lifumu*), whose duty it was to act as spokesmen for the people. Our neglect, due to ignorance, of this institution had already led to dissatisfaction, and when the crisis came, the people acted in the only constitutional way they knew. I need hardly say that further investigations are proceeding as to the exact position of the *amafumu*, and I do not doubt their place in that tribal society will be recognized by the government.

I find some difficulty in choosing my third illustration of what I have called the evolutionary character of the administration, because so many interesting examples crowd upon my memory. I think, however, that of the Lindi clans of the Wamakonde is worth selecting as a very helpful piece of administrative experience.

In south-eastern Tanganyika, partly as a result of disintegrating influence from the coast and partly of the battering-ram of the Angoni invasions and the hiving-off of the Wayao and the Wamakua, restless elephant-hunters who have managed to string themselves out all the way from the Zambezi to the Rufiji, the peoples have very little tribal solidarity, and in many cases the small clans live scattered and independent. There was no sign of a chief here; no one who could be made into a chief, and the first opinion in the administration was that nothing could be built out of such fine grains of sand, and that here the people must be ruled directly, by agents, or *akidas*, as the Germans had ruled in these parts. But no one concerned liked the idea of having an exception to a good system, and the long, difficult and laborious process was begun of putting these small cells under the microscope, of examining the claims of some hundreds of *wakalungwa* or clan-heads, deciding their boundaries, and of putting all decisions to the judgement of the people concerned. Upon this broad and true foundation a first story is being erected of associations of neighbouring *wakalungwa* in courts and councils, which can be carried further as the people become ready for wider co-operation. I emphasize this process because the argument is put forward that Kenya cannot adopt the Tanganyika principle because of the absence of chiefs. This small-cell organization, however, is the basis even where there are chiefs, and it may even prove all the easier with time and patience to build up really vital and democratic institutions where we have not the temptations which the office of chief presents to us and to which I shall shortly refer. (I need hardly say I use the word democratic in its most general sense.) It would seem that if an attempt should be made in Kenya to shift the basis of native local government more nearly upon indigenous foundations, then the experience so hardly earned in Tanganyika should be drawn upon. It is possible, even, that Uganda might find that experience interesting, in view of the problem presented by her less coherent Nilotic and north-eastern Bantu people, which she is trying to solve by rather different methods.

I have so far offered you only appreciation of what is being done in Tanganyika, selecting what I consider the more valuable features of the system. My standard of judgement has been that provided by my study of actual administration in southern and eastern Africa. There is, however, another and ideal standard from which the best system yet achieved must fall very short, and I think it is neither inconsistent nor idle to turn from appreciation by one standard to criticism by another.

I have spoken of the voluminous reports upon tribal history and institutions pouring into headquarters to form the basis for the dispositions of the government. Regarded as anthropological material, their quality is of course very variable. Few of the officers engaged in this work had received any training at all, least of all in anthropological technique, and though many of them were gifted with those qualities of mind and character that enabled them to train themselves and to produce valuable results, yet the very conditions of their work provided a further obstacle, in the constant transfers, in the wide varieties between the tribes, in the almost universal ignorance of their languages, and in the huge numbers and areas that make up most of the districts. We have, indeed, no standard by which to measure our own ignorance, or to guess at the proportion of the unknown to the known. Some sense of this is felt by experienced officers and is, in this work, the beginning of wisdom. It is tragic to think how many of our expensive administrative officers, and still more, perhaps, of our technical officers, through no fault of their own, are at this moment merely fingering the surface of their material, and in some cases actually rubbing it the wrong way. I believe that it is possible in Africa for the reports upon a district and even a province to be perfectly satisfactory while in fact the administration is being carried on in no kind of partnership with the people, and that this would not be due to any disingenuousness on the part of the officers concerned.

There are difficulties of another kind which are inherent in the policy of indirect rule. Perhaps we cannot with the best will – and we generally have that – surmount these difficulties, but it is well to recognize them. Under natural conditions tribal institutions were strong and supple, like the muscles of an athlete in training, because the hard necessities of war, of migration, and of self-preservation were using them to the utmost. We have come and have imposed our power above the chief's power, our peace for their conflict and danger, our crystallization for the fluidity of tribal movement. The change in the tribal body has been immediate and deep-seated; the muscles have gone slack, some organs are all but atrophied, and it is of this changed and weakened frame that we are asking heavy and strange tasks.

Let us take as a more particular example the position of the chief. I am no anthropologist and I speak with a deep sense of my own fallibility. It would seem, however, from a study of the ceremonies which attend the inauguration of a new chief, that his office was based upon a composite foundation made up of hereditary eligibility, religious sanction, popular choice, and something having the significance of a social contract, or a coronation oath between chief and people. Just at the moment when the effect of our civilization is to eat away the greater part of this foundation we are piling up on the institution a top-heavy structure composed all too largely of executive functions of a new and often distasteful kind.

This refers not only to chiefs but also to our Lindi clan-heads. We saw that by ordinary standpoints the Tanganyika Government has done great things here: judging by our ideal standard, we must have certain doubts. The position of the small clan-heads, or *wakalungwa*, depends upon their having obtained from the head of the clan from which they have hived off, or from that of the head to whose lands they have come, the right of *mbepesi*, or of conducting the ceremony of the sacred flour. At times of need when prayer to God through the mediation of ancestors is required, the *mkalungwa* goes with his people to the graves, and there flour is poured between the hands to make a cone. Over this a basket or cooking-pot is placed for protection, which in the morning is removed and the omens are read according to the shape retained by the cone. In these days, not only are the occasions for such prayers and ceremonies less in number, but education and Christian teaching are draining away their significance. The second feature of the *mkalungwa* was his judicial authority over his clan, which would have led to such a multiplication of courts if government recognition had been given, that a group of *wakalungwa* were put together to form a court, which, they say, is not at all the same thing to them. The third important mark of the position of the *mkalungwa* was that his people must build and maintain his house, and this has gone the way of all forced labour. I do not say that these changes are not necessary; only that we should remember them all the time that we are asking our Lindi headman to use the relics of his authority for the collection of taxation and the enforcement of various provisions for sanitation, the cleaning of cotton plots, and the like. The development must be attempted; it may prove possible, but it will not be automatic, and will need all the sympathy and understanding that we can give.

The question may reasonably be asked as to whether this dwelling upon difficulties, some of which seem unsurmountable, can do more than daunt and weaken us in our work in Africa. There are moments, indeed, when I think that we are like a man who in striding through a wood puts his foot through a beautiful cobweb, and, turning in regret, tries to reconstruct it. The next moment I throw the metaphor indignantly aside, for the stuff with which we are dealing is not gossamer, and it is living, and living vigorously enough to stand a great deal of injury and misuse.

I think, then, that it is worth while to dwell upon difficulties because we are thus reminded that the need is for study, and always more study. It is true that this is recognized today as never before. I only once came across a political officer in Africa who said, 'The less you know about these people, the better you can run them.' Yet the view is sometimes expressed that there are limits beyond which this study should not be pressed, and that those who do so press it may be regarded as sentimental and rather undignified, like grown-ups who have been caught on the floor playing bears with the children. It is, therefore, perhaps not unnecessary to repeat, not only that sympathetic study alone will break down the arrogance and complacency which cut free communication between ourselves and the African, but also that the realist and the practical man who takes up the other attitude is simply showing his own limitations in his own field, since he is willing to study all the materials he must use for the progress he advocates except that human material without which all the rest will, in the end, become mere dead things, unresponsive to the touch of his capitalizing energy. If practical results are asked, they can be seen in Tanganyika in the achievements, great and small, which are possible when the strong forces of tribal life are harnessed to a progressive social policy, and in the ease and peacefulness with which government is carried on from day to day in this vast and rather primitive country. I was deeply struck by a contrast in South Africa, where the strong tribal feeling of the Zulus, defeated, restrained and neglected, made me think of some large power-machine pushed on its side, still working, its energy running to waste, a sad, if not a dangerous, sight.

I think it is true to say that the more African society is studied, the more there is found in it to admire, not as a result of the first false reaction from our own complex and urbanized civilization, but because it contains certain solid elements which Europe would be glad today not to have lost. Most African tribes are true, natural democracies; they are the equalitarian societies of small peasant farmers rooted to the soil, and they have a solidarity that is powerful in co-operative effort. They have, in fact, many of the qualities that a Rome-weary Tacitus admired in our own ancestors. Vast changes will and must come, but I do not think that we need form the fatalistic conclusion that the African must tread every step of the long road we have trodden away from tribal society, and sojourn as we have done in the wildernesses of feudalism, despotism and individualism. Are we not today trying to create by political art some of the advantages we have lost by nature? Should this not qualify us to help the African to carry over into the twentieth century whatever was socially valuable of the first? It is no easy task; I think it is being attempted in some degree in Tanganyika, but it demands an increasing improvement of all branches of our African administration, and a far more intimate knowledge of the people whose future we are attempting to direct.

The Future of East Africa

The Times 13, 14, 15 August 1931

1. Settlers and Natives 1836–1931

The Joint Parliamentary Committee upon East Africa examined their last witness before the end of the Session, and their report may be expected in the late autumn.[1] Almost a century has passed since a parliamentary committee wrestled with this same problem of accommodating the claims of British colonists with the obligations of the Imperial Government towards the native races. The Committee of 1836 were provided with rather more precise terms of reference than the present Committee, being appointed

'to consider what Measures might be adopted with regard to the Native inhabitants of countries where British Settlements are made and to the neighbouring Tribes, in order to secure to them the due observance of Justice and the protection of their Rights; to promote the spread of Civilization among them, and to lead them to the peaceful and voluntary reception of the Christian Religion.'

The Committee sat with much industry during the shorter sessions of that time for a period of two years. Like the present Committee, they called before them officials, missionaries and settlers, with the representatives of the then new-fledged Aborigines' Protection Society, and African natives, Bantu and Hottentot, whom they examined with the help of interpreters. It is true that their terms of reference went beyond Africa, but the problem of deciding between the claims of the settlers in the Eastern Province of the Cape Colony and those of the natives, as put by missionaries and officials, was so great that twice as many witnesses were called from that country as from the rest of the Empire together, and the evidence took up an even larger proportion of time. In February, 1837, the Committee reported to the length of 85 octavo pages, in which they expressed a conception of trusteeship on a plane so lofty that, after a descent to the nadir of fatalistic indifference in the sixties, we are only just regaining it today.

Professor Macmillan's researches upon the great missionary Dr John

---

[1] *Joint Committee on Closer Union in East Africa. Vol. I Report No. 156, 1931.*

Philip (a prolific witness before this Committee) have served in part to still the voices which so long ridiculed the humanitarians of his day as merely ignorant and doctrinaire, and it might be interesting to see what answers the Committee, whose report bears the mark of the hand and the prayers of the devoted chairman, Sir Thomas Fowell Buxton, gave to the very problem which their parliamentary successors are now considering.

'The protection of the Aborigines [they said] should be considered as a duty particularly belonging and appropriate to the executive government, as administered either in this country or by the governors of the respective Colonies. This is not a trust which could be conveniently confided to the local legislatures. In proportion as those bodies are qualified for the right discharge of their proper functions, they will be unfit for the performance of this office. . . . But the settlers in almost every colony, having either disputes to adjust with the native tribes, or claims to urge against them, the representative body is virtually a party, and therefore ought not to judge in such controversies. . . . Whatever may be the legislative system of any colony, we therefore advise that, as far as possible, the Aborigines be withdrawn from its control . . . the initiative of all enactments affecting the Aborigines should be vested in the officer administering the government . . . and that the Governor of each colony should be invested by her Majesty . . . with authority for the decision of all questions affecting the interests of the native tribes.'

Later, referring to this system, 'the Committee could not be ignorant that it has been the plan generally, though not always, acted upon hitherto, and that it has failed because this power was lodged in the hands of inefficient men.' They did not scruple to name the three governors under whom the 'Caffres' were deprived of their land, and drew the conclusion—

'that the agency in whom this power is lodged is everything; that it must either be composed of men of high and tried principles, or much more responsibility must attach to it than has formerly been the case.'

This is as familiar as the statement of the great difficulty of the problem which both Committees in turn have had to face:

'To propose regulations which shall apply to our own subjects, and .. to those emerging from barbarism, and to those in the rudest state of nature, is a task from which your Committee would shrink, were it not that all the witnesses, differing as they do upon almost every topic, unite in ascribing much of the evil that has arisen to the uncertainty and vacillation of our policy.'

It is to be hoped that the present Committee will be led by the same consideration to attempt the same difficult task. Though the present Committee approach this problem by way of another, that of closer union between the East African Territories, it is nevertheless the racial question that makes their task formidable. If the racial question did not exist, if indeed Kenya were another Uganda, there would be no need today of a Joint Committee, and there would have been no Hilton Young Commission: the issue would either have been settled out of hand by the Colonial Office, or it would have been decided in 1924 by the Parliamentary Commission which first investigated the position. The real nature of the question soon asserted itself during the sessions of the present Committee, who, approaching it from the angle of a central constitution for the territories, and then from that of economic co-ordination, found themselves, like the Hilton Young Commission, brought up at every turn by the question of racial relations in Kenya.

The problem in Kenya, briefly stated, is to devise a constitutional structure that will allow full development to three races whose political capacity varies in inverse ratio to their numbers. There are about 15,000 European settlers, of whom about 2,000 are farmers; twice as many Indians, and nearly 200 times as many natives. Development has drifted along the conventional lines of a Legislative Council, in which, though an official majority is retained, there are 11 elected Europeans, five elected Indians (most of whom refuse to take their seats in protest against what they consider under-representation upon a humiliating communal franchise), and one missionary nominated to represent the native interests. The Europeans have, according to the Hilton Young Report,[1] exercised an influence over government even greater than the constitutional position seems to allow. Moved undoubtedly, in view of their small numbers, by not unnatural fears for their security, they claim to advance to predominance on the lines of 'ordinary colonial self-government', and, though in the latest official statement before the Committee they have modified their claims so far as to state that they

[1] *Report of the Commission on Closer Union of the Dependencies in Eastern and Central Africa, 1929, Cmd. 3234.*

are demanding no change in the constitution 'for the present', they have made it clear that the ambitions so often and so strongly expressed have not been abandoned. They are resolutely opposed to the Indian claims, and expect the natives to develop 'along their own lines' in the reserves, since they believe that for no time that can possibly be foreseen will any of them be fit to participate in a central legislature. They gave some support to the movement towards closer union because they hoped that, under the general control of a High Commissioner, they might be allowed an unofficial majority on the Legislative Council, and, being more than disappointed with the proposals put forward in the Hilton Young Report and the government White Paper,[1] they have decided for this reason, reinforced as it is today by financial depression, to oppose the project.

The evidence given before the Committee has shown how strong is the reaction against the settlers among the other races. They have no faith in any protection a High Commissioner might give them, and reject closer union almost entirely on the grounds that it might lead to an extension of the settlers' powers. The Indians of all territories are emphatically against it, and give as their reason (I quote from the mildest statement, that contained in the Government of India dispatch) their fear of 'the political ideals of the European settlers in Kenya'.

The native witnesses all spoke strongly against closer union; those from Tanganyika and Uganda expressing their distrust of the Kenya Legislature, of the system of reserves and the pass-laws, and their fears that in any closer association their own satisfactory position might be 'infected' from Kenya. The Kenya natives, dissatisfied with their present situation, were yet unable to imagine how a High Commissioner could better it. If they could not get into the presence of a Governor, how could they hope to penetrate to a High Commissioner? And, besides (with a sly humour which the leader of the settlers will be the very man to appreciate), 'Lord Delamere might get his ear.' The Baganda, progressive and confident within the four corners of their beloved Agreement of 1901, have, through their Kabaka, repeated at every official opportunity during the last few years their deep-seated fears of the European settlers of Kenya, who are 'continually asking for self-government that they may be independent of the Colonial Office'. Should they be granted a Supreme Council the settlers 'will inevitably think of their own advantage rather than of the advancement and wel-

---

[1] *Statement of the Conclusions of His Majesty's Government in the United Kingdom as regards Closer Union in East Africa, 1930, Cmd. 3574.*

fare of the natives, whom they will make laws to bring into subjection'.

The claims of the settlers are rejected not only by this vast majority of the inhabitants of East Africa; they have been condemned, directly or indirectly, by two Commissions and a series of governments. They are opposed by an important and growing body of public opinion in England, mainly on the ground that it is becoming increasingly clear that there is no place in East Africa for anything approaching a white Dominion, and that it is against British traditions and the best interests of all races to establish a minority and oligarchical system, a government of a black labouring class by their employers, under the disguise of a British representative parliament. The very principle of representation would be a standing invitation, first to the Indians, and finally to the Africans, to turn the sham into reality by all those ultimately irresistible processes with which our generation is growing familiar.

It would be unnecessary to discuss a claim that has so little chance of acceptance were it not that the leaders of the settlers not only appear to cling to it, but continue to turn away from the main body of criticism in this country. Directing their fire upon a scanty left wing of their opponents, they reiterate the complaint that a campaign of calumny has been carried on against them which it is the business of their delegations to combat by propaganda. The delegations will have served their constituents badly if they do not inform them that the opposition is composed of a large, important and growing section of informed opinion which cannot credibly be accused of sentimentality, malice, or, in view of the prolonged and public debate of the question, of ignorance. It is no answer to this body of opinion to say that the natives are treated well by the settlers, that they are not compelled to work, or even that they have sufficient land; or to reproach the British Government and people for not trusting their kin across the sea to give the native a fair deal.

There is no intention in any responsible quarter in this country either to injure the legitimate interests of the settler community or to depreciate their achievements. It is recognized that they are our own people, and that many of them typify the best in character, education and public spirit that this country can produce. If, owing to the plenitude of cheap labour, they have not been called upon to bear quite the burden of pioneers in other parts of the Empire, they have suffered greatly at the hands of their African stepmother, who pours her generous vitality not only into wholesome crops but into all those creatures and pests which prey upon them, and who is sometimes disastrously capricious in apportioning her rich measures of rain and sunshine. The small white

E

community, whose agriculture is only just emerging from the experimental stage, may well be proud when they survey the statistics of coffee, maize, sisal and wheat exported from their country. They have added to the revenues of the colony by their rapid exploitation of the soil, and their introduction of much that makes for modern civilization. They have a further claim upon the country which must strike anyone who has seen where and how they have built their houses and fostered their gardens, or has heard them talk of their adopted country. This is their love for a magnificent land and its wild life.

So much may be granted ungrudgingly, and if the colonists would withdraw their indefinite and excessive political claims no one in this country would add a syllable in qualification. Simply to combat these claims, however, it is necessary to remind the colonists that the dual policy has been fully implemented towards them; that they have had unfailing support, financial and otherwise, from this country; the advantages of extensive and cheap grants of land; of sharing in the services of a government largely paid for out of native taxation, and of the early concession of large elective representation upon the Legislative Council. When more is claimed it becomes the duty of this country to consider the numbers and to analyse the prospects of the community.

The recent intensive study of the situation has re-instructed us in the responsibilities thus undertaken, and has raised a doubt whether parliamentary institutions are suited to East African conditions and whether advantage might not be taken of the present opportunity to enter upon a modification of them which should progress according to the needs of a situation that is certain to change. It is a question that cannot be answered without understanding the interests of all three races. And here we are faced by our most serious difficulty. We know well the situation and claims of the Europeans; the Indians, supported by the august government of their mother country, have frequently explained their position. It is far more difficult to grasp the nature and needs of the 3,000,000 natives of Kenya, but the task must be attempted. The intention to do the natives abstract justice is not, and has not been, enough, and an ill-informed partisanship may do positive harm. We must endeavour, before trying to trace the lines of a constitutional alternative to representative institutions, to understand what the natives need from us in the sphere of government, remembering that the next half-century may prove, like the infant years claimed by the Jesuit teachers, the most impressionable period of their development.

II. *Working with the Native*

History will note that the European interest in Africa which developed
in the eighties of the last century was immensely increased by the war
and the establishment of the Mandates system. In this country the interest seems to have doubled during the last three years. It has its
romantic side, ably provided for by the American film industry, but is
in the main a serious interest in native society and native government
stimulated by a sense of the potentialities of our influence for good and
evil, and warned by a growing appreciation of mistakes in South Africa
and India. This new interest has been reflected back from Africa in the
richer reports sent in by all concerned with native affairs.

The government's *memorandum upon native policy*[1] should be read
in this light. It has been difficult to discover in any quarter objections
to the principles there laid down, in spite of widespread criticism of
some of the wording. The settlers, however, have protested bitterly
against the repetition of the Duke of Devonshire's famous 'paramountcy'
declaration,[2] though only perhaps in Africa would exception be taken
to the respectable democratic principle that the claims of the majority,
in this case one of overwhelming numbers, should prevail over those of
the minority. The document, which has the warm approval of all the
East African official witnesses before the Committee, expresses the
growing sense of the African's needs, and should be regarded not as an
attempt by one party to take something away from the settlers, but as an
addition upon the native side, and a reinforcement of principles accepted
by every British government.

In considering the position of the natives in their relation to the
constitutional issue in Kenya, it must be noticed that opinion is almost
solid upon the one point, that the political development of the natives is
to be in their own areas and 'upon their own lines'. This policy of
segregation – or, as Professor Edgar Brookes has renamed it, differentiation – changes character according to whether it is conceived in the interests of one or of both races. At its worst it offers only a temporary
escape from the intolerable sense of pressure which Europeans feel upon
their social and political life from the presence of a black majority: at its
best it is an attempt to provide full parallel scope to races at present
widely different in civilization. Since the industry and domestic life of
the Europeans are founded upon black labour, which forms a large

---

[1] *Memorandum on Native Policy in East Africa, 1930, Cmd. 3573.*
[2] *Memorandum on Indians in Kenya, 1923, Cmd. 1922.*

majority even in the 'white' areas, segregation can never be complete and it is probably undesirable that it should be so; it may, however, if conceived early and on proper lines, largely reduce the problem. East Africans might well study the situation in the south, where the policy has been attempted too late, and where even now the Europeans cannot bring themselves to take those measures which become more difficult every year, and which would, at least, alleviate the position. In so far as the European colony in Kenya are convinced that the natives are indefinitely unfitted to enter their society on terms of political and social equality, they should exert themselves to provide, at all costs, a sufficient alternative life in the native areas.

The costs may, perhaps, seem heavy. The natives must have ample land; they must be assisted to the utmost economic development, even if this affects the labour supply; there must be the most full and competent expression of the principle of indirect rule; and, lastly, all this must have as its background a sense of political security. The first two speak for themselves; the last two require some expansion.

The aim of our administration, if we are to succeed in developing native self-government, must be to find the true foundations of native society and build upwards and outwards from them. It might seem that this is today a commonplace, but in practice much of our administration in East Africa, as indeed in other parts of that country and of the Empire, appears to escape the guidance of this general principle and to halt between the old system of direct, and the new system of indirect, rule. Perhaps we are so convinced of our beneficence as an imperial power that it takes rude shocks to remind us that we are, in many quarters of the world, an alien government which has imposed itself upon subject peoples, and that we cannot move those peoples or reach their hearts and wills by endowing them from above with new and large ideals and loyalties, but only by stooping to discover the positive impulses that animate the smallest cells of their corporate life, and enlisting these in our work of civilization. Too often when the time has come when our subjects have expressed a desire to do things badly for themselves rather than have them extremely well done for them by us, they have shown an inefficiency and irresponsibility for which we are largely to blame. If we could remember that in relation to the Africans we are a foreign power with the functions proper to such, we should foster tribal society into an all-embracing organ of local government, through which all, and not merely a few, of our administrative activities would be expressed. This would automatically prevent us from attempting anything the people

either do not want or do not understand, and turn officers of all departments into teachers.

In some parts of Africa we are still carrying on expensive services,
medical, agricultural and the like, in no kind of partnership with the
people, although we are proving in other parts how well designed their
close-knit societies are for such co-operation. Similarly, the fact that
Africans are still unused to the handling of finance is in some quarters
made a reason for withholding from them the only effective training.
What a world of difference lies between the sentences which may be
uttered in different parts of Africa, 'That is the Government hospital,'
and 'That is our hospital' (or it may be 'our farm' or 'our school'). The
'our' means 'discussed and decided upon by our chiefs and elders, built
and maintained out of our tribal treasury, and administered in consultation with a committee of our people.' It is so that the white man
becomes the partner, not the dictator, and civilization ceases to dismay
since its services are taken and not imposed, while the foundations of
what may some day be an African nation are laid deep and true.

All this is impossible without knowledge. Perhaps only those political
officers with an anthropological bias, who through their whole period of
service have tried to study their people, can tell in what a dim light we
grope in this business of governing Africans. The political officer may
administer as many as 300,000 people, and even were he not for long
periods imprisoned in his office by routine work, his district would be
often difficult to cover. Owing to the conditions of the service, officers
are lucky if they spend more than six months before being moved to a
new district. They are, especially in Kenya and Tanganyika, almost
ignorant of the vernacular. It is especially hard for them to understand
the needs of the women of the tribes, who, since the government services
are staffed by men, and they themselves are largely ignorant of the lingua
franca of Ki-swahili, are doubly debarred from contact with the government.

Even if the natives were eager to instruct the administration in their
tribal history and institutions, instead of being most reticent, it would be
difficult enough, under these conditions, to feel very sure of the ground.
Yet the results of ignorance, where we are able to recognize them, are
striking enough, and tragic, comic or merely wasteful, according to
circumstances. In some cases we misapply Montesquieu's theory even
more than he did himself by a division between legislative, judicial and
executive functions which may leave the headmen as nothing but the
agents of government, so that it is no wonder a recent report laments

that some of them are 'unfortunately lacking in energy and need the constant supervision and stimulus of the administration in the carrying out of their duties'. Some of the native authorities we choose remain the puppets of the real power which lurks in the background.

These points are put forward rather to illustrate difficulties than to criticize. Native Administration is a branch of government in a state of rapid development; the best success can only be achieved by a trained and picked service, free from immediate political influences. Some of the European farmers have gone out of their way to gain a deep and sympathetic knowledge of their African neighbours, but many of them are too busy for such study and live remote from native areas, while the majority of the Europeans are townspeople whose knowledge of the native is confined to his most artificial and least favourable aspect as labour.

Inadequacies in the system of native administration in Kenya are not due to any lack of good will on the part of the settler community, whose delegates have, with justification, pointed out that the main responsibility rests with the Colonial Office, still less to any shortcomings on the part of a body of officers at least as able as any in the Empire. They result in part from the circumstances of Kenya's history in that the conscious and clear principles of indirect rule that were being worked out in West Africa were not generally available when Kenya was brought under the administration of the Colonial Office. In the last eight years or so political distractions have prevented a thorough and continuous policy, and produced a certain amount of distrust in some of the tribes. If reforms based upon research are to be part of a larger form of native local government in Kenya, the authority of the imperial government must remain unimpaired in the administration of the native areas.

A second condition is necessary to a successful policy of differentiation, if it is not to develop into another name for subjection. The hope that the natives will be satisfied to develop their own tribal institutions in the native areas will be falsified if there is even a fear that their destinies may be handed over to a parliament in Nairobi upon which the European colonists would predominate. The boundary round their lands, which under the imperial government might be their pride, would in this event appear to be their prison. Discontent and distraction would probably be the first results of such a situation, followed by a determined attempt to gain the predominance which our democratic theory gives to the majority. A Mosuto, when asked to consider the inclusion of Basutoland in the Union, remarked: 'If a horse is inspanned in a wagon together with a goat, the goat will be dragged and it will die.' Under East African conditions, the English horse might in the long run find that it was inspanned with an elephant.

We cannot, especially after the evidence given by the Kenya native delegates, shut our eyes to the beginning of native discontent in Kenya and of distrust between black and white. It has shown itself in a variety of ways, and perhaps most significantly in the united front shown by the Kikuyu on the question of female circumcision. Numbers of the natives read both the local and some of the English newspapers; they have formed political societies, and pool their political ideas in the slums and even the schools of Nairobi. I happened myself to come across evidence of the extent to which the natives of Kenya talk politics. I engaged a servant in Bukoba, who had been educated in a local mission school to the extent of reading and writing in Swahili, and I suggested to him that, as I was keeping a diary upon my travels, he might do the same. (Incidentally this diary, when handed to me before I left the country, revealed to me some of the mistakes and injustices I had myself, through ignorance, committed.)

It begins with a commentary on those parts of Tanganyika which were new to him. As a prosperous grower of robusta coffee, he was naturally interested in the valuable arabica coffee which he saw the Wachagga growing upon Kilimanjaro. 'Both planting and harvest make every eye that sees them jealous.' During his first journey in the train in Kenya, 'there were many people of various tribes in my compartment, and getting into conversation, as is the custom of travellers, they told me that they suffered greatly at the hands of the Europeans who live with them in the land of Kenya'. They proceeded to fill him with an exaggerated version of the land question and of the evils of the registration system. 'But I did not believe them. I thought it was just travellers' talk.' In the Kavirondo reserve, 'they told me they wept to think of Tanganyika because the conditions of their life in Kenya were so bad. But I, being benevolently disposed, was not able to believe these words.' Motoring through the Kikuyu reserve, he asked the native driver to explain what he saw and received this reply: ' "If you see a field planted with bananas and sweet potatoes, it belongs to a native, but if you see a coffee shamba, know that it belongs to a European." Then in very truth I was sorry for the people of Kenya, for I did not see that they had harvests from which to make trade, only food.' Among the Nandi, 'there was the same unrest among the people as everywhere else'.

This political consciousness will keep pace with the rapid spread of education and literacy, and will be played upon from outside by influences of all kinds emanating from London, Geneva, New York, Moscow, Durban and Johannesburg. South African native organization, indeed, is already reaching up to the Rhodesias, and it can only be a matter of time before the Bantu of the south and east draw together on the basis of their common interests. These need be no bogies; a contented people in a healthy political and economic condition will be immune from the mischievous contacts, and will find in the others much to encourage and inspire.

III. *Lines of a Solution*

In the preceding articles reasons have been given why the native areas of Kenya must continue under the administration of the imperial government and cannot be put under a Legislative Council upon which the European minority is predominant. If the Europeans cannot be kept under the tutelage of a crown colony government, while, in the words of Lord Delamere, 'two thousand years of evolution are enacted', then it would seem that two different kinds of government are required in the same country. We have already seen that the only point upon which there is almost unanimous agreement is that the utmost practicable degree of segregation should be maintained with the object of allowing differential development; where opinion divides is upon the settlers' claim that the Legislature upon which they hope to obtain a majority, shall be in supreme control of the whole territory, mixed and native areas included. The alternative is that the Legislative Council should develop towards responsible government of the settled highlands while the native areas should remain directly under the imperial government. This solution, which is generally called administrative separation, was put forward some years ago by Lord Lugard; it has been advocated more than once in these columns and received authoritative support before the Joint Committee, including that of the two officers who have had in their hands the practical conduct of native affairs in Kenya and Tanganyika.

There is, however, no easy way out of the situation in Kenya, and administrative separation, which in principle seems to solve almost every problem, presents certain practical difficulties. The first is that the country does not fall simply into divisions of black and white; and some means would have to be found of representing the special interests of Africans, both for the immigrant labour in the settled areas and for that undetermined number who are permanently detribalized. The problem of Indian representation would remain much the same as under present conditions. Whatever representation is given to Indian or native interests, there must be no doubt of the Europeans having political predominance in the settled area as far as the imperial government can guarantee it.

A further objection relates to the drawing of boundaries. There are two main settled areas, hinging upon Nairobi; west and north the great highland area that stretches unbroken from the slopes of Kenya mountain and the Aberdares across the lakes to the Kavirondo border, with a northward bend up the Uasin Gishu plateau to Mount Elgon; south and east, the smaller but also unbroken area of Machakos. These contain the bulk of settlement. The native areas also lie mainly in big tribal blocks. This fact would stand out more clearly if the present provincial boundaries, which were deliberately drawn to include native and mixed areas, were rubbed out, and, with them, the forest reserves, whose green intrusions on the map add a false impression of complexity. It would then be seen that the difficulties reduce themselves to three or four minor problems in the form of fragments or strips of settlement in native areas and the major problem provided by the Kikuyu reserve. This, while a continuous area from Nairobi to the eastern base of Kenya mountain, is for some miles near the capital penetrated by promontories and islands of alienated land.

A third difficulty is that of making a financial division. It is only increased by amateur guesswork before the materials for an analysis of revenue and expenditure are available. Possibly most of the objections, including that of prohibitive expense, arise from an exaggeration of the scope of the suggested measure. There is no intention to create two states, nor to cut all the departments of government in two overnight. Separation would extend to the largest practicable measure of local government. It is sometimes forgotten that this is a development that was begun when the boundaries of local government were drawn, and district councils were set up on the one side, local native councils on the other.

The Governor would continue to link these administrations together, and in those matters common to the whole country, of which communications and customs are the most important, he would probably have to be assisted by an advisory council on which the interests of both sides and of all races would be represented, but from which the possibility of a scramble for power on racial lines would be eliminated.

Here the constitutional issue in Kenya links on to that of East Africa in general. Kenya and Uganda, divergent as they are in some ways, are yet bound together by nature as the coastland and hinterland of a block of territory running into the heart of Africa, a single organism as far as communications are concerned, with Mombasa for mouth and the Uganda Railway for an alimentary canal. They have already common customs and postal systems. The services they share are much the same as those that would be common to the two divisions of Kenya, and the advisory council for the two might in time become the meeting-place for the three. Fears upon both sides at present make Kenya and Uganda suspicious of closer union, and any approach could only be with time and experience, and as a result of the new sense of security which it is hoped the development of administrative separation in Kenya might induce. Such an approach would only facilitate their co-operation in the fewer and less intimate matters which they have in common with Tanganyika.

It must be admitted that the settlers' delegates did not comment favourably to the Joint Committee upon the proposal for administrative separation. Their standpoint is that, until the time comes for them to ask for a further measure of responsibility, they are prepared to regard the present position as satisfactory. It is difficult to agree with this view, even if the more general considerations as to native development and the ultimate political future be disregarded for the moment, and attention be narrowed to the actual working of the Kenya constitution as it is today. The representation of native interests upon the Legislative Council is inadequate. The imperial government may insist that the scales be held even between racial interests; the local government may in all sincerity intend to do so, while the settlers in equal good faith offer their co-operation; but knowledge is necessary to secure more than an abstract and negative justice, and knowledge of native needs and ideas is not easy to come by. In the Legislative Council the official representation is largely made up of heads of departments who have little immediate contact with the natives. It is well known that this applies even to the Chief Native Commissioner who, during recent years, has rarely been able to get away from his department to visit the native areas. The main responsibility for representing African interests is thus thrown upon a single missionary, a busy man whose knowledge of the natives must necessarily be confined to those in the neighbourhood of his mission.

Is it surprising that the natives, watching from afar the mysterious workings of the central government, have a sense of being isolated and misunderstood, and expect no help from a conjectural High Commissioner? As for taxation 'they know that they are taxed and the money goes, and in the Executive and Legislative Councils it is divided up for different purposes, but they do not know how it is spent or why it is spent and they feel completely unsatisfied upon the subject'. This is hardly a situation that should be allowed to continue until the natives are ready to claim 'equal rights for all civilized men' even if the interval proves not quite so long as Lord Delamere's 2,000 years, nor is it one that can be adequately met by adding one or two more representatives of the same kind to the Legislative Council. Administrative separation would meet this problem by detaching native administration, and at least part of native taxation, from the central councils as at present constituted, and by putting them into the hands of officials able to concentrate upon their work and develop a system of native treasuries.

The settlers, upon their side, can hardly find the present constitution very satisfactory. It suffers from those inherent faults which Lord Durham revealed when he pointed out the difference between representative and responsible government and what comes of giving the one without the other. The settlers, then, are suffering from a recognized constitutional malady which England herself came through in the seventeenth century, which was fatal to our connexion with the American colonies in the eighteenth, and which we learned how to treat when our Dominions successively contracted it in the nineteenth. The symptoms are a continuous sense of instability, and, on the part of the representatives, an abnormal growth of their critical at the expense of their constructive faculties.

Administrative separation would allow a local application of responsible government as a remedy. At present the control of the government, which must be maintained in native affairs and in those common to the whole country, extends to matters which might well be released, and a second confusion is produced because the settlers are never sure where this control ends and their influence begins. The Hilton Young Commission considered that 'the present system of government has been undermined', and that 'Kenya unofficial opinion has in practice obtained a much larger influence in the counsels of government than accords with the strictly constitutional position.' This share, however, is subject to all the inconveniences, uncertainty, and friction which arise from lack of definition. Recent events in Kenya provide an illustration. The elected members have condemned the government in strong terms for taking certain action on its own responsibility, on the grounds that in so doing it had rebuffed the elected members and broken the convention of co-operation that had developed during the past years. Mr O'Shea stated that 'one had to be a member of the Council for a number of years to appreciate the fact that the Constitution under which they were working was an extremely difficult one, and it was only possible to work with success if there was proper understanding and co-operation between the executive and legislative side'. The *East African Standard*, while it admitted that 'the wide measure of co-operation which has existed in practice for a number of years has no constitutional foundation', asserted that 'responsibility was steadily growing in Kenya; if it should be replaced with irresponsibility – and that is the only alternative – there will be no question of where the blame lies'. The blame rests upon neither side and upon no individual; the trouble arises from a situation which depends far too much upon the personality of the Governor and his interpretation of a Constitution whose uncertainty invites misunderstanding.

The materials are here, then, not only for racial friction but for misunderstandings between the imperial government and the colonists which must have its own reaction upon the racial position. The South African analogy is instructive, but it must be used with care. The policy recommended by the Committee of 1836 may have been impossible there, but we must remember that it was never consistently applied, the home government alternating intervention and surrender with unfortunate results for all parties. We need not argue whether such troubles might be discounted if they could be regarded as growing pains in the youth of another great White Dominion which would spread over the larger part of eastern Africa. That dream has faded. Even if the colonists doubled or trebled, assumptions about their future must be made with reference to the map which shows the Kenya highlands in a relationship to black Africa very different from that of the two southern Commonwealth States. We must reckon with Tanganyika, where white settlers are few and localized and the best parts of the country are covered by 5,000,000 natives already well started upon a course of political and economic progress. Behind them lies the most heavily populated area of the Belgian sphere. To the west is Uganda, with its future assured as a native state or group of states; northward lie the unalterably native countries of the Sudan, Abyssinia and Somaliland.

The imperial government must do all it can to prevent the development of friction which, radiating from such a centre, might not only one day endanger the very existence of the white colony but might embitter and distract the relations between the imperial government and these African populations. This will seem no morbid fancy to those who calculate the rapid growth of communications in this region, still less to those who reckon with the advance of the African. The low estimates held of his powers have mostly been formed by those who have seen him in America and South Africa. To judge African potentialities for progress at their best it is necessary to see those tribes, of which the people of Bukoba in Tanganyika and the Baganda of Uganda are perhaps the best examples in East Africa, who have known little or nothing of subjection and disintegration, economic or political, and who are advancing with the help of European government as proud and healthy communities. Nor will they remain as tribes. Much has been said of the efficiency of the tribe as a unit of local self-government, but we cannot doubt that these small societies are no more than the foundations for larger edifices which will be held together by broadening social conceptions and which in some ways may compare favourably with the more top-heavy structures which are being run up in Asia. It is a development to be welcomed, since these units could provide the best kind of communal representation in some far-distant federation of East Africa in which, if the right decisions can be made today, the white settlers of Kenya may play the leading part.

The Times Leader 15 August 1931:

NATIVES AND POLITICS IN KENYA

We publish this morning the third and last of the articles in which a Rhodes Travelling Fellow just returned from East Africa discusses the future of native policy in Kenya. A large proportion of the time of the Parliamentary Joint Committee was occupied in hearing evidence on this topic. On the immediate question before that Committee – whether the closer union of Kenya with its neighbours Uganda and Tanganyika is feasible and advisable at this moment – the evidence and the financial position alike make an affirmative answer difficult. The conflict of testimony showed clearly that the general measure of agreement among the parties affected is too small to bear much of a structure at present. A policy which could have been put through ten years ago bristles with difficulties today. But the Joint Committee enjoys very wide terms of reference, and, whatever it may recommend about a High Commissioner, it can do a great deal towards settling the line of advance in native policy and towards forestalling the emergence of a political struggle between the different races in Kenya. The policy which would separate the native reserves from the rest of the Colony is open to various criticisms. A glance at any large-scale map of the Kenya highlands shows how inter-mingled the European and native races are, and to the argument from administrative difficulties there is added the psychological argument that any step which diminishes the responsibility of the European, through the Legislative Council, for native welfare might have the effect of making Europeans indifferent to that welfare and drive them to think and act in their own interests instead of in those of the Colony as a whole.

These considerations have not prevented administrative separation from gaining a steadily increasing support, because the greatest service that can be rendered to Kenya is to provide institutions which will minimize instead of promoting political controversy, and it is quite cer-tain that the demand of the natives, or of those who speak in their name, for more effective representation in the Legislative Council will grow. The bulk of the native population is politically ineffective and un-interested, but it does not require much intelligence for the many to give a general endorsement to the activities of the few. Those who think that the natives can be contented for long with representation by one or two missionaries, or even by a group of appointed Europeans, in the parlia-ment of the Colony seem to lose sight of the many influences outside the Colony, as well as inside it, which are stimulating political consciousness among the natives. Kenya is not a remote and self-contained island without neighbours, but lives in the heart of native as opposed to European Africa. To create tribal councils and native institutions that are subordinate to the Legislative Council of the Colony instead of being parallel to it might only afford a training ground for native politicians, whose natural ambition will be fixed upon entering the body in which the real decisions governing their welfare are made. Chronic controversy over the composition of the Legislative Council is something that it is of the first importance to avoid, and now is the time to arrest such a develop-ment and to provide an outlet for native political ability which shall enable it to be constructive. The alternative is to continue drifting towards a particularly dangerous and insoluble type of racial politics.

Nigeria Today

The Times 28, 29, 30 December 1932

1. *Studies in Racial Contrast*

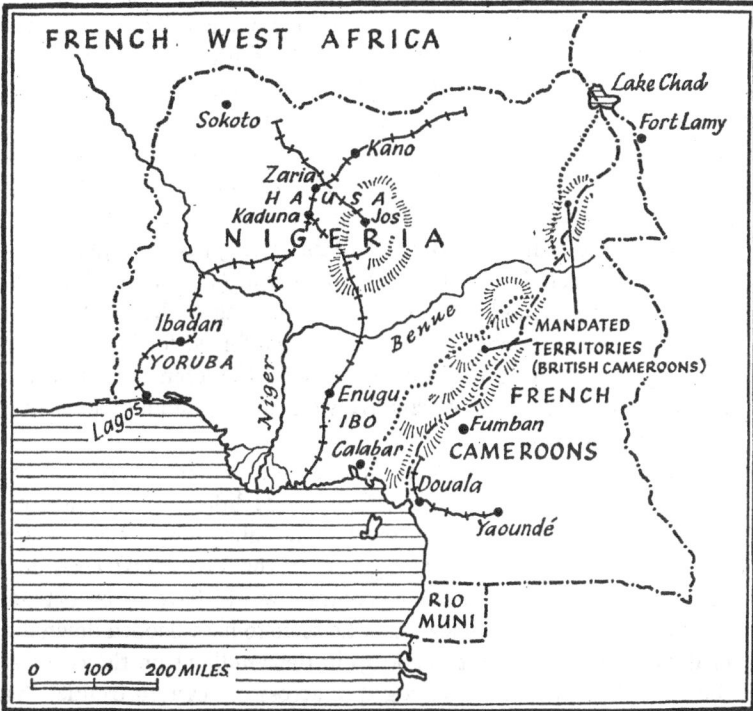

3 *Nigeria and the Cameroons*

In spite of all the penetration of recent years, Africa has not quite lost her old peculiarity of being more of a coast than a continent, and the British west coast is not only different, but still remarkably detached, from the rest of Africa.

It is so as regards communications; it is a *cul-de-sac* for the shipping lines, the airways ignore it, and the motorists on a dry-season trans-continental run still tend to regard Kano as their terminal adventure. It is so as regards racial contacts, if one excepts the rather brave trickle of pilgrims who straggle across to the eastern Sudan and so to Mecca. Its outlook, too, is different; its windows open upon Europe and, more distantly, upon the West Indies and America. Those of East Africa turn to Asia, while South Africa, like the old Dutch farmer, hardly sees the smoke of a neighbour's chimney. Yet, if the traveller, a little weary of the searching racial questions of the chequered countries, hopes to find a rest from problems in this all-black region, he will be disappointed.

Nigeria shares its first problem with the world. The revenue of the country has dropped from £5,973,822 in the financial year 1929–30 to £4,466,566 in the financial year 1931–32, while a profit on the working of the Nigerian Government Railway of £71,537 in 1929–30 has been turned into a loss (which is borne by government funds) of £316,626 in the financial year 1931–32. The situation is being met by drastic economies, the estimated expenditure for 1932–33 being £4,889,011, as against an estimated expenditure for 1931–32 of £6,358,189. The cutting down of estimates has led to a general stocktaking of the whole admini-stration. The importance of the event is reinforced for Nigeria by the opening of the governorship of Sir Donald Cameron, who returns to Nigeria after seven years of creative work in the administration of the natives of Tanganyika.

The twenty million people of Nigeria present a great variety of indi-genous culture. There is in East Africa a wide difference in the degree of political development between the Bahima kingdoms of Lake Victoria at one end and the little kindred groups of the Tanganyika coast at the other. For Nigeria the limits of contrast would have to be extended farther at each end. The Negroes, who seem to have flooded down diag-onally from the north-east to pile up in their millions on the coast, and the semi-Bantu peoples who edged in across the eastern frontier, have been played upon for thousands of years by conceptions of religion and kingship which are believed by some authorities to have come originally from the Nile. Imposed by superior immigrant castes, relayed from one tribe to another and crossed with primitive forms, these influences have resulted in societies of all shapes and sizes. But they largely failed to penetrate the deep forests or to climb the rocky hills. So at one end of the scale we find primitive groups whose social obligations hardly extend outside the family, while, at the other, the influx of Mediterranean or half-Mediterranean peoples bringing, in the last six centuries, the universalizing force of Islam, resulted in the construction of large kingdoms often out of the ruins of the older pagan chieftainships of Northern Nigeria. It so happens that these extremes occur in the far north and in the south, where the population is heavily weighted. And, using the whole of Northern Nigeria as their pasture, wander those Fulani herdsmen from whose ranks was recruited the Moslem aristocracy which, under the inspiration of Othman dan Fodio, seized nearly all the ruling places in the revivalist Jihad of the early nineteenth century.

It is inevitably the big emirates of the far north that first attract the traveller with their size and the prestige of their long history. It was in them that Lord Lugard made that act of faith the success of which has sent an influence throughout our native administration in Africa and beyond. It is here that he and his officers worked out the technique of indirect rule into a system that acts as a model, the main lines of which have been copied little by little elsewhere.

This northern country is not at first sight very pleasing. It is flat and dry and all but innocent of trees. But in Africa luxurious green beauty is too often the home of disease and the shelter of savagery. And soon the level, grey-brown fields, resting bare, as I saw them, between harvest and seed-time, acquire a charm. Their miles of unbroken tillage; their straight lines, and fences; their neat stooks of yellow cornstalks and little heaps of manure, grey with the ashes of the hearth; their onion beds, irrigated Egyptian fashion from wells in the dry river beds, are sufficiently impressive to anyone whose memory holds pictures of the meandering, makeshift cultivation of so much of Bantu Africa.

The way to see this country is to travel through it on horseback. The political officer on his rounds is, by rigorous tradition, always accompanied by the emir's representative, mounted and robed as befits his position, while behind him in single file will come the local district head and village head, a couple of mallams or so and one or two other anonymous horsemen, all with flowing, embroidered robes and bright saddle cloths, the leather of their harness brilliantly dyed and hung with coloured fringes and tassels. To ride with such a company, turning in, perhaps, upon the homestead of some half-naked peasant, who, with all his family, falls prostrate to the ground, is to understand what it meant to be a horseman in feudal Europe, particularly if you were the emissary of a great seigneur. Perhaps a Fulani nomad camp may be passed where these noble-looking people may be seen, content, while their cousins lord it in palaces, to follow at the tail of their white herds, living, in shelters of leaves or corn stalks, a life not unlike that of the Masai, and,

F

like the Masai, expressing a gypsy love of decoration in the designs of their milk calabashes and the fantasy of their gold braided hairdressing and huge ear-rings.

At night a lodging is found in a little rest-house of mud or wattle. Perhaps the district head will show you the quarters of his women, 60 or more of them, looking drugged with boredom in their crowded compound, and explain the different types and where he obtained them, until you imagine yourself in a stable rather than a household. At night the village girls may dance and sing, and then from under all the veneer of Islam the real tribal African breaks out. With the snobbery of the little market-town for the village, they sing rudely of the country girl and her lack of sophistication in matters of the heart, and, with an eye upon the pile of kola nuts with which I am rewarding them, they sing of my liberality and tell me (but I am not deceived) that my smile is like the lighting of a lamp and my eyes are as bright as the star that brings rain in August. And when the crowds have gone or remain a distant and respectful fringe on the night-sky, the notables may stay on, squatting round the fire and talk of the bad – or is it the good? – old days when the Harmattan, that cold wind in which we have shivered all day, and which brings from the Sahara a dust as fine as mist, was known as the Wind of the White Horsemen. For under its cover the dreaded bands from the desert, on mounts of chosen pallor, slipped down unseen until, from a hundred yards, they burst upon the terrified villagers.

Headquarters, the walled cities, have often been described, so much is there to delight the eye in the dignity of the ruling classes with their tall indigo turbans and embroidered gowns and the brilliant medieval horsemen trooped against crenellated red walls. Behind the colour the realities are solid. The emir and his councillors have a long day's work if they keep to their time-table, and the white-bearded Madaiki, Minister for the Provinces, who makes so restful a picture as he sits billowing upon the floor against an archway of red earth, is prepared at a moment's notice to jump into his old Ford and run out to any of the district headquarters. He collects over a quarter of a million pounds, not as a poll, but as an income-tax. Thirty per cent. of this goes to the government, 70 per cent. to the Maaji, or Treasurer. He sails in his wide robes out of his ancient, decorated treasury to prostrate himself in the sand beside your motor-car, and then shows you his robed and turbanned staff at work with their ledgers, notebooks, typewriters and all the paraphernalia necessary for spending a revenue of £230,000 without losing a penny of it.

It would not seem, so calm is the surface, that Northern Nigeria presented any pressing problems. The advance since Lord Lugard first marched up to these walled cities 30 years ago has been remarkable. As a result of his system, almost of their own momentum, the bigger Native Administrations have taken over one by one the activities of government, carrying out large capital works and employing and paying staffs of European experts until from the outside they appear to be approaching the position of self-contained native states. They are at present, however, limited in their authority. It covers natives ordinarily subject to the jurisdiction of native courts, a provision which exempts the European, the Asiatic – there are some considerable colonies of Syrians – and the southern natives. These last come from Supreme Court areas, and so the township where the mixed business community lives is a territorial enclave, under the Supreme Court.

Legislation was recently put forward which would have had the effect of making all persons within the area subject to native authority and jurisdiction, the Governor having power to exempt persons or classes of persons. It was expected that this would result in southern natives and even Asiatics losing their exemption. This was, however, withdrawn, and Sir Donald Cameron, at the Legislative Council of February, announced forthcoming legislation by which the authority of the Native Administrations and the jurisdiction of the native courts would be recognized as being, not territorial, but personal to their own subjects, and such other classes as the Governor should add by order. This, especially when read in the context of the Governor's speech, is not a distinction without a difference. It means, in fact, that a halt has been called in the rapid advance of the emirates toward self-containment. It is a halt, but it is certainly not a going back on the Northern Nigerian traditions; and it gives a valuable pause in which to consider the constitutional position of these units both in relation to the central government and within themselves.

II. *Rule of the Emirs*

It has been said that there has been a great advance in Northern Nigeria in 30 years of British rule. It is, however, well to understand its nature. The form has been the concentration of responsibility in the emir, whose autocracy, exercised through his council, his district and village heads, has been preserved and even increased by a tradition which debars British officers from any direct action. They supervise, tour, advise and report, but the only dynamic contact is between the emir and the single officer in charge of the emirate.

All northern political officers bear witness to the administrative ability of the Fulani; but none would maintain that they have undergone a complete change of heart in 30 years and have renounced all their old ambitions, some of which, as described in Lord Lugard's earlier reports and elsewhere, were, with fine and notable exceptions, to fill their harems and their stables; to make a brave show, at any cost of tribute, on all public occasions; to revenge themselves on their enemies and to entrench their families in all the more lucrative offices of state. Indeed, it is a striking tribute to the tact and devotion of the Residents that they have built up the present relations of harmony and confidence with an aristocracy so far removed from them in religion, ideals, and way of life.

Even so there is still a gap, which varies in each unit according to the personal factor, between the achievements of the Native Administrations and the ability and understanding of the native authorities. The gap is filled, and very ably and unostentatiously filled, by officers whose object it is to close it. This will take long, for here, as in many other places, we find ourselves obliged to enforce a policy upon native societies before we are able to communicate to them the social philosophy upon which that policy is founded. Such a communication must be delayed all the longer in Northern Nigeria, because a Muslim culture, backward but tenacious, has frozen them against outside influences, and in spite of all efforts education, as we define it, is only in its first reluctant stages. The attempt to advance too rapidly upon the road to self-containment would be to throw upon the political officer in control a responsibility greater than one man should bear, all the more as it is a responsibility in which he is given little help by the play of opinion upon the ruling class either from England or from the subject people.

A further advance towards territorial self-containment on the part of the emirate raises a more distant question as to the evolution of Nigeria; is it to be by consolidating the units until they grow together as a federation or by unifying them from above through the growing penetration of the central government? The balance of arguments seems to be on the side of the former policy; but it contains the danger, unless political officers continue to press liberal reforms from within, of crystallizing feudal monarchies which cannot indefinitely survive in the present world unless they are sheltered from its forces. It is for this reason that it may be asked whether the bigger and richer emirates would not be all the healthier for some measure of decentralization by which the village heads, the natural representatives of the people, might be brought into more active partnership with their Fulani overlords, especially as regards the local expenditure of some part of the revenues they raise.

A more difficult position than that of the assimilated Mohammedan subjects in the northern emirates is that of the pagans. As weather erodes the rock into desert sand, so the allied forces of Islam and slavery have for some five centuries or more been working upon the pagan tribal groups, turning them into the conglomerate Hausa-speaking masses of Northern Nigeria. Wherever the pagans found some shelter from physical conditions the process of erosion was checked. Even in Kano and Sokoto, where the forces were strong and the shelter slight, there are still remnants unabsorbed, while on the great central plateau more than 500,000 pagans have retained their peculiarities out of reach of the raiding horsemen.

The Nigerian Government in arranging boundaries had no difficulty in deciding, on the one hand, that the small enclaves should be subject to the emirates, where the inevitable and now painless process of assimilation will doubtless soon be complete; and, on the other, that considerable blocks such as the plateau should be recognized for what they are, independent pagan districts. There were, however, outlying areas, especially in the east and south-east, which, perhaps because they seemed too remote or too small to make convenient separate units, were included in the emirates which claimed them. The claim is in some cases open to doubt, and, so far as regards the eastern hillmen, would convince no one who has attempted to climb those scarps or seen with what desperate resolution these naked people have defended their independence and how, rather than venture into the plains below, they have forced the boulders of the crags into terraces on which they might grow their crops. Even on the lowest slopes of the hills the villages, which rise against the escarpment with the flatness of a drop-scene, have half-emptied before you can scramble up the first terraces, and while the headman is on his knees at your feet pouring earth over his head, the lowest rocky skyline is fringed with the peeping heads of his untrusting people.

The administration has in the last few years given a good deal of attention to these pagans. Officers are told off for months at a time to attend to especially backward areas, and frequently risk, and have lately lost, life in their determination to make a friendly approach and not to answer the first volley of stones too quickly with the rifle. Markets have been established at the foot of the hills to tempt these self-sufficient people into the outermost fringes of the world's economic system. A special school has been started at Toro where pagan teachers may be trained to the end that education may not, as at present, necessarily mean Islamization. In spite of all this the government is handicapped by its own system, which necessitates the administration of these difficult and remote people through an emir and district heads who, however efficient, are their ancient enemies and alien in religion and blood.

It would not be political wisdom to attempt to stereotype small, pagan groups in the middle of Mohammedan emirates. Islam, though often at first of a nominal kind, needs no proselytization to make it strong, especially as a social force. But there are outlying regions whose tenacious people would not easily be assimilated. It should be not so much a juristic question of proving conquest as of the best method of fulfilling our trusteeship, which, in the case of the eastern frontier districts, happens to be the specific one of the League of Nations Mandate over the Cameroons. To cross the border from these parts to the independent pagan districts of the plateau or the Benue or, indeed, to the Southern Provinces, is to realize what these boundaries mean in terms of administration. In these last areas the pagans profit by the direct and continuous attention of a district officer, of which they stand so much in need.

The Southern Provinces, a considerably smaller area than the Northern, though containing nearly the half of Nigeria's 20,000,000, runs from east to west in a curving strip, 500 miles long and about 150 miles wide. From the point of view of administration, it divides easily into three parts, the regions of chieftainship at each end, Yorubaland and the Cameroons province, and the central block of unorganized peoples.

The Yoruba and their kindred tribes are among the most sophisticated people of Nigeria. In Africa sophistication generally means disruption; but the Yoruba are fortunate in the possession of large and historic chieftainships, which we can administer very much on Northern models, and their tribal organization seems to offer a foundation broad and strong enough to stand the reconstruction on modern lines which the penetrating European influence demands. Examples abound of the extraordinary adaptability of these people. Ibadan, once the old war-camp of the Yorubas in the days when they were at odds with their neighbours and beat back the Fulani invasion from the north, was ruled by a council with a double set of titled members, for war and for peace respectively. The old camp is now a prosperous town of a quarter of a million inhabitants, and the old council is now a town council busy providing amenities for the citizens. The old Balogun, senior military member, sitting in an office of the magnificent new municipal buildings, will talk of his prowess in the wars and turn to the Balé, senior civil member, who is now the mayor, and argue with him as to how many guns they used to get for a prime woman slave. Only the other day there was selected as chief of the old centre of the Yoruba religion, a post which bears some resemblances to that of the Pope, an educated and 'trousered' Yoruba, an ex-station-master and a Christian. Clad in the traditional vestments, which include headgear strangely resembling a mitre, he officiates at pagan sacrifices while at the same time he is building a church in the sacred town, has an ambitious education policy, and is an authority on the production and marketing of cocoa.

The Yoruba *intelligentsia* who live in Lagos or Ibadan show, not scorn, but rather an affectionate respect for their chiefs, and it is this pride in their race, its customs, and its history, which makes it possible for the Yorubas, for all the violence of the changes working in them, to go forward as a people. Go forward they certainly will. Commercially they are strenuous beyond any comparison with the Bantu; their women will sit all day in the gutter offering for sale fractions of a box of matches or a bar of chocolate while the little girls of five or six run about their crowded markets hawking dried mice. The effects of sophistication upon this enterprising people are not all harmless, however, and one of the arts in which some of them excel is that of counterfeiting, while illegal distillation, an art imported from America, is beginning to make headway.

At the other end of the Southern Provinces lies the mandated territory, the Cameroons province, a country of hills presided over by the noble mountain of that name which rises almost from the sea. Here, too, there is considerable material for local government in the chieftainship of the semi-Bantu, who have a way, with their country, of winning the hearts of political officers.

III. *The Central Provinces*

It is the central provinces lying between Yorubaland and the Cameroons which present the most difficult administrative problem in Nigeria. It will be remembered that it was in this region that there occurred in September, 1929, that extraordinary outbreak known as the Aba riots, when thousands of women marched upon government stations, destroyed native courts, and looted stores, embarrassing mobs which in some places were only dispersed by rifles and machine-guns with considerable loss of life.

It had already been recognized that the system of administration, although the result of 30 and in parts 40 years of British rule, was unsatisfactory, and the movement flared up just as reorganization, which entailed the introduction of taxation, had begun, throwing a clear light upon the unusual lack of understanding between the government and the people. Since the standard of the service is, and has been, at least as high as elsewhere in the Empire, extraordinary difficulties must account for this extraordinary situation.

The five provinces of Warri, Onitsha, Ogoja, Owerri and Calabar, populated mainly by the Ibo and the Ibibio groups, contain about 6,500,000 people, or considerably more than the whole of Tanganyika. The single province of Owerri, perhaps the most difficult, contains more than 2,000,000, and here, as in parts of Onitsha and Calabar, they are massed in a way that has to be seen to be believed. The roads carry a constant stream of them on foot, bicycle or omnibus, and every mile or so the wayside markets are a dense crowd of women who nearly mob the stranger with their frantic greeting, and when one realizes how easily this kind of semi-hysteria could turn to another it is not difficult to picture the scenes described in the Aba report.

A recent estimate of density per mile over one division of nearly 1,000 square miles was 468, while there are areas of 20 square miles or so where it is over 1,000, figures which can hardly be approached elsewhere in the whole of tribal Africa. Nor do these figures relate to rich alluvial land, but to the mediocre soil of the palm-forest belt, and to an agricultural people who do not know how to fertilize their ground. Numbers alone, however grave their economic meaning, would not of themselves create the political problem. That in all its seriousness arises from a complete lack of natural organization beyond that of the groups of extended families. Just as the district officer, travelling this country, can never see a vista of more than 200 yards through the smothering palm-forest, so are the people in their massive numbers and their lack of leaders politically impenetrable. If in Owerri province the groups, and so the vital points of contact, numbered 200 instead of 2,000 (and indeed some investigations suggest a number nearer 10,000) the administration would long ago have got into partnership with these people. As it is, the almost inevitable attempt to make artificial groupings round selected representatives has led automatically to the corruption of the selected and the alienation of the people both from them and, to some extent, from us.

Numbers and incoherence do not exhaust the difficulties in these central provinces of Southern Nigeria. Upon a people so primitive and so unready for healthy development as communities, Europeanizing forces, economic and educational, have been playing intensively for 30 years and more. In the attempt to revive the natural authority of the family elders, half atrophied from neglect, there is danger of pitting the old against the young, the educated against the ignorant, the pagan against the Christian. It is, moreover, a paganism in which there runs a dark strain, lit up luridly from time to time by the discovery of murders, the object of which is the ritualistic mutilation and consumption of the victim.

Our peace, imposed from above, has allowed them to spill out of their small-cell organization, where their social obligation hardly extended beyond the family, and given them as individuals the freedom of a province and more before they have learned habits of association, with the result that they are in danger of becoming a mob before they have become a society. It is, however, impossible to despair of the future when one considers on the one side the vigour and malleability of the people, and on the other the devotion and sense of realities that mark the Administration in their present efforts to work out a solution. Research has been pressed forward, and already some promising experiments in the direction of courts and councils staffed by all family or group heads are in progress. Nothing could have been more fortunate at this juncture than the coming of Sir Donald Cameron with his successful experience of adapting Nigerian principles to meet the needs of some of the smaller and more primitive societies of East Africa.

There is the north and the south, but there is also, small in size and of an importance which is often debated, the coastal colony with the port and city of Lagos. Here a population of 150,000, under direct British rule, receives with their first force all the influences that come from Europe, from still more sophisticated colonies along the coast, from the West Indies and even from America. Already it is dividing into classes – an upper one of rich traders and of professional men who live in substantial houses and send a son or even a daughter to be educated in England; a middle-class of clerks, retailers and mechanics in the railway shops and garages; and the proletariat.

That the life of the first two classes is taking on an English colour need only surprise those who still believe in the essential dissimilarity of the African. Churches of 20 sects are filled each Sunday with well-dressed congregations; there are literary clubs and social functions where evening dress is expected. A well-planned suburban housing scheme has been a rapid success; the freehold plots are being filled up with houses built to suit purchasers by native contractors at a price of about £400 each; some have cost as much as £1,000 and more and have hard tennis courts. When they are barely finished, in go the lace curtains, the drawing-room 'suites', and the gramophone, while the householder will be seen in the evening planting flowers in the garden or putting up a fence to ensure privacy.

Half a dozen newspapers, all owned and, with hardly an exception, written and printed by Africans, are published in Lagos, and with all the faults of a young Press some of the leading articles, not excepting those which are critical of the government, claim respect. Some of the southern towns, in their degree, reproduce the characteristics of Lagos and have their libraries, sports clubs, and local newspapers. The district officer, with his well-beloved primitives in the bush, is apt to be a little scornful of the young African bourgeoisie; but they demand our sympathy and attention, not only because the standards they are following in hundreds, which will soon turn into thousands, have been set them by ourselves, but because the fact that they are just beginning to understand us gives them power to help or to hinder us in the business of government.

Nigeria with its deep differences between north and south and its fantastically uneven stages of development, is no easy country to administer. There is no clear-cut alternative between the policy of preserving indigenous institutions and that of superimposing an alien culture. The issue only presents itself in this simple form when we forget how deeply those institutions are already modified by the alien influence. In matters of justice, for instance, one single change in the south, the abolition of the ordeal, marks as great a revolution in their system as it did in our own. Even in the north, where changes were less necessary and far more difficult to achieve, important modifications in both law and procedure have resulted from our supervision.

To take an instance from another sphere, it would seem that by our preservation of native custom, as we have interpreted it, we have in certain places failed to recognize and so to regulate the development of that individual ownership which has been the inevitable result of the introduction of permanent economic crops. In these questions of the judicial system and the land laws, as well as in others, important reforms are already foreshadowed. It is difficult to judge the right moment for such advances; the policy of indirect rule automatically ensures that they shall not be too early; it is for the government to see that they are not too late. As modern influences penetrate they must find their reflection not only in purely native institutions but in our own administration, or both will be weakened by discredit.

The kind of paternal, amateur government in which the political officer, making the utmost of the comprehensive despotism allowed to him, became the father of his people, has produced in the district officer of today and yesterday one of those supreme types which history throws up when the opportunity and the genius of a race combine. In certain aspects in Nigeria the phase of government he represents is passing away. This need not be regretted when we remember that the preservation of native law and custom is not an end in itself, but a transitional stage by means of which Africans may in their own right become members of the civilized world, not as individuals, but as communities.

Nigeria Today

Letter to *The Times* 20 April 1933

This letter is an answer to Mr J. M. Fremantle, who in a letter to The Times *of 17 April 1933 suggested that my articles on Nigeria did not sufficiently stress the 'natural orientation' of West Africa towards the east and the north. He deprecated impatience with 'semi-institutions of the emirates', and with reference to the native states of India and to the legislation being promoted at that time by Sir Donald Cameron for the modernization of the judicial system in Nigeria, suggested that Britain should 'have enough imagination to hurry slowly'.*

Sir, – I am grateful to Mr Fremantle for his interesting criticism of my article on Nigeria. He believes that Nigeria's true orientation is East and not West. With his history and ethnology there can be no disagreement. The region we call Nigeria drew its human stock, its culture and trade from the north and east for all the ages before Europe knocked effective windows and doors into the blind wall of the southern coast. But Mr Fremantle speaks of a palimpsest; our administration must read the writing of today, and even that of yesterday records, partly as a result of the collapse of Moorish civilization in Spain and of the Turkish advance in North Africa, the loss of the old vitalizing communications with the north and east. Between the wall of the south and the closing Sahara to the north, Nigeria was cut off from the streams which once fed her culture from the Nile, from Arabia or Cordova, and was in danger of becoming a stagnant backwater. Pilgrims still seek Mecca and Toureg camels trace the old caravan routes to Kano and Bornu, but since Lord Lugard entered the red walls of Kano, the main current of trade and political influence has been from the West by the south.

What would Mr Fremantle have the government do? It is not in our power to do much to stimulate this isolated culture from within. Even if we could renew the old close contacts it would be a Rip van Winkle awakening since the West has come in full force to North Africa and in Egypt the co-religionists of the Nigerians, astonished at their conservatism, would hasten to indoctrinate them with self-determination and democracy. Yet the alternative cannot be mere restraint and preservation. This was not the policy of Lord Lugard, in spite of his wise directions to respect the religion and use the institutions of the people. Some northern officers, rightly determined that nothing must be allowed to weaken what is the greatest strength of the people, the self-respect they draw from the religion and history, are sometimes inclined to do less than justice to the far-reaching changes they have themselves helped to introduce. Had it been otherwise, the virtue would have gone out of their administration for surely we do violence to our reason in convincing ourselves that east of a certain longitude medieval institutions should be prolonged indefinitely under twentieth-century conditions, while the European who goes too far in repressing his own culture risks the loss of his integrity as an administrator.

I have spoken only of Northern Nigeria because I cannot follow Mr Fremantle in classing nearly all Nigerians (20,000,000) together in this matter. The non-Muslim Negroes of the south have greeted Western influence with eager receptivity and all their *intelligentsia* demand reforms on British lines. The Yorubas have been most affected, but there are signs that huge Ibo and Ibibio groups, with less history and social organization upon which to take their stand, will be even more impressionable. It is useless to sigh for the ideal of a slow, natural development of their own culture which we have made impossible. The factors are only partly under our control and reluctance to give of the best we have achieved for ourselves may cause a hindering distrust.

The antitheses of policy are not really so extreme as formal argument makes them. No one with knowledge of Africa is suggesting haste or pressure in Westernization. The proposals before the Legislative Council represent one of those readjustments in the balance between stability and progress that all human societies require from time to time, but with a dependent people the time and the measure must always be a matter of serious debate. Might not some of the opinion now so well instructed upon this issue in India be turned upon Nigeria, which however small and immature by contrast, is our greatest African dependency and merits more public attention than it receives?

France in the Cameroons

The Times 17 and 18 May 1933

1. *The Exercise of a Mandate*

By the treaty of Versailles the giant's share of the German Cameroons was allotted to France under Mandate. This slightly simplified a distribution which still leaves 16 international frontiers on the coast between Senegal and the Congo. For France the acquisition was important; all along the West Coast she is rich in hinterland, but poor in frontages. The Cameroons offers her Duala, one of the few good harbours on a surf-beaten coast. The two railway systems which feed the port will doubtless be extended one day to serve that most awkward mass of territory, French Equatorial Africa, which, from its narrow seaboard on the Gabon, stretches round the back of the Cameroons and into the heart of Africa for more than 2,000 miles to lose itself in the desert mountains of Tibesti.

The Mandated territory itself in tongue-shaped; from its broad root in the equatorial forest region it stretches through palm-belt and grassy plateaux to dry savannah set with granite bosses until the narrow tip thrusts itself between Nigeria and French Equatorial Africa to lick the reedy, brackish margins of Lake Chad. It carries a population of just over 2,000,000 at a density of five to the square kilometre. Each section is characteristic of its belt. In the south are the pygmies and the sparse Negro groups of the forest, increasing in numbers in the palm-belt; the intermediate hilly country supports numerous and industrious semi-Bantu; the dry savannah feeds the stock of the wandering Fulani and the Muslim tribes they dominate, while the black Arabs of the central Sudan pasture their cattle along the changing verges of the lake.

For a country that is only moderately rich, and sparsely populated, France may congratulate herself upon the success of her *mise-en-valeur*. The total trade of the country rose from 96,000,000f. in 1922 to 365,000,000f. in 1928, the three main exports, in order of value, being palm oil products, cocoa and timber. Although protests have been made at Geneva by the German members against the remission of shipping dues granted to French companies, the foreign mercantile community seems very well satisfied, on the whole, with the French interpretation of the economic equality enjoined by the Mandate. France furnishes about 30 per cent. of the imports, and takes 40 per cent. of the exports; Germany is the next largest importer, while England has 25 per cent. of the exports and 11 per cent. of the imports, the former figure being largely accounted for by cotton goods. Thanks to large capital and the large responsibility granted by our firms to their agents, a proportion generally estimated at about 75 per cent. of the total trade of the country passes through English hands. In fact, the only English complaint which I heard was that of an up-country trader against the administration of the cemeteries; he professed himself unable to sleep at night owing to the noise made by hyenas wrangling over the bones.

It is interesting, in view of the serious difficulties into which the economic crisis has plunged our African governments, to compare the situation of the French. The Cameroons Government has achieved marvels with a revenue which has stood, in the last few years, at the moderate figure of about 60,000,000f. It has not only carried the expenses of a government staffed by 800 Europeans, but has financed the entire cost of an ambitious programme of public works which would have been largely met from loan funds in an English colony. An extensive system of motor roads, many of them all-weather, has been constructed, radiating from the extremely difficult hill-country in the centre; 162 kilometres of railway have been laid through formidable country; while a deep-water channel and wharf with many other works, have been completed at Duala. On paper this has been accomplished by drawing up such pessimistic estimates of revenue that in one year the receipts doubled, and in another trebled, the surplus going into the reserve for extraordinary expenditure. The depression affected France and her empire later than England, and so far the effects have been slighter. For 1931 the deficit on a budget of 62,000,000f. was less than 5,000,000f., and that on the railways was negligible. Measures for the future include a reduction of salaries which, in contrast with our own practice, has had to wait upon metropolitan enactment of a general measure, while for the first time public works are being met out of a loan from France.

In raising this revenue the government has pressed hard upon the taxable limits of the natives, whose total liability has been quadrupled in 10 years. In somewhat tardy recognition of the effect of the depression upon them, the estimate for capitation tax for 1933 shows a reduction. The comparison is not easy to make, but as taxation is imposed on every person over 14 (a provision rigorously applied, to judge by the school-children who announce themselves taxpayers), and as extra medical, co-operative, and forced labour dues are levied, the native seems to be more heavily taxed than his neighbour in Nigeria, where taxation is lighter than in East Africa. Compulsory civil registration has lately been introduced, with a fee attached, which has called from one victim of this efficiency the remark that he could see some point in registering marriages but it was pretty hard that you should have to pay to be born and to die, neither of which you could avoid.

The Englishman, puzzling how the French have got so much more out of their revenue than could have been expected of an English government, is tempted to emphasize the part played by forced labour. The Cameroons Government gets the last unit of production out of the universal *prestation*, the enforcement of which, and its employment in roadmaking, must have formed a large part of the work of political officers during the past few years. Nor can it be denied that in Africa the use of forced paid labour for public works encourages economy in wages and amenities. The country was still full of grim stories of the extension of the railway through the unhealthy forest region to Yaounde. The able and humane Governor, who has just retired, M. Marchand, remedied these lethal conditions, but memory dies hard, and while I was in the Cameroons, at the mere rumour of further railway construction, a tribe much valued as 'labour' was dancing the gestures of shovelling earth, with the song 'How many of us will be taken for railway work?' and the counter question, 'How many of us will come back?' It is a hopeful sign that the Mandates Commission has been promised that, in the event of further construction, the workers' pay shall be trebled and their rations raised; and the construction cost a kilometre, through much easier country, is to be 880,000f. instead of 350,000f. There is always the danger, in the interests of 'development', of pressing too heavily upon the energies of an inapt and enervated peasantry, and the Commission has done well in its recent report to caution the Mandatory upon this point.

The Cameroons Government has been economical in far more justi-fiable ways. The overhead expenditure is less than with us mainly because salaries are lower. The average pay per head of the 71 political officers, with all their allowances and provision for pensions, works out at about 63,000f. a year, and these are the *élite* of the service, the *fonc-tionnaires* proper, who, unless patronage has excused them, have been through the École Coloniale and are transferable to other colonies. They are assisted by the 112 officials of the Service Civile, a lower grade recruited for the one territory.

It is only fair to say that, if the government gets the maximum out of the native, the maximum goes back to him. There is at present no racial division of interests. Much though the highlands resemble those of Kenya, there seems little likelihood of their attracting white settlement. When from the thousand unofficial Europeans the high proportion of women and children has been subtracted, with the traders and timber concessionaires, the number of true settlers would be small. A movement towards emigration at a later date might find the native peasant well entrenched behind the system of optional land-registration of which he is just beginning to make use. The last Governor saw the main hope of the country in peasant production, which has maintained itself through the crisis better than European enterprise, and he has been busy these last years turning the hill tribes into planters of Arabica coffee, which will benefit from the French bounty.

This central region, where multitudes of green hills rise into gaunt mountains at the English border, is the most promising area of the Cameroons. The people are plentiful and industrious; everywhere women may be seen bending black bodies over black soil, as naked as Mr Shaw's latest heroine except for a reticule containing their pipes and tax-tickets. Keepers of pigs, they must also be makers of fences, and as African fences insist upon becoming hedges, the settlements are tufted with foliage through which the curious tall houses thrust conical roofs. At the enterprising agricultural station of Dshang the French are experimenting in all crops that the natives might conceivably grow at an altitude of 3,000 ft. and more.

An equally vigorous policy is being followed at lower levels with regard to the oil-palm, with which the *prestataires* must line their roads and villagers make model plantations. There are several worse policies than this open to African governments, and if the urgency and compulsion of the methods followed, which make of the *Co-opérative agricole* something very different from what the name suggests, do not defeat their own ends, the natives will one day have their material reward.

The direct French methods are probably seen at their best when applied to the problem of disease. Outside capital cities, the Belgians can perhaps show the best-equipped native hospitals in Africa, but nowhere else have I seen a medical service so overwhelmed by its own popularity as in the Cameroons. Even in backward areas the hospitals and clinics were crowded, and the doctors and their native assistants were almost desperately at work. No fees may be charged to natives, a fact placarded on the hospital walls.

G

I had not travelled far in the centre of the Cameroons before the strong stab of the tsetse reminded me of the gravest medical problem of the country. Sleeping sickness, spread by the movements of the war, established itself along the central river valleys, to take a growing toll of life, and demand a most stubborn campaign. The French have put up a magnificent fight, and a special mission, assisted by grants from the mother country, under the inspired leadership of Dr Jaimot, has closely hemmed in the enemy. Evidences of the campaign are everywhere; in markets cleared for mass examination and in the travelling doctors and the uniformed native assistants met along the roads. The camps in the infected areas leave unforgettable pictures on the mind of huts where a dim fire just outlines the group around it, set in immovable postures of lassitude, expressing with their bodies the despair which, one hopes, they are no longer capable of experiencing in their minds.

II. *A Contrast of Policies*

It is not easy for an English traveller to pass a fair judgement upon French native administration. There can be few departments of government where we are more confident of our own achievements, yet across the border we find little but contrasts. Of these, perhaps the most striking is the position of the chief. In Northern Nigeria the palaces of important emirs and the native administrative offices are the real executive centres, thronged by large crowds and by horsemen from all over the emirate. Salaries of emirs, calculated on the basis of ancient tribute, are large; the more important chiefs draw as much as or more than the political officers who advise them; the Emir of Kano is paid as much as the Governor of Nigeria. I remember, by contrast, the meagre household of an emir across the border, once the peer of Nigerian rulers, into which the interpreter who was my guide entered unannounced and unceremoniously, making no secret of his own greater importance.

In the French Cameroons, as in much of French Africa, the chiefs, though their old sources of revenue are banned, receive no regular salary but depend upon the percentage they make out of head-tax. Emphasis is more upon their appointment by the government than the recognition of their traditional inheritance. Their ancient judicial powers have been strictly curtailed. Since direct rule in any literal sense is impossible where political officers are fewer than one to 10,000 natives (and even that ratio is high for tropical Africa), the gap is filled at first by the subterranean continuance of the old order, but, progressively, by a new type of native acting as government agent. Cooks and black sergeants are no longer put in as 'chiefs', as once in French West Africa, but even a chief of the blood can be turned into an agent. One of the old school, however, is likely to be less willing and less able for the part, so new chiefs come to the front, younger and more sophisticated, who in return for indispensable services in the collection of money and labour are given a free hand by authorities better able at first to judge results than methods.

As the grip of the government upon the country increases the big chief is no longer indispensable, and stories of abuse and oppression begin to find credence. The power of the big man comes to be parcelled out among sub-chiefs, but much of it falls to the uniformed native officials. Among these the interpreter generally plays the lead, as must be expected where, in the whole political service, only one man has earned the bonus for learning a native language and where continuity in posting officers is regarded as equally bad for them and for their district. Upon all these points the judgement of the English observer is assisted by a knowledge of our own mistakes in the same conditions and our half-success in a constant struggle to avoid them.

In the southern Cameroons, as in south-eastern Nigeria, native organization offers little foundation for indirect rule. But this is not true of the Muslim north or of the central region where the Bamiléké group are in the stage (paralleled round Lake Victoria and not without analogies with Norman England) at which immigrants of Mediterranean stock centralized and stimulated their subjects without destroying indigenous culture. In this prosperous hill-country the big thatched roofs of houses belonging to chiefs of the blood, more ambitious structures than any outside Buganda, can be seen peeping through the foliage. The Bamun, living farther north on mountains whose bold, treeless outlines are grateful to the traveller as he emerges from the muffling forest of the south, are even further developed. They acknowledged one king, who ruled from the remarkable city of Fumban. High in the lap of the hills, and behind 30 km. of walls and fosses, Fumban withstood the Fulani Jihad early last century and set a bound to Islam. The last king, N'Joya, was a man of parts. He set wise men to the invention of a language and a script with an alphabet of 435 letters with which to write the history of his line, while to settle theological differences he made a synthesis of Islam, Christianity and the local paganism. He has lately been deposed and exiled on grounds of oppression, and the country has been divided between a number of men responsible directly to the government. It is possible to credit N'Joya's misdoings and even his unpopularity, yet to wonder whether with more patient tuition at an earlier stage this interesting monarchy might not have been preserved to express the pride and serve the progress of the Bamun people.

The officials, from the Governor downwards, not only gave me the most generous help with my investigations, but discussed such issues fully and frankly. In spite of an item in their budget for translating Lord Lugard's 'Dual Mandate', I came to doubt whether the French can appreciate our African policy of indirect rule. The reasons lie deep in race and history. To their logic our system is inconsistent and indefinite; it is sentimental to their realism, while their ceaseless drive towards centralization strikes sharply against the exactly opposite tendency in ourselves. They professed themselves unable to understand how a people so humane as the British could allow so much responsibility to chiefs who must by their nature abuse it. Was it true that such and such irregularity had occurred across the border? That some of these emirs, bred in oppression and corruption, retained wide powers, and even inflicted capital punishment? I replied, for I had sufficient current evidence of the fact in French territory, that, so far as humanity was concerned, the anonymous agents of an all-powerful foreign government are as likely to commit abuses as established tribal authority and less likely to be found out.

Hard facts may have wrested so many concessions from the old extreme policy of assimilation that the French have been able to rename it association, but the assimilating genius of the French survives. It is clearly illustrated in their educational policy, with its insistence upon French and refusal to recognize teaching in the vernacular. Yet it is strange how pidgin-English has survived both French and German domination in the Cameroons. More than once, having lost my bearings far up in the interior, I have hopelessly tried, 'Parlez-vous Français?' upon some half-naked pagan, to get the astonishing reply, 'No, Ma, but I hear English.' The Frenchman does not preserve native culture because he does not share our respect for it. To him it is barbarism, and this in spite of an aesthetic appreciation of its externals which was brilliantly illustrated at the recent Colonial Exhibition in Paris. He will not now deliberately kill indigenous authority but why should he seek to keep alive what offends equally his conceptions of humanity, efficiency and centralization?

In seeking foundations upon which to build for the future we look for differences, the French for similarities. While native culture is even more certainly doomed in French territory than elsewhere to incomprehension and decay, unreserved co-operation with their rulers is open, and generously open, to the people. The French consciously aim at developing a gallicized native *élite* of government employees, clerks and planters. Though there has been a reaction against a policy of lavishly granting French citizenship, the idea behind that policy encourages the creation of the more indefinite but highly important status of the *assimilé*. In a circular issued last year the Governor-General of French West Africa stated: 'Although we have renounced the out-of-date policy of all-embracing assimilation, we have left a door ajar to permit individual accessions to French citizenship (*la Cité Française*). It is the fitting reward for successful efforts to raise themselves to our level.' The *assimilé* demands and obtains special consideration, and can distinguish himself in all those spheres where the rulers allow native partnership – government service, councils of notables and co-operative societies.

Moreover, the *assimilé* who has eyes to see may note encouraging signs, even if in the Cameroons they point, perhaps, beyond his own generation. Some of the most senior political officers, and most of the highest legal officials in the Cameroons, are men of half-blood from the French West Indies or Indo-China. M. Diagne, a Senegalese, ex-Under-Secretary for the Colonies, and married to a Frenchwoman, has recently toured French West Africa upon a special mission and been heartily welcomed by the natives at British as well as French ports.

Whereas British policy is concerned with the tribal masses, seeking to guide them through a slow integrated transition, the French system accommodates, above all, the *assimilé*. While the tribal masses are unable to formulate either appreciation or criticism, the *assimilé* is vocal in a political language understood by the world. In British Africa the emerging *assimilé* (for we assimilate in spite of ourselves) finds himself in a position socially and politically ambiguous, not without pathos at the moment but potentially dangerous for the future. In French Africa he is automatically incorporated as a collaborator in a work which, though it may fail to motivate us, is conceived on large and noble lines. The promise of social equality alone is enough to make French Africans forgive their rulers for any faults we may read into their administration. The policies of the two countries are so fundamentally different that there are limits to the degree in which one can learn from the other. Within these limits, however, France has of late years moved a little nearer to British indirect methods, though not so near in practice as in theory; and far-seeing Englishmen are wondering whether in our treatment of the *assimilé*, both in Africa and in England, we might not learn something from the French.

If the English attitude is that of a trustee, scrupulously respecting his ward's property and training him to be worthy of independence at his majority, the French attitude is that of a father who means to share among his children an inheritance long ago bequeathed to him by Rome; a French father, a firm disciplinarian, with no intention of indulging his children's vagaries or allowing them to grow up too quickly.

Only the future can decide between the two methods; we must content ourselves with unanswered questions. The French may ask whether we are not retarding progress by crystallizing primitive forms and narrow loyalties. We may ask whether the French may not find their assimilating forces strong enough to dissolve yet not strong enough to reintegrate. Both nations may well speculate on the future relationship of French and British West Africa when the peoples so arbitrarily and intricately distributed between them begin to draw together and find that the pink and yellow portions of the map are stamped with such different cultures and turned towards such different political destinies.

Protectorates in Transition

The Times 28 September 1933

Attention has recently been focused by events on Bechuanaland. The deposition of Tshekedi is still *sub judice*, but the limelight thrown upon an obscure corner of the Empire might be of greater service if it were not concentrated upon a single dramatic incident, but turned upon the background formed by the general position of the three South African Protectorates and our half-forgotten responsibility for them.

They are going through a difficult time. Two of them, Swaziland and Bechuanaland, have recently attracted the attention of a financial commissioner.[1] We need not assume, like the villagers whose neighbour was prayed for in church, that their case is now hopeless. Sir Alan Pim has diagnosed the trouble and proposed remedies which should lead to slow but certain recovery. Basutoland, by balancing her budget, has managed to escape this useful inquiry, but the territory faces many difficulties which are common to the other two, and beset countries depending upon the export of primary produce. Their production is mostly of low grade; their internal communications are scanty; markets and ports are far away; and they are embedded among countries which compete with the same products and control the lines and conditions of export.

Bechuanaland is, perhaps, in worst case. Its immense area is mostly mapped upon the Kalahari desert, on the fringes of which black and white pasture their cattle under menace of drought and disease. Huge areas of dry grazing lie untouched while the area round the waterholes is trodden out. Yet the problem of marketing to Durban or the mining areas is even more difficult than production and an embargo, placed by the Union because of foot-and-mouth disease in Southern Rhodesia, has had serious effects. Swaziland, that beautiful little country which goes down in three great steps from the high veld in the east, has the same export disadvantage, a dangerously capricious rainfall, and malaria in her rich low veld. Of the 500 white farmers who own three-fifths of

---

[1] *Financial and Economic Situation of Swaziland. Cmd.* 4114, *Jan.* 1932. *Financial & Economic Position of the Bechuanaland Protectorate, Cmd.* 4368, *March* 1933.

the land 40 per cent. are absentees, and a proportion of the remainder are poor whites and a liability upon the state. Basutoland, a purely native territory, is still able with its larger population of 500,000 to make both ends meet, but with increasing difficulty. The traveller who rides – and ride he must – in the high Malutis will see the hard, treeless shapes

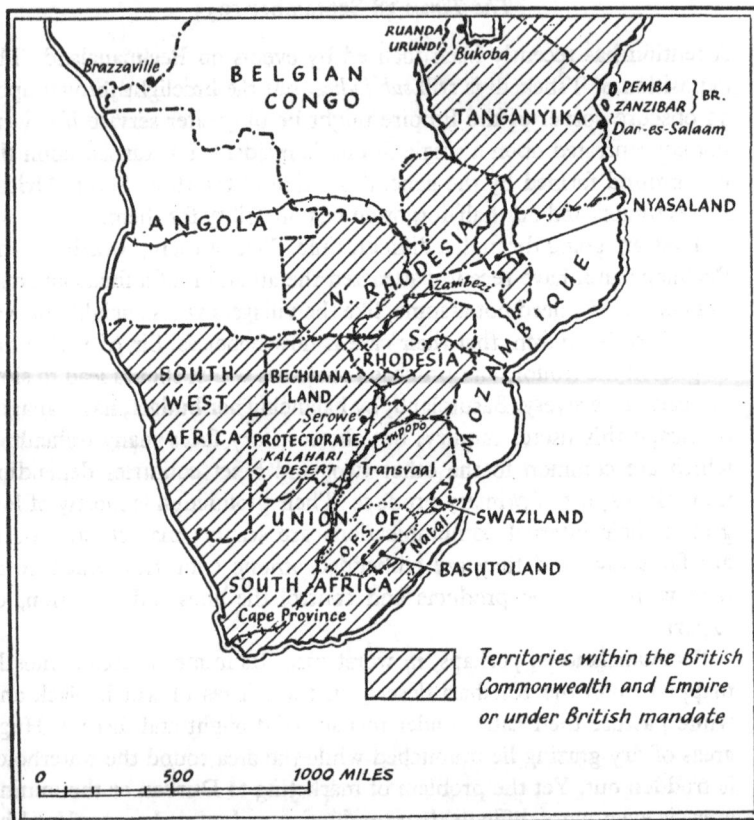

Territories within the British Commonwealth and Empire or under British mandate

4   *Southern Africa in the Thirties*

of the mountains softened by a running pattern of cloud shadows, blue upon green, with streams rushing zig-zag far below where he may refresh himself from a long day in the saddle in pools banked by irises and arum lilies. But from the heights he will see also the country's danger, the people forced up into the hitherto lonely mountains by increasing pressure on the soil, and the sores where the veld, bared by over-grazing to the tearing rains, is carried down every *spruit* to thicken the Orange River on its spendthrift way to the sea.

In all these territories semi-nomadic peoples, caught in the waves of European invasion, have been immobilized before they have learnt the the technique of immobilization. It is small wonder they destroy their soil. Penned behind this European innovation of frontiers and relieved from some of the conditions which keep down the numbers of men and stock, they try, without knowledge of paddocking, rotation of crops or manuring, to produce not only the old subsistence but the extra economic crops with which to pay taxes and buy the new necessities from the stores. The impossible is made possible by export of the one commodity for which the market is always ready, labour.

At any one time from 50 per cent. to 70 per cent. of the able-bodied men are away. All parties try to make a virtue of this apparent necessity, and certainly it is too well-established to admit of abrupt interference. Every economist, however, has condemned it. On the Union side the cheap labour of these temporary peasant-miners is, in the end, the most expensive. At the same time the labourers, being based on family subsistence in the Protectorate, and asking only tax-and-pocket money, debase the whole rate of native wages, thus injuring the permanent black proletariat and depriving the Union of the home market which 5,000,000 moderately prosperous peasants and artisans would provide in any other country.

On the Protectorates' side, while all experts, including Sir Alan Pim, agree that the territories could progress if the natives were taught to make a better use of their soil, what educational advance is possible for a people whose sons having spent their boyhood herding cattle, interrupt their prime of life by distant excursions of nine months to two years into unskilled industrial labour? The ultimate remedy for this complementary wastage of human power, though it lies in exactly the opposite direction from the mirage of segregation, is to build up by slow parallel degrees on the one side a permanent population of efficient and contented labour round the industrial areas, and, on the other, more productive and self-sufficient native territories. A start has been made with the last policy, but its fulfilment waits upon a recovery of the world markets.

The prospects of such an advance in the Protectorates are closely bound up also with political and administrative problems. Native administration, with its preservation of tribal institutions and the wide powers left to the chiefs, bears a superficial resemblance to the indirect rule of tropical Africa. It is, in reality, something very different, and might be distinguished under the name of Protectorate policy. It is the product of circumstances rather than principle.

In the confused three-sided struggle of the last century in South Africa, tribal belligerency was not enough to save African kingdoms, as the Matabele and Zulus learned to their cost. Two other things were needed. The first was the alliance of nature. Khama made an ally of the desert, Moshesh of the mountains. Urged by the Frenchman, Casalis, to settle beside his mission, the great Suto leader, pointing to the magnificent natural fortress of Thaba Bosiu, said, 'That mountain is my mother.' He was buried on its summit under a cairn of stones, and when I climbed the mountain I felt it a privilege to set up the fallen splinter of rock, roughly scrawled with his name, which serves as headstone to his grave. It is mainly to the wisdom of Khama and Moshesh that Bechuanaland and Basutoland owe their existence today. Over the heads of the various local authorities, provincial, Dutch or chartered company, they appealed steadily to Caesar, resolutely handed themselves over to the Great White Queen, and were reluctantly accepted by the imperial government.

Neither party was then able to understand the situation, both thankfully assuming that a guarantee of frontiers, with a minimum of interference inside them, was all that was wanted. Today we realize that only the surface of the past has been preserved. Underneath its whole content has been transformed. Tribal society cannot be kept unchanged when all the conditions it was developed to meet have disappeared. This is most obvious in the case of the chieftainship. Relieved from the test and discipline of their old responsibilities, the chiefs draw their authority from the alien government above, which cannot replace the controls from below which it has unconsciously destroyed. Since there were limits to the amount of grain, beer, milk and meat that one man could consume, the riches of a chief in the old days were necessarily a common benefit; the great individualizer, money, has changed all that.

The visitor from Nigeria or Tanganyika, versed in the true gospel of indirect rule, will find much to shock him in the Protectorates, especially in the lack of supervision over the chiefs, who record neither their cases nor the emoluments of justice they retain, and who have considerable and not very closely defined rights to levy tribute and labour. He would remark the absence of the basic institution of the Native Treasury. It would be short-sighted to impute blame to either the chiefs or their advisers for this state of affairs. It was not in these small Protectorates, with their special limitations, that the technique of indirect rule could be developed. They can, however, take advantage of the moral taught by today's experience in tropical Africa, that it is not by mere non-interference that tribal institutions can be carried over in working order from the old into the new Africa, but by vigorous leadership and continuous administrative education.

The error, perhaps, has been upon the right side; over-interference in uninstructed days might have destroyed the great asset the tribes have preserved, their sense of solidarity centred upon their chiefs. The traveller who crosses the Basutoland border must be struck at once by the free bearing of the natives, even if it is the pride of beggars. Dressed in their gorgeous blankets and big grass hats, they ride their little ponies with the high heads of men who still own their country. In Serowe the national sentiment gathers about the red-gold crag round which the native town is spread. On the summit, above the tomb of the great chief Khama, rises the delicate bronze form of a *duiker*, the emblem sacred to the tribe, while below, on their stools in the Khotla, the chiefs administer their form of justice until lately under the presidency of the great Khama's son, Tshekedi. This tribal solidarity has so far acted mainly as a shelter; its dynamic capacity is still latent. Reform is in progress in all these territories under the stimulus of a High Commissioner and of three Resident Commissioners with wide experience of other native countries. It will, however, be a delicate task to break with traditions which half a century has hardened, and to press supervision upon conservative chiefs in such a way as to strengthen and not impair their powers.

Conservative to fanaticism the chiefs certainly are, but there has been a reason for it and for the almost too unquestioning allegiance of their people. This has been the constant uncertainty as to the political future, caused by rumours of imminent transfer to the Union. Such rumours have also had a disheartening effect upon the administrations. Lord Strathcona's recent statement in the House of Lords, with its repetition of promises to safeguard native interests and to consult both the natives and Parliament before considering transfer, will do something to clear the situation from this side. Upon the Union's side the new Coalition government is a guarantee of moderation, and moderation is not likely to raise a question which, in view of the passionate attachment of the tribes to the imperial connexion and our reiterated commitments to them, would cause serious embarrassment to all parties.

This seems all the more evident now that a decision has been made to leave the whole controversial question of Union native policy in continued suspense. Many South Africans, especially among the young and

by no means only those of British descent, impatient at the old sterile
policy of repression, are beginning to think out native policy on entirely
new lines. It will be some time before their thoughts can affect policy. It
will take at least as long for the reforms in the Protectorates, representing
for South Africa a valuable alternative experiment in native administration, to work themselves out. When these two events converge, and not
before, will it be possible to arrive at a settlement acceptable not only to
the Union and the imperial government, but to the Africans whose
destiny it will decide.

Future Relations of Black and White in Africa

The Listener 28 March 1934

The outstanding fact about tropical Africa today is the greatness and suddenness of the change that has come upon it. Half a century ago modern Europe broke in upon peoples many of whom had been living in a state of virtual isolation for the few thousand years in which much of the rest of the world had been civilizing itself. I suppose that in the whole of history no people has ever had to pass through a more critical century of development than these tropical Africans in the fifty years that have just passed and the fifty that are to come. And we in this country have undertaken the responsibility of guiding nearly fifty millions of them through this crisis. What kind of change is taking place in the Africans themselves? How quickly has it been happening, and how quickly is it likely to go on happening, and how are we going to deal with it?

Let us put two contrasting pictures side by side. We find ourselves in front of a village set in the middle of rolling bushland; a rough palisade of branches round a circle of about twenty huts, with mud walls and thatched roofs. We are greeted by the patriarch, the grandfather of the hundred people who live in the enclosure – an old, bearded, very dignified man, naked, like all those round, but for a narrow piece of hand-woven cloth round his loins. He is not only head of this large household, but as the senior of his line, of three or four more neighbouring households. This little community of some few hundreds is almost completely independent of the rest of the world. The household heads, and especially this senior one, have authority over the others because they are in close touch with the ancestors, whose favour is vital to the very existence of the group. Our old friend here, when he succeeded, had the heart of his predecessor served up to him in a human skull. He ate it solemnly, that the power of the dead might live on in him. He refreshes this power by eating human flesh from time to time; also the hearts of all dangerous animals killed in the hunt. A young man is smearing himself all over with a kind of liquid clay. He is going courting and this is a magic to make him seem strong and beautiful in the eyes of his beloved. The women are returning from the fields with their hoes, or carrying pots of water on their heads: we notice their stately walk and the elaborate patterns cut almost all over their naked bodies; the young boys are driving in the goats that they have been herding all day; the girls are tending the still smaller children. Everyone here, it seems, has his or her exact status and duties according to age and sex. Keeping order among them is not very difficult. The discipline of tradition – the daily co-operative struggle with nature for a living, their equality in poverty – all this makes for order. And few dare risk the automatic punishment of magic that most offences bring into action, and the disfavour of the ancestors. For the visible village life is ringed about by invisible forces, and these must be placated or combated by magic. The gravest responsibility that lies upon the elders is not the control of men and women but of natural forces. In times of crisis, when the food crops upon which their lives depend are in danger, they follow, in their obscure little corner of Africa, a tragic custom as old as human history. They take a young unblemished child, and sacrifice him. At night, secretly and in silence, some of the blood is mixed with earth and scattered on the fields to restore the power of earth and bring on the crops.

And now turn to look at the other picture. We are in a west Coast town, seaport and capital. We set out to pay a call upon an African gentleman. His house is large and it has an excellent view over the water. A servant answers the door and we enter to find ourselves in so completely European an interior that it is with a shock of surprise that we notice the family photographs are of black people. We know our host; we met him having tea with the Governor the other day at the races. One of his horses won the big event. He is a merchant, a rich man as riches go in these parts, a member of both the Legislative and Municipal Council. He comes in now, an extremely dignified and courteous host, speaking good English though with an accent, and we settle down to talk and tea. We discuss English politics; he has been to England several times. Last time he and his wife took their younger daughter and settled her into a new school. His son and older daughter are both there at the University; the son has just taken his Finals at Cambridge. If we were in the mood we could go on a little further where we might call upon a well-to-do lawyer who is part-owner of the best daily paper in the country. It is his brother who writes those leading articles criticising the follies of Europe, or perhaps our own policy with regard to, say, the Kakamega goldfields in Kenya.

Here, then, we have two extremes as they exist in Africa today. How many people do they typify, and how many more are at different stages in between? The families which have become Europeanized to the extent of those we called upon are probably to be counted only in tens. They are to be found mostly on the west coast – they hardly exist yet in the east. Below them are perhaps some hundreds of families partly Europeanized. They are, as it were, candidates for the top grade. In the next class we shall find a good many thousands scattered all over British tropical Africa. They are made up of teachers, clerks, government employees, small contractors, and so on. They talk English fairly well, wear European clothes, read a newspaper, play tennis, belong to a debating society and live in a sort of bungalow-cottage with a tin roof and curtains in the windows. Below them comes a much larger class of people living in certain areas, exposed to European influences, round a town or a big mission station. Or the area may be one where a profitable economic crop is grown – cocoa in the southern Gold Coast, palm-oil in parts of Nigeria, cotton in Uganda, coffee in Tanganyika. In these prosperous areas there are probably plenty of schools, plenty of markets, and good roads. A family income far above the usual African rate has allowed them to buy some of the treasures out of the shops, some European garments, if not a complete outfit, a bicycle, a sewing machine, a wrist-watch, packets of sugar and tea, or, perhaps, gin and patent medicines to restore virility. It is in such areas that the younger genera-tion which has been to school grasps eagerly at the new freedom. Nominal Christians, half-emancipated from the fear of magic and ancestors, they are apt to flout their elders' authority. Small wonder that Dr Audrey Richards, the anthropologist, heard an old man saying to his son, 'Now you are a Christian you think you can do any wicked thing.'

Finally comes the great mass of Africans who have not been exposed to quite such strong influences. The coming of the European has changed their lives in many ways. Yet those best qualified to judge, the anthro-pologists, reveal to us societies that have clung to their old customs with great faithfulness. In spite of many changes imposed upon them, the pattern of life remains much the same.

We see from this that civilization for the primitive African is bound to mean to a large degree, and especially at first, Europeanization. The French call the process assimilation. It is as though the two cultures, African and British, were two thick fluids of very different colour and character. Each population, like millions of little absorbent objects, lies soaking in its own culture, as in a great vat. For the most part we sprinkle our culture widely over the great African vessel in the form of schools, and mission, trading and government stations; in this way it cannot dilute the African culture very quickly or uniformly. But if you take and drop single individuals, as with our Negroes educated in England, into the British culture, then assimilation will go further; if they stayed there it might become complete. Assimilation is largely bound up with economic progress. The question is – will African trade advance at the rate it did in the decade before 1929 or remain static or declining as in the last few years? That is for the great financiers and economists of the world to answer – if they can!

Even a moderate advance in Africa means change at a rate unknown before in history. Must we go through here all the painful incidents that have accompanied rapid change in our Near and Far Eastern dependencies? The feverish young nationalism: the fierce internal conflict between parties and religions: the premature demand for Western institutions: the bitter racial hostility towards ourselves, answered on our part with reluctant repression in the interests of order?

We naturally look to the form of government to see if it is any better devised in Africa to stand the inevitable strain. I explained in my last talk that the dominant form in British tropical Africa was known as indirect rule. Its object is to allow change by growth rather than by mere substitution – growth of familiar tribal institutions into more modern forms to suit modern conditions. This is surely the soundest way to build upwards towards a real unity: to keep the native foundations even if the central forms are ultimately on the English model.

'But', I seem to hear a voice interposing, 'can you really assume so readily that Africans have the capacity to advance like this. Why did they never build any civilization of their own? Have not scientists proved that the Negro brain is inferior in capacity and quality? And why should these savages leap 2,000 years and presume to take the culture and the institutions that we hammered out painfully century by century for our special needs? No, let them develop on their own lines. Let them be good Africans, not bad imitations of Europeans.'

Neither science nor history as yet gives us a clear-cut decision on this question. But you cannot travel about Africa without realizing vividly certain things. Negroland was barricaded from the rest of the world by desert and forest; and nature added her handicaps to this isolation. In some ways her indulgence sapped human effort: in others her violent alternating moods of drought and flood made it useless beyond a certain point: she bred an abundance of wild beasts and pests and diseases to prey on men's crops and livestock; she kept man himself diseased, half starved and ridden with fear. It may be the average African brain is smaller than ours. It is by no means proved. Nor is the exact significance of size. We are told that the brains of Esquimaux are larger than ours, but we do not contemplate sending to Greenland for our next batch of dictators. The brains of English women are smaller than those of English men and yet – but I must not start on that. It would take too long. And you can imagine all I might have said. As for the 2,000 years' argument, there is all the difference in changing by slow effort your own environment, and in having it changed for you, as it were, overnight, with nothing to do but adapt yourself to it. The figure 2,000 years is quite irrelevant. There are examples – I know one or two of them personally – of Africans 'civilized' by our standards in one or two generations.

And lastly, this curious modern tendency – though it has been known in the world before – to monopolize culture or civilization. As if civilization were not a common stock which has slowly accumulated throughout history. All the important elements of civilization had been contributed by other people long before we savages began to squeeze in next to France for our share. And since then, can we claim to have given back as much as we have taken? It would be pretty poor, now that we happen to control the access of so many Africans to civilization, if we tried to edge them out. It would certainly compare badly with the generosity of our French neighbours who express pride and joy because they are handing on to Africa the torch that Rome gave long ago to Gaul.

Some of you may be wondering why I have seen the future relations of black and white as a matter between only the British government and the Africans. What of white settlement? Numerically the thousands of white settlers in East Africa still make small showing among the African millions, though their wealth and ability give them an importance beyond mere numbers. The settlers dream of a British dominion from the Nile to the Limpopo or the Cape. Will they increase? Probably, but it is difficult to count upon any very large increase because there are important limiting factors – lack of land; lack of labour; and the competition of blacks in skilled and semi-skilled work.

But even if white settlers will never form more than a small minority in East Africa, race-relations in black-and-white Africa may affect our relations with black Africa. There is no need for me to tell you of the conflict of principles that has marked the history of Kenya. A series of governments, a series of visiting commissions, an all-party committee of both Houses of Parliament, have all refused to consider handing over the political control of the African population to the settler minority. They

H

have not done this because they have any prejudice against the settlers, but because, as Sir Edward Grigg and Dr Oldham explained in their broadcast debate, minority rule would begin with injustice to the Africans and would probably end with the submergence of the whites. African and Indian delegations to England have expressed almost passionate opposition to such a step. As the Africans advance in education and unity and in the sense of power that numbers give – a Pan-African movement is inevitable some day – their opposition will become formidable. The only hope of satisfactory racial relations in the long run is for the settlers to renounce a political ambition that causes such tension and consider the alternative of co-operation. Yet it must be difficult for the Kenya settler to imagine any form of co-operation with Africans today. He must see them as abysmally backward and often very tiresome, stealing or infecting his cattle, misunderstanding his orders, breaking labour contracts. It is greatly to his credit that he is generally such a just and kindly employer. Yet in the long run more is needed than a happy master-and-servant relation. Will that more be possible? Or will it be checked by that psychological barrier which is not peculiar to settlers, nor to Africa, nor to white people – colour feeling? It is upon this that the whole future depends.

This colour feeling is no mysterious, almost sacred, instinct which it is impertinent to analyse. It is made up of reasonable elements, each of which can be exaggerated into unreason. There is the sense of difference roused by colour and features so unlike our own. But this sense of difference may be exaggerated by mass-suggestion into an indiscriminating repulsion which will prevent any approach to Negroes as human beings. Another element in colour feeling is the sense that the Africans' culture is lower than our own and in some ways distasteful. This is reasonable. But it may be magnified into the view that all Africans are and always will be an inferior species. Anthropology can correct this view by revealing the reasonableness, the richly human character, of their old social life; and history would remind us how recently, as mankind's history goes, the disgusted Romans hewed down the Druid Groves and the altars strewed with human remains. As for the savagery of inter-tribal raids, we should not forget the vast, the literally incalculable, losses by war, famine and disease which we Europeans inflicted upon Africans by forcing them to fight each other in a quarrel which had nothing whatever to do with them.

What really turns a rational appreciation of the differences between the races into an irrational colour prejudice is fear. It may be only a slight sub-conscious fear – fear of economic competition: fear of racial mixture. Only the latter could make us so unreasonable as to refuse to have any social contact with even the most civilized African. That is why it is impossible to dine with an African in Johannesburg and possible in Lagos. Yet all our experience teaches us that these relations are less likely to develop on this level of mutual respect: mixed blood on a large scale has mostly resulted from the men of the superior race taking advantage of the subjection of the inferior.

The Joint Committee on East Africa looked forward to the appointment of Africans to Legislative Council. But how can this or any other form of co-operation develop if the eastern Africans are mostly so backward? The slow working of the educational system will not normally produce leaders in the near future. A special arrangement is needed to give some picked men and women the completest possible education. Half-education with its hindering inferiority complex is useless for this purpose. One can see already that we are in for endless misunderstanding with those who are educated enough to understand their own point of view but not enough to understand ours. Dr Aggrey was one of the few Africans – perhaps the only one – to go further, indeed all the way.

Moreover, I believe that such Africans could profoundly influence race-relations. Every European who meets them would shed a load of prejudice in the first ten minutes. He would get a sudden vision of what Africans can and will be. He would realize that co-operation is not only possible but valuable. Only experience can show that: the settler is not going to listen to pious exhortations from outside.

Africans have always suffered from being regarded as a huge, incomprehensible, vaguely menacing black mass. They gain on emergence as individuals for the simple reason that they are such likeable people. They have their faults but they have some very useful virtues – kindliness, tolerance, humility, a great zest for life. And they smile better than any other people in the world. I wish I could break off there so as to end upon a cheerful note. But we cannot hope to leave this difficult question in a spirit of easy optimism. It is useless to pretend that there is not a conflict of principles in Africa today. Those who are struggling to give the Africans scope to develop to their full stature as civilized human beings, rather than as servants of our civilization, will need the moral support of this country. We have declared ourselves against a policy of racial discrimination. If we go back on our word on the grounds of defending white civilization, then white civilization will become so much the less worth defending. It would be a sad thing if African scholars writing the history of the British Empire a thousand years or more ahead should describe our magnificent achievements up to this point, and then go on to relate that it was just here and in Africa that we began to go back upon our great traditions.

Some Problems of Indirect Rule in Africa

Address to the Royal Society of Arts 24 March 1934
Published in the Journal of the Society for 8 May 1934

I have included this talk for two reasons. One is that it reflects, not without some criticism, views held when the so called 'indirect' principle of Britain's African administration was working up to its climax. It will be seen that, contrary to views held by some of its critics, and especially by Africans, the principles of indirect administration were not, even in 1934, held as immutably fixed or permanent. The second reason for inclusion, and for retaining the report of the discussion, lies in the character of the audience. It included Lord Lugard himself; Mr F. H. Melland, former native commissioner, in Northern Rhodesia; the leading anthropological official of Nigeria Dr C. K. Meek; the distinguished historian of Africa, Professor W. Macmillan; Sir James Currie who had been director of education in the Sudan, and Mr McGregor Ross former director of public works in Kenya who had become a severe critic of Britain's policy there. The record illustrates also the part which African students in this country could play at this early stage in discussions of this kind. Miss Thomas was, I think, the first African woman called to the Bar in Britain and Mr Dowuona became one of the first two African administrative officers in the Gold Coast and was later a member of the staff of the University in Accra. Dr Drummond Shiels, Labour Under-Secretary of State for the Colonies 1929–31, was the Chairman. The talk and the discussion therefore reveal something of the spectrum of ideas about African administration held in 1934.

The paper I am to read to you this evening deals with a large and difficult subject. There are several people here who have spent a working lifetime in the practice of native administration, and who may rightly question by what authority I comment upon their work, still more criticize it. My reply is that I do not claim to speak from some external eminence of intellect or experience. I see my function (to which the fascination of Africa lured me from my settled course) as the humble but necessary one of synthesis. The Colonial Office, perhaps wisely, has never inclined to the French practice of standardizing administrative forms or methods. Very wide discretion has been left to the African governments. These until very recently pursued their own methods with little reference to the experience of their neighbours. Even now the fruits of that experience cannot fully be gathered from official papers; native administration more than any other must be studied in action. Yet Africa is a large continent, and our territories are scattered. Through the generosity of the Rhodes Trust I have been able to travel fairly extensively in order to study native administration. In such a general survey I could place little reliance upon my own observations. Such knowledge as I have is largely a total of the contributions of others, and, above all, of those political officers, from governors down to assistant district officers, who have received me in such a friendly spirit and have been such patient teachers. I think I understand something of the difficulty of their work and the many handicaps under which they carry it out. Such criticisms as I may make have generally been the agreed conclusions of discussions I have had with their own more thoughtful members. With so much personal explanation, I can approach my subject with less sense of presumption.

I am not taking indirect rule as a general principle in the government of subject peoples; as such, of course, we can find examples of it all through the Empire and all through history. I take it in the narrower sense in which it is more usually employed, the application of that principle according to a special system in parts of British Africa. I cling to the term, though some of high authority seem inclined to abandon it, because I think it would be difficult now to withdraw it from circulation, and because it is one we can easily stamp with its proper meaning. We owe the inception of this system to Lord Lugard and the administrators who worked under him in Northern Nigeria. He made a lasting virtue out of the temporary necessity in which he found himself in the first years of this century. If there are any who still imagine that the system was quickly born in a moment of inspired opportunism, let them re-read not only his *Dual Mandate* but, even more, his early annual reports and his political memoranda.

I will cut short my explanation of the term indirect rule, because, even if the explanation is not superfluous to this audience, its meaning will become more clear after we have dealt with some of its problems. I have not yet seen a short definition which wholly satisfies me. In default of such I offer you a provisional one. It is as brief as I can make it – too brief, perhaps, for clarity. Indirect rule is *a system by which the tutelary power recognizes existing African societies, and assists them to adapt them-*

selves to the functions of local government. This recognition is a legal one. It is the great merit of the system that while it gives to native institutions the fixity and status that only detailed statutory recognition can give, it yet allows that wide variety both in the forms and in the degree of authority delegated which is absolutely necessary under present African conditions. Following the Nigerian model, it is normally built round three aspects of government, judicial, executive and financial. It might be expected that the third would be legislative. Its absence is only partly due to the subordinate position of native societies: it also arises from the unfamiliarity of the African with the legislative process as we understand it. Nor is it quite true to say that it is absent; most native authorities are granted the power to make rules or by-laws, but, so far, except perhaps in Uganda, there has been little spontaneous utilization of this power.

The judicial aspect of indirect rule is not only the recognition of native law and custom, which, of course, obtains and must obtain even where there is direct rule, but the recognition of native law courts. On the executive side either a chief, or a chief in council, or a council of elders, is gazetted as a Native Authority under the Native Authority Ordinance, with the powers and duties it confers. Native Treasuries, which are the aspect furthest removed from natural forms, are set up to receive, for local expenditure, a rebate of the taxation paid by the group. In every aspect the powers granted can be, and generally are, graded according to the size of the society and the competence of its rulers. The unit recognized is generally known as a Native Administration.

Such, in brief outline, but in its completest application, is the system of indirect rule. It started at much the same time at two points, Uganda and Nigeria. In Uganda it sprang almost inevitably out of the conditions of the Uganda Agreement of 1900 and, to a lesser extent, from those with Toro and Ankole. There is evidence to show that, before the treaty, the officers concerned differed as to the form our guardianship should take. But the agreement stipulated in considerable detail for the maintenance of the Buganda kingship and council, courts and local government, and for the payment of all the native officials. This agreement was elaborated and extended from time to time. Apart, however from these agreements and the necessary legal structure of the system, there has been little published documentation on native administration in the form of reports and instructions. This was doubtless due partly to the small size both of the country and the service, which enabled officials to keep in close personal touch with each other and with head-quarters. The Uganda system does not seem to have had much influence beyond its own borders. The native administration of its neighbours, Kenya and Tanganyika, shows little sign of such influence.

It is from Northern Nigeria that the formative influences in native administration have come. Perhaps the main reason is that Lord Lugard was not only a great practical administrator, the success of whose work was its own advertisement, but had the capacity to rationalize his achieve-ment, and articulate its principles. Certainly their rapid advance in the last few years has been the main fact to record about native administration in Africa. It looks as though indirect rule may become almost an alterna-tive term for native administration in British tropical Africa. This is doubtless partly due to the growth of interest in this country in all African matters, entailing a discussion of administrative principles with a general endorsement of the Nigerian system.

The most sweeping advance was that carried out by Sir Donald Cameron in Tanganyika. In the six years of this governorship he intro-duced the Nigerian system, but in a form adapted to the different condi-tions and the different racial stock of East Africa. In his Native Admini-stration Memoranda he re-stated the system, incorporating the general lessons learned from the long experience of Nigeria with the provisions specially applicable to Tanganyika. At the same time he infused into the administration the qualities of sympathy, patience and faith without which indirect rule would be a paper façade. Our mandate for the Cameroons meant the extension of indirect rule to the peoples there.

Some years ago the Sudan sent a political officer to study the Nigerian administration, and in the last few years the Sudanese Government has been remodelling its administration, especially in the pagan south, on indirect lines. Sir James Maxwell, who went as Governor to Northern Rhodesia with experience of Nigeria, introduced there a system of native courts and authorities in 1929. In 1930 the Governor of Nyasa-land, Sir Shenton Thomas, sent his Secretary for Native Affairs to study the Tanganyika system, and a beginning has been made in the reorgani-zation of Nyasaland on more indirect lines. Sir Richmond Palmer, who did so much, especially upon the Treasury side, to build up the Northern Nigerian system, went as Governor to the Gambia and applied his experience to the little river-territory. In view of projected reforms in the Gold Coast, the Secretary for Native Affairs was recently sent to Nigeria to study and report upon the system there. And, to bring the wheel full circle, the return of Sir Donald Cameron to Nigeria has seen the model itself remodelled to meet changing needs, and its principles applied as never before to the peculiarly intractable conditions of the south-east.

But even where the Nigerian model has not been consciously followed, the ideas upon which it is based have affected native administration. It may not, perhaps, be too fanciful to imagine that the slight advances made recently in the Union towards the recognition of native chiefs and courts owe something to distant inspiration from this quarter. The reforms proposed for Bechuanaland will probably show traces at least of such influence. Both the French and the Belgians have expressed increasing interest in our methods, though it is doubtful whether they would find it easy to apply such a peculiarly British compromise.

It is in these years of rapid extension that the system has been subjected to a growing volume of criticism. This seems to me an almost unqualified good. The Colonial Service is in the peculiar position of a bureaucracy which can hardly be checked from above or below. Its operations are too remote and specialized for proper comprehension by the home government and too inscrutable for that of the people it is guiding. Yet without comprehension there can be no control. The absence of criticism – and I use it in the sense in which it is more often applied to literature than politics, as including appreciation – has been a weakness to the Colonial Service. It works in a dim light and upon rapidly changing material. Constructive criticism can stimulate it to the re-adjustments that are almost continually necessary in its work, and even the attacks of the unconstructive may force it to re-define its policy and so increase its self-knowledge. It suffers, however, the same limitation as the English Civil Service in that it cannot very easily defend or interpret its own work.

I propose to consider what seem to me the one or two most important criticisms of indirect rule that have recently been made. The legal recognition of native institutions is dependent upon their actual recognition. The criticism has been made by Captain Rattray and others that this recognition has often been faulty and incomplete. There is much truth in this. Political officers were not qualified to carry out what is, after all, expert anthropological research. In the past when most of the research work should have been done they had little or no opportunity of acquiring technical equipment, though many individuals went a long way towards making up the deficiency with those personal qualities without which technique remains barren. An increasing number now receive training. But the initial faults here were more than a matter of technical equipment: unavoidably or not, officers were often denied the time or the conditions in which to carry out their preliminary investigations. They had to make rough-and-ready arrangements with the groups as they annexed them.

Let me give some examples of these mistakes. They will also bring out the extreme difficulty of the task we have set ourselves in Africa. Captain Rattray, in his study of the tribes of the northern provinces of the Gold Coast, points out that in certain parts the original, or earlier, inhabitants were divided into totemic clans ruled over by priest-chiefs, Ten'dana, who relied upon spiritual sanctions and were dependent upon the support of the elders. Over these an invading people established a political suzerainty of the type we can more easily translate into our terms. But, as so often happened in Africa, they did not venture to displace those who had the spiritual guardianship of the earth, with all the duties that guardianship involves. But, when we came, we accepted the claims of the political overlords and overlooked the position of the Ten'dana. In some cases where the Ten'dana had not been subjected they feared for the effects of contact with these impatient, revolutionary white men, and sent unimportant agents to face the music. These became 'chiefs'. (This frequently happened in Africa: Mr Driberg records it of the Bari, and there are other instances.) I do not want to enter into the merits of what may be a very difficult case with two sides to it; I have not the knowledge. It may be that the overlords are now so firmly established as to be the only authorities with whom (and this must always be the test) co-operation is practicable. But the instance shows the possibility, perhaps even the probability, of making initial mistakes in the recognition of native authorities.

Let us turn for examples to Nigeria. It contains by far the largest population of any African territory and it is not surprising that it shows the greatest range of social groupings. In the great emirates of the north we find the most advanced political organizations of tropical Africa, while in the hills, often only a short distance away from the emir's capital, and in the southern forests, we find some of the most backward and atomic groups under our rule. When you get, as in the south-eastern provinces, six or seven million people in this stage, the administrative problem becomes serious. It is telling evidence of the difficulty of the recognition of such groups according to the principles of indirect rule, that, in the very home of the system, it is only today that it is being properly applied in these parts. In the densely-populated Ibo country it is roughly true to say that extended families of a few scores of people were practically independent, though for certain purposes a neighbouring group of such families (officially known in these parts as a kindred) acted in concert, while upon still more exceptional occasions there might be an even wider collaboration. In groups of this size and character there can be no concentration of authority of the kind that we recognize as executive. It is not only that it is dispersed between the hierarchy of groups from the biological family to the group of kindreds. Even if you take a single group, the kindred, authority is not, as appears at first, simply a matter of gerontocratic succession. We shall probably find that to seniority must be added the highest grade of certain titles, while other functions are distributed among the priests of the earth-deity, the priests of the local fetish, the diviner, and associations of the middle-aged and younger men. Is it surprising that a government whose agents could not talk the almost insuperably difficult language of these people, were so long unable to take them into any effective articulation? Increasingly careful efforts were made to choose men acceptable to the people. But the promotion of an individual from societies where everything was transacted in council acted as an automatic disqualification. His position became the more impossible when he was made to act for a section of the population which, if it was the smallest conceivable to government, went far beyond their restricted social boundaries. From these conditions arose the significantly named 'warrant-chiefs', men whose chieftainship depended solely upon the warrant they received from the foreign government and the cap of office they wore upon their heads. The increasing difficulty, and in some cases the breakdown, of administration after 30 years shows that the recognition of the natural authorities is not always a matter of anthropological pedantry. During the last few years, as a result of prolonged inquiries and discussions with the people concerned, experiments are being made in recognizing the heads of kindreds, and even, in some cases, of extended families, and of allowing them to act in council under the most natural and elastic conditions. It is hoped that, when we have at last got down to the ultimate authorities, they will build up voluntary federations where our artificial ones have continually broken down.

What I have said applies mainly to the Ibo. I could illustrate the point with examples from other tribes of similar constitution. To take only one instance from Northern Nigeria, a careful investigation of a very large and primitive group recently revealed that in almost every case the official headmen were those who had no claim to primacy. I had the good fortune to visit these people with the officer (who, incidentally, is a trained anthropologist) who was carrying out these investigations. He spent an evening discussing affairs with a group of very old men, heads of kindreds. They were not much to look at as far as clothes and cleanliness went, but their faces were marked with a shrewd and humorous appreciation of all that they had experienced in their long lives. Presently there arrived the official district head, a considerably younger man, well dressed, and wearing an embroidered cap. He attempted to sit down among them where they crouched on the ground opposite to us. He was greeted with an outburst of refusal, half indignant, half amusedly sarcastic, 'What, that little boy sit with us! Not much! Let him sit over there by himself. Such impudence!' It was, of course, a tribute to the sympathetic and tactful attitude of their officer that they felt able to show him their feelings in this way.

In East Africa similar mistakes have been made. In Uganda these could hardly be called mistakes. When the administration there, having organized the affairs of Buganda, began to deal with the rest of the country, they found no comparable political development outside the three other Hima kingdoms. The Nilotic peoples of the north, and the Bantu of the east, differed from each other in many ways but were alike in being divided into small clans, whose affairs were in the hands of councils of elders and who offered no authoritative individuals who could be gazetted as chiefs. The government set to work to extend the Buganda system as far as it could. Buganda 'agents', as they were called, were sent to the Basoga and Bagishu to train chiefs and teach efficient methods of administration. In Busoga, a Lukiko, or central council on the model of Buganda, was introduced and for a time a Muganda was actually created President of the Basoga. I happened to be at a meeting in Busoga just as the last agents were being withdrawn, and saw something of the relief and satisfaction of the people. In the Nilotic districts an attempt was made to create a class of chiefs of the kind desired. There, too, some Buganda agents were sent, and a simplified form of Buganda local government was introduced. Opinions still differ among political officers as to whether this admittedly artificial development was necessary, and whether it has justified itself. This, with the subsequent question as to whether it is now too late to follow the example of Southern Nigeria and work back again to the original foundation, are of the kind that probably require anthropological investigation. The Uganda policy in this respect would appear to be out of harmony with the principles of indirect rule, however satisfactorily it can be explained on grounds of the administrative necessity of the time.

Kenya, though a system of native courts was established fairly early, has never adopted indirect rule in the sense that I have been using it here. Its administration can therefore hardly be judged by the same standards. The main feature of Kenya native administration in the last ten years has been the introduction of local native councils upon a model imported from Fiji. Yet the general claim is made of building upon native institutions. Among the Kikuyu and Kamba groups there seems to have been a clan organization in which functions were distributed among age-grades, and which might have proved a very workable basis for local government. (I speak tentatively because we still wait for a really definitive anthropological study of these people.) Unfortunately, but very naturally, the early administration looked for chiefs and encouraged them into existence. Lindblom shows us the disruptive effect of this upon Kamba society, while the Routledges found the Kikuyu quite ready to describe the powers and privileges of a chieftainship which they had only invented six years before to suit our convenience. The Chief Native Commissioner, in his evidence before the Joint Parliamentary Committee on Closer Union in East Africa, admitted that, as a by-product of inquiries into land tenure in Kikuyu and North Kavirondo country, he had gained the impression 'that a great many wrong head-men have been appointed through ignorance of what was really the native custom'. He also explained that the 'official head-man really owes most of his authority to his government position and not to his personal influence'.

Similar mistakes have been made in Tanganyika. Here, as in Nigeria, the sequel to the discovery of mistakes has been a sincere attempt to rectify them. Perhaps one of the most valuable lessons to be learned from the last ten years' work in Tanganyika is that the recognition of the native institutions which the people desire is a continuous, or, at least, a prolonged task. Accurate information is not to be achieved by questioning a group of influential natives for a day or two and writing down their replies, but by patient research. But patient research is only part of the work. The skilled anthropologist may discern the prophet or rain-maker in the shadows into which he has retired. But he will not be able to call him out or to foresee how far and in what ways he can still claim to lead his people. It is by winning the confidence of people who think they have only too much reason to distrust us that they can be induced to tell us, or, more usually, to show us what they really want. And they can hardly know what they want themselves until experiments in co-operation have actually begun.

There is a tribe in Tanganyika which, after repeated invitations to disclose its constitutional wants, put forward a young district clerk who fully understood the ways of the white man as their chief. He was arrayed in what was understood to be suitable insignia, a scarlet cloak and a busby-like head-dress of black vulture feathers. He had not been long at work before it was discerned that a sardonic old man in a blanket was the real moving spirit and the prompter of the chief. Instead of making a fuss and scolding all parties into exasperation, the administration has very sensibly allowed a situation which seemed satisfactory to all parties, and which worked, to continue. If, later, there should be general agreement that their priestly authority should be officially recognized as chief, or as president of a council of elders, I am certain the government would meet their wishes. And this may very well have happened since I last had news of them.

The development of indirect rule in Tanganyika has been a story of perpetual changes and readjustments. Sometimes the right authorities, having seen the wrong ones properly treated, have come forward and proclaimed themselves. Groups hastily included under their neighbours have found courage to protest and have been given their independence. The divided have dared to claim unity. Apparently simple chieftainships have slowly revealed themselves as complex constitutional systems. The administration was taught to work for ends other than convenience, uniformity and finality. The result was a collection of 200 different native administrations showing the greatest possible variety as to form, area and population. These have decreased in number by voluntary federation. The moral for those territories which are now embarking upon indirect methods is that the preliminary reorganization and the passing of the necessary legislation is only the merest beginning of the reform.

The tendency to misunderstand and the temptation to mishandle native institutions spring from the same fact, a dissimilarity so great between the two societies in contact as to make mutual comprehension or co-operation extremely difficult. This is not the time to develop the contrast, even if I were competent to do so. There was a time when anthropologists confessed their failure to understand how primitive societies regulated their affairs by assuming some mysterious, automatic 'group-instinct'. Dr Malinowski has taught us to look further and to recognize the forces of social cohesion which are to be found in kinship-relations, in magic, religion, economic reciprocities and other aspects of primitive life. But he would not deny the difficulty for the hard-worked district officer of discovering these forces, still more of linking them up with his own activities.

When the agent of our society approaches the African society he looks at once for the seat of executive power. He wants someone who can carry out orders which are generally strange and distasteful. Executive power in our sense seldom exists except where, in faint anticipation of the conditions we impose, one people has subjected and centralized another and has introduced a distinction between the political control of the overlords and the traditional, spiritual authority of the indigenous leaders. I think we must admit that even the best-informed and most sympathetic government cannot ask the co-operation of an African chief without modifying his position. It wishes him to act, and to act quickly, in collecting tax, producing labour and clearing roads. It wants him to be constantly accessible, and not to keep disappearing in order to make rain, to visit ancestral graves, or to consult diviners. In the native administration ordinances we can read a list of the duties which native authorities have to perform. If you run your eye down the list you will see mention of sanitation, noxious weeds, the regulation of gambling, prohibiting the cutting of trees, restricting the carrying of arms, exterminating tsetse fly, with many other duties which the chief at first either does not understand or of which he cannot approve. In order to induce him to use his authority we tend to rely, more or less consciously, upon the hold we have over him through his dependence upon us for his position and salary. He, on his part, must endeavour not to strain an authority which at that very moment is being undermined as a result of our influence. The old authority of the chieftainship, in fact, tends to drain away from below while we pour in our new authority from above. By the standards of indirect rule native administration might be judged by the degree to which a process, inevitable up to some point, has gone. Where it has gone as far as it has in some parts of French territory it makes little difference whether the chief was originally a natural authority or is merely an appointed agent.

It is for these reasons that some critics (and notably Mr Tagart, who writes with the authority of a former Chief Native Commissioner of Northern Rhodesia) believe that African chieftainship is essentially unsuited to the functions we put upon it. It may be that among the many expressions of African chieftainship about which we are generalizing there are some which are so sacred, so completely detached from what we call practical affairs, as to offer no possibility of co-operation. But, for the rest, I believe that if the partnership is approached with a proper sense of the difficulties involved, it can be made effective in the interests of the people. There are generally one or more aspects of chieftainship – the leadership in war or the hunt, the right to certain dues, in kind or labour, the presidency in court or council – which offer a basis for a working compromise with our own conceptions of government. Nor must we forget that African institutions showed themselves to be remarkably plastic long before we came to Africa, and are still showing it.

We cannot speak of proof in these matters, but there is certainly circumstantial evidence to show us that African chieftainship can adapt itself to the responsibilities we have put upon it. Chiefs whose main function was to maintain fertility, who symbolized to the tribe, as the ba-Thonga said, what the bull is to the herd, or whose title and greeting was 'Rain', have adapted themselves to very different duties without, apparently, losing the allegiance of their peoples.

It is, perhaps, on the judicial side that co-operation with the chiefs has been most fruitful. In Africa the development of law and judicial procedure seem to have gone far beyond that of other primitive peoples. Almost from the first we could recognize, with comparatively little adaptation, their law, their courts, and much of their procedure. This is the feature of indirect rule which works most normally and successfully. I believe this has been of the utmost value in promoting mutual understanding and in predisposing both sides to extend co-operation into more difficult fields.

To all this, however, one important condition must be attached. Some of you may already be criticizing my unqualified use of the word 'chief'. Let me say at once that I would be ready to substitute for it at almost every point 'Chief-in-Council'. As Captain Rattray said in his recent article in the *Journal of the African Society*, it was almost inevitable that the first societies to be recognized in Africa should have been highly centralized ones. A study of Lord Lugard's political memoranda would show the distinction between the principles of indirect rule and his most notable application of them to the emirates. In spite of this, indirect rule has suffered at the hands of those who have assumed that a somewhat despotic chief is a necessary ingredient of the system. Our slowly increasing knowledge of African society shows us that despotism was the rare exception; that many chiefs were 'constitutional' in a sense not so far removed from that in which we employ the word to describe our own king; that they were largely dependent upon popular approval; that they acted with and through councillors, and that, as an additional check, authority was widely diffused among the constituent family-cells of which society was constituted. Yet even where the position of the chief has not been misinterpreted from the first, the daily need of the political officer for rapid and efficient response to his advice is a perpetual inducement to him to exalt and isolate the chief. It is from every point of view a most serious mistake. It not only causes immediate injury to the tribal constitution, it introduces a form of government which, however convenient to us at the moment, is going to block by far the most promising line of future progress. It is surely by strengthening and broadening councils that we can encourage the expression, in a form more suited to changing conditions, of the old corporate or democratic spirit of African society. It will also allow the co-operation of educated and Christian people who are at present often left outside. Indeed, the time may soon come when more efficient and highly centralized societies, such as the emirates, will find it necessary to graft upon themselves the elements of conciliar control and decentralization which they have lost.

The criticisms we have been considering are directed towards defects in the system of indirect rule. There are others that seem to bring the system itself to trial. It has been urged that primitive society, from its nature, cannot be preserved in the modern world except by questionable artificial measures, and that most Africans who are educated enough to understand the position of their people today reject the control of conservative chiefs and demand as rapid an initiation as possible into the culture and political forms of the civilized world. If we withhold this initiation they will suspect that we have reasons other than their own well-being for holding them back. I could add the protest which an African made to me the other day against being protected from the possible dangers of too rapid an advance. 'We do not wish for any special treatment. We do not wish to be protected; we want to be allowed to make our own mistakes, and to work out our own salvation, as you did.'

This point of view deserves great respect. It certainly seems as though some of the most vital elements in African society cannot indefinitely survive the influences that are attacking them. Captain Rattray has written of the almost ideally democratic character of the old system of Ashanti, which was that of 'concentric circles of loyalty' radiating outwards from the family patriarchate. But how long can the patriarchal system survive? We cannot foresee. The introduction of money and of economic specialization weakens the necessity for co-operation which holds together the small kinship groups. The greater ease with which that money is earned by the young than the old upsets the characteristic

I

African balance of authority. At the same time the old customs may prove far more tenacious than we foresee today. I will not go on to discuss the effects of contact, and especially of education, upon the other social bonds, such as magic and religion. A great deal has been written lately to demonstrate these effects, and will be familiar to this audience. I would rather suggest that the speed and extent of the change have, perhaps, been a little over-emphasized. A group of younger anthropologists, some of whom have been trained by Dr Malinowski in the functional method, and who consider changes produced by culture-contact as fit subjects for study, have lately been at work in Africa. Their first investigations, as represented in the writings of Dr Richards, Dr Mair, Dr Hunter, Dr Schapera and others, seem to me to bring out the conservative power of African society. They reveal Africans as no passive sufferers of our influence and all the effects it should logically produce in them, but as showing considerable initiative in taking what they want from us and keeping what they want of their own. And they write of peoples exposed to considerable European influences. I have sometimes wondered, in view of the character of that vast Africa which lies off the main road and railways and away from the labour markets, what alternative form of government the opponents of indirect rule would propose. They would not have had us break up the old Moslem kingdoms of Nigeria, or suppress the Kabaka and Lukiko of Buganda? And yet it is possible that the effects of direct rule upon these more politically advanced peoples, once subjected, would be less disruptive than upon smaller and more primitive societies. For the latter the adjustment of their social conceptions to the new conditions is a longer and more difficult process. It is unlikely to be successful if the relation of the one to the other is not demonstrated in the most practical possible way.

It may be that in criticizing the defects and pondering over the difficulties of indirect rule we sometimes forget its main objective. It attempts to make possible a development by which Africans keep the stability and pride of their community-life and extend their existing social forms to meet new needs and serve wider unities. My survey of different systems of administration has convinced me that the desired progress is actually more rapid where Africans advance in social groups and from a familiar starting-point than where, as so often happens in the more direct methods, they are turned adrift in strange country as a crowd of individuals.

Yet criticism of the kind we are considering will always be necessary to correct the constant tendency of indirect rule to deteriorate into a policy of mere preservation. It is not only that development should be allowed: it should be stimulated and guided. The South African Protectorates provide an example of what indirect rule is not, or should not, be. Tribal institutions were recognized, and were left to continue their functions under circumstances quite other than those they had been developed to meet. Chiefs conducted their courts, retained fees and fines, made levies, and in Basutoland 'placed' new sub-chiefs, with little systematized supervision. We might compare the almost static conditions in these territories during the last half century with the rapid advance in Tanganyika during the last decade. Here change, which I believe in this case has been progress, has been constant. Small units have voluntarily federated with their neighbours, and their forms have been modernized. Above all, the Treasury system has enabled the native administrations to make all kinds of new activity their own. Council halls, schools, roads, bridges and model farms, even where their use is not yet fully understood, are the visible expression of their own tribal unity and of their partnership with the government. I believe that the Treasury is a fundamental part of indirect rule. By teaching practical finance and economics, it introduces the authorities and ultimately the people into the modern world as nothing else can do. But the lesson is not learned quickly. We sometimes forget, I think, taken up as we are with our own good intentions, how little these can be understood, or even credited, by most tribal Africans. Many district officers have told me of their discovery that their people believed the poll-tax went straight into their own pockets. I remember on one occasion talking to some old men near the Rovuma River, which marks the border between Southern Tanganyika and Portuguese East Africa. They had lived under the Germans until they fled south at the time of the great Maji-Maji rebellion. Some years before they had returned to Tanganyika. I asked them, somewhat complacently perhaps, under which of the three governments they preferred to live? After some discussion they replied very definitely, 'the Portuguese – because their rate of tax was lighter!' I remember asking another tribe how the Wahehe had ruled them when they had been under their domination. The reply was, 'As the Germans ruled us; as you rule us – by the spear!' We have not only to expect their misunderstanding of our motives but also ignorance of the ends towards which we are trying to guide them.

It may be that in countries where the white colony is dominant, indirect rule cannot perform even the transitional functions we ask of it elsewhere. I have noticed that many of the doubts about the wisdom of indirect rule are bred in South Africa among those who care most for the progress of the native. They see the danger of attempting to build up two states for black and white upon mutually exclusive principles. Yet a proper system of indirect rule in the reserves might be made the best civic training for the tribal natives, so long as it is not made an excuse for denying citizenship to those who have become, in fact if not in name, members of the white state. It is impossible to visit Zululand and not believe that those fine people would have progressed further in every way, even in civic capacity, if they could have expressed their deep tribal feelings through institutions of the kind we have discussed.

You may think that I have made out a poor case for indirect rule. I seem to have dwelt almost exclusively upon its defects and difficulties. I have done so because I realize that in complacency lies its greatest danger. Perhaps, so as not to leave a mistaken impression, I had better state my profound belief in it. I will conclude by drawing attention to one great advantage we may expect of it in the future. When one people is dominated by another and superior people they show at first an eager receptivity. There comes a later stage when they feel the effects of disintegration, when they grow tired or disappointed with the new things and ideas they have acquired, or become embittered by the exclusive and dominant position of their teachers. They turn back to seek the shelter of their old institutions, trying to gain self-respect and the respect of others by exalting their past history, or reviving and flaunting their old arts. If they are too late, and their culture is beyond revival, there comes a sense of despair or, at best, a fatalistic acceptance of cultural absorption. It has even been maintained that the relics of British art during the Roman period illustrate aspects of this cycle. It is clearly illustrated in Maori history, as Dr Firth has pointed out in his study of Maori economics. It is not, moreover, confined to primitive societies. Few people have been subjected to more complete and sudden cultural domination than the majority of Africans. If we can apply the principle of indirect rule at its best, not only to government, but to all aspects of our contact with them, we may be able to save them – and ourselves – from the worst effects of this reaction.

DISCUSSION

The Chairman said that the audience would be happy to know that they had Lord Lugard with them that afternoon. He had been variously referred to as the creator, inventor or instigator of indirect rule. Whatever their attitude was on that subject, they knew that Lord Lugard was perhaps their greatest authority on Africa, and they would hear his views with great respect and attention.

The Right Hon. Lord Lugard, P.C., K.C.M.G., C.B., D.S.O., said that Miss Perham had no need to apologize for venturing to address an audience largely composed of people who had been in Africa. She belonged to neither of the two classes whose opinions on African administration are discounted for opposite reasons. On the one hand, there was the local administrator, of whom it had been said that his ideas were parochial, that he had lost his sense of proportion and was the victim of hide-bound formulae. On the other, there was the casual traveller – known as 'Paget, M.P.' – who claimed that he had a wider horizon after a few weeks in the country, and was prepared to tell the British public how the thing ought to be done, but he never had the responsibility of carrying out his theories. Each of these had a contempt for the other. Miss Perham's claim to express an opinion was based on a happy combination of the best attributes of both. She was neither a flying visitor nor a local administrator. She had spent the best part of a year in Tanganyika and the best part of a year in Nigeria, and was able, by her sympathy and understanding, to get the local administrator to feel that she was a colleague, and to place the best of his experience at her disposal. Her paper showed what the result had been, because she spoke as if she were an experienced administrator rather than if she were a travelling critic.

He did not think he was the best person to open the discussion because he agreed so heartily with everything the lecturer had said. She was kind enough to mention his name in connexion with indirect rule, but in Nigeria in the early days they had an exceptional opportunity. They started with a clean slate. They had no fixed regulations or Colonial Office experience of any kind behind them, and Mr Joseph Chamberlain had trusted the 'man on the spot'. He thought that Sir Charles Orr, whom he was glad to see present, for he was one of the early administrators of that time, would agree with him when he said that indirect rule, as it grew up in Nigeria, was not the work of any one man; it was the work of all the Administrative Staff, who co-operated together, and he, as the head of the government, endeavoured to co-ordinate the ideas and suggestions he received from his various district officers as a coherent policy. As regards indirect rule, it was, he supposed, the task of anyone who opened the discussion either to criticize or to ask for information. He would say, therefore, that he would have liked to have heard more about Miss Perham's views as to the part that the educated native of the future would play in the development of indirect rule. They would look to the educated native for leadership in social development and not only in the sphere of indirect rule. No community was worthy of participation in rule unless it could produce leadership in every department. The system of indirect rule covered much more than questions of administration and ruling. It covered the question of participation and co-operation in every branch of civilized progress, and any community which was bound to look to aliens for leadership in education, health, judicial procedure, etc., could never claim any right to anything approaching self-government. Unless the educated African would endeavour to become a leader in those branches, by qualifying as doctors and in other branches, he could not expect to be given anything like self-government. He saw many African gentlemen present at the meeting, and he had no doubt they would be able to put forward their own criticisms and suggestions, and he would like them particularly to answer that question.

Professor W. M. Macmillan, M.A. (Professor of History, University of the Witwatersrand), was filled with admiration for the excellent exposition which Miss Perham gave them, and for the way in which she was able to isolate these problems of indirect rule. She was studying the subject as a synthesis, as she had called it, yet she could do what he found it so difficult to do, look at things in separate compartments. It was just possible that she laid a little too much stress on the machinery of indirect rule and forgot the human material with which that machinery must work.

Like Miss Perham, though with a different emphasis, he must profess himself a whole-hearted believer in the useful possibilities of indirect rule. They had something in common as they had both started as humble historians, and both of them had drifted away from the teaching of history in the effort to study the great problems of modern Africa. As a historian he would express also his regret that Miss Perham was forgetting the historical spirit in her excessive regard for that extremely useful specialist study of African institutions, anthropology. Anthropology, he was afraid, was going to lead us astray in dealing with human material. There was especially a danger in sending out as specialists persons who, unlike Miss Perham, had no knowledge of our own history and institutions. Let us understand the African by all means, but there was a real tendency in this modern world not merely to study, but almost to worship, African institutions. African institutions must be judged by how far they had made for good African life. Train the expert in history as well as in anthropology and they would not have what seemed to have happened sometimes in south-eastern Nigeria, experts finding institutions which never existed.

Another impression was that the dominant opinion among experts was not always progressive, or at least that it was taken advantage of by reactionaries. South Africa was possibly flirting with indirect rule for conservative reasons. To some South Africans indirect rule was welcome as an excuse for leaving the African very much as he is, and leaving him to deteriorate in his own way. Yet in South Africa anyhow complete segregation was impossible, contact was inevitable and could not be merely ignored. We must not merely break up African society. But even indirect rule was our rule, and the ultimate responsibility was therefore some of it ours. We had sometimes got to impose better ways. At what point were we to cease to impose? That was the real problem.

In trying to discover African institutions there was some tendency to shy off from the educated classes as not real Africans. It was essential rather to get alongside thinking Africans who were the Africans of the future. They were the moving factor in the mass. What did we mean by indirect rule? It seemed to be not always to find African institutions and develop them, teaching Africans to lead fuller lives; to the 'new' Africans it sometimes seemed to mean putting them back in the same position as when we first went there. Indirect rule – or in the Nigerian phrase, which he preferred, Native Administration – ought to mean *local government*. A good deal could be done by starting at the beginning and teaching them to be responsible for their own affairs. England led the world by laying the foundations of its political machinery in the local council, and it learnt its political sense locally. That could be done in Africa, but at present most educated West Africans could not see further than Lagos or Accra. He would suggest, particularly to his African friends, that the strong point which they were apt to overlook in this development was that there was an honest attempt in West Africa to achieve a real African authority with the best of African officers. The ideal was most certainly to give Africans of ability a share in the management of their own affairs. Only then would the African attitude to government become that of the Londoner to the 'bobby', not that of the most law-abiding natives to the Johannesburg police.

Miss S. J. Thomas, (a law student from West Africa) agreed with the views of the last speaker because he had defined the progress of indirect rule. Indirect rule was making puppets of African chiefs, who were men to be respected. They were in a way higher than the government, but they were chiefs in name only. If the chiefs were called agents it would be a better name because they were carrying out the orders of the British Government. The chiefs represented the people no longer, and the Africans did not want their chiefs to sell the people to the British. That was what indirect rule was doing instead of helping them to govern themselves. That was the motive, or at any rate ought to be – to help them to get some practice in self-government, which was what they needed. When the British left Africa what would the people do? They would be in trouble because they had never had any experience in governing themselves. If only indirect rule would carry out its real aim they might be able to have this experience so that when they had self-government they would not be unprepared. The Legislative Council had no power, and had to do what the Governor wished, and therefore they did not represent the real Africans. They wanted to be represented and to be given training so that they would be able to express themselves. That was all they were asking for. There must be real co-operation and real understanding. At present the British were dictating to them, and the Africans had to do what they were told. They could not go against it because they had not got the power.

The speaker was not in favour of anthropologists. Africans were not curious to be studied in order to find out from where they came. If British rule meant to help them, the first thing to do would be to educate the chiefs. They did not want illiterate chiefs, because then, on account of their ignorance, they easily fell into the hands of British administrators. They wanted sound education, to be able to understand and to express themselves as they would like to. Once they had that, and knew what was good and what was bad, they would be in a position, when they were given self-government, to look after their own institutions and to judge for themselves the merits of those institutions.

Sir James Currie, K.C.M.G., K.B.E., said he was in complete sympathy with what the last speaker said. In the various parts of Africa he had seen he did think there was a risk of the system, as it was being run at present, serving as a sort of counter cry to reasonable educational demands. He had formed that feeling, and he held it very strongly. A great many of our younger school of African administrators gave one the impression that, God not having called them to be the obsolete type of country squire in England, they thought they had a good chance of duplicating the part in Africa. He thought that that was how the thing was working out, and it was certainly not with that objective that Lord Lugard or Sir Donald Cameron had started it. It stood a very great risk of becoming identified with a policy of the advocacy of complete educational and economic paralysis, and he did not believe that that was what the African wanted, just the contrary.

Mr Joseph T. Sackeyfio (Gold Coast) said that Miss Perham's remarks as to the recognition, legal or actual, accorded to African institutions in order to stabilize them, were erroneous. The institutions had been, and would continue to be, independent, and they needed little or no definite recognition by the British, for they would continue, as in the past, to adapt themselves to local needs, and to adopt from new cultures what they might need in so doing.

The introduction of indirect rule into Africa, as was evidenced in the parts affected, had resulted in the divorcement of the people from their chiefs and elders. The sacredness of the Stools, and the sanctity of the person occupying them were losing their sway. If ever there was anything which the pure African would never forgive the European for, it was that act of defiling the sacredness of the Stools. Miss Perham had spoken about the chiefs being agents, and said it diminished the prestige of an African paramount chief, sub-chief or elder, to be nominated as an agent of the British. That was one of the results of indirect rule.

The greatest evil which could be done to African ideals was found in the widening of the gulf between the chiefs and their subjects. The sacredness referred to the Stool, but the occupant for the time being, like Caesar, had a sacred person, the violation of whom spelt punishment. At present in Africa there was not the respect, not even an ordinary respect, accorded to the chief, for he, being an agent, had lost the confidence of his people, although in return he obtained recognition from the British Government in the form of honours, such as O.B.E., K.M.A.C., etc. Such awards were to be wholly condemned, for their likely influence was to raise doubts and distrust in the minds of the people, and not unwarrantably so.

The Gold Coast was being visited with the pest of indirect rule, and recent legislation there showed how the feelings of the people towards the British were being strained. The government on the spot kept on stressing the old tune of trusteeship, which was a weariness to the people and a camouflage to rob them of their freedom and liberty of speech.

All that Africans asked of the British people was that they should be given a chance – a chance to show the world what they could do to further the progress of Africa, and that the British should not, by bamboozling them and keeping the people 'in their place', force them to swallow what they did not want.

Mr McGregor Ross, (former Director of Public Works, Kenya) thought that in the extremely interesting address they had heard from Miss Perham the portion which pleased him most was the story of the district officer who had so much liberality of spirit in his régime that it was possible for a young African official, although appointed by the government as 'a chief', to be told, upon appearing at a village council, by the elders there assembled to take a back seat while they carried on the business upon old-established tribal lines. Many African tribes possessed elaborate systems of democratic control, perhaps antedating local government in England. He thought he was right in saying that, when Lord Lugard met the Kikuyu people some forty years ago, he entered into friendly relations with a notable chief, Waiyaki or Eiyaki, who was acting as chief-in-council for a large part of the Kikuyu tribe, and he (the speaker) thought that investigation would show that self-government was more or less general among the tribes at that time. That particular chief, after Lord Lugard had unfortunately severed his connexion with East Africa, was exiled from his tribe and country by the colonial government for voicing the aspirations of his people in a manner which we should probably regard as proper and meritorious today; and the lands which had belonged to his family were given to a Christian Mission, which still possesses them. However, the joy of Africans at the reinstatement of their old forms of government, to which Miss Perham had alluded, was a joy which it was still open to the British Government to extend to Africans under our rule. The Kikuyu tribe at the present moment had sent a representation to the Secretary of State in which they asked that a paramount chief might be re-established in their tribe, the occupant of the post to be chosen by the people. That petition was a notable one, because it was signed by five or six bodies of organized African opinion among the Kikuyu of widely differing attitudes towards government. They varied from the extreme left-wing group, the 'Kikuyu Central Association', a body not always entirely polite, to a right-wing group, calling itself the 'Kikuyu Loyal Patriots'. For the occasion of this petition they had all joined forces to make a joint representation to the government that they would be extremely grateful if they might again have a paramount chief in Kikuyu. Although the wording of the petition was not quite all that it might be, because it came down sometimes from the word 'request' to 'demand', he hoped that any infelicities of expression would be overlooked by the British Government in dealing with this petition, and that they might be accorded the right to re-establish within their own area some such form of government as prevailed in the days before we knew them.

Mr F. H. Melland (former Commissioner for Native Affairs, Northern Rhodesia), said he would like to emphasize a name which Miss Perham did mention, but one which had been rather overshadowed by Sir Donald Cameron, and that was Sir James Maxwell. In Northern Rhodesia the indirect rule which he started had, in some ways, gone even further than that in Tanganyika, except as regards treasury matters, and there was now, thanks to the policy which he had introduced, a sound form of local self-government in that country.

The lecturer had given them a very illuminating example when she spoke of the natives who told her of the government of three nations which they had sampled, of which they preferred the Portuguese. That suggested a real lesson to be learnt by us. We were fond of thinking that our ideals must inevitably be acceptable to other people, and that what was good for us was also good for them. It reminded him of the story of two contractors in Africa. One was often very drunk, and the other, a Scot, was always very sober and hard working. The drunken man managed to get all the labour he wanted, and was able to cut all the wood he wanted, but the hard-working Scot could not get half as much out of the natives. Natives did not always look at things in the same way as we did. There was a danger in trying to get them to want the things that we wanted, for that way lay disappointment.

Mr M. Dowuona (Gold Coast; St Peter's Hall, Oxford, later Registrar of Ahmadu Bello University, Northern Nigeria), said that in the first place, he wished to associate himself with the previous speakers who have expressed their thanks and appreciation to Miss Perham for her, if he might say so, admirable and illuminating lecture. She had shown a wide knowledge of the system of which she was perhaps, the best and ablest unofficial advocate. The last time he had an opportunity of discussing the question of 'indirect rule' with Miss Perham, she seemed to have an open mind on the subject. Now, it seemed, she had gone a long way towards accepting it as a workable system, with, of course, some modifications. She might yet depend upon those who were not wholly converted for kindly criticisms which, he was sure, she would receive in good spirit.

In the second place, he would like to answer the question raised by Lord Lugard as to the part which educated Africans should play in African administration. It was customary to call educated Africans 'detribalized'. He was not going to discuss that term here. But one thing which the use of that term brought about was to set a premium on ignorance. It was a pity that that should be the case, especially when it led to the exclusion of the educated African from taking part in shaping the progressive policy of his people. No one denied that the illiterate African had enough common sense and ability to decide on a good policy. But it was doubtful whether he could interpret English administrative methods and legislation adequately. That was where, he thought, the educated African was indispensable. The African peoples would not and should not rely solely on the interpretation of English administration and legislation by English administrators. By that he did not mean to impute any dishonesty to the latter; he rather wished the masses of the people to be enabled to see a possible point of view in matters which vitally affected them.

The educated African had, he thought, two rôles to play in African administration. First as a member of the African civil service. He did not mean his position as an ordinary clerk. Lord Lugard, in his *Dual Mandate*, raised the question of training educated Africans for administrative posts. He hoped he would develop that point more fully in the next edition of his book. In theory there was no reason why qualified Africans should not be appointed to higher posts in the African civil service. But there had not been lacking practical difficulties. Even in the case of the appointments of professional men, e.g., doctors and engineers, certain irritating and discriminatory treatment had kept out of the service men who might be of great service to their country.

The second respect in which educated Africans could be of use in African administration was by allowing them to take an increasing responsibility in the municipal administration of the larger urban areas. The hold of central government officials had hitherto been, he thought, too strong. In the minds of many a European there lurked the fear that administration by Africans would lead to corruption and inefficiency. But corruption and inefficiency, he ventured to say, were not peculiar to the African, as the present and past history of administration by white peoples abundantly showed. It was the continuous vigilance of the public and the growing scientific method of public administration which had diminished corruption and inefficiency in white administration. He thought similar publicity and method would reduce corruption and inefficiency among Africans to a minimum. What was needed was a bold policy whereby increasing responsibility would be given to Africans. If the African public realized that the government was theirs, they would, he was sure, deal effectively with their own people who betrayed their trust.

A word about the anthropologists. Professor Macmillan appeared to limit anthropology to the study of the so-called primitive peoples. He (the speaker) would extend that definition to include the study of the white races, whose manners, customs and institutions were not always easy for Africans to understand. Miss Perham had referred to the work of the young anthropologists of the 'functional school', trained by Professor Malinowski. He would like to see, at no distant date, young Africans similarly trained, who would study the white peoples, especially the English, their customs and institutions, and interpret them to the world. It would be interesting to see how they would be received by the educated English public.

The Lecturer, in reply, stated that the discussion endorsed her view that they must not be complacent about indirect rule.

She would like to say a word in defence of anthropology. The new anthropologists, the younger generation, were no longer looking at Africans as specimens, nor seeking to preserve the past for the convenience of their researches. They lived with the Africans and made friends with them, and their interpretation of existing conditions would be of the greatest value to Africa. Nor should Africans imagine that anthropology was applied only to them; there was in process an anthropological survey of the different parts of London. It would be most interesting to carry out Mr Dowuona's suggestion for anthropological research in this country by Africans, but the Africans would have to be properly qualified.

The whole object of indirect rule was to train people in self-government. It was, perhaps, a pity, from the point of view of criticizing the system, that the majority of the Africans present were from the Gold Coast, where it had not hitherto been so fully applied as elsewhere. It was essential to the success of indirect rule that it should enlist the co-operation of the educated native. She felt this so strongly that in speaking on the wireless the other evening she put up the suggestion that, as it was so necessary for us to get African co-operation in East Africa, we could hardly wait for the slow working of the educational system there, and should consider training selected natives so that they could interpret their own people to us. They alone could show us how we could carry out indirect rule as they want it, and not as we think they want it.

The discussion had been most instructive to her, but she felt it was necessary to remind the educated natives who criticized indirect rule that there was a serious responsibility upon them to make a very careful study of it; to go into the hinterland, away from the towns, and realize what was being done there. Their opinions would gain in value when they learned to understand not only their own difficulties, but ours.

The Chairman, in moving a vote of thanks to the lecturer, said that everyone would agree that the subject they had been considering was one of the most important of African questions. Miss Perham spoke about the lack of constructive criticism in this country, and one of the great benefits of such a meeting was to bring aspects of our colonial policy to the notice of the people of this country. There was no doubt that we did lack articulate public opinion here on the proper methods of carrying out our imperial responsibilities.

It was clear that native administration by indirect rule was specially suited and was almost inevitable for large territories of undeveloped communities, and if it allowed expression of any change in the outlook of the people on the form of government, it would be, in many places, the best system. Numerous Africans, however, for geographical or educational reasons, were practically detribalized, and, as Lord Lugard had pointed out, the great problem was how to get the co-operation of educated Africans in whatever system of government they had.

He would suggest to their African friends present that they should not be content with purely destructive criticism. That was a very natural temptation to them. Let them try to be constructive and show how government could be improved, and they would find a very large audience in this country willing to receive their suggestions with sympathy and to advocate their adoption if they were practicable as well as progressive.

Personally, he had always looked on indirect rule with some apprehension. There was rather too much feudalism and aristocratic privilege in it for his liking. He agreed that it was desirable to preserve African institutions and methods of government natural to the people, but they did not wish to stabilize procedures and relationships which the people themselves – in the absence of British compulsion – might have modified or abolished.

He, like Professor Macmillan, was a little suspicious of the anthropologists. He knew that many of them were good and helpful both to people and government, but they tended to look backwards rather than forwards. He had never been able to feel that there was such a cleavage between the essential outlook of Africans and ourselves as to make it necessary to delve deeply into local superstitions and folk-lore in order to devise proper lines of progress in government and administration. Democracy appeared to be natural to the African, and he hoped that advance would be along the lines of the development of democratic institutions. They heard a good deal about the dangers to democracy in the world today, and he did not see why those who believed in democratic institutions should not get some assistance from Africa, if development was in the right direction.

They should, therefore, he thought, recognize indirect rule as a wise method and a useful instrument in many territories, but insist that it be made subject to progressive influences, and not remain a refuge for feudal and aristocratic systems which had served their purpose.

He would like to assure Africans that there was a tremendous amount of goodwill towards them in this country, and that the British people, as a whole, were anxious to discharge properly their trusteeship and to assist Africans to learn, ultimately, to govern themselves. No doubt there was a minority in this country which was afraid of such an objective, but it was a minority, and African co-operation in constructive statesmanship would steadily diminish its influence.

They were very grateful to Miss Perham for giving them such a comprehensive paper and for covering so many aspects of that difficult subject. He had great pleasure in assuring her of their gratitude for the trouble she had taken, and in wishing her success in her further study of the subject.

He would also like to thank the Royal Society of Arts and the African Society for arranging that meeting. He hoped it would be only one of many which would be held to study the problems of the great continent of Africa, whose right solution was of great importance for the future welfare of humanity.

The vote of thanks having been carried unanimously, the meeting terminated.

Dr C. K. Meek (former Resident and Anthropological Officer, Nigeria) writes: In the course of his remarks on indirect rule, Professor Macmillan is reported to have said, 'Train the expert in history as well as in anthropology and they would not have what seemed to have happened sometimes in south-eastern Nigeria, experts finding institutions which never existed.'

It is not clear what Professor Macmillan means by 'experts' (he might be classed as one himself), but as I had, prior to my retirement last year, worked as government Anthropologist in south-east Nigeria for two-and-a-half years I thought he might be referring to myself, though I am not altogether ignorant of history. He assures me, however, that he was not alluding to me or to any other individual – he was using the term expert 'in a collective sense'. But who were the experts 'in a collective sense' who 'seemed' 'sometimes' to have found in south-east Nigeria institutions which never existed, and what were the institutions? Serious statements of this kind, if based on nothing but uninstructed gossip, are liable to do a lot of mischief, more particularly in an area which has recently experienced considerable political trouble.

A great deal of rubbish is being talked and written about indirect rule and anthropology as though they were some subtle device for keeping Africans and others in a state of subjection. Indirect rule is only another name for local self-government on evolutionary lines, and does not imply and should not entail a condition of stasis. Anthropology is neither an esoteric science solely concerned with the past nor yet a panacea for all present ills. It merely endeavours to tell you as much as possible about the people you are trying to govern. Rightly applied it takes cognizance not (like Professor Macmillan) of one section only of the community, but of all sections, and although not directly concerned with questions of policy, it ranges itself naturally on the side of a broad dynamic policy, seeking to maintain all that is useful in native culture, but opposing attempts to use as instruments of government institutions which are losing or have lost their validity. Every intelligent Administrative Officer in the Colonial Service is necessarily an anthropologist.

The South African Protectorates

The Times 5 and 6 July 1934

The preceding article upon the South African High Commission Territories, published in The Times *on 28 September 1933, reproduced on pp. 77–82 was mainly descriptive. It ended with an optimistic hope that the question of their transfer to the Union, which had been raised even before my article was published, had been fully answered by our government's reminder to South Africa of the pledges we had given to the Africans. But the pressure from General Hertzog continued to mount during the succeeding months. Those of us who had knowledge of the three territories and concern for their peoples, with Lord Selborne and Lord Lugard in the van, did what we could to inform public opinion upon the issue. This was the reason for my writing these two articles.*

1. *Legacies of History*

General Hertzog has asked this country to transfer the three South African Protectorates to the Union. The question at once arises, 'What exactly is the nature of our connexion with them?' The answer, somewhat unfortunately perhaps, lies in a long, complex, threefold history which most of us have forgotten, though every item of it is bitten into the memory of the tribes concerned.

The Protectorates are a legacy of the last century when colonists of both races were spilling over the frontiers and falling foul of the native tribes they found there. The British Government, torn between the dictates of order and humanity on the one side and the fear of responsibility and expense on the other, alternately reached out and withdrew the hand of control.

Basutoland first claimed our attention. Here, in the mountains, Moshesh gathered up the refugees of Zulu and colonial wars and built them, as much by moderation as strength, into a nation. He first repulsed the Zulus from his stronghold and then, characteristically, sent food after them. In the forties the Boers on their Great Trek rounded the Drakensberg and began to press Moshesh upon his vulnerable northwest, where the mountains go down to the prosperous flats about the Caledon River. He resolved to turn, where he was to turn so often with

K

such varying hope, to the paramount power in South Africa. He had provided himself with a scribe. Some years before, hearing rumour of mysterious but helpful beings called missionaries, he had dispatched a half-bred trader with 200 cattle to procure one and had so drawn M. Casalis, of the Paris Evangelical Mission, to his mountain stronghold of Thabo Bosio. The Frenchman met the chief, and noted, for all his naked torso and leopard skirts, the 'intelligence and softness of his eyes'. 'I felt at once that I had to do with a superior man trained to think, to command others and, above all, himself.'

Now began the long and honourable task of bringing Christianity and Western education to the Basuto, of which the Mission celebrated the centenary last year. 'If we still have our chiefs,' said one of the orators then, 'if we exist as a nation with our own red flag with the black crocodile on a white ground, it is thanks to Casalis, Arbousset and Gosselin.' But at the date of which we are thinking the nation was still to make and still to save. Casalis was told to write to the Governor of the Cape that Moshesh had marked the generous policy of the British Government towards African tribes and was 'convinced more and more that neither independence nor existence is possible except under the protecting shield of the Sovereign you represent'. The Governor, well intentioned but powerless to control the emigrant trekkers, could only warn them against encroaching upon native tribes. In 1843 this was followed by a treaty of alliance and friendship with Moshesh. A few years later Sir Harry Smith, tempestuous in movement as in personality, rode north of the Vaal, met Moshesh, showered compliments upon him, wrestled with him for his soul, committed his reluctant government to a sweeping proclamation of British sovereignty from the Drakensberg to the Vaal, and rushed away to scatter the ensuing Boer rebellion at Boomplaats. 'Trust to me,' he urged Moshesh, 'and no one will dare to raise a hand against the Great Chief of the Basuto.'

This was all very well. But warnings, treaties and proclamations of sovereignty were on paper; Moshesh was left to deal with the realities. These included the colonists still pressing upon his country and his own wild borderers who pounced upon their cattle. Who is to blame where pioneers and tribesmen straggle along an undefined and unpoliced frontier and where the aggrieved take their own compensation with interest? Soon the Basuto were in disgrace with the British Government, represented by men who did not know their African tribes and who regarded Moshesh as despot enough to levy compensation in cattle by the thousand at a few days' notice. Expeditions were sent against him in 1851 and 1852, but they failed, like the Zulus before them, to take Thabo Bosio, and the second time they fell back leaving forty Lancers dead on the field.

It was at such a moment that Moshesh showed his statecraft. A messenger sped after the unhappy commander. 'I entreat peace from you. You have shown your power – you have chastised – let it be enough I pray you, let me no longer be considered an enemy of the Queen.' Two years later, a cold fit following the hot, the British Government abandoned all their troublesome subjects, white and black, north of the Orange and left them to fight it out for themselves. And, since we left them without settling the bitterly disputed boundary, fight they did, the Governor watching gloomily from the Cape. Moshesh could not credit his abandonment. 'But the Queen,' he told his people, 'has not left us for ever. No Sovereign ever did throw away subjects. . . . Some day Queen Victoria will come back among us. On that day I shall rejoice as I rejoice at the rising of the sun.' But Queen Victoria tarried, and the desolating war dragged on year after year, the combatants growing ever more exhausted and more embittered. The Basuto committed atrocities; the Boers destroyed the French mission and razed the crops. Able and humane Governors, Sir George Grey and Sir Philip Wodehouse, importuned by the Basuto, pleaded with the Free State, offered their impotent arbitration and chafed to do more. The Boers were thrown back from the very summit of Thabo Bosio with the loss of their commander, but Moshesh, despairing of the end, appealed with growing desperation for British protection.

At last the government gave way and, to the very natural exasperation of the Free State, proclaimed the Basuto British subjects. 'I have become old . . .' Moshesh wrote in reply; 'I am glad that my people should have been allowed to rest and lie under the large folds of the flag of England before I am no more.' And, to the Queen: 'My country is your blanket, and my people the lice in it.' Moshesh died, in peace indeed, but worn out in mind and body; no barbarian saint, for he had learned something more than diplomacy in a bewildering and perilous world, but partaking of greatness by the courage and tenacity with which he preserved the nation he had made and the drive (there is no other word) of his resolution to become a British subject.

But this was not the end for his people. In 1871 the Cape received responsible government and with it the mountain territory. The Basuto said they could no longer reach her Majesty's government and that 'silence like the darkness of night has descended upon the people'. In

1879 the Cape Government decided to disarm the Basuto, who were still deeply disturbed by the memory of their previous abandonment by Britain. Rebellion and the Gun War followed, prolonged by the threat of the Cape Government to break up a portion of the country into farms to pay for the war. The Basuto, as usual, fought well. The Cape failed to assert its authority over them and they appealed, as always, to the imperial government. The rising young politician, Cecil Rhodes, was sent up to Basutoland in brilliant but bizarre partnership with Chinese Gordon. Gordon said he would not fight with tribesmen whom he admired so much, and Rhodes told the Cape Government that they had had the worst of it at the cost of more than £3,000,000: that they had attempted to 'put the best boy among the native races in the stocks' and that they had better hand the responsibility back to the imperial government. So it was done, and a native orator told a rejoicing assembly of the nation 'We are a new people, being born a second time'. In 1898 Lord Milner, a staunch defender of the Protectorates, went up to Basutoland. The Basuto agreed to double their tax in order that they might dispense with the Cape's grant of £20,000 a year and with the degree of control it might still represent. Since then Basutoland has remained under the British Government and, except for their participation, through a grant of men and money, in the Great War, have enjoyed at last the happiness of having no history.

If Basutoland owes its national existence to the efforts of strong chiefs, the Swazi very nearly lost theirs through the follies of a weak one. In the seventies, the Boers who pushed north of the Vaal began to look east to the sea. In their way they found a tribe akin to the Zulus from whom they obtained a strip of land and with whom they made a treaty. When, after annexation, the Transvaal was retroceded by the British, the independence of the Swazi was one of the conditions of the accompanying Convention. Under King Umbandine such a guarantee availed his people little. Of the proffered sweets of civilization his preference was for greyhounds and champagne, and he became the helpless prey of concession-hunters to whom for trifling sums he made away rights of every conceivable kind. Monopolies for photography, for auctioneering and selling spirits; concessions, duplicated and overlapping for mining and grazing; concessions for collecting the Customs and the revenue, and concessions, it was even said, for granting concessions. The Swazi spoke of 'the documents that have killed us. We hold the feather and sign: we take money but we do not know what it is for', British subjects were concerned and the need for British intervention was urgent.

In 1890 the British and Transvaal Governments held an inquiry and set up a government representing the three parties. This, it need hardly be said, did not work and in 1894, overriding the wishes of the Swazi, who sent a deputation of protest to London, we recognized a Transvaal Protectorate. After the South African War the Governor of the Transvaal administered the country until the grant of responsible government in 1906, when the High Commissioner took charge of Swaziland.

In 1906–7 the administration of the country was at last reduced to order. A commission was set up to hack its way through the jungle of concessions, and, on the basis of saving one-third of the country for the natives, managed to produce a compromise between the claims. The Swazi found themselves separated into 31 different reserves, the rest belonging to 500 concessionaires of whom 60 per cent. live in the country. Historically and economically, Swaziland is in a very different position from the other two territories.

The Bechuanaland Protectorate, which forms the huge central block of southern Africa, has experienced fewer vicissitudes than its sister Territories. Not one but a row of chiefs rule its peoples, who cling to the eastern fringe of the Kalahari. Most important numerically and politically are the Bamangwato, whose chief was the famous old puritan, Khama. The possibility of German extension from the west and Boer from the east threatened the 'Northern Road' which was vital to Rhodes's imperial strategy while the humanitarians feared for the fate of the tribes. In 1885 Sir Charles Warren led an expedition to the north, annexed British Bechuanaland, and proclaimed a Protectorate over the larger area to the north. But this was exactly where Rhodes wished to run his railway to Rhodesia and beyond, and he was determined to get the country for his Chartered Company. Khama and his fellow chiefs, however, who had been watching events in South Africa and Rhodesia, had other views: like Moshesh they were determined to offer their allegiance solely and directly to the imperial government. In the face of strong official discouragement they sailed to England, put on top-hats, and called at the Colonial Office. 'Shall we,' asked Chief Bathoen of the Bangwakatse, 'be given into the hands of a company whose work is to hunt for gold and the wealth of the land only?'

There was much correspondence and many interviews. The chiefs hung on month after month in the strange city, resisting all the persuasions of the officials and even the redoubtable Secretary of State himself. When Chamberlain went away 'resting in another land' they waited patiently into the cold autumn for his return in order to tell him their

fears all over again. They pointed out that the Company wished to take
the best parts of their country. 'Do not let them take away the land which
is the life of your children . . . or bring liquor into the country, to kill
the people speedily.' 'The Company wants to impoverish us so that
hunger may drive us to become the white man's servants who dig in his
mines and gather his wealth.' Assured that the Company was under the
Crown and that conditions favourable to them would be demanded, they
protested that even if the government should try to protect them 'with
words which are written in the agreement we shall lack peace in our
hearts . . . we have no voice which can be heard in England.'

The truth was that Britain, by the high principles she had proclaimed
and had to some extent acted upon in South Africa, had brought upon
herself the grave responsibility of having won the trust of the natives.
'We have seen the justice and the kindness with which the Great Queen
seeks to govern us. There is no government we can trust as we can trust
that of the Great Queen. We pray you, therefore, not to throw us away
as if we were troublesome children who would not listen to their
mother's words.'

The chiefs got their way. They agreed to provide the company with
a strip for the railway, but for the rest, by a somewhat vague agreement,
they were 'to rule their own people much as at present' under an officer
who (for only explicit assurance on the constitutional point would
satisfy the chiefs) was to receive his orders from the Queen through the
Secretary of State and the High Commissioner. A promise was made to
recognize the right of the chiefs to collect the tax and their jurisdiction
over natives in civil and minor criminal cases. The chiefs went home to
their arid country well satisfied with their work and unaware that anything more was needed for the future but a sleepless defence of the *status
quo*.

II. *General Hertzog's Demand*

It is impossible to consider the treatment of the Protectorates at the
Union apart from the whole question of South African native policy.
The issue is controversial, but we cannot avoid it: it is one of the two
main *motifs* of South African history, and the very reason for our connexion with the Protectorates today. Nowhere has it been more often
proved than in South Africa that difficult issues are not to be solved by
the kind of moderation which consists in obscuring awkward facts.

The peculiarity of South Africa, compared with other Dominions, is that it made divergent claims upon our liberalism and our humanity: we could never, it seemed, do justice at once to the claims of white and black. At the time of Union liberalism was in the ascendant. By the standards of history the grant of responsible government to the Transvaal in 1906 was a generous act, and in 1909 our statesmen felt a natural pride in an Empire in which two peoples so recently at war could meet round a table to plan their union as a self-governing nation.

How stood our other obligation? The natives had shown extraordinary loyalty and orderliness during the war and Chamberlain had written to Lord Milner that the enfranchisement of natives qualified by education would be among his list of the conditions of self-government. But at Vereeniging this difficult issue was postponed, wisely perhaps, though Lord Milner afterwards regretted it. 'The question of granting franchises to natives', ran Clause 8 of the Treaty, 'will not be decided until after the introduction of self-government.' When in the 1906 Constitution the Transvaal refused to give any political rights to natives, the British Government laid down that 'pending any grant of representation to natives . . . no native territory now administered by the Governor or High Commissioner will be placed under the control of the new Responsible Government.' Swaziland was therefore transferred at this time to the High Commissioner.

The interdependence of the two issues was thus already clear, and it was made still clearer to the Convention by its chairman, Sir Henry (afterwards Lord) de Villiers. Having recently visited England, he announced that the imperial government wished to give the delegates a free hand in everything but the native franchise and the Protectorates, since 'it regarded itself in a special sense as a guardian and trustee of the natives of South Africa'. He warned them that if the 'settlement of the Franchise question was regarded as unsatisfactory then the Protectorates would not be handed over'. Sir Edgar Walton, himself a delegate, wrote that the Convention was made to realize early in its sittings that if the Protectorates were to be included 'then the native peoples must find in the Constitution such provision for their protection and for their interests that they would be induced of their own free will to be included in the new State about to be created'.

The other provinces, however, rejected the Cape Franchise, and even any limited form of it, and persuaded the Cape to abolish the right of its coloured and native citizens to sit in Parliament. The Cape representatives, and especially Colonel Stanford and Mr Sauer, put up a great fight for the extension of their liberal traditions, but succeeded only in entrenching their own native franchise behind a two-thirds majority of both Houses.

The Protectorates question was treated in a clause permitting transfer at some future, unknown date, and in a Schedule containing safeguards which should operate in that event, the Convention being more interested in the permission and the British Government in the safeguards. These consisted of guarantees to the natives regarding their lands, their tribal institutions, and the liquor traffic; a form of administration by a Commission under the control of the Governor-General in Council, and in the reservation to the Crown of any legislation affecting the Schedule. These last conditions were strongly contested by some of the delegates, and it was necessary at last for the High Commissioner, Lord Selborne, who had instructions from home and also the difficult task of reassuring the uneasy tribes, to write a very frank letter to the Chairman:

'The obligations of His Majesty's Government to the tribes inhabiting Basutoland and the Bechuanaland Protectorate are obligations of honour of the greatest possible weight. These tribes surrendered themselves under the dominion of Queen Victoria of their own free will and they have been loyal subjects ... ever since. The history of the connexion with Swaziland is different but the obligations are only different in degree.'

In a final and even stronger letter he declared: 'It is no question of policy we are discussing: it is a question of honour and one to which every section of public opinion in the United Kingdom, government and opposition alike, is keenly sensitive.'

The compromise at last achieved, a delegation brought the Bill to England and heard it debated in Parliament. Speakers on both sides openly regretted the exclusion of natives outside the Cape from any political rights, but few felt that it would be either practicable or justifiable to endanger union on this issue. The government assured the House that it could regard the Cape Franchise as absolutely secure, and there was a general expectation that the Cape tradition would in time leaven the whole Union. On the Protectorates issue the government were pressed hard. Their spokesman, Colonel Seely, interpreted the Schedule as purely permissive. 'It does not bring transfer an hour nearer. In fact ... it makes it more difficult.' He emphasized the strength of the administrative safeguards. 'Under its terms, transfer, should it come ... may well be hardly perceivable to the natives themselves.'

Put thus in its contemporary context, the Schedule appears not as a promise but as a permission, and one dependent upon conditions and safeguards. Since the conditions are bound up with the question of South African native policy we are obliged to review its course since the Union. The northern delegates at the Convention had perhaps a good case when they reserved the vital issue of native policy for the decision of the nation-to-be. But the comprehensive settlement that was to follow Union has never come. The interruption of the Great War and the hesitation to grasp so difficult and so controversial a problem have led to successive postponements, and still another postponement forms part of the recent agreement between the Nationalist and South African Parties. The only definite suggestions before the country are still the so-called Hertzog Bills containing proposals, which have been emphatically rejected by the natives, to abolish the Cape Franchise in return for a limited communal representation for the whole Union. Meanwhile a number of important Bills have been passed. The Land Act of 1913 prohibits natives from acquiring land outside their reserves; the Mines and Works Act gives statutory expression to the customary colour-bar; and the Urban Areas, and Native Service Contract, Acts closely control the movement of natives in town and country respectively.

Though some attempt has been made to develop native institutions in the reserves, the vital problems of land, labour and political rights remain unsettled. There are, however, encouraging signs for the future in the independent and liberal attitude of young South Africans to the problem, while the new Ministry has begun, by a generous grant, to provide for native health.

If in 1909 we hesitated to transfer the Protectorate tribes against their will, there is an added reason for hesitation now. The Statute of Westminster and the South African Status Act (against which, we may notice, the Transkei natives protested) have rendered the safeguards in the Schedule constitutionally worthless. The powers of the Governor-General and the reservation of Bills exist no more as checks on a Dominion government, and we must delude neither ourselves nor the natives with the belief that the Schedule or any other conditions we could devise could bind future South African governments.

However good our case, we are not excused from making a very real effort to appreciate the South African point of view. With the passing of the Status Act the Union has fulfilled its nationhood. It is only by the fullness of its independence within the Empire that the ambitions of some of its people for secession have been met. The status of the Protectorates alone mars the completeness of the picture. And the limitation touches a very sore point. British intervention in native affairs is a century-old grievance, and not only with the Dutch. South Africans feel that the native problem is *their* problem; one of life and death which they alone can understand and for the mishandling of which they alone will suffer. They cannot allow it to be settled on abstract principles by people who sit in impartial security 6,000 miles away, who do not know what it means to feel their civilization threatened by a huge, black and still half-barbarian majority. Would England, it has been asked, submit the determination of her naval policy to South Africa? And is not the logic of the policy of trust to trust entirely and to remove the last vestiges of imperial control south of the Zambezi?

This argument has proved strong enough at various times in the past to outweigh that of the humanitarians. But is it really so relevant today and to the present issue? The time has long gone by – it had gone in 1909; even in 1902 – when anyone in this country imagines that, even though we are bound to be keenly interested, we either could or should dictate South Africa's native policy to her. The status of the Protectorates, when South Africans call it to mind, may act as a slight irritant to dominion nationalism, but it can hardly be maintained that it constitutes a serious check upon the Union's freedom of action. Meanwhile the claims upon the other side do not seem to have lost any of their force. Those who know the history of our reiterated pledges, above all those who have visited these peoples and have seen as human realities the strength of their loyalty and trust towards the British Crown, would hesitate to coerce or cajole them into abandoning their allegiance. Recent messages to *The Times* confirm what all previous evidence would lead us to expect, that they unanimously reject the idea of transfer. With native opinion in this state, that consultation of their wishes to which we are pledged might prove extremely embarrassing, if no worse, to all concerned.

It had been suggested in the Union that economic and administrative conditions in the Protectorates are such that they could hardly lose much by transfer. The Protectorates can probably stand comparison with other native areas of South Africa, though the lack of official information about the Union Reserves makes such comparison difficult. But it must be admitted that they do insufficient credit to a country which rightly prides itself upon its government of subject peoples. In parts of tropical Africa our Colonial Service has succeeded in discovering and taking into effective partnership those social forces which exist in even the smallest societies. Isolated, poor and paralysed by the uncertainty of the future, the Protectorates have never yet drawn adequately upon this valuable experience. True indirect rule has yet to come and should find magnificent material in the unbroken pride and tribal patriotism of these people.

Reforms, however, are already in progress, and with the future cleared for a period, with – it must be faced – some financial help for the two poorer territories, and with the expert administration we have to offer, it might be possible at some later date to transfer the Protectorates in a state in which they would be a credit to us and to themselves and an asset to the Union. Nor has the Union any reason to distrust the success of such an experiment. Successful administration on tribal lines touches no controversial issue; all parties, and most of all the segregationists, who are probably in a majority, desire to see the utmost possible development of native institutions in Reserves. It is just here that British experience could be put at the service of South Africa, and where contact and mutual understanding might be effected with regard to the two divergent systems of native policy which are developing in the black, and in the black-and-white, parts of British Africa and which may otherwise, with the linking up of the continent, meet in absolute and dangerous opposition.

Two points remain. This complex and delicate issue cannot be settled without the good will of the Union which has the Territories economically at her mercy. Secondly, if these arguments are good, it is for a postponement of the transfer and not for an eternal refusal. We need not anticipate that the South African government will be unreasonable and will refuse to appreciate the intimate obligations which bind us to the tribes. If it has become almost a convention for this country to defer to the wishes of the Dominions, it has been out of fear of abusing our primacy. How could South Africa make a more effective assertion of her new equality than by deferring to us in a matter which lies so near the honour of our country?

The Protectorates of South Africa

During the controversy over the Protectorates (more correctly the High Commission Territories) which continued after the date of the preceding articles those of us who were fighting for their retention by Britain were opposed by a formidable British antagonist. This was Mr Lionel Curtis, who wrote three articles in The Times *on 13, 14, and 15 May 1935, urging a prompt acceptance of the South African demands. These authoritative and uncompromising articles could not be left unanswered. I therefore wrote a further article for* The Times, *published on 16 May 1935, to controvert them and to remind the public of the history and character of our obligations to the peoples of the three territories. To gain still wider publicity I proposed to Mr Curtis that our articles should be published within the same cover. To this he agreed and generously allowed me, in the arrangement of the articles, to have the last as well as the first word* (The Protectorates of South Africa, M. Perham and L. Curtis 1935). *The concluding pages were as follows:*

The issue of the Protectorates has been set out in all its difficulty. It is in a very exact sense a legacy of history, and that a history of which there has always been, and perhaps always will be, two interpretations. I know as I write that my own conclusions are shared by many thoughtful people in South Africa as well as in England. My correspondence since my views were first published testify to that. I know, too, that there are many in this country who are exercising considerable restraint during these preliminary discussions but who, if they suspected that moderation meant any tampering with the principles involved, would make an outcry that would assuredly waken extremists in South Africa to a counter-demonstration. The issue might then pass out of the hands of reasonable people anxious to understand each other's point of view.

The course I have suggested asks sacrifices from both the Union and ourselves, and, indeed, from the tribes as well. From us it demands a resolute and intelligent effort at reform in a situation which offers no time for half-measures, and an expense of money which will, however, represent an inconsiderable item in our vast budget. I believe that when the situation is explained our people will be willing, as they have been before, to redeem our past pledges and our past mistakes at this cost.

From the Union it demands a generous appreciation of difficulties which to us seem very real, and a willingness to co-operate with us in their solution.

South Africa was laid out by nature upon a grand scale and it has a way of moulding large minds. Among the dead, Mr Curtis has reminded us of General Botha, and of the supreme greatness of the way in which he kept his word in 1915, which has been too easily forgotten in this country. Neither do we perhaps sufficiently appreciate how great an achievement the present united government represents in view of South Africa's past, or the significance of General Hertzog's presence at the Jubilee. It is because Mr Curtis knows so well what all these things mean that he wants us to do what seems to him the big thing in return. He asks us to act along the lines which he and his fellow-workers of the Milner school have always urged, of teaching political responsibility by trust, and of respecting nationality so that the very force which would otherwise destroy the Empire strengthens and enriches it.

Is this liberalism to be applied only to the white races? Assuredly not, we can reply for Mr Curtis, remembering his work for India. On what grounds then are these other communities to be excepted? Because they are African? Because they are small? Because they are so inconveniently placed? Or because they have 'no voice that can be heard in England', and so their case is allowed to go by default? The reply that it is because they have not got responsible government is hardly tenable. It could not have been applied to a country that was powerful like India, or white like Southern Rhodesia, as a justification for overriding their wishes in the most fundamental issue which can face a people. We should not allow the often unconscious arrogance which can be bred by our colour, numbers, wealth and power so to distort our perspective that we fail to recognize the element of nationality in a small, black and backward society.

Taking the Basuto as an example I maintain that they are that mysteriously formed entity, a nation. Their common life is bound up with all they share, the memory of their past endurances and triumphs, their high country and their reverence for the name of a great man. If this common life of theirs can be guided for a little longer through a difficult world by those they trust, it may become strong enough to maintain itself. It will not only offer those who share it greater opportunities for self-expression and for progress than they can hope to have without it, but ultimately in joining it will invigorate the main stream of Bantu life in the Union. When a small and primitive nation is destroyed, which may happen though no member of it is killed, not only do those who participate in the destruction injure themselves but something, the potentiality of which cannot possibly be gauged at the time, is lost from the world. The community-life of these tribes in any full sense rests upon what still remains of their pride and independence of spirit; and these are highly vulnerable and can be undermined by the neglect or contempt of the ruling race or by unimaginative administration as easily as they can be broken by force. Would it not be better to delay transfer a little longer while the new sympathy among South Africans towards native needs grows stronger and more effective and with it the realization, already present, that the Union has an interest as well as a duty in developing strong tribal government?

General Botha's people know what it is to defend their nationality in peace and in war, and they have been through the experience of defeat as well as of victory. They are mostly farmers and have a deep love for the soil of their adopted country. They are able therefore to appreciate better than those of British descent what the Africans have endured and what they need. These smaller communities who have been defeated or surrounded by the Europeans are in a far more unfortunate condition, for they can see little ground today to hope not only for equality but for any place but that of servants in the nation-state which has developed above them. Their need is therefore all the greater for a home, geographical and cultural, where they can develop fully and freely to the utmost that is in them. That is why the natives of the Union, watching these events so earnestly, wish to see their kinsmen in the Protectorates keeping the lamp of freedom alight. If in the past we have treated the Dutch of South Africa not well – Heaven save us from complacency! – but a little less badly than would have been the case if we had not been striving, with the help of Mr Curtis and others like him, to act upon certain principles, it would be a melancholy climax if in order to keep their friendship and that of their fellow nationals (for opinion on native affairs does not run on racial lines) we should be obliged to abandon those principles and so become something a little less than our own better selves. Yet do we not fall into complacency if we imagine for a moment that these principles are a national possession? Let us turn to that prayer which Botha scribbled, with a reference to the date of the Peace of Vereeniging, upon a slip of paper as he sat at the Versailles Conference table, and which has waited sixteen years for publication: 'God's justice will be meted out to every nation in His righteousness under the new Sun. We shall persist in prayer in order that it may be done unto mankind in love, peace and Christian charity.'

Native Lands in South Africa

Following this exchange with Mr Curtis the South African pressure continued to be so strong that those of us who were defending the case of the tribes did not feel able to urge an absolutely uncompromising negative but we got as near to it as we could. The immediate sequel was an attempt by Mr J. H. Thomas to arrange some measure of administrative co-operation with the Union (Cmd. 4948 1935). In our hopes that the attempt might prove the beginning of a solution Mr Curtis and I thought we had at last found some common ground and we wrote the following letter to The Times, *published on 30 May 1935.*

Sir, – Our articles on the South African Protectorates to which you refer in your leading article of the 24th were written because we both feared decisions injurious to native interests, though for different and opposite reasons. One of us feels that native interests would not be served by an early transfer of the Protectorates to the Union Government. The other believes that an early transfer would be in native interests.

We should like to say, therefore, that we both agree that the policy, foreshadowed by Mr Thomas and General Hertzog, of close co-operation between the British and South African Governments for the furtherance of native interests in the Protectorates, leading ultimately to their transfer to the Union with the willing consent of the natives themselves, would offer the best possible solution. Its successful issue would reflect lasting credit on British and South African statesmanship. It is to be hoped that public interest in this question will not die down, as an urgent responsibility lies upon us to make the utmost possible use of our new opportunity.

We should like to have said this in the preface to the book from which our articles were extracted; but the book was already in print and ready for issue when the announcement to which we refer was made. As its readers will find, we see eye to eye on another important matter, which for reasons of space had to be excluded from the articles published in *The Times*. The lesson of the Pim reports seems to be that such inquiries, with all the enlightenment they bring to the government and the public, ought not to be resorted to only when conditions have almost gone beyond the reach of the remedies they evoke. The possibility of developing, with due regard to all that is best in our traditions of decentralization, some system of regular inspection in our colonial empire seems to us to be worth serious study.

Yours, &c., MARGERY PERHAM, LIONEL CURTIS

Our hopes proved unfounded partly because the Africans were unwilling to accept help from the Union and partly because General Hertzog revealed an interpretation of the proposals as a stage towards a transfer. British governments, therefore, retained their sole control over the territories until their graduation during 1966 into an independence which, in view of their geographical and economic relationship with the South African Republic, may be full of hazards.

An excellent account of the long involved story will be found in Lord Hailey's The Republic of South Africa and the High Commission Territories 1963.

The Conquest of Ethiopia

Letters to *The Times* published 5 October and 22 November 1935

On 2 October 1935 the Italians had launched their invasion

Sir, – The main issue between the League and Italy is one of principle bound up with the Covenant. But it has an African background and it is just this background which Italians and some Frenchmen see in such a different light from ourselves. Mussolini is reported to have asked why Britain refuses to allow Italy to do what she has done so many times herself, while in certain French quarters we are accused of perversity or self-interest in exaggerating the importance of a merely colonial war. There is an answer to this and it is not, as our critics assume, a defence of our own past record, which would at once lay us open to the retort of hypocrisy.

The Covenant was the expression of a general desire to secure better dealings between peoples: it applies to colonial no less than European relations. Does Italy wish to drag our generation back to the standards of a past age? If her people study our policy towards subject peoples, they will see mistakes of judgement and abuses of power. But they will also see, whether in India, Ceylon or Africa, a growing tendency to respect the social individuality of the nations and tribes under our rule, and to repair the mistakes of the past by helping them to develop through their own local patriotism towards self-government as well as civilization. We have, however, no claim to be complacent: we have still too many selfish tendencies to suppress for that. And we have been late in realizing that nationalism, on however small and backward a scale, is a constructive force which it is sheer waste to destroy. But these are the reasons, which both Italians and Frenchmen, with their assimilative ideals, may not find so obvious, why we should regard the seizure of Ethiopia as a crime.

Holding these views, we cannot regard Ethiopia as the last unclaimed slice of Africa. If she were not unique in that continent she would not be the last truly independent community there, and as such a symbol to Africans throughout the world. Her semi-civilized Amharic peoples, brave, Christian and proud of their long and rather noble history, are the nucleus of a nation. A new chapter has already been added to that history by the dignity of the Emperor and the restraint of his people

L

under their ordeal. Of course Ethiopia is backward. She has been cut off from those influences which have softened our own medieval savagery, and which led us, little more than a century ago, to abandon a slave trade of a far more extensive and cold-blooded kind than hers. But it is not necessary to idealize Ethiopia to believe that in these days of the League there is no need for a backward country to be bombed into subjection to another power before she can be allowed to draw upon the assistance of the civilized world.

If Mussolini crushes Ethiopia he will destroy the vital forces through which she could best be civilized. Italy will find herself the gaoler of sullen prisoners whom she will only be able to cow by methods which will demoralize herself as well as them. These are the hard-earned lessons of our own colonial experience. And this is the interest, as opposed to interests, that we have in the African side of this conflict.

Yours, &c., MARGERY PERHAM

Sir, – While we congratulate ourselves upon having saved the principle of collective security, the aggressor with 'supreme contempt' continues to invade Ethiopia. All over the world the calculation is being made, with satisfaction or anxiety, that in the clearest conceivable case of aggression, and in circumstances in which the aggressor is unusually vulnerable, 50 nations cannot prevent war dragging on from weeks into months. We can dismiss the rumour that the government is weakening on the main question of principle. But can we be convinced that, ruling out unilateral or military action, the most effective sanctions have been chosen? It is to the interest of all nations, not excepting Italy, that the war should be stopped quickly rather than slowly. Definite information on this point is hard to obtain, but we can at least ask questions. Who is supplying the petrol which moves Italian lorries, tanks and aeroplanes against the Ethiopians? Who is feeding the Italian troops? Can we be regarded as wholehearted in our desire to stop this war so long as we make no proposal to cease, after adequate notice, from providing supplies to maintain the armies of the aggressor and facilities for ships bound on that errand? League nations have not a monopoly of the necessary supplies, but non-League nations might hesitate to be left with the clear responsibility for supplying them.

It is possible that the issue has lately become a little obscured. We have been distracted by our general election; Italian propaganda has been both obviously and subtly active while the Ethiopians have no skill to counter it or to appeal to our imaginations. War correspondents are showing us the campaign through Italian eyes. A section of our Press has taken a line totally out of keeping with our old traditions of humanity and of sympathy for oppressed peoples. Yet surely nothing can blur the central fact. A great western nation has decided in cold blood to concentrate all the science and resources of 'civilization' upon the destruction of men and women whose crime is to be 'backward', and whose only policy is to defend their homes. It is attacking a ruler who had begun the reform of his country and who has taken great risks by his reliance upon the League of Nations. The war news cannot be read without a sense of shame. And at any moment now the Ethiopians must begin their defence, and then, whatever the result, their losses must be immeasurably heavier than those of the invaders. What modern battles mean in terms of human anguish is only too fresh in our minds. We are committed to action. Can it not be action which will save both peoples from imminent carnage?

Yours, &c., MARGERY PERHAM

Obligations of British Policy in Ethiopia

Letter to *The Times* 29 April 1936

In his letter in The Times *of April 22 Professor Toynbee had concluded his eloquent appeal to British honour with an appropriate quotation of Greek verse.*

Sir, – Professor Toynbee has put into fine words the deep feelings entertained by many of us about the plight of Ethiopia. In a complex and difficult situation what practical action do these feelings suggest?

Circumstances, chief among them the hesitation of France to keep the Covenant, have hitherto hindered any immediately effective action to stop the war. Is the alternative, in default of that complete unanimity which we can hardly hope to have this side of Utopia, for all those powers loyal to the Covenant to sit back in a new kind of neutrality and watch the aggressor exterminate his victim? The desperate situation of Ethiopia reminds us that, outside the sphere of the Red Cross, no practical assistance of any kind has been given to her, and her modest requests, such as those for League observers and for a loan, have been dismissed, apparently with little consideration. The reason, of course, was that effective international action to stop the war would make all lesser measures superfluous and all national efforts – of the kind we have taken before in history – improper. Instead of such action we have watched a prolonged game of musical chairs in which the powers have walked round each other determined not to be left alone in doing the right thing. News from Geneva and other countries is not very full, but it seems certain that if the Assembly were recalled and given a courageous lead by Britain a large number of powers, including the Dominions, would be prepared to express their loyalty to the Covenant in action. Full sanctions by all these powers, some of them important for the products they supply or the position of their ports, must materially worsen the position of Italy. The past history and present courage of the Ethiopians combined with the rains make it likely that the war is by no means over. A loan for the supply of food and arms and the improvement of the communications across the Kenya and Sudan frontiers might prolong resistance beyond the financial endurance of Italy.

For Britain, quite apart from her great share in the need for international justice and security, the forward policy has become especially necessary. The layman realizes that the government must have very grave reasons hitherto for its hesitation to take this course independently of France. But the layman, shut out from the secrets of the council chamber, has an eye upon the horizon and sees even graver dangers there. One is that the refusal to take risks in the clearest imaginable issue of international right and wrong today may increase the risks of an old-fashioned balance-of-power war tomorrow. Another is that the apparent discrepancy between our words and actions at Geneva may cost us the trust of the world, and especially that of the coloured people upon whose loyalty our Empire stands.

Finally, in the event of the League breaking down over this issue, it is important that Britain should be clear of responsibility for that failure. Otherwise she will have disqualified herself for the task that must be hers in another generation, that of helping Europe to rebuild a more effective international order.

I am, &c., MARGERY PERHAM

Lines published anonymously in The Spectator's 'Notebook' *15 May 1936 upon the death of Dr John Melly, leader of the Red Cross Mission to the Ethiopian war, murdered when trying to save lives in the riots in Addis Ababa on the night following the Emperor's flight.*

JOHN MELLY

We stayed. Was there not busy reckoning to be done at home
Of fears, of costs – how many long, sharp nails go to a cross?
The ignorant dark people on their hills said 'They will come.
Are they not strong who gave to us their pledge "your loss, our loss"?'

He went – with those dark armies. They came on, the white, winged
    foes
In strength to work their will; with art to burn, to blind and rot.
He had no weapon; yet, clear-shining, merciful, arose
His purpose like a sword, defeating them – they know it not.

He went, young, smiling, urgent, with those happy few who said –
But not in words – of one flesh is mankind: who ran to give,
Unreckoning, the best they had, their lives (and he is dead).
We count our wealth of safety, yet – are we so rich who live?

Our Task in Africa

The Times 10, 11, 12 February 1936

These articles were prompted by the German claim for colonies. The first has been abbreviated as it contained some repetition of previous articles.

1. *Administration of Natives*

The question of colonial claims was recently discussed with great authority in this column by Lord Lugard[1]. He dealt mainly with Africa, the continent to which the questioners mostly turn, and there confined himself chiefly to economics and emigration. Government, viewed from the standpoint of African interests, has not been given much attention in the discussions of the last few weeks except in very general terms to which the subject does not lend itself.

We characterize British policy as one of 'trusteeship'; but this is a legal term blurred by transfer to the political sphere and, in its meaning of unqualified service to the interests of our wards, we must admit that it still remains an ideal. The much-quoted 'mandate principle' carries us a little farther. For while it seems that a self-appointed imperial trustee would be free to decide that it was in the best interests of his wards that they should never attain their majority, Article 22 of the Covenant assumes that the task of the mandatory is temporary, that of developing backward peoples until they can 'stand by themselves'. Further, specific conditions in the interest of the governed are elaborated in the terms of each mandate. While it may be assumed from official statements that the British Government accepts the standards of the mandates system for the rest of British Africa, even this is not enough; since in the methods through which the mandatories perform their obligations we find wide differences, not only as between British and foreign powers but as between members of the British Empire itself.

If then this is an appropriate moment to review the present character of our African administration we must be prepared to study our methods in some detail. But we are faced with a difficulty. The map confronts us with 15 territories, each with its own government, moulded, British

[1] *The Times*, 13 January 1936.

fashion, according to local peculiarities of ethnology, history and economics, and by the administrative personalities of its various governors, the whole collection, in foreign eyes, shockingly unco-ordinated even in essentials. Yet, across all this heterogeneity can be traced, with a clearness that increases in recent years, the expansion of a single administrative principle, that generally known as indirect rule.

The name was first used to describe Lord Lugard's system of admini-stration in Northern Nigeria. As the Colonial Office was not accustomed to impose even methods of proved success upon its governors, the Northern Nigerian principles had to wait for self-propagation by the chance of men and events. Their extension was begun in Southern Nigeria when, in 1914, Lord Lugard amalgamated the two parts: with the acquisition under mandate of a strip of the Cameroons, they crossed the eastern frontier. Shortly afterwards the appointment of Sir Donald Cameron, with his 16 years' experience of Nigeria, led to a resolute and intelligent development of indirect rule to suit the conditions of 5,000,000 East Africans. Uganda already had its own somewhat static system of indirect rule derived from the treaties of 1900-1, but had never rationalized it into a form suitable for export outside its four advanced States.

Farther north the Sudan Government had evolved order out of the ruins inherited from the Caliphate by firm bureaucratic government tempered by the sympathy and good sense of an exceptionally able staff. From about 1926, after sending one of its officers to make a comparative study of the Nigerian system, it began by gradual steps, leading from the judicial to the financial sphere and from the Arab north to the Negro south, to introduce a more devolutionary system. Northern Rhodesia, Nyasaland, the Gold Coast, the Gambia and Sierra Leone all adapted their systems to the prevailing principle.

The system, thus stamped with the empirical endorsement of the men on the spot, received the official blessing of commissions to East and West Africa and was crowned in 1931 by the approval of an all-party Joint Committee of both Houses of Parliament. It has been given the less obtrusive, but even more valuable, if critical, commendation of nearly all the very able group of anthropologists who are at present interpreting African society to us. Modern social psychology has en-dowed it with wisdom after the event.

There are other ways of administering Africa, and at the present stage they show strangely little difference in the surface presented to Europe through official reports or even to the eye of hurried travellers.

Almost everywhere in Africa 'chiefs' can be found. Under the most conscientious system of indirect rule the anthropologist will detect certain corruptions of the old status, but where a 'direct', or the pretence of an indirect, rule obtains he will find much more. Impatience, even when benevolent, combined with ignorance, finds it is much more expeditious and 'efficient' to dictate than to teach.

And with most Africans it is all too easy. Behind a façade of chieftain-ship the self-interest of chiefs and their subordinates may be set working against the common interest for ends which neither they nor their people comprehend. Nothing unseemly need occur at the administrative head-quarters. A look or a gesture is enough to remind a chief, or it may be a policeman or an interpreter acting ostensibly for a chief, that his posi-tion and salary depend upon his execution of an order. While the officer turns back to his table to write a glowing report, illustrated with impres-sive statistics, about the prosperity of his district and the efficiency of his chiefs, these set off to get the white man what he wants, and to get it quickly, whether it be a burdensome tax, 'voluntary' labour, or increased production of economic crops. They are armed with an irresistible weapon, the power of the foreign government, and in handling it they have lost their own traditional restraints, and have not yet learned ours. The peasant knows that it is useless to complain to the white man against his agents who are also his eyes and ears.

Indirect rule cannot wholly check a tendency towards the 'black agency' policy inherent in the African situation, but it provides safe-guards. Chiefs must be the free choice of their people according to their own process of selection, however prolonged and elaborate, and must not be deposed by the government without the people's concurrence except for the gravest reasons. The constitutional functions of coun-sellors, sub-chiefs, priests and elders should be maintained. The political officer should advise but never dominate; should not, as a rule, cramp his people's initiative by sitting upon their courts and councils; should have his headquarters near, but not too near, those of the tribe. Above all he should be free enough of routine to be constantly on tour and to know his people and their language well enough to be able to detect suppressed pathological symptoms.

It is Africa's misfortune to evoke generalizations about 'the African', yet none of these can be even approximately true if they are not based upon a study of some at least of those hundreds of societies within which the lives of most Africans are still set. Information about these societies and the disintegrating effects upon them of European contact is now available. No government is equipped to legislate for Africa, nor any politician to generalize about it, without at least some of this knowledge. The practical man will object, if he has read so far, to all this detail about pettifogging chiefs and administrative minutiae. 'Africa,' he will say, 'is a vast, undeveloped continent to be seen as a whole, and as part of the present world problem.' This is the kind of realism which deals with people as if they were things until the time comes at last when they assert their own humanity, and then they are probably too difficult to be dealt with at all.

II. *The Colonial Structure*

The British, judged by the best of their administrations, are today offering Africans an effective training in self-government. This is directed towards developing communities through their own local institutions rather than by attaching advanced individuals to ours. Nationalism, where it finds legitimate scope, can be one of the strongest constructive forces in the world, as it is the most ruinous where it is frustrated, and tribalism is nationalism in miniature.

There are already signs that white rule will force the growth of a wider African nationalism. Under skilled and sympathetic government this growth can be turned to constructive ends from its first stirrings. Clan is encouraged to co-operate with clan, as in the example given in a recent article in this column from British Togoland: tribes are already beginning to enter into federal relations with their neighbours, and if this spontaneous movement is fostered even larger groups, and so more effective local governments, will gradually come into being. The apparent readiness of many educated Africans to throw away their past runs counter to a deeper desire, already manifest, to assert their cultural identity. Indirect rule leaves them some freedom to make their own synthesis of the old culture and the new one we have brought.

The association of the system with primitive institutions is only incidental to a transitional stage towards whatever forms first of local and ultimately of central government Africans shall themselves develop to meet their needs. Meanwhile the task of guidance is nearer to education than administration, and officers have, like good teachers, to cultivate patience and sympathy, and, like them, to lead their pupils towards the unknown by way of the known.

Functions of this kind are not performed to order. Whether or not in his dealings with Africans an officer in a remote station approaches the ideal standard of devotion and courtesy – honesty and the will to be just can generally be assumed – is largely a matter of character. It is unlikely that the people will reveal his shortcomings. Since character is largely formed by education we must look nearer home for the basis of our African system and ask how our administrative service is recruited. There were always able men to be found in the service, but in recent years the general standard has risen. Of the 603 entrants since 1926, 510 have been graduates from Oxford and Cambridge. While to some this may seem a fact for criticism, it must be remembered that through the system of state and other scholarships, especially in the subjects most usually taken by these men, these Universities attract the pick of the schools throughout the country. Analysis of examination honours would show that the academic standard of entrants has risen markedly, especially in the last five years.

The Colonial Office, however, ranks this as only one among the desired qualifications which, according to the report of a 1930 Committee upon this question, include 'vision, high ideals of service, fearless devotion to duty born of a sense of responsibility, tolerance, and, above all, the team spirit'. Agricultural, veterinary and other departmental officers are mostly recruited from the newer universities which specialize in these subjects. These entrants, like the administrative cadets, generally undergo a year of post-graduate training for their service. Bureaucracies always invite attack; but these facts show that Britain, which has never shared the prejudice of some Colony-owning countries against oversea service, endeavours to give of her best.

Once appointed, administrative officers – for the other branches on their present scale are a post-war creation and have still their traditions to make – are trusted with a stimulating measure of responsibility. Brought up in similar traditions they are able to understand one another, a very important matter in conditions where misunderstanding is so easy, although of course uniformity of type can be carried too far. The Governor, upon his side, knows what he can expect of his officers in the way of loyalty and of appreciation of his policy. Detached, like all English civil servants, from politics, and reasonably comfortable and secure in their positions, they can afford to preserve that *sine qua non* of good native administration, their consciences. Their seniors are nearly always men who have served the same apprenticeship; they generally understand their difficulties and give them scope and time, though never so much as the good district officer demands, in which to produce results.

Enthusiasm for sport, though sometimes indulged too far as a distraction, sweetens conditions of life not always very healthy; and a sense of humour corrects the besetting sin of native administration, the tendency to take oneself too seriously. It is surely a healthy symptom, in a recent Tanganyika report, that a provincial commissioner should have incorporated in it the account given by a district officer of his own visit when, after he had harangued the assembled notables upon their civic responsibilities, one old man got up, in the pause succeeding the peroration, and remarked, 'I have brought some eggs.'

The Service, which had the strength and weakness of having grown freely according to the needs of different periods and regions, has lately been reformed and co-ordinated. Since 1930 the Colonial Office itself has been reorganized for its task of recruiting and administering the Service and of applying the best technical skill to the needs of different territories. Behind the whole system lies more than 300 years of continuous experiment in the government of colonies in general, and of more than a century in that of Africa. Colonial administration is a technique which requires a long apprenticeship and in which subject humanity is the material which has to suffer the blunders of the beginner.

The form of administration I have described had to be conceived by individuals and worked out by a picked Service, but it has flourished only because it is in harmony with our constitutional tradition. This, expressed at its highest in Parliament, running through our vigorous institutions of local government, and through hundreds of unofficial bodies, national and local, down to the village institute, is to evoke to the utmost possible degree the consenting will and the active co-operation of those concerned in any undertaking.

This tradition, in spite of many mistakes, has enabled us to create that new political institution, the British Dominion, and it is only because we are so lacking in foresight that we are a little surprised to find ourselves today on the edge of what a recent correspondent to *The Times* has called the era of the brown Dominions.[1] The process of transferring responsibility has seldom in its early stages been a very easy or graceful one, and so far as Africa is concerned, it is much too soon for promises or pronouncements as to when or how the distant objective will be reached. But in this continent at least we may avoid some of our Indian difficulties. We have corrected the nineteenth-century complacency about the universal superiority of our own ideas and institutions, and

[1] E. Wench letter to *The Times*, 20 December 1935.

instead of enervating by over-paternalism have begun to work self-government from the bottom upwards.

The vitality of British democracy not only guarantees the destination but also safeguards the course of this native policy. It is difficult to imagine how such a policy could exist, much less advance, in a country where there was not the utmost freedom to criticize the government, and where an energetic public opinion was not constantly playing upon colonial problems. Without suggesting that the whole electorate is alert to these issues, there is a growing body of informed opinion in England which watches them keenly. Much of it is concentrated through those societies which in meetings and periodicals discuss colonial or specifically African topics. Certain larger bodies existing for other purposes, religious or political, and certain newspapers, are traditionally sensitive about the interests of subject peoples. There is a very salutary tendency to regard any outbreak of disorder less as a symptom of vice on the part of the ruled calling for punishment than of maladministration on the part of the rulers calling for investigation and, possibly, for reform. Dubious incidents get immediate publicity and become the subject of questions in Parliament, deputations to Ministers, and, possibly, Commissions of Inquiry. Sometimes an incident is exaggerated and a good deal of unnecessary embarrassment caused to the authorities. But it is generally felt that such a mistake is upon the right side and that without continuous criticism, constructive as well as destructive, the department and the Service which administer remote and almost voiceless people might become static or worse.

The classical rights of our rule of law enable Africans to join in this protection of their interests, though few educated Africans would admit that they are sufficient, and some of them are generally engaged in protesting against what they regard as an infringement of one of those rights. On the West Coast, where education is older than elsewhere, Africans, elected as well as nominated, play an active part upon Legislative Councils, as the minutes of those bodies would show. In the Gold Coast especially they have more than once modified government policy by their outspoken opposition. Native newspapers on the West Coast are many and vigorous, subjecting governments and often individual officers to the freest criticism.

East Africans have not reached this stage of political education. They found, however, some expression in 1931 when African delegates were invited to give evidence before a Committee of both Houses of Parliament. Those from Tanganyika and Uganda impressed all who heard them with a grasp of administrative realities that comes only from practical experience. The Kenya delegates, though not the most extreme critics of government that could have been found, were no mere tame nominees, but freely ventilated their grievances. After the unfortunate Aba riots in Nigeria in 1929, Africans were put upon the Commission of Inquiry which examined the various officers with regard to their conduct and reported critically upon certain aspects of government policy. A very novel portent has been the appearance of Africans in the constituency of the Colonial Secretary Mr Ormsby-Gore during the last general election. But, for all this, African political opinion is only in its first faint manifestations. With the gradual spread of education and the linking up of the continent, it will increase in strength until it provides a safeguard for African interests for which the self-restraint of even the most humane rulers is a poor substitute.

III. *The Line of Advance*

In the preceding articles I have laid myself open to a charge, which foreign readers would be especially quick to make, of complacency. Let me confess that had I been writing in any other context but that of colonial claims I would rather in every aspect of this subject have dealt with our shortcomings than with our achievements. This does not mean that the achievements have been overstated, but that since they fall so very far short of the large and difficult task we have set ourselves in Africa, undiluted self-congratulation is dangerous. Let us then consider for a moment certain of these shortcomings.

We must first admit that though the somewhat altruistic policy discussed here is that declared by our government, it is not unanimously supported in this country. Other things are said and other things are sometimes done which give foreigners excuse to charge us with hypocrisy. But in the lively conflict of opinions in England today there are signs that the altruistic conception is gaining at the expense of the others.

Secondly, it might be well to dispose of one misconception which seems to distract many of our foreign critics from the main issues of today. It is that we pretend to a blameless record in the acquisition of our colonies. Like all other imperial powers we expanded by force and like them we have in the process committed our crimes; as an older and more extensive imperial power we may even have committed more than other nations of those crimes which an earlier morality condoned. Historians must calculate the more and the less according to their perspective. We believe these errors are best remembered in order that they may never be committed again. It is our object today to change the basis of our rule from one of force, which has never given us the satisfaction promised by some continental philosophies, into one of co-operation and ultimately of partnership.

The principle of administration by which, as I venture to suggest, this change can best be brought about has been described. But, though the process of levelling-up to the best standards seems likely to continue, the achievement in British Africa is still very uneven. Those territories, especially where the administration has only recently been remodelled, have found that the legislative forms of indirect rule are easier to import than the technique. Much greater knowledge of the people we are guiding is necessary, and it cannot be said that we are yet making sufficient attempts to obtain it.

Apart from the general level of administration there are several large problems that we have still to solve. One of these is to find a place in a system designed for the backward masses for those groups of educated Africans who have progressed far beyond them and who are already claiming an immediate advance towards British parliamentary forms. While the French, with their conception of a more assimilative and centralized empire, can endeavour to satisfy their *intelligentsia* with civic privileges, we have to attempt the harder task of helping them to identify themselves with their own communities in an inevitably slow advance. We shall fail unless we can convince them that the present system leads towards, not away from, their ideal of national self-government.

Eastern Africa presents a major problem of its own. White settlement and industrialization have not so far proved very compatible with the development of strong native local government. The main reason is that in a mixed state such as Kenya the government finds it difficult to give to the political education of Africans that absolute concentration and devotion that the task demands. Friction between settlers and Africans over questions of land and labour has been allowed to develop, and a constant fear, vividly revealed before the Joint Committee of both Houses in 1931, haunts the African leaders lest the settlers should gain control of the government. All this reacts upon the relations between government officials and Africans, and makes it difficult to create that atmosphere of mutual confidence and respect which is essential if administration is to be educational.

There is no need here to impute blame to any party. The official, whose career for the 25 years or so he passes in the country is bound up with the well-being of his African charges, begins their political training by virtue of that same democratic tradition which stimulates the settler to demand complete self-government for himself. The objectives at this stage are incompatible, and in Kenya Great Britain has recently refused a demand which would mean the government of the Africans by a small minority composed of their employers, and this in the most authoritative way possible, by an all-party committee of both Houses of Parliament. Yet the problem remains in that the attempts of the settlers to obtain in practice the control that they are denied in theory unsettles the political atmosphere and discourages constructive native administration.

We have also still to solve the related problem of the effects of white industrialization upon native well-being. The Report upon the recent riots in the copper mines of Northern Rhodesia reveals something of these effects.[1] Even Tanganyika is not immune, and a recent report expresses some fears for the future of the famous Nyamwezi tribe in view of the drain of labour to the coastal plantations.[2] These problems are not easy ones, since the poverty of Africa handicaps welfare work for Africans, but 'development' which frustrates legitimate progress or even results in social damage or bitter political conflict cannot ultimately be in the interests of any party. Informed foreign opinion fastens upon this issue and watches to see how our government will harmonize these conflicting interests.

In spite of these qualifications the situation in our African territories as a whole supports the conclusion that their inhabitants would have nothing to gain, and possibly much to lose, by being handed over to another power. Braving the charge of hypocrisy, let it be said that true internationalists in this country must come to this conclusion with regret. We do not undervalue the effects of a generous gesture, or of an example of peaceful readjustment. But we are not dealing only with goods and with land, but with subject people, and a sacrifice at their expense could hardly raise the standard of international ethics.

Even those who believe that we may have been mistaken in retaining Tanganyika after the war must recognize that it is not a mistake that can easily be retrieved. The period of our rule there may seem short in years, but it has been of profound importance to Africans. In this period African local governments have passed out of the stage of occupation and of consolidation, and, provided with resources of increasing money

[1] *Report of the Committee into Disturbances in the Copperbelt, 1935, Cmd. 5009.*
[2] *Annual Report of Provincial Commissioners on Native Administration for the year 1934. Western Province section, p. 45.*

and personnel and an enlarged conception of the scope of government, have participated in almost every sphere of administration. It is difficult to see how even the most liberal and experienced nation could take over from us that fruitful experiment in local self-government in which African and English constitutional ideas are now so closely fused.

It would take us outside our subject to ask why it is always Africa, not very rich in primary resources and not very suitable for colonization, which must always take first place in discussions of colonial claims rather than land elsewhere in the world that does not carry a subject population. Even for Africa, however, the response to the so-called 'have-nots' need not be wholly negative. We are entering here upon new and difficult ground, but some landmarks at least may be discerned. It would be a retrogressive step for Britain to hand over without or against their will peoples to whose interests she is now deeply committed. But two steps forward are possible. One, is to commit herself still further in African interests, and to obtain international endorsement for this commitment. The other, along the lines suggested by Sir Samuel Hoare at Geneva, is to share freely with the rest of the world such economic advantages as belong at present to trusteeship.

Those who realize the danger to Africa lest these two aspects of African and European interests should be divided advocate the extension of the mandates system to colonies and protectorates. We must not entertain exaggerated hopes of this system. Its main function is the provision of a sounding-board of international criticism at Geneva, but this is effective only in so far as public opinion in the mandatory country is sensitive enough to provide an echo. To visit countries under mandate is to observe certain limitations of the system which are perhaps less clear in the voluminous literature of Geneva. It is regulative, not creative, in its function, and even this regulation is most easily applied to definable points in the mandates which mostly fail to cover the essentials of native policy. Yet the system does represent an immense advance upon the old sole Imperial irresponsibility, and points the way to further advance. A simple extension of the existing system may not, however, be practicable. The juridical status of a mandate – debatable though that is – could hardly be fitted upon a colony. Some of the more advanced peoples concerned would violently resent a complete change of status being made over their heads. Nor, on their part, would all the African powers be ready even for the discussion of such an abrupt and far-reaching change.

A more evolutionary and flexible system would accord better with political realities. Might it not be found along the line of conference, committee, investigation, report and convention which has been followed at Geneva in the case of native labour and other subjects? Questions of economic equality and those regarding naval bases and the militarization of natives are clearly susceptible to such treatment. Applied to the linked questions of the opportunities for European emigration and the rights and future needs of Africans with regard to land, it might dispel some dangerous illusions. In these and other subjects which suggest themselves it would be necessary to assign a large arbitral function to expert and impartial opinion; and here the experience of the 'neutral' members of the Mandates Commission might be invaluable. In the face of world opinion it would be difficult for an African power which was unable to agree to any transfer of territory to refuse indefinitely to ratify these conventions. The practical and laconic Englishman may recoil from the projection of all this international talk and print into what he has so long regarded as his own business, but let him ask himself what alternative is offered in the situation of today.

If an international colonial service is impracticable there lies outside the executive functions of government a vast and increasing field for research where foreign help might be encouraged. British governments in Africa have lately invited a distinguished German scholar to advise them upon linguistic problems and have welcomed a number of foreign anthropologists. Machinery might be set up to further a wider recruitment of foreign scientists. And though we need not deceive ourselves that any of these measures would appease the most dissatisfied powers, they would be the first steps towards an internationalization of imperialism which might one day deprive imperialism of its present attractions.

Trusteeship, which for Britain means, in large part the training of subject peoples in self-government, does not easily lend itself to international regulation, but it should be the mainspring of our policy in all other aspects of government. It would impel us to associate African opinion so far as possible in all these international proceedings. In this matter of the part to be played by the coloured races we have no choice but to combat in deed and word the very different ideas apparently held in Italy and Germany. Only the other day Herr Hitler, as reported, proclaimed the indefinite indulgence of the white race's 'urge to rule' as necessary to the basis of the European economic structure, while he derided our policy of trusteeship as a 'weak conception' and a 'pacifist idea'. Britain's answer must be to pursue that policy, as it has been defined here, even more openly and deliberately. It is the only policy

M

which can justify her to herself, to most of the world, and to her own subjects in retaining present control of such large areas. And it is the only policy that promises in the end to remove one of the causes of world conflict by enabling Africans to take charge of their own destiny.

The Times Leader 12 February 1936:

WHITE AND BLACK AFRICA

Miss Perham sums up this morning the results and the lessons of the remarkable development in British administrative policy in Africa during the past twenty years, the origin and progress of which she has described in her two previous articles. Although it was not her purpose to discuss the idea, put forward by some hasty and ill-informed enthusiasts, that international unrest might be appeased by a redistribution of Colonial possessions, yet it is worth noting that, speaking with admitted authority on the subject of African native administration, she rejects it outright as detrimental to native interests. She points out that 'we are not dealing only with goods and with land, but with subject people, and a sacrifice at their expense could hardly advance the highest interests of internationalism'. She does not claim that everything is perfect. Indeed she emphasizes the difficulties of the task undertaken by the new school of administration and the imperfection of the results so far achieved. But, in spite of all the necessary qualifications, and surveying the situation of the African territories as a whole, she comes to the conclusion that their inhabitants 'would have nothing to gain, and possibly much to lose, by being handed over to another Power'. The growth of the system of 'indirect rule', training the African to govern himself and to develop his own traditional institutions, has gone so far, Great Britain has committed herself so deeply to the interests of the native peoples in Africa, that it would be a retrograde step to hand them over to some other authority without or against their will. Nor does she think that a simple extension of the mandate system would be practicable, even if the other African powers were ready to discuss such an abrupt and far-reaching change. She suggests that a more flexible line of advance might be found by using the machinery of conference, committee, investigation, report, and convention for the discussion and settlement of African problems.

There is no need to go into this suggestion at the moment, for the main object of Miss Perham's articles is to describe and explain the change in the spirit and methods of British native administration since Lord Lugard first applied the principle of indirect rule in Northern Nigeria. It is not a simple story, since it concerns no fewer than fifteen territories scattered over the east and west of Africa, each with its own separate government, which has grown into its present shape under the influence of local peculiarities of ethnology, history and economics, and of the personalities of its various governors. The Colonial Office is not accustomed to impose upon the administration of any Colony methods adopted elsewhere, even when they have admittedly proved successful. To the foreign eye there must seem something almost shockingly unsystematic in the existence of these fifteen unco-ordinated governments; but this very lack of co-ordination, the heterogeneity of the different administrations, makes it the more striking that, each in its own time and in its own way, they have all adopted the methods first developed into a system in Northern Nigeria. These methods, applied by the men on the spot, have since received the official blessing of Commissions to East and West Africa and the approval of the Joint Committee of the two Houses of Parliament. The essence of the principle is the recognition by the white administrator that his function is not to dictate but to teach, even where dictation would be more expeditious and apparently more 'efficient', and that no hurried policy of economic development must be allowed to cut across the slow primary task of political development. To work effectively under such limitations demands not only a carefully planned technique, but also high qualities of patience and self-restraint. By careful selection, however, the Colonial Office has succeeded in building up a school of administrators, recruited mainly from Oxford and Cambridge, who have already justified themselves and are gradually establishing a new tradition in native government.

Progress has not been uniform in the different territories. In some of them the principle of indirect rule is harder to apply than in others. There are complications introduced by white settlement and by industrialization which vary in intensity. In one sense there is not one native problem but many. At the same time everything which affects the native in one part of Africa has its repercussions all over the continent. In this connexion let it be added here that there is every reason to welcome the new prospect of a compromise on the Native Representation Bill which is now before the South African Parliament. As it was originally drafted, the natives of the Cape Province were to lose the right of registering as new voters, which they have possessed for eighty years, though natives already on the register were not to be deprived of their right to vote. This proposal, supported by most of the representatives from the Transvaal and the Free State, where there has never been any native franchise, as well as by all the Malanites, has been strongly opposed by a large body of opinion in the Cape. It was felt that to disfranchise the native would be a reactionary measure which might embitter relations for generations to come. The compromise which General Hertzog is reported to be considering is on the basis of a separate electoral roll and separate representation. This suggestion also has its difficulties, and it is, of course, far from satisfactory to the champions of the native franchise; but it would be infinitely preferable to the original proposal of sheer disfranchisement.

Introduction to Ten Africans

A collection of biographical studies, six of them taken down by expert recorders and four written by the subjects themselves.[1]

We have grown accustomed to the peculiar condition of empire under which we control the destinies of people we do not understand. In Africa, especially, our agents regulate in considerable detail the lives of some tens of millions of human beings of whose languages and ways of life they still know little, and with whom they have none of those ordinary social relations through which people come to know and to like each other.

The main reason for this is the 'backwardness' of Africans. It is an obvious and fundamental fact, but one upon which we are apt to lean a little too hard in order to make ourselves comfortable in a difficult situation. In default of true knowledge we too often make do with assumptions: the primary one, that Africans are backward; next, that they are all almost equally backward; even that they are inherently, and so permanently, backward. Cut off, as most of us are, from any contact with Africans as individuals, we think of them or deal with them in the mass, according to our various standpoints, as 'natives', even as the 'heathen', as 'hut and poll taxpayers', or as 'native labour' or even as 'the native problem'. We see the strange, stupid or cruel things they do and, ignorant of their motives, forgetting what we ourselves did yesterday, what, alas! Christian nations are doing today, think them relatively more stupid and cruel than they are. We allow black skin and Negro features to shut Africans off from those perceptions which we turn upon members of our own race. When, here and there, an African differentiates himself from the mass in a way we cannot ignore, he often rouses in us a kind of resentment. Is this, perhaps, because it is troublesome to adjust towards an individual an attitude which for our convenience or our prestige we habitually turn towards a race?

The very poverty of the Africans is a barrier between them and peoples who have enriched – some would say complicated – their lives with the innumerable products of modern industry. We see semi-naked

[1] Faber & Faber 1936, second edition 1963.

peasants living in mud huts, satisfying their elementary wants apparently in the most primitive ways. Surely, we think, people living like that cannot have personality as we reckon it! Forgetting for a moment the most obvious facts of anthropology, and the long ages of evolution during which we shared, until yesterday, their primitive culture, we may even make the unscientific remark that they are near to the animals. And, yet, perhaps, if at night some of the elders should come and sit round our camp-fire, and its flames should suddenly paint their faces as they talk, we may be startled by a sudden doubt. For these faces are all different; each has taken the stamp of life in its own way. Naked torso, foul rags, outlandish tongue, greedy hands stretched for tobacco or coins, cannot hide the truth. There is the authentic sculpture, that of human experience working upon genuine and sometimes fine material. In the middle squats the elder statesman – or is he, perhaps, a bishop? – white beard, thoughtful eyes, grave lines, still posture. There is the man of action, the renowned hunter, straight-lipped, keen-eyed, restless, assertive. Next to him is the humorist with roving self-conscious glances, and puckish twist to mouth and eyes. These are people of full human stature, rich personalities some of them, and it is our loss as well as theirs that we do not know them.

This lack of mutual individual knowledge has its consequences. There are certain methods we find it quite natural to employ towards masses which would seem quite inappropriate or embarrassing if we tried to use them towards groups of individuals some, at least, of whom were known to us. In India all the competence and integrity of our administration has not been able to compensate for this lack of individual, mutual understanding. In many parts of Africa we see a clumsy dictation in place of the experiments in partnership which are open to us and which in one or two places are actually being begun. The dictation may be inspired by the best intentions. It is possible to work in a spirit of high altruism *for* 'natives': it seems more natural, on the other hand, to work *with* 'individuals'. Their wishes and feelings begin to come into the picture as well as our standards of what is right and efficient.

This division of man from man means loss of a less measurable kind. People who are shut off from communication with human beings around them, whether it is within their own wealth, rank, nationality, or race that they are confined, begin in time to impoverish themselves. A purely negative attitude, a vacuum, cannot be maintained, and prejudice fills up the void. And in those made to feel themselves outcasts unfortunate qualities grow rank. Their injured self-respect makes for hypersensitiveness, and they seek compensation in self-assertion. Some of the most valuable human qualities are denied growth in them or distorted in growing. The defence or exaltation of their depreciated race becomes a will-o'-the-wisp in pursuit of which intellectual power is wasted, facts dodged and history perverted. Bitterness saps the power to appreciate or to co-operate. There is no exercise for the sense of responsibility. There is no room for that dual foundation of man's belief in his own value as an individual person and as a member of his community, upon which alone he has hitherto been able to build up his contribution to civilization.

I do not for a moment suggest that this situation is due entirely to human perversity or that a little right sentiment will open a golden age of mutual understanding. The barriers between the civilized and the less civilized are there, and they are solid. Nothing of course need hinder us from achieving reasonable relations with fully 'educated' Africans, except certain fears which do little justice to our dignity and common sense. But the fully 'educated' (I am using the word in our own somewhat arrogant sense) are few. Only those who are exceptionally patient and disinterested will succeed in getting on friendly terms with Africans in all the awkward fractional degrees of education. As for the very primitive, perhaps only saints or scientists can learn to know them well. Are we then to sit down comfortably upon our side of the barrier, or, recognizing the present waste and future danger it represents, shall we make some effort to cross it?

The young athropologists are doing much to sap that ignorance of Africans which is chiefly responsible for the disdain in which these are held. They have done much and will do much more in the next few years to reveal tribal society as an intelligible working whole, rather than as a field for the collection of strange customs or quaint handiwork. Yet it is not all anthropologists who can breathe upon the dead bones, nor is it everyone who will read works which are labelled anthropology. Other means of insight are needed.

My own work in Africa demanded much travelling. I could know few places or persons intimately. Yet from time to time, in Africa or in England, I have been able to make contact, and in one or two cases to make friends, with Africans. In the light of their opinions, old cherished assumptions began to look strange. To explain ourselves and our policies to them was instructive and sometimes uncomfortable. But it was an adventure, a new kind of African exploration coming as the old kind gives out, to discover for myself behind all the admitted differences of race and culture what in theory I knew to be there, our common nature, easy to know, and sometimes easy to like and respect. I almost blush as I write this, knowing that I may offend some of the initiated among my own people by committing to paper something at once so personal and so obvious, while some Africans will be offended that it should be necessary to speak of it at all.

These were the ideas that prompted this collection. I wanted to share my experience; to introduce English readers to a group of Africans, individuals and individualities, so that they might obtain a sense of that intimacy which few of our people can achieve in life. That, let me hasten to say, is the extent to which this book is propaganda. I maintain here no theory about Africans unless, in the eyes of some, what I have already said constitutes a theory. These Africans have not been carefully selected to represent any special virtues or qualities. Still less – and here I can only offer my word – have their stories been tampered with, and light, shade and colour redistributed so as to build up the picture that my collaborators or myself might wish to present. There is, I think, sufficient internal evidence of the truth of this. That knowledge of Africans as persons makes it impossible to dismiss them all as savage or backward is a truth which has its reverse side: it is also impossible to regard them all as uniformly good, simple, unfortunate, or oppressed. These Africans, like any other ten persons, vary in character and also reveal contradictions in themselves.

Although it would be against the principles expressed in this introduction to say that the subjects of these lives are typical, I must own that we have endeavoured to present people who have undergone widely different degrees of European influence. By that standard the stories have been arranged as far as possible in an ascending scale, with effects which will not escape the discerning reader. At a certain point across most of them runs a band rather like that igneous intrusion which forces itself among the old sedimentary rocks, altering their character and all the contours which form above them. Has this European intrusion been for the happiness of these individuals? Have its effects been deep or superficial? Perhaps the three stories that start below the line may in part provide an answer. But it is not for me to instruct the reader as to what he should find: each will discover different things according to his knowledge and perception.

Kenya revisited

The Times 17 February 1937

Though the depression imposed a dismal thrift on Kenya and severely tested its economic structure, and though the yellow gleam from the new goldfields has not heralded the Golden Age that some expected, yet the last six years have been far from barren.

In Mombasa and Nairobi many new buildings catch the eye. Some must be credited to Indian enterprise in business and social service. The European cathedral in Nairobi has grown two tall spires, and in their tribal area nearby the Kikuyu have built their magnificent Church of the Torch under the guidance of one Scottish mason. In the middle of the town the onion domes and minarets of a large new mosque stand in somewhat unhappy neighbourhood with the sober, classical Macmillan Library and a very modern chunk of flats in the fluid concrete style. The suburbs, swelled by retiring officials, reach out to the borders of the Masai and Kikuyu Reserves and are now linked to the centre of the town by an efficient omnibus service manned by Africans and free from 'Jim Crow' restrictions. Justice and the Municipality are housed in large new buildings, but the nerve centre of the administration, the Secretariat, still functions in a decrepit tin shanty. Gardens are much richer, and the great bunches of lilies and delphiniums marketed by Africans for a few pence and the English peas and beans, celery and lettuces, almost compensate for fever, amoebic dysentery, red dust, and the sanitary system.

In the Nairobi native location the main addition is a large stadium, centre of a great development in African athletics. Last year 8,000 natives – an orderly crowd – watched the cup final against Uganda. They appear to be natural football players, though their respect for the prestige and the boots of white men – their own feet are bare – prevent them fairly matching their prowess. They have not yet evolved for themselves that advanced product of civilization, the referee. Athletics are not so popular as football. Yet I saw a Kikuyu teacher win the seven miles (37 min. 50 sec.) for the fourth year in succession immediately after winning the three miles (15 min. $15\frac{1}{2}$ sec.).

On the European side of the town the only native to be seen now in the streets in savage undress is one whose shield bears an inscription about genuine native curios. Europeans' hats, where they have not been discarded, are no longer of broncho size; there are fewer bright shirts and belts; revolvers are no more seen, and alcohol plays a much smaller part in stimulating the gaiety of equatorial nights. Some of the personalities who set the tone in the old carefree days are no more, and others have felt the effects of time and economic depression. Yet not all the glory of the pioneering atmosphere has departed. Women do their shopping in corduroy trousers, and the farmers arrive in cars battered with their conflicts with the Kenya roads. And at nights zebras crop the gardens of the outlying houses, and pursuing lions sometimes dispute the way home with returning diners-out.

Kenya appeared true to form. A constitutional crisis was raging when I left, and another broke out soon after I landed. Once again elected members stumped the country, local associations passed resolutions against the government and pooled their indignation at a Nairobi convention. Large headlines on the Kenya crisis dwarfed those other crises troubling far-away Europe and Asia. Yet – and this is one of Kenya's mysteries – it was difficult to find a single European who privately was not entirely reasonable. Income-tax, the burning issue since 'Mr Pim passed by',[1] is not an innovation to arouse enthusiasm; but a considerable majority of Europeans and Indians were in favour of it, and it has since been accepted.

It was upon the constitutional aspect of this, as of other issues, that the elected members, off the platform mostly as reasonable as they are hospitably charming, rallied support. They apply the old English slogan 'no taxation without representation' to the exotic conditions of Kenya. They do not claim political supremacy. Not now. But they do claim an advance by instalments which would gradually undermine the constitutional position as defined for unanswerable reasons by the Joint Select Committee of 1931 and accepted by the imperial government. This claim keeps the other races uneasy and puts the government on the defensive. It is not difficult to sympathize with the European leaders. The virile political qualities of their nation are in many cases reinforced by administrative abilities developed in one or other of the imperial services. They are conscious of a more intimate and enduring relationship with the colony than that of the official class. They fail to appreciate the preponderant influence over policy which their ability already gives

[1] 1 October 1935 Sir Alan Pim was appointed and reported in the Report of the Commission on the Financial Position and system of taxation in Kenya, 1936. Col. No. 116.

them. Confident of their own good intentions, they refuse to recognize the points where their interests clash with those of the other races and the reasons why these races cling to the imperial control for its very remoteness and impartiality which the settlers condemn. They will not admit that minority rule would be an immediate injustice to other communities and an ultimate danger to themselves. No single act would do more to bring about the political stability they say they desire than a statement by themselves that now and for some period of years to come they are prepared to abide by the present constitutional position.

Kenya has not done herself justice over the income-tax crisis. Beneath the surface of almost continuous political controversy changes are at work for the better. I gained the impression that race relations had improved during the last six years. Except for the regrettable personal attacks upon the ex-Governor Sir Joseph Byrne this has extended to the two races of officials and unofficials. At 11 o'clock in the morning politicians will interrupt their invectives in the Legislative Council against the inefficiency and high salaries of the officials to share a pot of tea with them in the neighbouring café. Their conflict is caricatured on the cricket pitch and sweetened by mutual gibes at dinners. In the Districts personal relations are almost always good. Credit is due to both sides, but more perhaps to the officials, who have so frequently to balance their actions between conflicting claims. It is upon the maintenance of their high standards of training and of impartiality that the welfare of the natives largely depends.

Europeans and Indians maintain an astonishingly complete detachment from each other, though they work, and in many cases live, close together, and may soon find themselves competing for jobs of the same kind and of limited numbers. Feeling seems much less bitter. The Indians seem more confident that the India Office, with the new India behind it, will not allow their position in Kenya to be worsened. Most noticeable is the growing appreciation among Europeans of the part that the African must play as a producer, and of his urgent need for social services. This appreciation is not universal and does not always extend to the administrative and educational developments of the Reserves. It is unfortunate that most Europeans know Africans only as 'labour'. Administrative officers have a pretty full programme, but an additional item of great value to the country would be conducted tours in the Reserves for sympathetic settlers.

The Reserves are well worth visiting. Beauty and interest are there as well as problems. I camped on a high, cold green hill in the Kiambu

District of the Kikuyu Reserve. It was so high that when the rain and the mists lifted I could see the immense blue foundations of Kenya mountain on one side and Kilimanjaro, with its ill-matched yet noble peaks, on the other. It was so cold that I had to keep a log-fire burning all day. Not far away was the native court, built like a Greek theatre, with the office like a Greek temple, unusually solid results of the classical education. The cement tiers were crowded with the public, which always attends Bantu litigation. The Bench sat on the stage, in the shade of a fig tree, while the litigants squatted arguing their case before them with the help of twigs which represented either telling points, the boundaries of their land, or goats, most of which had been dead many a long year. Or I could ride among the little farms that covered every inch of the surrounding land. One of the thousand Kikuyu hillocks was crowned with a five-roomed brick villa of a kind that may be seen five miles out on any road leading into London. This had been built by a native farmer, Masharia, from the proceeds of 20 acres.

Beauty and interest – but problems also. The local chief and headmen sat around my fire and talked of their people. The dominant subject was land. They told me their people were obsessed by the fear of losing more land to the Europeans. Nothing they could say would allay this fear: the retort was that they were paid by the government to say it. Would it not be possible, they urged, to have a document, signed and sealed by the King himself, that their lands would be inviolable? Nothing less than this would ever satisfy their people. The omens are a little better. The recent Land Commission[1] had admittedly a difficult task: they did not err upon the side of generosity to the African. But it has been found possible to modify many of their recommendations in his favour and these modifications – this is the encouraging feature – have all obtained the agreement of the European representatives.

One difficult question remains. The Kiambu natives lost, according to the Commission, nearly 100 square miles of excellent agricultural land to Europeans. They have had a larger area in compensation, but much of this is pastoral or even waterless. As there is no more land of the kind lost available in the area, ideal justice would demand restitution. But it lies under a costly dark green blanket of coffee and this solution has been ruled out. The position is further complicated by some thousands of native right-holders still living in the middle of European farms, whose claims cannot be extinguished, as is proposed by Order in Council, until they are given suitable alternative holdings. And what of

[1] *Report of the Kenya Land Commission, 1933, Cmd. 4556.*

their brothers and cousins, evicted before the Commission? The new legislation for the control of squatters in the White Highlands cannot be enforced because that unsatisfactory status is held by some 60,000 Kikuyu, and if many of these tried to crowd back into the congested Reserves, where land is owned by individual families, the results would be serious. Population density is relative to agricultural methods. The Kikuyu, industrious cultivators, are already beginning to learn how to conserve their soil, but a primitive people needs a generous margin of time, and therefore of land. The Kenya administration is alive both to the smaller problem of rights and to the larger one of needs. No one who has studied the problem could maintain the old view that the Kikuyu are so unreasonable that they can never be satisfied. There is every hope that the European representatives understand the need for generous settlement and for exorcizing a dangerous bitterness.

This is only one of the questions that have to be solved if the four races in Kenya, Africans, Indians, Europeans and Arabs – in order of numerical importance – are to develop harmoniously. There are some encouraging signs. Sir Joseph Byrne, in spite of the depreciation which he has met, and the economic difficulties under which he has worked, was able to present a good account of his stewardship. Progress has been especially notable where there was most leeway to make up, on the side of native production of economic crops, though Kenya is still far behind her neighbours in this. The medical department has shown vision in handling the vast problem of native hygiene and correcting a balance hitherto overweighted upon the curative side. Great help has been given by organization and research to European farmers and special machinery set up to relieve those in distress. The new Governor (Sir Robert Brooke-Popham) – and in Kenya Governors are all-important – will be assisted by the good will that meets a new appointment and by a rising revenue. He may even be inspired by the hope that in Kenya it is still just possible that an equitable solution may be worked out for those racial problems that in another part of Africa appear to have reached an almost insoluble deadlock.

Tanganyika Now

The Times 5 August 1937

To pass from Kenya into Tanganyika is to experience a sudden sense of calm. Only now do you realize how restless is the political atmosphere of the colony you have left. You mark with surprise the serenity with which administrative officers, untroubled by criticisms of their conduct or their pay or by the intricacies of racial finance, concentrate upon their work, the care of some 5,000,000 Africans.

It may seem strange that calm should characterize an ex-German territory at this moment. True, many British residents have combined with prominent Indians and Africans in defence of the *status quo* and have issued a manifesto with that object. But they know it is not in Africa that the answer to their question will be given. In the meantime they cannot easily prove that political uncertainty is keeping capital out of the country since capital is certainly coming in to nourish well-founded enterprises. Foremost among these is the Geita Goldmine, which promises to be the biggest thing of its kind north of the Rand. And Lord Chesham has chosen this moment to demonstrate his faith in the future by sponsoring, on new co-operative lines, a scheme of British settlement in the southern highlands. Meanwhile British and Germans work together amicably in the Chamber of Commerce and dine and dance together, as at the gathering of sisal planters in Tanga. It is no secret that the Germans are deeply divided among themselves. The word of command has been given by the local agents of the Nazi Party, but neither the older generation of ex-officials and aristocrats nor the newer one which has recently found it advisable to emigrate has fallen very readily into the ranks.

To the traveller returning after six years perhaps the most striking feature of the mandated territory is the great increase in native production. This is in tobacco, in groundnuts, in coffee – mainly a native crop – above all in cotton. Credit for trebling this last crop in the period is largely due to the docile, cheerful and industrious Wasukuma, who are cultivating their plain south of Lake Victoria to the very rocks. The increase in production is due to the 'plant more crops' campaign launched by the last Governor, Sir Stewart Symes. Like all developments in this abnormal continent, it has its attendant dangers. Drought and tsetse force two-thirds of the population to live in one-tenth of the total area. The enhanced demand made upon the favoured parts by the primitive cultivator threatens to exhaust or erode the soil; while his stock, more destructive than his hoe, is assisted by peace and veterinary science to increase daily.

An alarm, however, has been sounded, and officials, scientists and sociologists are gathering to the defence of Africa's soil. The Tanganyika Government has made some small beginnings to deal with this great problem. Some native authorities were advised years ago to plant belts of trees against wind erosion: others have revived ancient taboos to preserve forest around the sources of their streams: the Wachagga have forbidden cultivation of the steeper slopes of Kilimanjaro. A political officer has been seconded to make a thorough study of the land tenure, agricultural methods and grazing system of the Wasukuma as a basis for action. All this shows that the government, true to its traditions, is making a bid for the co-operation of the natives in a matter which, however urgent, can hardly succeed by coercion. There is another more obscure erosion set up by our urgent materialism, that of the whole delicate co-operative pattern of primitive life. But from this we turn away, doubtful whether we have the power, or perhaps the will, to arrest it.

Increased native production brings another problem. The main European agricultural enterprise in Tanganyika is sisal. For many years before the slump growing streams of men were drawn from the virile tribes of the west and south to tend this repulsive vegetable, which has spread inland up the Tanga railway, a dark green smudge on the pale landscape. Now the price has risen again, and the industry, which was turning away labour in the slump, wishes to restore past neglect and make new plantings, and so demands more labour. But in the interval the African has been taught that he can pay his tax and buy his shirt and trousers, his hurricane lamp and even his bicycle, by working with his wives on his own little farm in the healthier highlands. The Wanyamwezi, the great porters of East Africa, who have perhaps suffered most from a drain upon their manhood which began long before the days of sisal, are beginning, much to the joy of their officers, to repair their society. They turn a deaf ear to the wiles of the recruiter. The gold mines compete with the planters and are forced to turn to Northern Rhodesia or even to the feeble immigrants from Ruanda for their supply.

A committee has inquired into this deficiency of labour.[1] The sisal and gold industries are important and play a large part in the economic life of the territory. They claim to offer the peasant a better cash return than he can get from his own fields. But is it more than, by better methods, he will get from those fields tomorrow? And is it a greater return in terms of human welfare? The Nyasaland report[2] on emigrant labour says 'No' with emphasis, and few Tanganyika officers who know their people give any other answer. A system which injures African society at its very source cannot in the long run benefit even those industries based upon it. Nor is it in the interests of the world that it should be flooded with the products of cheap labourers who, at the East African rates of about eight to 15 shillings a month, cannot be effective consumers. In Tanganyika the problem may be postponed by applying less wasteful methods of employing and transporting labour and by offering better wages. The conditions of labour, too, have in places been allowed to deteriorate and could be made more healthy and attractive. It seems that sooner or later the issue, which is not peculiar to Tanganyika, must be met: whether, in the presence of a limited labour supply, peasant production is to be regulated in the interest of European capital, or vice versa. Tanganyika, with its special status and traditions, is likely to give an answer different from that which has been given in some parts of Africa, both to the north and south.

One interesting item in the increasing native production is the 2,000 tons of arabica coffee marketed by the Kilimanjaro Native Co-operative Union Limited. Of the 36,000 farmers on the coffee-bearing slopes, 24,000 are members, divided into 26 societies which correspond with the chieftainships into which the streams, running down from the snowy summit, cut the mountain-side. Each society has its own office, store, and weighing-shed, and here a queue may be seen in the picking season, from men with sacks down to little children with baskets. They pour their hulled coffee into the containers of a machine which registers the weight upon a large dial for all eyes to see. The producer then draws a proportion of the estimated price, returning for the balance when the whole crop has been sold. The members engage their own clerks and staff for spraying against disease and elect their own local committee and their representatives to the union. Their British secretary is, inevi-

---

[1] *Report of the Committee Appointed to Consider and Advise on Questions Relating to the Supply and Welfare of Native Labour in Tanganyika Territory, 1938.*

[2] *1935 Report by the Committee into Emigrant Labour.*

tably at this stage, the keystone of the system. The product has the advantage over some neighbouring European plantations in that it is grown round the homesteads and has the advantages of the manure from the cattle stalled in the dusk of the little dome-shaped huts, and of the shade and mulch of the banana groves which make one green cloister of the mountain slopes. The wide variety of soil and climatic conditions over the wet half of the great mountain gives the pooled crop a uniformity in quantity and quality that a single estate can hardly maintain.

So much for the experiment. What – inevitable question in Africa – are the problems? They are many, too many to discuss here. But, on balance, the arguments seem to favour the project. The Chagga tribe, penned between forest reserve above and white settlement below, are, like the Kikuyu, land-hungry and assertive almost to nationalism. The training upon the economic side in unity and constructive democracy should steady rather than excite them. And on the material side, apart from the more immediate advantages, this union may enable the Chagga to become economic citizens rather than helpless instruments in the commercial world of which they are now a part.

Economic questions have necessarily been in the front of men's minds in recent years. But the traveller who returns to Tanganyika after six years will be impatient to know the answer to another question. For six years ago Sir Donald Cameron was just leaving the territory after the great constructive effort by which he built up native local government upon tribal foundations. Has his system stood the first test of time, and of an economic strain that might well have warped it? The answer is, I think, reassuring. It is not a long answer, for native administration here is happy in having no history but that of quiet development, of the gradually increasing efficiency of courts, of the co-operation between chiefs and their officers in fighting the tsetse fly, in countering erosion and improving production. Everywhere officials reaffirmed their faith in a system which Sir Donald Cameron's two able successors, Sir Stewart Symes and Sir Mark Young, have maintained, and without which we could not fulfil the spirit of the mandate. Now, however, that the urgency of construction is over – and African governors who mean to build must work with an eye on the calendar – some of the faith that was needed to move mountains of official doubt and of native suspicion has given way to a more objective attitude. Yet for me the surprise has been that the first plan has been so slightly modified and the first enthusiasm so little dimmed.

I met many old friends among the chiefs. Two who came to England

N

for the Joint Parliamentary Commission showed me the histories of their people that they had been inspired to write. One Sukuma chief, in spite of advancing age and weight, had just been camping out in a distant part of his country to teach his people to make cattle troughs. I watched the Bukoba Federal Appeal Court at work in their new court house overlooking the downs which fall to Lake Victoria with its blue landless horizon. I met a young ex-schoolboy chief who had offended his people by erecting a cement dais and throne in his royal cattle-hut. A formidable old chieftainess rebuked my curiosity by the economy of her replies. Asked why she kept dozens of white rabbits in her bedroom, she replied, 'To eat,' and an inquiry whether she had a husband she countered – only too reasonably, I fear, for one in her position – with 'Why should I?'

But in Africa problems haunt even one's enjoyment of personalities. Some of the best chiefs are those whose characters were hammered out in hardier independent days and who are yet willing to work with their new masters. In one district I was given a vivid picture of the contrast between the generations. An aged chief, now set aside, received me with such dignity that his soiled cotton cloth became a toga and his stick a staff of office. The strong lines had been drawn upon his face when he had to fight for his people against a world of natural, human and superhuman dangers. His son, the present chief, like him in feature, was in every way a smaller man, and went about his supervised duties with an air of nervous anxiety. The schoolboy grandson pressed upon my attention his excellent clothes and less excellent English, and referred contemptuously to his grandfather as 'an old *shenzi*,' which in his context meant a dirty old bushman. (I doubt whether my reproof went home.)

Fortunately this picture is not universally typical in a country where some educated young chiefs are operating successfully between the old order and the new government. But it does illustrate one aspect of the main problem created by Europe's rapid mastery of Africa. In this, as in other matters, there can be no going back, no preservation, perhaps no re-creation, of the better elements of the past. The only policy is to go forward; to give larger, not smaller, responsibilities; more, not less, education, until Africans develop for themselves the virtues of civilization in place of the lost, always virile, and sometimes noble virtues of barbarism.

The Model Baganda

The Times 25 August 1938

Fifty years ago *Punch* published a cartoon in which a distracted John Bull, finding a black baby deposited upon his doorstep, exclaims: 'What, another! I suppose I must take it in.' He did so in spite of Sir William Harcourt and the old Liberals grumbling about having their hands forced by 'militant bishops and hare-brained *militaires*' (a dig at a certain Captain Lugard). For the British public were fascinated by stories of this astonishing kingdom in the heart of Africa, with its seemly, courteous people, who, a few years after our coming, produced men who were prepared to die at the stake for Christianity, and others who volunteered to fight for their new rulers against our own mutinous Sudanese troops.

Uganda then generally meant the kingdom of Buganda, which curves round the north-west of Lake Victoria, centred upon the royal house at Mengo. Buganda still dominates the rest of a territory mapped by treaty round the sources of the White Nile. Upon each return visit the traveller must be impressed anew by the harmony, unusual in Africa, which the Baganda seem to have achieved between the tribal past and the twentieth-century present. Compared with other prominent African groups they seem to be more ductile than the Yoruba or the Gold Coast Colony peoples; more open to Western influence than the Muslim city dwellers of the Sudan and Northern Nigeria; more disciplined in their political unity than other east African groups which we call progressive. Their British officers rather deprecate praise on the analogy, perhaps, of Africans themselves, who give the best child an opprobrious name to outwit the jealous spirits.

The basis of the Baganda advance has been a soil and rainfall that allowed of settled cultivation. It is exciting to watch this mapped from the air as you pass from the browner, less peopled lands of the north above ever richer greenness as you approach the Lake, and it is a refreshment to see in Africa this ordered luxuriance chequered by the waiting tilth of purple-red soil, dark with rain most of the year.

Every mile farther south are more and better homesteads, set back from the road and reached by neat little paths bordered with flowers and shrubs. Common in the 'home-counties' is a two- or three-roomed bungalow with a tin roof, a cement floor, wooden doors and window frames, a fenced yard, and often a separate kitchen and fowl-house. There will be a bicycle under the little veranda, and in the house chairs, tables, beds, mosquito nets and perhaps a sewing machine. Round the house is the dark banana grove. It provides the Baganda's staff of life, nutrition which, to judge by his physique, has been rather maligned. The garden will also show sweet potatoes beautifully planted on steep little mounds, ground-nuts, peas, beans, pumpkins, cassava, perhaps some chillies and maize, or even a fruit tree. Then come the cash crops, one or two acres of cotton for the average peasant, and a small plantation of *Robusta* coffee. (The tribes on higher ground grow the more valuable *Arabica*.)

The farmer with a wife or two, and perhaps a temporary labourer – one of the hungry little men who file in thousands along the roads from Belgian Ruanda – can manage this farm, which will cover from five to 10 acres. He feeds his family from it, and last year he made between £3 and £5 gross on his cotton, and perhaps a pound or two on his coffee. Out of this he resignedly pays the rather high and complicated taxation, which is being reduced and simplified by the present Governor, Sir Philip Mitchell. He pays for his children's schooling and dresses the boys in khaki shirts and shorts. His wife goes out in a dress of bright silk which flows from bare shoulders to bare feet, caught at the waist by a wide sash and bow of some skilfully contrasting colour. Walking in these dresses through the broken light of the forested roads, these women give Buganda a garden-party atmosphere. It may be that this peasant, whom, with our historic incapacity to appreciate any system of land tenure but our own, we turned in 1900 into a rent-paying tenant, now owns his farm in registered freehold. Thirty thousand out of Buganda's 270,000 men have already bought their farms at prices ranging from 10s. to £3 an acre, and the process is accelerating.

In education also Buganda is the centre for Uganda, and, as a result of the recent Commission upon Higher Education, will be the future university centre for the whole of eastern and central Africa. Kampala is to be the seat of the new Higher College, which will crown 60 years of missionary education, and this will enhance the influence the Baganda must wield as the most advanced African group between the Zambesi and Ethiopia. The Commission made history by drawing Europeans and Africans into conference from half a dozen territories, and a recent inter-territorial conference has confirmed the impressive academic plans

presented by the Governor, who from the first has promoted the scheme
in its widest and deepest possibilities.[1]

These developments have stimulated the intellectual activities of the
linked commercial and political capitals, Kampala and Mengo. They
were already considerable. Not long ago I attended a debating society
at which a West Indian communist lawyer urged the rendition of the ex-
German colonies on the grounds that there was nothing to choose
between one imperialist exploitation and another. He was a brilliant
speaker, and some Europeans – there was only one other present – might
have shivered to watch all those dark faces and bright eyes absorbed by
his arguments. The issue was a triumph for the policy of allowing freedom of speech and political responsibility to African people. The
Baganda answered the speaker soberly with reasoned criticism and
reasoned defence of British rule, and voted him down by a majority of
ten to one.

The Uganda bookshop in Kampala throws another sidelight upon
education. The Bible is still the best seller here: 11,000 Bibles and
15,000 Testaments were sold in 1936, about a quarter of them in English,
and many in expensive bindings. Large numbers of other books are sold.
During the Ethiopian war some hundreds of relevant books, costing
from 12s. to 18s., were bought by Africans.

Girls' education, as the Commission pointed out, is still very backward in quantity and standard. Among two or three post-elementary
schools the Baganda can send their girls to a 'Domestic Science College
for African Ladies', a boarding-school where the food is only 'semi-
native', and where they can learn, for £5 a year inclusive, child-welfare,
the piano, social etiquette, manners and deportment. Those who feel
alarmed at reading this will be comforted to learn that among the things
they must bring from home is a hoe. In fact, working to a time-table from
5.30 a.m. to 9 p.m., the girls, putting in five and a half hours of lessons
and one of chapel, do all their own housework and grow their own food.
All this represents a revolution, but it was not enough for a group of
leading Baganda whom I met at the house of an African friend. Prepared
as one must be in Africa for the unexpected, I was yet startled by the
view they all strongly expressed: 'There is too much emphasis upon
domestic science just now. Of course, we realize its importance, but we
don't want all our women to be prepared just for marriage. We want
some of them to have the chance of standing on their own feet in the
professions and playing their part in public life.'

[1] *Higher Education in East Africa, 1937, Col. No. 142.*

On the political side, beneath the pleasing surface of a model government, problems have been accumulating. Agreements, written or unwritten, may sometimes save African institutions from our ill-considered attempts at adaptation. To Africans, inevitably conservative and suspicious, they tend to become a sheet anchor, and an anchor is not the most suitable implement for modern Africa. The famous Uganda Agreement of 1900 has shown increasing signs of strain these 38 years, in spite of one or two agreed revisions. Today there is need to review the constitution, both as to the internal relations between its parts, the Kabaka (the ruler), the Ministry, the Council and the district organization, and also as to the relations between the native government and our own. One result of defining too jealously the sphere of an African State as it was is that the interesting welfare functions which develop later and which in Nigeria have been taken over by the larger Native Administrations have been lost to the Baganda, whose traditions have discouraged intimate co-operation with the central government. On the credit side, however, the native government has, within its limits, retained a very real responsibility in a sphere not always, in Africa, devoid of shams. The ministers especially have shown great ability and devotion in an extremely delicate position between their British advisers and the Kabaka. The present Governor, who was Sir Donald Cameron's Secretary for Native Affairs in Tanganyika, is exceptionally qualified to help the Baganda to clarify and strengthen their constitutional position and adjust this most remarkable African government to modern needs.

I have dwelt long upon Buganda, the educational and economic centre, the Mecca of the emigrant labourer, the model administration. North and west lie the other 'kingdoms', Ankole, Toro and Bunyoro, the last-named the relic of the once large Empire of Kitara, and an example of honest government under its enlightened Mukama. Outside these lie the kingless, almost chiefless, peoples, Bantu in the east, Nilotics in the north, at all stages of development down to the pygmies on the slopes of Ruwenzori. Most of these have an inferiority complex towards Buganda, whose agents were sent, not without some damage to their own more primitive but vital institutions, to teach them the business of administration. Lately, however, with more sympathetic study and use of their own institutions – a movement which has still further to go – with the diffusion of the remunerative crops of cotton and coffee, and the beginnings of education, the balance begins to be righted.

Financially Uganda compares very well with her large East African neighbours. In 1937 there was a surplus balance of nearly £2,000,000 on a revenue of the same amount, and though £370,000 of this was spent upon capital works, a surplus on current revenue of nearly half a million more than restored the balance. This is a good record for a country where production is 90 per cent. African. Cotton, it is true, at £3,500,000 out of £4,000,000 worth of exports, plays a disproportionate part, but coffee is creeping up, and may soon touch the half-million mark. Blessed with a light loan burden, Uganda, with the generous start of £100,000 from England, and the promise of a like sum from Tanganyika, can afford the heavy expenditure contemplated for the capital and endowment costs of the new Higher College. In a country where there is taxation without representation, it is satisfactory to feel sure that upon this item at least the tax-payer will not grudge a penny of the money.

Educating Africa

The Spectator 11 November 1938

On 3 November the Duke of Gloucester cut out a sod on Makerere Hill which stands near Kampala in Uganda. The ceremony, which was carried out with a native hoe made of silver and ivory, was the first step in the construction on the foundation of the existing school of the future Higher College for East Africa.

This project arises immediately out of the report of a strong and very hard-working Commission which visited East Africa early last year and reported the same autumn.[1] The Commission realized the boldness of its own main recommendation, for the report continues, in the next sentence: 'We are aware of the present very flimsy foundations of primary and secondary education upon which such institutions will need to be based, and realize the possible risks of too rapid advance and of a top-heavy structure.' That the College is premature, is indeed, likely to be the main criticism which must be met.

The College must first be related to the map. It is to be built in Uganda and it is expected to serve the whole block of territory which lies in east–central Africa between the Indian Ocean and the chain of great lakes, Nyasa, Tanganyika, Victoria and Albert. Here lie the territories of Tanganyika, Kenya and Uganda, with the island of Zanzibar, centre of the old Arab coastal Empire. To the south are Nyasaland and Northern Rhodesia, whose political destiny is at present being considered by the Bledisloe Commission.[2] These territories contain 15,000,000 Africans and cover an area about the size of Western Europe.

In terms of civilization and of European influence, which are not always synonymous, the 15,000,000 present very wide differences, which are partly inherent, and partly due to the differing degrees of European influence which they have attracted by their accessibility and their economic geography. At one extreme today we have the pygmies of the forested slopes of Ruwenzori, Uganda's Mountains of the Moon; the sparse, semi-nomads of the Kenya–Ethiopia border, and that handsome, proud, but conservative racial group which contains the Masai

---

[1] *Higher Education in East Africa, 1937. No. 142.*
[2] *Rhodesia – Nyasaland Royal Commission Report, 1939. Cmd. 5949.*

and the Nandi. At the other end of the scale we have the tribes which have not only felt the full force of European influence but have reacted in vigorous and positive manner. The Kikuyu, who curve round Kenya mountains and into the very suburbs of Nairobi, are politically alert, eager for education – they even run their own independent schools – and astonish the intermittent visitor by their advances in agriculture and housing.

On the Kenya shores of Lake Victoria are the more docile, perhaps more industrious, Kavirondo group whose representatives at the present Makerere College run their Kikuyu fellows hard. In Tanganyika, too, groups in Bukoba and upon Mount Kilimanjaro have raised their social standards upon a material basis of coffee, but other groups, competing with the help of a more varied production, are advancing. Uganda, however, holds the leading place and, in Uganda, the ancient kingdom of Buganda. It is by no mere accident that the site of the new college is to be in the heart of Buganda, on a hill next to that where its old capital stands. This fertile and populous African state, almost isolated in the middle of Africa, reached a surprisingly high standard of civilization. The Baganda, from the well-mannered peasants working among their banana or cotton plantations to their leaders who fill the hierarchy of offices recognized in Sir Harry Johnston's Treaty of 1900, give the impression of people who have already a good start upon the road towards civilization.

Viewed educationally, East Africa reflects all these varieties, and does not present, as a whole, a very advanced picture as compared with the southern and western parts of the continent which knew a European school-system some generations earlier. In Uganda, in some ways the most advanced part, about a third of the children of eligible age do in fact go to school, but, for five-sixths of these, this means a bush-school, where most of them spend a year or two mainly engaged in learning their catechism from a native evangelist. This is no criticism of the missions, without whom there would today be hardly any education at all in East Africa, since government has only come in at a very late stage to supervise and assist and to play some part in providing secondary and urban schools. For secondary education, the present Makerere College is the only full secondary school for the whole group of territories, though five or six others, mostly mission-schools, and some of them excellent, will shortly achieve that status.

These, then, are what the Commission recognizes as the flimsy foundations upon which, following the example of Sierra Leone, the Gold

Coast, and Nigeria, the Commission recommend the creation of this higher college. The conclusion may seem to be that faith has here out-run discretion. But there are certain features of the African situation which suggest another view.

The first is the urgent need for the new college on a utilitarian social plane. For man and the animals and plants upon which he lives there is a pathology of the tropics which probably accounts for African back-wardness. Measures are needed to study and to guard against the hos-tilities of nature, which range from the sapping operations of her multi-tudinous parasites to the dramatic caprices of her meteorology. And the people in the mass have to be helped to re-order their lives so as to meet nature upon more equal terms. This demands a large campaign, in which the African peasantry cannot afford expensive Europeans except as a general staff. It is for the training of African field-officers, already begun in Uganda in medicine and veterinary science, that the college finds its most obvious justification.

Less obvious, perhaps, is the need of Africans for leadership in adapt-ing their lives to the revolution which European intrusion has brought into the old tribal way of life. The reconstruction can be guided only by Africans who have passed beyond amazement and admiration to an understanding of the civilization that has so abruptly invaded their continent.

There is a further aspect of the College. 'The considerations,' writes Lord Hailey in his *African Survey*, 'which decide the character of higher education are largely political, for the type of instruction given depends on the view held of the place in society which the educated African may be expected to fill.'[1] This raises a question about the East African College which can only be answered by looking to the precedent of Achimota and considering the spirit which informs both the Commission's report and also the first measures which have been taken to fulfil it. All these point to an education which is something very much more than the manufacture of subordinate cogs in an imperial machine. The plan from the first has not been imposed upon Africans but has been developed in discussion with them. An African held an important place upon the Commission: African witnesses played a very large part in the instruc-tion of the Commission: African delegates were called with Europeans at an Inter-territorial Conference convened in May to consider the immediate tasks arising from the Commission's report. The same pro-mise is held out in the proposed constitution of the College. Following

[1] Lord Hailey. *An African Survey*. O.U.P. November 1938, p. 1288.

English precedents it is to be no government-controlled institution, but is to have a status of independence based upon a large settled endowment and an automonous governing body. The establishment of such a College suggests that, however gradually, the era of paternal government must pass into a new era of co-operation between Britain and her African subjects. British administrators know very well the risks that attend such a policy. Yet the risks may be less where they are so willingly taken.

The Sudan

The Times 6 and 7 June 1939

1. *North and South Contrasts*

The traveller who comes from British Africa to the Sudan will naturally be alert for contrasts. The first of these will be presented by the capital, viewed against memories of the modest or makeshift quarters of most of our colonial centres. The buildings strung along the Blue Nile – the palace, the departments, the official houses – seem surprisingly large and have the air of being built for all time. Kitchener and Cromer planned the new Khartoum that arose over the bones of Gordon, and they were both men of large views and the grand manner. It should in fairness be remembered, however, that they could not have expressed themselves so characteristically in bricks and stones had they not had the Egyptian revenues behind them. They had assistance also from nature, for what other colonial capital has such a dramatic geographical setting as the place where the two Niles meet and for a space refuse to mingle their light and dark waters?

Within the secretariat the archives reveal a history of administration which shows further differences from that of our colonies. The Sudan administration was for long markedly direct and bureaucratic. There were four reasons for this. It was in its main outline an extension of the Egyptian system. As in India, and in contrast with tropical Africa, it could command educated, or at least literate, natives for subordinate posts. On the British side the personnel was almost entirely military. Firm and paternal government was the main need of peoples who, already half ruined by the oppression or inefficiency of the Mahdia, had yet by their superb courage invited the destruction of their finest man-power in the Omdurman campaign. But 'direct' and 'indirect' are, fortunately perhaps, never very exact terms when applied to British administration, and almost from the first provincial governors made piecemeal use of such responsible authorities as they could find.

In 1921 a new direction was given to policy. Lord Milner recommended that greater use should be made of tribal organization, and shortly afterwards a senior official was sent to make a comparative study of the system in Northern Nigeria. In 1926 Sir John Maffey came to the

Sudan and made 'devolution' his main objective. Since then it has gone steadily forward, and today in all parts of the Sudan native courts and authorities have become serviceable parts of the machinery of government, and the ten most advanced Native Administrations have now their own treasuries. Tribal organization, broken by the Khalifa and long neglected by the Anglo-Egyptian Condominium, has quickened again in active relationship with the government.

Yet here again the Sudan presents native administration with a difference. Some of the tribes are nomad or semi-nomad. Even where they are in process of becoming sedentary under ordered and scientific government, they retain much of the nomad polity. The peculiar combination of the Nazir's patriarchal rule with a large degree of independence on the part of section and tribesman is not easily harnessed by ordinance to the tasks of modern local government. The people, shifting their herds and cultivation at the dictates of a stern but capricious nature, elude administration of the kind possible in much of Negro Africa. It is not easy to centre them upon a tribal headquarters. The ascetic tradition of the desert, reinforced by that of the desert religion, inhibits interest in the buildings and other outward forms which, for us and the negroes under our charge, give to pride of community a local habitation and a name.

Moreover the northern Sudan differs from tropical Africa in that tribalism is not the only social cement. The northern tribes are members of three fraternities which transcend tribal divisions: that of the local sects or *tarikas*; that of the Arab world, now stirred with a new self-consciousness; and that of Islam, with its 250,000,000 from China to Senegal. In the Sudan Islam, like medieval Christianity, regulates the whole of life, and is a culture as well as a religion. Cultural has been followed by some political unity. The nineteenth-century rule imposed by Egypt was preceded by secular empires which broke and mixed the peoples, and it was succeeded by the violent pulverization of the Mahdia. A still newer bond has been provided by education upon Western lines in Gordon College, and its so-called 'graduates', mostly well-paid servants of the central government, abjure tribalism, suspect 'devolution', and claim to be Sudanese *sans phrase*. This group was stirred into its first effective impulse of nationalism when in 1936 it saw the future of the Sudan decided in a treaty between its co-rulers. An article[1] in this column last July brought out the moderation of this Young Sudan and its remarkably good relations with the

[1] *The Times*, 29 July 1938. 'Young Sudan – A Nation in the Making' by Khartoum Correspondent.

government. The Sudanese add to their valour a courtesy so deep-rooted as to affect their whole attitude towards their present rulers. Their infant Press has already described the treatment of Libyan Moslems by the Italians and quoted the views of Sudanese that Britain is 'the best imperialist Power'. This does not mean that their nationalism will be a feeble growth, for the Sudanese are a vital and brave people, but that its development may be accompanied by less friction and more understanding than experience elsewhere has led us to expect. Such is the hope of British officials, whose own traditions of courtesy and sympathy are largely responsible for these good relations. They are now planning the establishment of a centre in Khartoum based upon a library and lecture hall where the races may meet for even better mutual instruction and understanding. All this, however, increases the gap between the urban and official few and the rural many, and it falls to the foreign government to supply by art the normal political adjustment and development which its presence tends to check.

All this applies to the northern Sudan and little of it to the southern. In the distinction lies one of the country's main problems. The abruptness of the contrast has struck all travellers, from the earliest to the latest, who have made their way up the White Nile past the twelfth latitude. Two memories mark it vividly in my mind. The first is a visit to a well-centre of the southern Baggara, those robust cattle Arabs who were the strength and sinews of the Mahdi's revolt. The evening was spent watching the fine-looking young Nazir do justice among his people. There was no mystery and no despotism about his office. His tribesmen were independent in their bearing, the women litigants strident. At night the old men told the saga of the Mahdia with that apparent lack of bitterness that rouses the wonder of Europeans. After a night in a grass shelter, made sleepless by the barking of dogs and the lowing of cattle, we watched the herds being watered in wide basins moulded out of the earth itself. Although my hosts were dark from drawing freely through slavery upon Negro blood, this was the authentic Dar al'Islam with its turbans and flowing robes, its ceremonious hospitality, its coffee drinking, and its dominant call to prayer. There can have been little change in the scene presented by this cattle camp since the later middle ages, when Arabs, pressing down from Egypt, won these lands for the Prophet.

Yet, only a few miles upstream, you pass into the land of the blacks, the pagan, half-naked Nilotic Negroes known as the Shilluk. It is difficult to understand how these people, strung out in a long line of villages on a ridge beside the Nile, could have survived Baggara raids, the oppression and slavery of the Turkish rule, and the rush of the Mahdia. Perhaps it was through the protection of their great founder Nyakang, who is worshipped in shrines on the sites of his continuing revelations, and whose spirit lives in his descendant, the divine king, or Reth.

The present Reth is a man of great composure. He wore, like all his subjects, no more than a kilt of cotton, the ends looped over one shoulder. On his head was a navy blue beret, worn like a crown. My reception was in a round native hut, far superior to the careless improvisations of the Arabs. We squatted on the floor. An attendant offered the Reth a calabash of cool native beer, and then, as with another divine king I had seen 1,500 miles west in Nigeria, he turned away his head, for gods do not thirst. Next came my turn, and not knowing whether I, too, partook of the divine nature, he compromised by turning half away. I wondered whether the most sympathetic foreign government could transform a divine king into a local government authority, and that in a single generation.

Farther south again, through banks of *sudd* and walls of papyrus which, from the air, can be seen almost choking the great river on its long struggle to the north. The *sudd* looks livid against the dearth of the plains, which are swamps in the wet season but in the dry are alternately bleached and scorched in great tigerish stripes with sun and fire. Here the other two Nilotic groups, the naked Nuer and the Dinka, make their pastoral cycle with their beloved cattle. Their district commissioners, though their hearts are with these conservative people, must enforce the rule that none may escape payment for the good order brought by the government, however little that order may be welcomed. They are therefore trying to coax these herdsmen out of their arrogant self-containment. Even the Nuer, last and least tamed of African tribes, recently sent their warriors to handle, with comic unsureness, the strange weapons of pick and spade in the making of Malakal aerodrome. Big, naked, long-shanked men, looking wild and shy, they gladly downed tools to show us how they could dance and sing. Unfortunately a Shilluk gang near by was inspired to compete in a song which affirmed that the kingdom of Nyakang would never come to an end. Fearing lest the Nuer might volunteer a different historical forecast and emphasize it with their picks, the District Commissioner suggested a return to work.

This illustrates the character of the south as compared with the Moslem north. The south is different in race and in religion, whether pagan or Christian. Its peoples first enter history in Egyptian tombs, bowed and chained in frescoed file beneath the heel of Pharaoh, and this was still their role 5,000 years later when the European conscience, itself newly converted, reacted against the horrors of equatorial slave-raiding. The tribes are still confined each within the boundaries of their exclusive languages, customs, and loyalties.

South of the Upper Nile province the old Bahr-el-Ghazal and Mongalla have been combined to form the vast, backward province of Equatoria. A thousand miles broad and 400 deep at the widest points it embraces the broken tribes Baker and Gordon tried in vain to save from the northern slave-raiders and other predators. These tribes are all isolated in the very depths of Africa from any external influences but those of a handful of officials and of Italian and British missionaries. The economic problem is that of finding crops that will stand a long haul and the communications to carry them.

The southern Sudan still needs the old sympathetic paternalism of the District Commissioner. It is being given this with something which is new and, indeed, on this scale, unique – the application of anthropological knowledge to native administration before rather than after the disintegration of tribal life. The knowledge is of an unusually high standard. This is due partly to the employment of anthropologists, and partly to continuity in the posting of commissioners, some of whom have stayed eight or ten years in one district. It is to be hoped that the government will be allowed the long uninterrupted period which it requires in order to bring this skilled and humane policy to fruition.

11. *Planning for Native Prosperity*

The present Governor-General of the Sudan, Sir Stewart Symes, has summed up the main problems of the country as 'distances and diversities'. These are not only between north and south. West from Khartoum lie the red plains of immense Kordofan. This, the richest and most populous of the provinces, from which the world's main supply of gum-arabic is drawn, has still no more than an elementary system of communications. It has its full share, also, of diversities. To the north are the camel-breeding, nomad Kababish, asking little more from the government than its help in settling accounts peacefully with their many neighbours. South come the more sedentary Arab tribes, which, responding to good government, represent the Sudan's most effective local administrations.

Farther south, in isolated rocky clumps, are the Nuba mountains. Up these, as in Nigeria, the pagan blacks have been swept by the tide of enslaving Moslems. Only slowly and painfully have these independent hillmen been taught that a government could demand submission without stealing men for soldiers and children for slaves. Now their welcome is effusive: every naked man, woman and child scrambles out of the craggy villages to shake your hand, and few tribes I have seen in Africa present such a picture of vitality, of good cheer, and of industry in the cultivation of their huge crops of tasselled millet.

Farther west lies the ancient kingdom of Darfur, independent until 1916, when the Sultan of a sixteenth-century dynasty, tempted into a *jihad* by the Turks, went down with his medieval levies before an expedition from the Sudan. Here, too, distance makes its problem. All goods, when they leave the Kordofan railhead, must go hundreds of miles on lorries, often skidding and roaring through deep sand in bottom gear. Yet, given good rains, Darfur cares little for this, since it has not unlearnt its medieval self-containment. Its granary is the mountain mass of Jebel Mara, home of the industrious yet fanatical Fur. These mountains seem surprising and precious after the dead levels and drought of the Sudan. Climbing their escarpments with pack-mules or camping and bathing in valleys brilliant with irrigation, it is possible to capture that sense of Africa's strangeness and remoteness which Europeans seem fated equally to desire and to destroy.

East of Khartoum distances are better served by the railway system than in the west. But human diversity meets us again. Here, beyond the Arabs, are the Beja – Kipling's Fuzzies and the ethnologists' pre-dynastic Egyptians. They speak their own language and live their own harsh life with their camels and goats. Like all Eastern Hamites, they are beautiful, though they seem of coarser build than the Eritrean Beni-Amer or the hawk-like Somali. Their dour conservatism has for some thousands of years turned the edge of foreign influence, but their latest government has got under their guard. Schools, nuclei of slow change, have appeared among them. Not only that. A plan to harness the wild spate of the Gash River for irrigating cotton and to build the necessary railway was started some 14 years ago by the government and the Kassala Cotton Company. Quick returns would have demanded that the Hadendoa, the local Beja group, should have been edged out of this fertile stretch to make room for people more apt with the hoe and more interested in its rewards. But the local officials strove with the Hadendoa and for them: the government, compensating the company with alternative opportunities in the Gezira, took over the scheme, and slowly the

O

herdsmen have learned that cotton is a plant to be diligently cultivated, not used as God-given forage for camels. This cotton, thanks to the rich Eritrean silt, is among the finest in the world.

The Gash, though perhaps the most romantic, is not the only flood-cotton scheme. The Nile also does its share. Even after Egypt's chartered pre-emption has been met, its waters still supply, not only the buckets dipped by the hand-worked *shaduf* or the ox-drawn *sagia*, but a number of power-driven pumps which irrigate grain and cotton. One of the most interesting pump schemes is that run by Sayéd Sir Abderrahman el Mahdi. Aba Island, with its cave from which his father issued to raise the Sudan against the Turks, is now stamped with the unromantic mathematical pattern of irrigation. Here, from a fine house, the Sayéd, a leading notable of the new Sudan and active in public service, directs a large business enterprise, and offers productive work to the pilgrims who throng to him from the ardent, unsophisticated west.

All these activities, however, are statistically insignificant beside the Gezira scheme. For this the waters of the Blue Nile, with their heavy deposit washed from the Abyssinian mountains, are held up at Sennar to irrigate an area the size of Somerset. This land is rented from its tribal owners. The scheme is a three-sided partnership. The two companies, the Sudan Plantations Syndicate and the Kassala Cotton Company, have invested some £E.5,250,000 of capital in ginneries, canalization works and the finance requirements of the scheme. They carry out the management of the enterprise and receive 20 per cent. of the profits. The government, which out of loans guaranteed by the British Treasury, and out of revenue, has sunk nearly £14,000,000 in the major irrigation works, gets 40 per cent. The 21,000 tenants, cultivating up to 10 *feddans* of cotton a year on a tenancy of 40 *feddans*, bring their labour and draw the remaining 40 per cent.

The cotton market has proved an unstable basis for so large a financial and social venture. Beginning with the high prices and yields of the late twenties, in 1930 the scheme encountered simultaneous and severe falls of price and yield. Its collapse would have gravely affected a poor country heavily involved in one large commercial venture. Economies in working, a slight improvement of the market, and a better understanding of the pests which were diminishing the crops, just saved the situation. The scheme has since been made less vulnerable by the bold policy of greatly increasing its area to reduce overhead costs per *feddan*. The result has been that in each of the three seasons, 1935–36–37, between £2,000,000 and £3,000,000 worth of cotton has been sold.

Before the bad years tenants' individual net profits often ran into three figures. For 1937 the average is reckoned to be £E.29. Such returns, by tropical African standards, seem large. Yet the tenants show far fewer results in better living conditions than, for example, the Baganda with their average *per capita* gross return of between £4 and £5 a year for rain-grown cotton. This is because the Arab spends much more upon sugar and coffee; upon ornaments of precious metal for his wives, and, as an ex-slave-owner, upon hired labour.

The scheme, for better or worse, represents a social revolution. Upon the monotonous geometry of the irrigated area are gathered the local tribesmen who a few years ago stooped only to the light seasonal cultivation of their precarious rain-grown millet. Complaints of those who have to wrestle at close quarters with their agricultural inadequacies are many. From a wider point of view, however, it seems almost a miracle that these fatalistic semi-pastoralists should endure at all the almost ceaseless time-table of work.

The Sudan Government has worked hard to protect the interests of the local population both as landowners and tenants. Yet, looking to their future as a community, the scheme does not seem very constructive. Each of the 21,000 tenants is a unit directly responsible to a white inspector, himself carrying out an inflexible centralized routine. The tenant has no sense of responsibility towards the scheme which dominates his life, and little understanding of it. He has no link with his fellow tenants as such. Atomization and ignorance have dangers, which have been illustrated lately in more than one part of the British Empire. Aware of this, the government is experimenting to discover whether village life cannot be integrated with the cotton production.

The Gezira is probably the Sudan's main internal problem. The present Governor-General has made a general overhaul of the Sudan administration enlarging the provinces and revising the local government, rural and urban. The remodelling of the education system, culminating in an advanced academic prospect for Gordon College, will be costly, but the Sudan Government is proceeding with it in spite of falling cotton prices and the loss by stages of the Egyptian subvention.

Looking outwards from the Sudan two questions attract attention. The Sudan has to adjust herself to her new neighbour in Ethiopia. The recent war and the conquest have hitherto produced extraordinarily few effects along an extensive frontier, but they have made her the aerial highway for another empire. Second comes the working out of the Anglo-Egyptian treaty of 1936. The Condominium was defined in 1899, when one partner was almost wholly under the control of the other. This condition lasted until after the war, and the increasing restiveness of Egypt only served to strengthen British control by giving cause, in the 1924 mutinies, to remove Egypt's troops and most of her personnel from the Sudan.

The treaty reaffirms the Condominium in terms of Egypt's new independence. Already Egyptian troops have marched back to their barracks in Khartoum; and some Egyptian officials have taken up their posts. Others, doubtless, will follow. There is nothing, however, in the treaty to promise that Britain will relinquish her present predominance in the work of administration except in favour of the Sudanese. It is justified by her experience and by the use she has made of it. True, Britain went to Egypt for economic, and stayed for strategic, reasons. Through Egypt she went on to the Sudan. But Britain can offer subject peoples valuable services in compensation for her intervention and the Sudan has an especially favourable balance-sheet. Moreover, Britain has given some of her best sons to the Sudan service. Nowhere, certainly, has the writer seen more friendliness and trust between rulers and ruled.

In the modern world the helplessness of backward peoples is a danger to themselves and to those who compete over the control of their lands, but as they achieve identity and a voice the sphere of control diminishes and that of co-operation extends. This development in the Sudan should ease our partnership with Egypt, which from its nature cannot attain perfect harmony. The very dissimilarity of the two powers, however, can enrich their giving; and by increasing the sphere of co-operation for and with the Sudanese the two Condominium Powers should find safe and honourable ground for their partnership, and one day, perhaps, for its dissolution.

The Future of the Rhodesias–Divergent Systems of Government

Letter to *The Times* 29 July 1939

In July, 1939 Sir Godfrey Huggins, Prime Minister of Southern Rhodesia, visited Britain to discuss the findings of the Bledisloe Commission on the future of Central Africa. A debate on the subject was to take place in the House of Lords on 31 July.

Sir, – There is danger lest the crisis may distract attention from the deep significance for Africa of the issues which Mr Huggins is now discussing with our government. These relate to the future of Southern and Northern Rhodesia and Nyasaland.

British Africa today contains two divergent systems. In areas where the European minority is considerable and has political control, the political, economic and social measures crystallize its present superiority and lead to a stratified or caste type of society based on colour distinction. In the other system, which obtains where European residents are few or absent, British officials assist Africans to develop in all aspects of life towards a position in which they may ultimately stand by themselves. Discussion of this contrast would be simplified if it could be detached from questions of vice and virtue. The only virtue of the Colonial Service is that it is composed of temporary, expert officials responsible to an impartial, strong and experienced government. Admittedly the system has defects and is liable, especially in small territories such as the two now in question, to periods of inertia. For these the inadequate interest of the British people and Parliament is largely responsible, and suggestions to remedy this are being considered.

On the other hand, there is no vice in the British community of Southern Rhodesia, least of all in its attractive leader: it is composed of much the same sort of people as ourselves and our Colonial officials. But its position prevents impartiality: it is impelled to its courses by the strongest immediate motives of economic interest and by fears, often subconscious, for its own ultimate preservation. Its most high-minded individuals seek to mitigate the policy of the majority and alleviate it with social services. But those who know what Africans can achieve where they are encouraged to reach to their full stature as persons must

contrast this with a system where they figure mainly as cheap, unorganized labour and – the decisive test – where the least qualified white is
given the full citizenship and economic opportunity denied to the most
highly qualified African.

For Southern Rhodesia, with about 60,000 whites and 1,250,000
Africans, the issue is settled. It has almost complete 'self-government'.
The question is as to whether the first steps should be taken to extend
the Southern African system to Northern Rhodesia, with 10,600 whites
and 1,366,425 Africans, and Nyasaland, with 1,800 whites (largely
officials and missionaries) and 1,619,530 Africans. A Royal Commission
has recently reported in somewhat inconclusive form, and with important reservations by half its members, that these steps should be taken,
and that the white minorities of the two northern territories should be
given even fuller representation than the considerable measure they
possess. Two members of the Commission hope that this, together with
closer association with Southern Rhodesia, will lead to the amalgama-
tion of a 'solid *bloc* . . . under one democratically elected government
imbued with British ideals'. This is not in harmony with the report of
the highly authoritative Joint Select Committee upon the basically
similar problem of East Africa. The great differences in racial numbers
and culture in both areas require the continuance of an arbitral impartial
government which can hold the balance between conflicting interests,
encourage actively the advance of the Africans, and progressively adjust
institutions to that advance.

The representatives of the 3,000,000 northern Africans, who know
southern Africa well from their labour-migrations, have protested
strongly and unanimously against the steps proposed. In this dilemma
we cannot evade the main issue by compromising upon one modest step
when the next ones will be automatic. We cannot salve our conscience
with safeguards in native interests, since experience has taught that
such safeguards upon otherwise 'responsible' governments do not work.

Our leading ministers have recently made before the world very large
claims for our Empire as one where subject-peoples advance towards
self-government. The steps proposed are not compatible with this claim.
They would remove what many of us regard as our only moral justification for retaining so large a colonial empire. We may be sure the European claims will be fully and ably voiced. The future interests of the
unrepresented Africans are wholly dependent upon the willingness of
people in England to study and to urge them.

Yours faithfully, MARGERY PERHAM

War and the Colonies

The Spectator 6 October 1939

'Over 40 administrative and labour officers in the Colonial Service are attending a fortnight's course of instruction in London on labour problems in the Colonial Empire. The course is the first'. [*The Times* 4 October.]

The war has its special problems for the colonial empire. Fortunately, if Italy remains neutral, our subject peoples need not this time be involved in bloodshed. They may, however, suffer in less dramatic fashion simply from being so very much out of the news.

It is only a few weeks ago – how much longer it seems! – that it was generally agreed that the colonies were being neglected by a Parliament which allocated a derisory amount of time to their affairs and met that time with almost empty benches. Recent events in the West Indies, in West Africa, and to a lesser extent in East Africa, have shown how much these territories need attention. Many of their peoples are backward, and unrepresented: in some parts they are confronted with powerful, conflicting interests. It cannot be expected that government officials, whether in the colonies or in Whitehall, or even the Colonial Secretary, can always right the balance of administration and policy in their interest without the additional weight of public opinion in this country. Yet now this opinion, recognized as inadequate in volume and in its expression through Parliament even in peace-time, will be diminished by the urgent distraction of war. If those who are interested in the welfare of the colonial peoples recognize this danger from the outset, they may work to counter it.

Fortunately there are indications that, as far as the war and colonial finance allow, the motto in Downing Street is to be 'Trusteeship as usual'. The hope is that administration and the social services will be fully maintained. The bulk of the work of the Colonial Service is necessary routine; it is a very small extra margin of men and of time which allows that routine to be enriched by sympathy and knowledge and infused with constructive purpose. The withdrawal, therefore, of even a

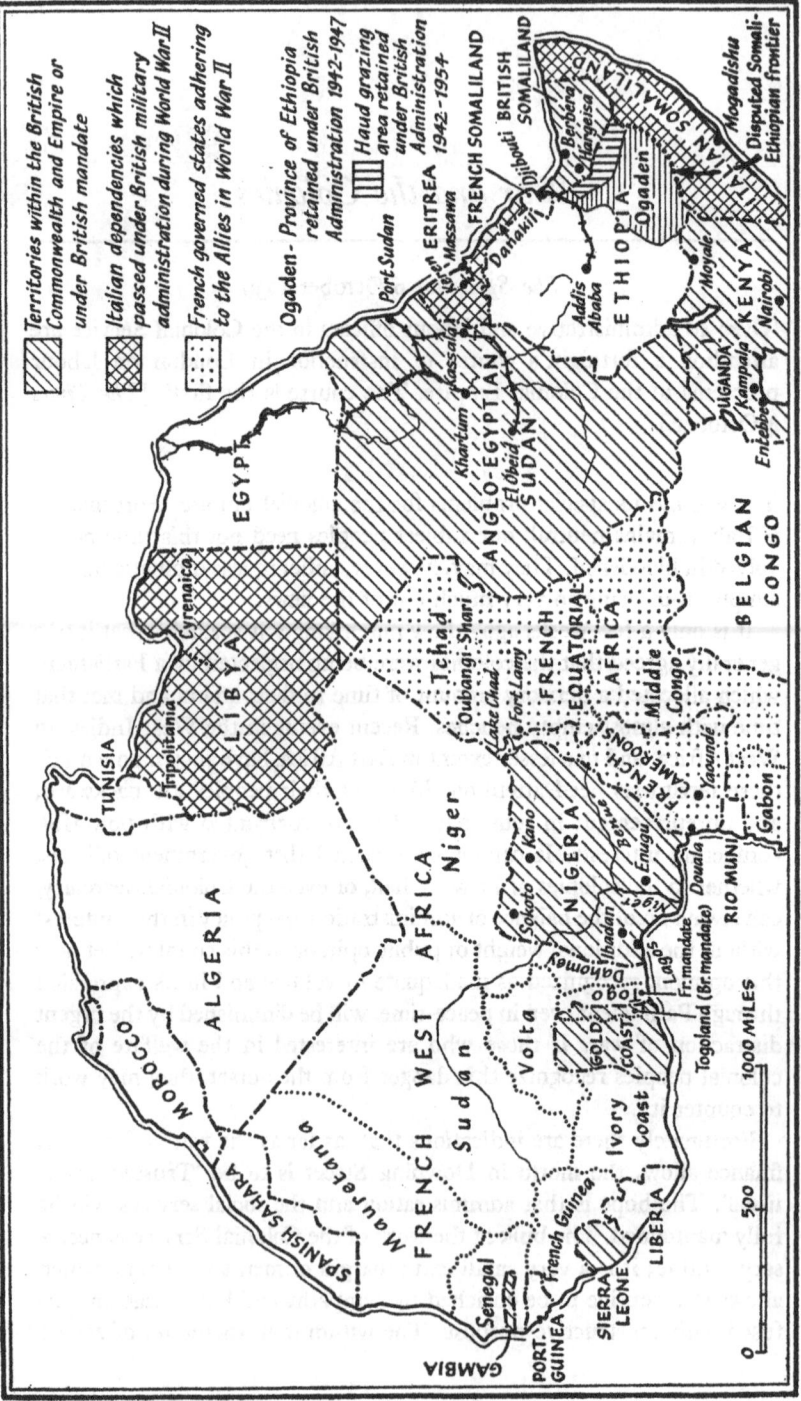

5 Northern Africa at the end of World War II

small percentage of staff throws the rest back working, and indeed over-working, upon mere care and maintenance.

It is not possible to devise a sort of colonial moratorium for the dura-tion of the war. Our colonial governments are engaged not so much in stimulating a general advance which can be slowed down for a given period, as in belatedly devising institutions and services to meet social disintegration and urgent physical dangers, such as soil-erosion and sleeping sickness. Against this general background of colonial needs certain current problems stand out which are certainly not solved by the outbreak of war. There is the labour unrest in the West Indies, which is much more than a question of labour. There is the problem of the Gold Coast cocoa-growers, which is only one part and one local example of a whole complex of problems which centre upon the colonial peasant producer, and which concern his social and economic organization, his land tenure, the financing and improvement of his crops, their marketing and – ideally – price-stabilization. There is the large question made immediate in Central Africa by the Bledisloe Report, but always with us in Kenya, how a full sphere for the political and economic development of the African millions is to be kept open against the immediate pressure of European minorities for predominance.

Thirdly, we must be prepared for a series of new situations produced by the war itself. Even in Africa there are urban centres and developed regions where large groups are self-conscious and politically alert. For many of these the word 'war' has still vivid and unhappy associations, and a degree of restlessness, however slight, may appear among them. We learned in India during the last war that when the spell of the normal is broken (if, indeed, imperialism can ever be regarded as a normal state of affairs) the choice may lie between more co-operation or more sup-pression. This was on the grand scale, but the same issue may present it-self upon the small scale in some of our colonial territories. Suppression is becoming, for the British, an impracticable weapon: after being used once or twice it breaks in our hands. This is mainly because we have lost faith in it ourselves. We have, especially in recent months, solemnly declared through the mouths of our political leaders, that not only the Commonwealth, but also the colonial empire is based upon respect for freedom, and leads, however gradually, towards self-government for its peoples. With whatever qualifications when applied to our heterogeneous possessions, such statements must mean something, and war is an occa-sion when we may be asked by subject peoples exactly what they do mean.

The conflict with Germany means that our high claims for our empire will be forced upon our attention from without as well as from within. So long as empire appears mainly a matter of national monopoly and prestige it is loot which the strong man armed must defend from the stronger man with little support from his own conscience or that of the world. One way of escape from this weak position is in the direction of international colonial administration. This has already been discussed in England, and we may expect the discussion to be stimulated by the war. The idea is attractive both in itself as an exercise in international co-operation and as removing subject people from the position of stakes in Europe's game of power-politics. But even if Europe could develop a new international spirit stronger than that which for a few years made Geneva such an exciting and hopeful place, the difficulties at the colonial end are formidable. An international government might provide a high-minded secretariat, devoted social services and a planned economic development. Colonial administration means all this, but it means some-thing more, a tutorship in civilization. This tutorship, as exemplified at its best in certain places and at certain times, is a warm, human relation-ship in which European civilization is offered in the rich peculiarity of a national embodiment through a national language.

It is unfortunate that the accidents of partition should have striped one part of Africa alternately with French and British culture, but it serves to demonstrate that France and Britain hold very different views of the nature and destiny of the Africans. The mechanical parts of colonial administration might be standardized for international use, but what of the cultural? Backward people are very 'human' and extravert: an international government might prove cold and rigid and so arrest their psychological adjustment to civilization. At the worst, it might prove itself effective mainly in securing equal rights in exploitation and in prolonging imperialism by syndicating it.

There is another aspect. International government would not be introduced into a vacuum: it would have to replace, even in mandated territories, some positive appreciation of our rule and political ideas, which has been strengthened by widespread knowledge of Hitler's racial theories. Outside the few fully educated this appreciation may be vague and emotional, but a year of crisis has helped to define it.

In the long run the only sure way of saving backward people from the dangers to themselves and the temptations to others of their position is to press on their education and development with all speed, and to enlarge in every practicable way the sphere of co-operation with them.

This, with ample 'straight' news, will be the best, and indeed the only, propaganda they will need. But it requires money, public support and, even at the expense of some of our old tradition of imperial decentralization, a more positive lead from Downing Street.

Italian Operations on African Desert Frontiers

The Times 10 August 1940

On 4 August the Italians began to advance into British Somaliland.

Italy is operating on four African frontiers, and a number of unfamiliar names are coming into the war news. Strangely enough, they are the names of places where conditions are very similar, dry stony country where backward pastoralists wander in search of water and grazing. It is a military advantage that many of these nomads can remove themselves and their stock from the path of the invader and leave him with little refreshment. It is also a humane comfort. We may hope that the African proverb 'When elephants fight the grass is trampled' will not be fulfilled.

Attacking from her vast mountainous base of Ethiopia, Italy is in somewhat the position of a wounded buffalo bursting out of cover upon her hunters. How much damage will she be able to do before she begins to lose strength? Italy has been wounded by British blockade and air-raiding, how seriously we cannot yet tell. Petrol is her life-blood, in country without rail or regular river-communications, where the sea-ways are denied. For the moment she has great superiority in numbers of men and machines. She has probably large numbers of riding and pack animals, but tropical campaigns are cruelly wasteful of these. Since it is British policy in this war to face hard facts, let it be admitted that the Italians also have some advantages of terrain. In the western Desert, in the Sudan, and in Kenya, as over the precarious barley fields of the Egyptian Bedouin, fairly level routes lie in front of Italy's mechanized columns.

The Northern Frontier and the Turkana Provinces of Kenya contain about half the total area of the country and carry about one-twentieth of the population. They stretch for 800 miles along the borders of Italian East Africa and run down like a great trough between the Ethiopian mountains and the Kenya highlands. The present is the dry season, and it is probably wise to allow Italy to extend her lines of communication through this worthless wilderness of thorn-scrub rather than do the fetching and carrying ourselves. From Moyale the Italians will have nearly 300 miles to cross before they reach country which offers them much hospitality. This may not worry mechanized columns which can have a free run to their goal with a picnic on the way.

But will they have a free run? The South African air force will help to escort them. At the end they will meet positions prepared to defend the ways up into the highlands. Kenya is not quite the sort of military or geographical proposition to be taken easily by columns at the end of semi-desert communications of this length.

British Somaliland is quite another story. This is rather a Cinderella among British colonies. An arid plateau of 68,000 square miles, it supports with difficulty about 300,000 wandering Somali herdsmen. These Moslems are a conservative, proud, fierce and handsome people. Man and camel seem to look with equal contempt at the white stranger who visits their ungracious country. It has been by no means a land of peace.

The Mad Mullah provoked us into four major campaigns between 1900 and 1920. In these the supply and transport officers were the key men, even though a dozen aeroplanes assisted to drive the Mullah from the country in 1920. The writer had such distinction as may be claimed for the first European to hear of his death. As I trekked with a companion along the Ethiopian frontier, an excited messenger from the Arussi country rushed up to our camp with the news. The British Government must have spent millions on men and missiles for his destruction, but he was finally killed by a mosquito.

It is across the frontier where we were camped that the Italians have marched to take Hargeisa. Commentators who call it a collection of mud huts hardly do justice to this station. It is, for these parts, a fair-sized native town, and some bungalows for military and Colonial Service officers stand along the banks of a river-bed, where a lion-coloured torrent races for a few hours at a time in the short rainy season. It is this water, absorbed in the sand, that the Italians will be baling up through the deep wells in the river bed.

Supply and transport problems are not what they were even in 1920. The Italians know the country. They have a Somaliland of their own next door and were fighting yesterday in Ethiopian Somaliland. From Hargeisa they have an easy run northwards over the stony sand of the plateau. Thorn-scrub and aloes should give chances for cover and camouflage against air attack, while the richer growth which trims the *wadis* offers solid shade. Some commentators seem too optimistic in their hopes of a mountain barrier. It may be remembered that in 1937 the Italians were allowed to pay for the building of a motor road from the frontier through Hargeisa to Berbera to carry two-ton lorries. Even if this can be destroyed there are no serious and unavoidable natural obstacles for a column until it reaches the rather abrupt descent of the escarpment down to the maritime plain where Berbera shimmers in the burning August *Khareef*. Here dynamite should give Italian engineers some work. But some of them are already in the plain, having probably taken the easier descent down the escarpment where the ancient caravan route leads to Zeila. They have taken this humble but historic port, which fell into dignified Arab decay with the opening of the Jibuti railway. There is nothing but sand between Zeila and Berbera.

Somaliland in itself would be no great material loss. Both country and people were too hard to take the impress of our civilization easily. An educational scheme started a few years ago had almost broken against the suspicions of the Mullahs. But its loss as a Moslem country would cost much in prestige and must give pause to potential allies in Ethiopa. Even if its harbours would be a mere luxury to Italy, the 450 miles of coast would provide an extension for air-bases to plague the Gulf of Aden.

In the Sudan more immediately valuable objectives are threatened. There the Italians have taken Gallabat and Kassala. This last is a famous African town. Here during the Mahdia the Ethiopians, responding to the call to rescue the Egyptian garrisons, fought with the Dervishes and only lost the fruits of their victories on the death of their Negus John. The Italians took Kassala in 1894 from the Dervishes, but handed it back to the British in 1897 as part of a general agreement.

Kassala stands just apart from the Eritrean foothills. Outlying fantastic rocks throw waves of heat on the large dusty native town. It is the headquarters of the immense Kassala province, which reaches from the Red Sea almost to the Nile. The town stands on the railway built in 1927–29 to tap the Gash cotton-fields and runs on into the rich cornlands round Gedaref. Kassala stands within a radius of 200–250 miles of important objectives – Khartoum: the rail and river junction of Atbara; the Gezira cotton scheme; the great Sennar dam which feeds it with the Blue Nile waters; and the new Egyptian dam on the White Nile at Jebel Aulia. The country between is the level plain of the Butana, where Arab and Hadendoa nomads herd their camels and cattle. The land is so flat that when the sun comes up in a cloudless sky the prospect is more like a geometrical pattern than a landscape. The only obstacle is the Atbara River. It is rising now to its fullest height, but will quickly diminish to a string of blue pools in white sand. We may expect that the Italians will not be allowed to extend at their leisure from Kassala into the heart of the Sudan, and in the coming conflict we shall have the great asset of a positive and enthusiastic Sudanese loyalty. The Sudanese are great fighters. The tragedy is that their promising apprenticeship to civilization should be interrupted by the wasteful folly of war.

In conclusion, on all the African fronts upon which Italy is attacking she has a fairly clear run geographically. Such natural obstacles as there are – drought, escarpments and rivers – will need human reinforcement before they can be really effective. Until yesterday the British African empire, secure in the affection of its subjects, had a barely sufficient police force. Much has since been done to change this state of affairs, but we have been warned to expect initial reverses, and before we reach fuller strength, it is in the lengthening communications of an enemy cut off from his home base that we must find our first advantage.

'Free France' in Africa

The Times 14 September 1940

On 26 August Chad was the first French dependency in Africa to declare for de Gaulle.

Those who go to the map in order to assess the significance of the declaration by French Equatorial Africa and the Cameroons in favour of Free France will be answered only in part. They will see that our four west African territories, whose obtrusive pink always catches the British eye, are separated from each other by a mauve background which, in spite of these and other coastal intrusions, forms one continuous block over the whole north-west quarter of Africa. In fact, however, this mauve block is not so solid as it looks, since the Sahara, filling the centre, makes French Africa less a block than a circle of territories, lately, and only slightly, linked by the aeroplane and the Trans-Sahara motor route. The circle falls into three sections: the Mediterranean territories and the two sets of provinces of West and Equatorial Africa, each under a governor-general.

There are four parts of Equatorial Africa. The Gabon, on the Atlantic, was the nucleus from which expansion began to radiate about the middle of the last century, until it fused with that from the north and west at Chad and was checked on its way to the Nile and the Red Sea by the Fashoda incident. The middle Congo runs down the north bank of that river and is served by the newly equipped deep-water harbour of Pointe Noire. Ubangi-Shari lies inland round these two rivers. Chad is in the belt between the Lake and Darfur, where savannah turns to sand, and it runs up to the desert mountains of Tibesti, in which Senegalese tirailleurs of the Camel Corps watch upon Italy's Libyan frontier. These parts were federated in 1912, and in 1934 were further centralized under the Governor-General at Brazzaville. The huge distances and poor communications made close centralization impossible, and the provinces have kept much of their old individuality. In Chad especially, where the administration, confronted by tenacious Moslem nomads, is only now being finally shifted from a military to a civil basis, the service has a sense of independence and a fighting tradition which may explain its having been the first to reject Vichy. The French Cameroons, based upon the roomy estuary-harbour of Duala, is constitutionally separate as a Mandate, but its Commissioner is a member of the Equatorial Conseil de Gouvernement.

As it would be perilous in this war to support ourselves upon illusions, let it be admitted at once that Equatorial Africa, for all its immense size, is perhaps the poorest and least developed part of the French empire. Its greatest poverty is in man-power; it has only 3,500,000 inhabitants, against French West Africa's 15,000,000 and Nigeria's 20,000,000. French authorities have admitted that for many years the man-power of this region was severely overstrained. It had the fourfold task, after producing its own food supply, of working for the many forest concessionaires, of providing porterage, and of building the railways and roads that should eliminate this wasteful means of transport. In recent years many reforms have been made and a more humane and balanced development pursued. The Cameroons is, by contrast, more fertile, compact and populous than its large neighbour, and its administration has gained mostly commendation from the watching Mandates Commission. These territories are administered by about 1,000 officials and contain about another 4,000 settlers, traders and missionaries within their wide borders.

The map suggests at a glance the importance of this territory. Covering over 1,000,000 square miles of central Africa which could separate Nigeria from the Belgian Congo and from East Africa, it now connects them and makes a continuous stretch of Allied territory from the Cape to Cairo and from the Atlantic to the Pacific. It is necessary, however, since the map's suggestion is a little over-optimistic, to inquire into the nature of the links which equatorial Africa provides.

African transport systems have been developed to evacuate the products of the interior to the nearest practicable port. So in this territory four separate railways run one or two hundred miles inland; they are economic arteries each with its own system of veins and capillaries in the form of motor roads and tracks. Only a small proportion of these roads, especially in Equatorial Africa, are first-class all-season roads, and the whole system has little inter-colonial importance. On our side of the border roads are generally inferior to French or Belgian, owing to our tenderness about forced labour. Our approaches, for example, into both sides of Chad Territory, from Nigeria and the Sudan are – or were until very recently – seasonal and elementary, indeed, almost painful. The best transport across equatorial Africa is provided by road, rail and river through the Belgian Congo.

P

We need not expect, however, that we shall be sending a stream of bulky traffic across the continent. What Equatorial Africa does offer is the resumption of air services for important personnel and mails. The French, and still more the Belgians, were quicker than ourselves to realize the part aeroplanes could play in a backward continent, and their territories are well equipped for the purpose. The French Aéro-maritime circled the west coast to Pointe Noire every week, while Air France, in alternation with the Belgian line, cut boldly across the Sahara to Gao and on to Brazzaville by Fort Lamy. Both routes took three to three and a half days. Our connexion with the west from the main East African line was from Khartoum. The traveller could leave the Nile giving its fish-like gleam under the stars before dawn; cross the pink scrub-patched steppes of Kordofan, Darfur and Wadai, and reach Fort Lamy and Kano by night.

What of material resources in these countries? They produce, in ever-increasing bulk, the same coffee, cocoa, palm oil and ground-nuts which we have hardly the shipping to carry from our own colonies. The only important exception is the valuable timber of the forest region, that primeval forest made familiar by that great missionary and great man Schweitzer. In a letter to General de Gaulle on August 28, Mr Churchill promises to extend to colonies which joined the Allied cause economic assistance on a scale similar to that applied to our own colonies, and trade with them is now open. These represent very solid reasons why French West Africa should change allegiance, and every week in which her bulky crops are piling on the quays or rotting on the ground will be added incentive. In the more backward parts Africans who have only turned to economic crops under strong official pressure may fall back upon the old subsistence economy with relief, but in parts where a higher standard of life has been built up on oversea trade the shock will be severe. In either case the whole economic system will be strained, the revenue will decline, and it is difficult to see how advice from Vichy will prevent financial collapse.

It follows that the political future of the French empire which adheres to Marshal Pétain must be precarious. Effective imperial government today requires self-confidence on the part of the rulers and good will upon that of the ruled. There can be little confidence among officials humiliated by the almost incredible news from France and anxious about the hostages to fortune they have left there. Divided among themselves, uncertain of their future, their pay, and their leave, they will not find it easy to handle Africans who will be even more bewildered than themselves. Picture, for example, the state of mind of the advanced Senegalese, whose connexion with France was first formed in the days of 1848 liberalism, who were represented by one of their own race in the French Parliament, and whose minds, widened by military experience in Europe and elsewhere, are filled with fear and hatred of Nazism. With the increased call made upon them in this war went even greater promises than before. As M. Mandel, the Colonial Minister, told them: 'The efforts that are thus demanded and freely accorded must find their necessary counterpart in the granting of more and more extended rights to the protected populations, in their ever more complete assimilation to the bosom of the French city.'

This question has a wider significance than the immediate difficulties of the French empire. French and British tend to be critical of each other's colonial methods, which differ in response to deep differences in history and temperament. In spite of some recent changes of emphasis in French policy, the work of their Lyautey, unlike that of our Lugard, remains a brilliant exception rather than a model, and their centralizing and assimilative policy still contrasts with our plans for local self-development and self-government. It must, however, be remembered that the French offer backward people the gifts their educated members most ardently desire. There is room in the world for both our policies, because both are based upon a belief in the potential equality of the races, but there can never be any compromise between this belief and the revived tribalism of our enemies. Already the men of Vichy are attempting in their first racial measures to destroy something much older in their national tradition than the liberalism of the Third Republic from which they are trying to dissociate themselves. It was in the middle eighteenth century that a British officer in North America admitted that the French had sufficiently proved to him 'that a civilized member of society and an Indian hunter are not incompatible characters'. It may be our privilege, in helping France to become herself again, to ensure that her characteristic and generous contribution to the great problem of race-relations shall not perish from the earth.

The World, the Commonwealth and Dockland

Londoners and colonials in the great fire raid on the city

The Spectator 10 January 1941

Christmas morning, 3 a.m. in the shelter under the church. It's a shelter-de-luxe, this, compared with most, but even here, as night goes on, the air becomes thick with the sickly smell of unwashed bodies and bedding. Three hundred pairs of lungs use and use again their small ration of air. The lights are on, and fall upon the stacked humanity in the bunks and the garish decorations looped over them. Many sleepers snore with great power: sometimes there is a word or a groan. In the babies' corner little pink forms lie in the dainty cribs they owe to American kindness. Above them presides a lighted Christmas tree.

Christmas Day, and dinner-time. The shelterers have come up from their refuge into the hall above, and sit at the long decorated tables. Turkey, sausage and Christmas pudding are served to them, the solid realization of an idea conceived in Hollywood. Undergraduates, male and female, pacifists, responsible matrons from among the shelterers, social workers, permanent and migratory, wait on them with the scrambling eagerness of beginners. The feasters do their part stolidly amidst the altruistic bustle; dockers, labourers, city office-boys and char-women, factory-hands. They pull their crackers and wear their caps and accept their cigarettes. Of what are they thinking? Of the donors in Hollywood? Of their broken houses? Of their evacuated children? Difficult to say. They seem only half aware of what 'they' are trying to do for them. Most of them seem to accept 'their' services as fatalistically as the bombs.

Christmas evening. There is a pantomime in the shelter. *Cinderella*. It is a home product. One of the clergy has written it – perhaps not up to the highest Hollywood, but admirable for its purpose, none the less; another plays the buffoon most excellently. The pantomime is true to tradition with its topical jokes and its knock-about fun. The ugly sisters, with the properly improper display of underwear, monopolise the cellar in an air-raid, and Cinderella is sent to sit, not in the cinders, but on the roof as spotter. At the royal ball it is not her slipper but her gas-mask that she leaves behind. Hitler is requisitioned to take the part of the bad fairy and appears at intervals in a flash of green spot-light to the music of the sirens, only to be worsted by two clowns with more than professional vigour. Ministers and officials who make wonderful promises about shelter reform get their share of caricature. 'Where's Mrs Brown? I want to see her at once.' 'She's just gone off on the government evacuation scheme.' 'Oh, that's all right. She'll be back tomorrow.' The audience, perched thickly on its bunks, screams with delight. It catches up other jests too personal and local for the stranger. It joins with strength in the chorus of the dominant song:

> There'll always be a Christmas
> Whate'er the year may be,
> So let old Nasty try his tricks,
> He won't stop you and me!

That is only one shelter. There are plenty of others in this dockside borough. And shelterers need food. So it's cheering to see a large and fully equipped canteen coming down on tow from the West End. 'From the People of Sierra Leone to the People of Britain.' Admiring groups read out the inscription and pool their resources in geography. The Freetown Creoles in their cabins and the tribes inland must have put together their coppers and small silver for this welcome gift. So hands from Hollywood and Negro Africa reach across two oceans to meet in London's battered dockland.

A few days later the new mobile canteen takes the road. It gets its baptism of fire, for this is the night of the great fire raid on the City. The East End receives its share. Those invisible pulsating machines spray their incendiaries as they pass, and the temporary stars which the shells add to the heavenly pattern descend in spatters of shrapnel. It's not the best moment to break down on the road. The young Indian barrister – bringing help from yet another continent – and the medical student, who makes up our canteen crew, do their best in a darkness lit up only by the neighbouring fires. Two calm and effective locals, leaders in the near-by church, spring out of the pavement and lie on the muddy cobbles to coax the organs of the towing car. Here as elsewhere in England, the little human creatures at work under that incalculable sky are bound together by an excitement, almost an exhilaration.

On again, to the great shelter under the arches beside the docks. The canteen is very late. There are about fifteen hundred shelterers here, and many have had no evening meal. They do not know why 'they' bring a canteen or who 'they' are or where 'they' come from. But 'they' are late and that is cause for annoyance. There is a rush, and the table, set up with difficulty in the shelter to take the tea-urns and food, rocks dangerously. Hands tug at the canteen party, reach and clutch and wave their mugs in the dim light. Cockney voices shrill their orders. Appeals for restraint and discipline are not understood. Even the grown men do not respond. Disraeli's Two Nations are still two, and how is this one to learn courtesy, to feel a sense of solidity with the other from which 'they' of the canteen have come?

The rush dies down. There is time to look round. The air reeks from the crowds and the unsavoury bundles of bedding, some of which – for there are not yet bunks to go round – still lie on the damp floor. Water drips from the arches and down the walls. The Lascars foregather in one bay. Bill from Jamaica lies in his usual place with a pipe that contributes richly to the atmosphere. His house has been bombed. His wife lies in hospital with both legs broken. His own ankle has been smashed. His blanket has just been stolen – yet he smiles upon the scene with the benign humanity of the African patriarch. His low musical voice and gentle manner strike a deep restful chord in the Cockney crescendo. ('Yes,' admits a talkative matron, 'I've got good friends among the blacks and we say they make better 'usbands than our men. But some'ow I'd jest abaht kill my girl if she walked with one. Each class should marry into its own class – that's wot I say.') The mother of eleven justifies the whirlpool of dirty and tired children – it is nearly ten o'clock – which surrounds her by a drama of evacuation and of ill-treatment in far-away Cornwall. A dozen boys led by a magnificent little blue-eyed brigand worry through the crowd like a pack of dogs among sheep – so much voltage of human energy and intelligence running to waste or to mischief. The fifteen-year-olds, boys and girls, from such factories as are not charred shells, prick the blackness of the corridor with their cigarettes and enliven it with sudden giggles. When one of 'them' drags the canteen equipment through the passage with 'Excuse me, please – would you mind making way there,' the words are not out before the 'toff's' voice is being lavishly caricatured by a dozen unseen humorists.

'How is morale down there? Are the people really taking it?' 'Yes.' 'How splendid they are!' To those who have had even a glimpse of the grey proletarian square miles of dockland, seen the children playing in streets made but little more dreary by the casual devastation of the bomber, this conversation seems insufficient. The 'Yes' is true, but it is too short an answer. The real answer is a long story of which the most important chapter should be written immediately this war ends. Indeed, is it too soon to start writing it now?

The Copperbelt Report

Letter to *The Times* 3 March 1941

In March 1940 there were riots at the copper mines in Northern Rhodesia in which a number of Africans were killed. The Report of the Commission to inquire into the Disturbances on the Copperbelt *was published in Lusaka in July 1940. This report, the Governor's statement upon it of 18 February 1941, and* The Times *leading article of that date raised the issue of migrant versus resident labour, the former system being at that time generally accepted as economically and socially desirable.*

Sir, – The Copperbelt Commission's report demands, even at this moment of the war, our serious consideration. There are especially two points in your leading article of 18 February for which I would urge further consideration.

You say that the policy of accommodating more married African labourers at the mines is not consistent with that of maintaining the tribal system and may develop a rootless population. Is it not time for us to inquire whether the present form of labour migration is not destroying the roots of the tribal system in a more subtle way? Some tribes are deprived of a high proportion of their men in the prime of life. Do the little boxes of trade goods and the generally diminishing trickle of cash which go back to the tribes compensate for the effects of this deprivation upon their family, social and political life or upon their subsistence agriculture? There is also the question of the effects upon the men of their unnatural life at the mine, some of which may, perhaps, be shown in their riotous conduct. The migration from the land into industry in England was in some ways a painful process, but at least the workers did not have to break up their family life, and they could, as time went on, look to the state to provide, partly from taxation of the industry, good social services for their wives and children and their own old age. Above all, they had the hope of improving their position in a steady job, perhaps of climbing high up the economic ladder or even to the very top.

This brings me to the second point. It appears from the published summary of the report that the government, in effect, rejects the Commission's proposal that the African worker should be given the opportunity to advance from his present stage of low-paid, unskilled labour. It is no longer practical politics for the British Government to challenge the colour-bar which has spread from the Union into Southern Rhodesia, but is it now to confirm its advance still farther north? Northern Rhodesia is still a brown colony: the white workers are still very few and localized: they have not been there many years and it is probable that most intend to retire to more attractive regions. We have still, then, the opportunity to draw the frontier to the colour-bar along the Zambezi. We have certainly good reason to do so. By the economic colour-bar, because he is an African, a man is artificially prevented from rising to the position he is capable of filling. This issue should not be confused with that of barriers to those equal political or social rights which Africans in a backward country like Northern Rhodesia are not yet capable of using even if they were granted.

The economic colour-bar is inconsistent with the speeches which our leaders have made distinguishing the spirit and racial policy of our empire from that of the Nazis. It is inconsistent with our practice in other parts of Africa and it is not allowed by our Belgian neighbours on the copperbelt. I am fully aware that, in view of present events in East and South Africa, this is a very difficult question. But postponement only allows white labour to make the position more difficult. There have been imperial problems which, under our treatment of delay and compromise. have settled themselves. But this is not one. It is a deep and clear conflict of interests and principles which, in default of just settlement, is likely to endure as long as black and white retain the colour of their skins. It will become graver with every advance in education and self-consciousness of those African millions who, relying upon the spirit of our promises, are offering us in this time of danger such great loyalty and courage.

Yours, &c., MARGERY PERHAM

The Future of Ethiopia

Agenda January, 1942

In 1941 Ethiopia was reconquered. In January, 1942 Britain and Ethiopia signed an Agreement and Military Convention.

The re-conquest of Ethiopia from the Italians has placed in British hands the task of re-establishing the first country to be freed from Axis aggression. This African kingdom therefore assumes an importance much greater than its population and material development would seem to warrant. Watching Britain's action in Ethiopia today the world will try to estimate the ideas and the spirit which our government is likely to bring to the construction of the promised new order of tomorrow.

Other causes have contributed to give Ethiopia a high symbolic importance in international affairs. Italy's aggression gave her a significance, ably emphasized by her Emperor, as the main test-case of the international order which was set up after the last war and which finally broke down with her conquest. Many violations of the rights of small nations have since occurred and have indeed raised the question whether their restoration to full independence upon the old model will be practicable. But the extreme cynicism with which Italy violated the rights of Ethiopia, and the failure of the attempts by the League of Nations to protect a fellow member, have endowed the status of Ethiopia with very special historical associations. On the plane of imperialism Great Britain, as the holder of a great colonial empire, is peculiarly tested. Ethiopia, from its situation and its stage of development, is, as Italy tried to demonstrate, potentially 'colonial' territory, even if it is almost the last and the least digestible of such territory in Africa. It is almost surrounded by countries under British governments;[1] it is well-watered and fertile and it is at the moment wholly in the power of Britain's imperial forces. The temptation is obvious. The British Government, it is true, has renounced in general, and specifically with regard to Ethiopia, the annexationist ambitions of her enemies. But will she be

---

[1] The Anglo-Egyptian Sudan may be regarded as being at present under predominantly British rule.

able to keep these promises in the spirit as well as in the letter? This question will be asked above all in the United States where there is a background of anti-imperialist tradition and a somewhat critical attitude towards the British position in India and the colonial empire.

This question is also being put from another quarter. The significance of Ethiopia reaches its highest intensity in the eyes of politically conscious Africans both in Africa and throughout the world. This sentiment is unaffected by the fact that the Amhara are not Negroes, a race which they have always despised and enslaved. Inquiries have been made about Ethiopia's restoration from the depths of the Nigerian bush – and men from that bush have now marched and fought across Ethiopia – but the degree of interest is generally in proportion to that of education and racial self-consciousness. The inferior status which is imposed upon Africans in several parts of the world, and the social discrimination which acts against nearly all Africans who are in contact with Anglo-Saxon societies, have evoked in response a psychological complex which fastens strongly upon the compensating idea of an independent African kingdom. Hence the word 'Ethiopianism' has come into use to describe activities which spring from the longing to assert African independence of white government or tutelage. It has elements akin to what is known as 'spiritual Zionism'. It is especially in West and South Africa, in the West Indies and even in Haarlem, that the word Ethiopia strikes deep chords of racial awareness. The Italian invasion was the cause among certain groups in these areas of intense interest, a flow of subscriptions, and even, in the Western Hemisphere, of demonstrations and riots. The successful re-establishment of Ethiopia would increase the self-respect of all the more advanced Africans and would confirm their confidence in Britain, while even the appearance of going back upon our word would foster their antagonism towards white, and especially British, imperialism. More widely and with less intensity, the cause of Ethiopia has interest for all coloured and subject people.

Opinion in Britain itself is more difficult to interpret. There can be little doubt that at the time of the Italian invasion the British people felt, perhaps more deeply than any other European people except the Swedes, who had special ties with Ethiopia, the sentiments of sympathy and indignation. There was also, for many, some sense of responsibility because of the widely-held belief that sanctions had not been applied with sufficient resolution, and that arms and other help had not been supplied to Ethiopia. The reaction against the Hoare–Laval proposals testified to the character of British interest, which, with the sense of admiration for the bearing of the Emperor, found their strongest and most definite expression in the founding of the Abyssinia Association. On the other hand, in certain humanitarian circles, such as the Anti-Slavery Society, there have been, for obvious reasons, more mixed feelings. On the whole, however, it may be assumed that most British people regard the Ethiopian campaign not only as a victory over the enemy but as the righting of a great wrong, and an opportunity for generous action on the part of their government.

This, then, appears to be the background of opinion in the world and in this country, against which Ethiopian affairs must be handled. It is clear that a highly altruistic policy is expected of Britain. The government has, indeed, accepted such a policy in a statement in the House of Commons on 5 February 1941, by Mr Eden, in which five obligations have been undertaken. They are:

1. The re-establishment of Ethiopian independence.
2. The restoration of the Emperor Haile Selassie.
3. The renunciation for Britain of all territorial ambitions in Ethiopia.
4. Temporary measures of military guidance and control in consultation with the Emperor, to be brought to an end as soon as the situation permits.
5. The provision of outside assistance and guidance in economic and political matters, which has been requested by the Emperor and which should be the subject of international arrangement at the conclusion of peace.

It will be the object of this article to show, from examination of the character of the country and people of Ethiopia, the nature and the difficulties of the task which Britain has undertaken. Some of these difficulties stand out at once in Mr Eden's statement. One may arise in the attempt to reconcile the first two obligations with the last two. The second difficulty lies in the fact that between the period, even now ending, described in 4, and that envisaged in 5, a third period must intervene, which will inevitably be somewhat undefined in time and character. It may last for several years of war and peace-making, and during this time the British, who have conquered the territory of Ethiopia, hold it in military occupation and are also the *de facto* or *de jure* rulers of all the surrounding countries (with the small and precarious exception of French Somaliland), must bear a large responsibility for the affairs of the territory. Our immediate problem and the main theme of this article is that of Anglo-Ethiopian relations in this interim period, though it must be remembered that what is done in the next few years may set the stage for the third and international act which is to follow it. We know that an agreement to cover this period is at present being negotiated between the Emperor and the British representatives, and this may have been published before this article appears. It will need, however, for its interpretation an understanding of Ethiopian conditions and of the problems which will probably be encountered by both sides in carrying it out.

The European who wishes to understand a country such as Ethiopia, and who has not been accustomed to studying societies, past or present, which are very different from his own, needs to make a special adjustment of his mind. This is the more necessary for Ethiopia because strong feelings have been roused by her dramatic rôle on the international stage. On the one hand she has been accused by the Italians of being backward and barbarous and, as such, meriting conquest and subjection by a civilized power. An attitude of something like moral disapproval for certain elements of backwardness may sometimes be discerned in our own country and has appeared in some of the books written about Ethiopia. Upon the other hand we find an attitude which is the extreme opposite, one of passionate partisanship which measures Ethiopia's merits in proportion to her wrongs and deprecates even the attempt to make an objective appraisal of her social conditions, and, above all, of the Emperor and his policy. Both views do credit to the hearts of those who hold them, the one group being moved by the wrongs they have seen done upon the slaves and subjects of the Amhara, the other by those inflicted upon the Amhara by the Italians. The people of Ethiopia, both the rulers and the subject peoples, need the help and interest prompted by such sentiments, but this is not likely to be given wisely unless, in this question, the head reinforces the heart. Ethiopia, however, provides hard work for the head, with its long history, its variety of peoples, conditions and religions, and, for the student at least, the incomplete and unsatisfactory nature of much of the available information.

It is not within the scope of this article to attempt even a summary of Ethiopian history. Yet there are certain questions that must be asked by all who approach the question of our present relations with this country, and the answer to these is to be found, in part, in her history. The first of these will certainly be how far Ethiopia is, or is likely to become, a nation. To answer this we must first consider the character of that part of Ethiopia which is inhabited mainly by Amharic-speaking people.

The name Amhara is loosely given to the Ethiopians proper who form the historic nucleus of the present kingdom. They are concentrated upon the high, mountainous region which makes a rough inner square north of Addis Ababa and well within all the frontiers of 1935, except in the north, where the Italian boundary cut across the ancient kingdom of Tigre. These people are of Hamitic-speaking stock upon which, in prehistoric times, Semitic influences and language were imposed. Jewish, Greek and Christian contributions were afterwards made to their civilization. There was a powerful and martial kingdom of Axum in the first century A.D. and its people were converted in the fourth century to Christianity, their Church being afterwards linked with the Egyptian Coptic Church from which they have since drawn their Abuna, or chief bishop. In the early Middle Ages the old Ethiopia rose to a standard of civilization which was probably a good deal higher than that of contemporary England. There were times when she dominated the whole eastern horn of Africa, when she conquered the Yemen and developed her sea power. When the first full light was thrown upon Ethiopia by the Portuguese priest Alvarez in the early sixteenth century, we see a country of ordered government, with an autocratic monarchy, an elaborately ceremonious court with courtiers dressed in silks and jewels; priests and nobles eager to debate theology and church history with a stranger, and thousands of churches and monasteries, with their stone buildings, ornamental vestments and collections of manuscripts. The rise of Islam had already cut Ethiopia off from her contacts with Europe and Asia. She was encircled by Moslem states and, shortly after Alvarez's visit, was overrun and pillaged by Ahmed Gran, ruler of the neighbouring Adel, to the south-east. With astonishing resilience, and with some help from Portuguese musketeers, she threw off her conquerors, and restored the historic and Christian Ethiopia. She showed the same tenacity in throwing off Roman Catholicism which was brought to her by the Portuguese in the seventeenth century.

Ethiopia then can boast a longer Christian civilization than we can ourselves, and a legendary and historic past well known to her people since it is preserved by the Church, reflected in its hagiography and expressed in the many ancient monuments, churches and monasteries of the north. The people themselves believe that their present dynasty, to which history allows a possible seven centuries, can be traced to the union of King Solomon and the Queen of Sheba, and the historical and religious sanctity which attaches to its present representative are important factors in the immediate situation. Maintaining their independence and religion for centuries of bitter warfare, the Amhara developed great pride, self-confidence, and conservatism, with a distrust of foreigners which has found an increasing justification in their recent international relations and in the character of many of the adventurers and concession-hunters who have entered Ethiopia in the last fifty years.

The mountainous and broken character of their country not only helped to defend the Amhara from foreign conquest but divided the parts from each other, and gave considerable independence to the frequently warring *rases* and kings who yet, if sometimes only in theory, acknowledged the sovereignty of the Negusa Nagast, or King of Kings. The apparent disorder and disunity of their history should not blind critics to the underlying social and cultural solidarity of the Amhara which has always prevented their complete dissolution under the action of centrifugal forces. It is also wise to be on guard against drawing too facile conclusions about the backwardness of this people from their material poverty and the semi-savage nature of some of their customs. Much that offends European standards in this country is due to the long isolation of Ethiopia behind the physical barriers of mountain and desert and the cultural barriers of hostile and backward Moslem peoples. Ethiopia is, moreover, from certain aspects a twelfth-century kingdom preserved into the twentieth century and many of the defects of her system are due not, as is sometimes suggested, to inherent, still less to blameworthy, faults in the people, but to a medieval equipment of economics and communications such as necessitated similar methods of government in early England.

The simile must not be pushed too far. The monarchy, though it was theoretically more absolute than in England, an absolutism defined by almost every traveller in extreme terms, did not in all the 2,000 years of its existence build up a system of centralized administration such as that so well and truly founded by our Henry II and Edward I. Yet though the monarchs were often challenged and humiliated from within by their subordinate kings and *rases* and occasionally defeated from without, the throne itself was never overturned, and any man able enough to reassert, through civil war, statecraft and politic marriages, its absolute power over all rivals, met with no institutionalized opposition. The kingship was based less upon a system of civil government than upon personal leadership of the Church and the army. The Church was inseparably linked to the State but was mostly subservient; its head, as one ruler expressed it, in a moment of anger, was only 'a slave brought from the Turks'. The army was perhaps the supreme expression of the people's tradition and energies – warfare, internal or external, was almost continuous and the soldier was a man of prestige and privilege. The government was founded upon the military organization: the monarch was the commander-in-chief and nearly all officials held military titles, governors being the equivalent of generals, while their subordinates were colonels or less. The provincial governor's main function, and one for which he retained most of the tribute, was to maintain and lead his provincial army. The cultivator, himself liable to service in a general levy, carried, by an elaborate and heavy system of dues in kind and labour, the whole unproductive hierarchy of Church, army and officials. His position was known as 'gabar', one who pays gibr (tribute), from which the professional classes were largely exempt. In Amhara country peasants of the ruling race, living unconquered, often upon their ancient tribal lands, were, in spite of onerous dues, by no means serfs, but had in some parts substantial powers of local self-government and could leave their lands and their lords at their own will.

This independent people, static for many centuries yet virile, in the second half of the nineteenth century found their continent changing around them with the coming into it of the Europeans. Once again they reacted vigorously to outside pressure. Under Menelik they took the offensive, defeating the Italians at Adowa in 1896 and, joining in 'the scramble for Africa', they carved out, with the help of Europe's new weapons, an empire of their own – of which more presently – just before their European competitors could annex it. There were, however, other and deeper adjustments required which were less easy to achieve. Menelik, for example, tried to strengthen his internal position, not by building up a system of administration outwards from the centre, but by importing from abroad the system of ministries and adding them to the centre. But his ministries remained without effective administrative connexion with the provinces, and his own royal duties remained personal, undelegated and physically crushing.

After the unhappy interlude of Lij Yasu's minority and reign, Haile Selassie, Menelik's second cousin and by no means the obvious heir, step by step built up his position and, as much by patience and shrewdness as by force, attained the imperial throne in 1930. Son of the progressive Ras Makonnen, and a pupil of the French Roman Catholic Mission at Harar, the present Emperor understood the significance of Western methods and inventions better than any of his people. He had a short race with time. Held back by his fear of alienating a conservative Church and ruling class, yet urged on by the growing menace from Italy, he struggled to modernize his army, to reform his central administration with the help of European advisers, and to meet foreign criticism by promising the reform of slavery. As with Menelik, the lack of an administrative system or the men to staff it, threw the whole burden of a new and rapidly expanding kind of government entirely upon his shoulders, already burdened by difficult foreign affairs.

The Italians have come and gone but this constitutional problem, with many others, remains. How, both by Ethiopian action and British advice, they will be met depends partly upon the psychological climate now obtaining in the country. The people have passed through a series of disturbing events – a reforming Emperor, a terrible war in which their ancient military pride was crushed by mechanized and aerial aggression; their Emperor's flight; five years of Italian rule, and a second war, this time of liberation, by Britain's imperial forces. What has been the effect of all this upon the mind of the Amhara people, especially of the clergy and upper classes? Are they prepared for deep political and social changes? Has their old sense of isolation and complacency deserted them? Do they understand the lessons of the two wars and are they ready to accept reforms and effective foreign assistance? It is probable that with a people unaccustomed to rationalize their feelings there can be few observers, even in Ethiopia, who can yet answer these questions with much certainty. It would, however, be wisest to assume that the old sentiments of independence, conservatism and distrust of foreigners have not wholly disappeared and that in a country where leaders have always quickly arisen to turn hopes or grievances into armed insurrection, it will be necessary to encourage royal reform and offer foreign guidance with great discretion. The roads themselves which the Italians, rising in this one thing to Roman tradition, have left behind them, might be made to carry such disturbing passengers as royal agents and European officers all too swiftly into these ancient, remote and semi-autonomous provinces. The Emperor himself possesses the tradition and experience of royal power and of this, since he attained it by his own efforts before 1935 and regards it as the expression of his people's independence, he is jealous. There seems no good reason why he should not be given full opportunity to exercise it in the Amhara provinces, and to find by practice a balance, which no foreigner could strike, between monarchy, Church, aristocracy and people. The reverse side of independence is that no Emperor should be able to rely upon British support for the maintenance of his rule if it should become plainly and widely unpopular with his people.

So far this article has been written as though Ethiopia were confined to the great triangle of mountains that lies north of the Blue Nile and south of Eritrea. But this is only the Amhara nucleus of the present empire, and we must now consider its other component groups and the problems they present.

The Amhara themselves, according to recent estimates – and we have nothing to go upon but estimates – are actually in a minority in Ethiopia. A recent Italian estimate puts them at about 32 per cent. of a population of 8 millions. The largest group in the country is that of the Galla who may represent about 42 per cent. They came in from the east and south, and in the sixteenth century, in the wake of the Moslem conquest, over-ran almost the whole country. They penetrated even the highlands and reached right across to the present Sudan border, thus dividing the Semiticized Amhara from the earlier Hamitic population to the south which they were beginning to influence. Large numbers of the Galla, who are themselves Hamitic-speaking, are still probably pagan, and have maintained the democratic age-grade organization of their small disunited pastoral clans. A large proportion, coming under influences carried from the Red Sea Coast or the Sudan, have become Moslem, though not as yet of a very advanced or fanatical kind. Some of these, south-west of Addis Ababa, are also monarchical, having grafted upon their own democratic and atomic forms the kingship of the earlier Hamites, sometimes called Cushites, into whose country they intruded. Others, again, especially round Addis Ababa, have become Christian through their contact with the Amhara.

The main part of the Galla areas was brought under Ethiopia by the Shoan branch of the Solomonian line to which the present Emperor belongs. This dynasty, during the past two centuries, thrust out in all directions from the mountains of central Shoa, subjugating Galla tribes. The process culminated with Menelik, who in 1889 seized the imperial crown for his house. He built up a great army, and after his defeat of the Italians, he turned his soldiers south and south-west. With their immensely superior weapons imported from Europe, they easily subjected in the next few years, not only the remaining Galla groups but the 'Cushite' kingdoms and tribes, the negroid peoples of the south-west. Thus, by an effort comparable to the simultaneous annexations of European powers, which had indeed stimulated the Shoan ruler, Menelik practically doubled the population and area of Ethiopia, and greatly increased his own power, since he regarded these areas as the appanages of his own house.

Q

It is clear that the Galla are likely to play an increasingly large part in Ethiopian development. They cannot, however, be regarded as anything approaching a solid, homogeneous group. Still less is there, as yet, a self-conscious Galla nationalism. They are geographically distributed almost in a great half circle south of Shoa, with some outlying groups in the north, and a wide projection to the west. Religion is another important dividing factor. Christianity denotes a degree of assimilation with the Amhara rulers. Islam gives its own sense of solidarity and self-respect. Paganism generally spells isolation and backwardness. The Galla are divided, too, in their way of life: in the southern and eastern lowlands they remain semi-nomadic pastoralists, while on the fertile hills which they have overrun further north and west they have shown an astonishing adjustment to their agricultural opportunities. A people subject to so much dispersal and fissure is not likely to have a unified attitude to the ruling Amhara. They have, indeed, received no uniform treatment from these rulers. War, massacre, subjection, serfdom and gradual assimilation seem to have formed the sequence where Amhara and Galla have lived in close neighbourhood, as along the southern frontier of Gojjam and in and around Shoa. A certain degree of autonomy has, however, been allowed to groups such as those in Jimma and Leka, which were strong enough to ask and to use it. Jimma, indeed, remained under its own old ruler until 1933 and his country, partly because of his encouragement of trade, upon which he levied exceptionally light taxation, was most prosperous. Upon the other hand, exaction and oppression at the hands of Amhara soldiers and landholders has often been the lot of the less accessible and less organized Galla, such as those of Bali. On the lowlands skirting the Amhara mountains in the north-east, groups of fanatically Moslem Galla have for centuries maintained a turbulent, and at critical moments, a dangerous semi-independence.

There is not any rigid conventional Amhara–Galla attitude, or any social or economic barrier against the Galla to prevent them rising from the status of a conquered people. They have for centuries mixed in marriage as well as concubinage even with the leading Amhara families, and have held the highest posts. Lij Yasu, the last king, had a Galla father, who was made a Negus (or king), and the present Empress has Galla blood. On the other hand, while some Galla seem to have fought well, both in the Italian war and in the recent campaign of emancipation, it would be true to say that others showed more indifference to the advance of the invader than did the Amhara, and groups of the northern Galla, corrupted and armed by the Italians, actually turned against the

Ethiopian army in its retreat. The two peoples may be likened to two fluids: there is nothing at present in their composition to prevent their ultimate coalescence: they are already intermingling where they are in contact and it is a condition of the very future of Ethiopia that no new element should be introduced that might prevent that coalescence. Religious intolerance upon either side would turn the Moslem Galla and the Christian Amhara into very refractory components of the future Ethiopia. It remains to be seen whether the Italian flattery of Islam at the ancient Moslem town of Harar has revived the old religious antagonisms of this area.

The Galla must take first place in any attempt to answer the question as to whether Ethiopia is, in fact or in promise, a nation. The other subject peoples are by comparison small minorities. But they bulk large in their importance as a political problem. The first reason for this is that, even more, perhaps, than the backward elements of the Galla, they have endured maladministration and enslavement. The Hamitic people of the south, of whom the best known, perhaps, are those of the mysterious, vanished kingdom of Kaffa, suffered terribly at the hands of Menelik's armies. The negroid peoples further south and west were an easier prey.

Such evidence as we have about the process of conquest suggests that it caused the numbers and prosperity of these peoples to drop sharply. Amhara government did little to heal the sores. The methods by which soldiers and officials were maintained by the tribute and services of those cultivating them were customary, as we have seen, in Amhara provinces. But in the conquered regions, these methods, unregulated by ancient custom and unrestricted by the common culture of rulers and ruled, took on a harsh and destructive form. The 'gabar' system, which in the north was at its best a form of tenure and a method of taxation, became in much of the conquered south a personal servitude, in the exaction of which there was little to restrain the greed of military governors and their soldiery. These were allotted so many gabars for their upkeep, from two or three families to an ordinary soldier, ten or twenty to an officer, and anything in the region of several hundred for a governor. Customs varied locally but in most of these provinces the gabar had to provide his master with grain, honey, firewood and fodder for his mule; his womenfolk had to work in the soldiers' hut and he had to follow him as an attendant when he went to war. There was little to restrain the soldiers from further exactions, and in practice, in these depopulated provinces, the gabar was not suffered to leave. It is this system which a recent proclamation of the restored Emperor admits to be little better than slavery. Such was the misery of the people in parts of Maji and Goldea that they fled to the hills and forests, fighting their neighbours and selling the captives, or even their own children, as slaves in order to buy rifles to defend themselves or join in banditry or the slave-trade.

This question of slavery is inseparable from any discussion of the south-west. The institution was, of course, recognized throughout Ethiopia, and slaves were to be seen everywhere in the households and working on the estates of the Amhara. The south-west 'Cushite' and Negro provinces were, however, the source from which the constant replenishment required was mainly supplied. There seems to have been more opportunity for the extensive use of slaves on the estates carved out of the fertile and depopulated south than in the bleaker north. The Moslem Galla, especially those of Jimma, were important slave-traders and slave-owners. Negroes were largely used as slaves and had the advantage of being easily recognized and reclaimed if they ran away. There are, however, no reliable figures about the numbers and distribution of slaves. Estimates can have little value where the number of the total population is not known.

The policy and achievements of the Emperor in combating slavery in fulfilment of his obligations to the League of Nations and his promise to the British Anti-Slavery Society have been, like so much in Ethiopia, the subject of controversy. There can be little doubt that the reforms were better upon paper than they proved in practice. The Emperor, however, was fighting almost single-handed in a country in which opinion had not yet been affected by those ideas which, it should always be remembered, moved us to abolish our own more oppressive form of slavery little more than a century ago. He was working also, as we have seen, with very inadequate means of making his will felt in the far-away provinces where slave-trading continued up to 1935 to find sources of supply, though it was reduced and driven into the obscurity of night or of leafy by-paths. One of his most effective steps, taken late in 1935, was to appoint a progressive governor to the oppressed province of Maji, on the borders of the southern Sudan, with Colonel Sandford as his adviser.

It would appear that it is in these conquered and oppressed provinces that the Emperor will chiefly need advice and assistance from Europe. We may note that since his return to power, he has prepared a proclamation in which he has abolished both the legal status of slavery and also the gabar system. It is probable that slavery throughout the country will be abolished gradually by the judicious stages which Lord Lugard and other practical experts have advised. The trade, which depends upon the institution, will decline with it, though both will probably linger in less accessible parts as they have even in territories under direct British rule. The problem of provincial maladministration in the south and south-west is, however, much wider than slavery and is bound up with the lack of a central revenue for the payment of soldiers and officials and with standards of conduct and attitudes of mind deeply implanted in rulers and ruled. No stroke of the Emperor's pen, no piece of advice offered in Addis Ababa, can transform this situation in a few weeks or months. Even the British political officers at present distributed in the provinces will not easily find a tempo and technique which will not antagonize the very men through whom they must work, and who cannot be expected to visualize the ideals of good government towards which their foreign advisers are looking. It is this which has provoked the opinion that these subject provinces should be separated in some degree from Ethiopia proper and given special administrative treatment. The practical difficulties against forming an island of separate government in this region are, however, great. Moreover, most, if not all, of the peoples of these provinces might under wise government be assimilated in time, and their fertile lands would play a valuable part in building up the economy and revenues of the future Ethiopia. Equally important is the impossibility of explaining such a partition in terms which would disarm the indignation of the Ethiopians and the criticism of world opinion, in the face of what would be a grave breach of faith. There are stronger arguments for assisting, from within the Ethiopian kingdom, those reforms of administration in the subject provinces which the Emperor had already begun in selected areas before the Italian war and which, under no conceivable form of government, could possibly be anything but a slow and difficult task.

There is, however, one group of nominally subject people to whom the above arguments do not apply. The Somali and Danakil of the eastern and south-eastern semi-desert lowlands, though included within the Ethiopian boundaries, pursued their wandering and ascetic life with little interference from the Amhara. These mountain people hate to enter the torrid depressions which surround them and there was little fat for them to squeeze out of the lean and fierce nomads who occupy them. Intermittent levies of stock were made from the Somali, but even this exercise of sovereignty was impracticable in most of that Danakil country, which is one of the last parts of the world where the blue ribbon for intrepid travel could be won.

It would be no easy task, especially since the Italians raised Somali levies to fight, with success, against their old enemies, to put the Ogaden tribe of the Somali back under an effective Ethiopian control. It is probable that much the same applies to the Danakil people who lie between Ethiopia and the Eritrean port of Assab, which has been developed by the Italians, and linked to Ethiopia by a road.

The question must be considered as part of a much larger situation. The future of these semi-desert areas can hardly be separated from that of the coast-lands to which they lead. Ethiopia's main commercial outlet is down the railway to Jibuti in French Somaliland and less important outlets, but capable of much further development for local trade, are by British Somaliland to Berbera and by Eritrea to Massawa, as well as by the route already mentioned through Danakil and Eritrean territory to Assab. Ethiopia needs a guaranteed access to all these ports on the Red Sea and Indian Ocean. They are however of very great strategic and commercial interest to several nations, as they lie upon a narrow stretch of the main sea route between Europe and the East. The coast, and the hinterland to varying depths, is unproductive semi-desert land, carrying a sparse, nomadic population, and wholly unattractive to the Ethiopians. Two of the parts into which this area was arbitrarily divided, Eritrea and Italian Somaliland, have been conquered by Britain. The future position of the third, French Somaliland, is very ambiguous. It is nothing more than the port of Jibuti, a toll-gate built to tap Ethiopian trade at the railway terminus, and a port of call for French shipping. When all these features of the situation are reviewed together, it seems possible that these ports and their hinterlands might form a very suitable subject for an experiment in inter-Allied and ultimately, international, administration. The populations affected amount to only a few hundred thousand and their country is not susceptible of much development. The Somali tribes, however, as a people constantly migrating across the present arbitrary political boundaries, and often at odds among themselves, have much to gain immediately from being given a single administration, which might also help them in the future to develop a sense of unity which does not at present exist and even to build up some form of self-govern-ment. Politically and materially backward, they are people of high individual pride and energy and of fine physique, great fighters and traders, with a strong sense of being superior to all their neighbours. Hitherto little has been done for them by European governments which drew no revenues from them, but a unified administration, drawing upon the dues from the ports and transit trade, might be able to offer more constructive services. Ethiopia's loss might look large upon the map, but it would be negligible in fact and she might be compensated with the Eritrean highlands which are culturally part of Ethiopia. Under this plan, Ethiopia, Italy, France and Britain would all have made their contributions of territory to the experiment.

It will be clear from this review of some of the main problems of Ethiopia that it will be no easy task to offer this country with one hand independence and with the other advice and assistance. The difficulties may be summarized from three aspects, military, financial and administrative and political.

The military is the most obvious and perhaps the simplest problem, and it is the one most likely to be appreciated by the Emperor and his people. The campaign in and around Ethiopia is now concluded. But until the Allies gain peace with victory there can be no assurance that the war may not swing back again into north-east Africa. It is necessary that the British command in the Middle East should be able to treat this whole area as a hinterland of war for communications and supply and as a possible theatre for further campaigns. They cannot afford to allow conditions of serious insecurity to develop there, yet they cannot afford to maintain large forces for its prevention. This probably means that Britain must, at least for the moment, co-operate with the Emperor in organizing a centralized and modernized army as a police force, and must keep the existing roads and aerodromes in good repair. It has been stated already that a British military mission is to work with the Emperor. Precedents from Iraq and Egypt suggest the lines for an arrangement and it may be presumed that the cost would be regarded in the main as one for the imperial war exchequer. Military control at a crucial moment of world conflict must entail a degree, which will vary according to the situation inside and outside Ethiopia, of political control.

The second aspect is that of the closely related financial and administrative problems. It would be impossible to maintain the physical equipment for modern administration, which the Italians had built up at vast metropolitan expense, upon the Emperor's ordinary revenue. Still less would it be possible to encourage the introduction of reforms in administration which must imply the encroachment, already begun in a small way by the Emperor before 1935, of centrally paid agencies upon the independent position of provincial governors maintained by local tribute in kind and in labour. There was nothing resembling a budget in the old Ethiopia. A possibility – it can hardly be called an estimate – based upon a list of calculations and guesses is that the cash revenue was in the region of two to three hundred thousand pounds which, owing to the self-supporting position of the provinces and the amount of tribute in labour and kind used for the upkeep of the Palace, does not, of course, represent the true revenue. The Italians, in addition to their long-term appropriation for public works of £130,000,000, made further budgetary provision for current expenses in Italian East Africa, most of which would go to Ethiopia. Judging by other African territories of comparable size and population, a British colonial government after years of developwould expect to spend and to raise a revenue of £3,000,000 or £4,000,000 a year. It is probable that when her economy and taxation has been shifted fully on to a money basis, and her resources in coffee, hides, wax, etc., fully developed, Ethiopia might follow the example of other tropical countries and rapidly increase her revenues. But this would depend upon the conditions of world trade following the war.

All this will in any event take some years. The immediate choice which faces the Emperor and his British advisers is the standard of administration that is to be attempted now. It is obviously desirable at least to maintain the roads and other material equipment bequeathed by the Italians. But this, for a time at least, must mean the employment of foreign personnel. It is highly desirable to start paying at least a certain number of officials and soldiers even before the system of tribute can be so reformed as to support them. It is obviously essential to develop the economic resources and the social services of education and health, and both, in Ethiopia's condition, will be slow to give their returns. Temporary subsidies are clearly required and it seems that in the immediate future they can come only from Great Britain. Financial aid has generally been proportioned pound by pound with financial control. This is the dilemma which can be solved in part if the Treasury in this instance relaxes precedent and the Agreement is framed so as to allow of British influence but not of a control incompatible with independence. A small financial alleviation might be found in annual payments from the Sudan or Egypt, or both, for concessions in the Lake Tsana and Blue Nile areas which are so vital to the future security and development of these countries. This question has so long been the subject of negotiations with Ethiopia that such an agreement should be beyond misunderstanding and criticism.

Finally, we come to the practical aspect of our new relationship with Ethiopia. This, defined or implied, will be the central part of the forthcoming Agreement. If the outline given here of Ethiopian conditions is true, there will clearly be need not only for financial help but, at least for a time, for European advisers and technical assistants. The Emperor used these before and has stated that he needs them again. Is it desirable for the old situation to be revived in which, as the Emperor's employees, they had neither outside sanction nor support? The Emperor and his people, with their long history of independence, will say 'Yes', and those in this country who discount the difficulties of Ethiopia's conditions or who distrust British imperialism will support them.

The problem is a real one, about which those of equal good will towards Ethiopia may differ, all the more as so many factors in that country are still obscure. Reforms inspired from within will, of course, be of more value than any imposed from without and the historic pride and initiative of the ruling people should be harnessed to the work of reform. But this will be a slow educational task. Authoritative help may be needed in the immediate re-settlement of this disturbed country in order to diminish the possibility of Britain being drawn in later when she might incur the charge of interfering in defiance of the Agreement. This document will, presumably, cover only the war period, since Mr Eden has pledged Britain to make the provision of outside help the subject of international arrangement at the conclusion of peace. This, if the post-war settlement meets our hopes, may relieve Ethiopia of some of her fears and ourselves of some of our responsibilities. The fears might be lessened even now if the Emperor were encouraged to choose some advisers of other than British nationality.

The liberation of Ethiopia invites us to plan for the coming world at a moment when we cannot even guess at its shape, and when nothing more is possible than an interim plan founded upon our hopes. It may, therefore, be well, in conclusion, to remind ourselves that the war which, in this context, may be said to have begun in 1935, has wholly changed the meaning of the word independence, especially when applied to small and weak states. More than ever before their separate existence is dependent upon the will of the larger industrial powers. Most countries are now potentially 'colonial' territory in the sense that they are open to the armed mastery or exploitation of the few strong states. Even if the Allies obtain a very substantial victory their peace settlement may for long rest upon the maintenance of their physical superiority. Upon this level of high politics we encounter another problem. So long as the opposed groups of nations retain their present principles the interests of Ethiopia, like those of other small states, appear to be bound up with those of the Allies and, especially, in this case, of Britain. Ethiopia needs a strong Britain, yet herself, as a weak 'independent' neighbour,

represents a possible danger to her ally's strength. Ethiopia thus antici-
pates the call which will be made upon the political and moral capacities
of the Allies. On the political side they have to deal with the problem
left unsolved after the last war and now presented in an even more
difficult form, of reconciling the self-determination of small countries
with the needs of a world system of security and economic order. Upon
the moral side they have to appreciate the claims of even small and backward communities to achieve, by the release of their own energies, the
highest possible standard of cultural and material life. It lies mainly
with Britain to tackle this problem as it presents itself in the horn of
Africa and this task will need all her political art and the most liberal
and altruistic traditions of her imperial and foreign policy.

The Colonial Empire

On 16 February Singapore surrendered

The Times 13 and 14 March 1942

1. *The need for Stocktaking and Review*

The Malayan disaster has shocked us into sudden attention to the structure of our colonial empire. Events such as we have known in the last
few weeks are rough teachers, but our survival as a great power may
depend upon our being able to learn their lesson. It is not the intention
of these articles to discuss the explicit charges made with reference to
Malaya and Singapore. Whatever explanations or even corrections may
later be made with regard to them, most people in this country have
been startled into a sudden questioning, or rather into an intuitive certainty that our colonial administration needs adjustment to the new
conditions of our world.

This is the more required since our allies are turning anxious and
critical eyes upon the empire they are helping us to defend. Total warfare has to be met by a solidarity that neither hammer-blows nor wedges
of intrigue can split. It seems unreasonable to expect a colony of which
the very status is a mark of backwardness and lack of unity to come
whole, even in defeat, through this terrible test. Yet elsewhere peasants
and workers, almost if not quite so ignorant and backward as those of
our colonies, have fought as men fight only for a cause they recognize as
their own. This forces us to ask the long-range question whether British
rule does develop that solidarity which society needs for health in peace
as well as for strength in war.

Dutch colonial experts have classified the strange composite communities which have emerged under modern imperialism as 'plural
societies'. Of these Malaya and Kenya are striking examples, but other
colonial territories have some of their characteristics. Over those countries the imperial power imposes the steel frame of its imported state
system. Relying upon its strength and in harmony with its main economic purpose, diverse groups, native or immigrant, pursue their material
ends. Outside a few points of economic interaction they can minimize

contacts with the other groups. Held secure and separate in the steel frame, they can indulge themselves in the enjoyment of their own social life and culture and the increase of their own political solidarity. They need never find their true relative positions because the government will allocate powers and define relationships, sheltering this community and discouraging that, according to its own policy. In its brief strokes this picture may be overdrawn; there are, of course, some contacts and some joint political machinery. But the main lines will stand as true.

It needs the brutal hammering of war to make us fully realize the weakness of such communities. Since we ought not now to shrink from applying this test in anticipation, let us imagine – what is not unimaginable – that Japanese transports and aircraft carriers appear outside Mombasa harbour. How would the 'plural society' of Kenya respond? The small settler community would know very well what they were fighting for. The disciplined professional African troops would show the same remarkable bravery as they did in Ethiopia. But would the Indian community, in its political and social segregation, find it possible to rally shoulder to shoulder with the Europeans and join with them in common discipline and sacrifice? Would the Kikuyu, still unsatisfied about their land and with some of the leaders of their political societies in prison, give the wholehearted co-operation that would be needed? Would the coastal Arabs, or the Kavirondo dock labourers, who not long ago rioted against the admittedly indefensible conditions in which they had to work, carry on in the face of hardship and danger?

Perhaps they would, for it can never be prophesied how human beings will react in a crisis. But even to imagine Kenya in the throes of desperate war is to set us wondering whether it is wisdom to encourage separate communities to develop on 'their own lines' upon parallels that will never meet. Can we afford the assumptions that a common citizenship is impossible and that the steel frame will be there to hold the groups in their uneasy suspension for all time? These assumptions are now abandoning us, and it seems time to take those few first practicable measures which will hold out at least a future hope of a more equalitarian society.

A revision of the time factor is needed for all aspects of our colonial policy. Some of its principles and methods were laid down in the leisurely days of the last century and the first decades of this, and into these even the last war did not break with the same mental violence as have the totalitarian revolutions. We regarded empire as part of the order of things, at once beneficent and enduring. We developed towards our backward charges a paternalism that could hardly conceive of their coming of age. We established at the top standards of administrative purity that we could not bear to see diluted by too much possibly clumsy and corrupt native participation. With our cult of 'thorough' and our belief that human institutions are not made but grow, we set ourselves to bring change by gradual development from the old order rather than through the rapid imposition of the new. Some of these were merits in their day, and have not become defects overnight. But since modern inventions and administrative methods have changed the whole tempo of human affairs, they, too, need some revision.

The exhibitions of imperial dynamism in the last years by Italy and Germany have so repelled us that we have been inclined to reject all the new techniques the age has put into their hands. Yet some of these techniques which they have used for selfish or degrading ends might equally be employed to speed our own purposes of enlightenment and political education. They have been so used elsewhere. While we have been working out careful plans by which, for example, literacy would spread in some centuries through our dependent populations, other rulers have set themselves to achieve this not, indeed, in one generation, but, by a revolutionary conception of education, for both generations at once. We might enrich our own experience and revise our ideas of time, scale, and scope in education by careful study of the measures taken in Russia, China and Turkey. The colonial peoples are quick to grasp the connexion of poverty and subjection with ignorance, and there is no service for which they ask with the same passion as they do for education.

In this sphere, as in others, some of our achievements and some of the plans we are slowly maturing are thorough and have been conceived in the truest human terms. But our Adviser on Education at the Colonial Office needs to be chief of a general staff of able men and women who would go on tour in order to collect the dispersed experience of our own and other empires, and offer the resultant stimulus and information to our governments and teachers. And since no foreign rulers can supply from above the dynamism we observe in this field elsewhere, much greater efforts should be made to evoke and to harness that which is waiting below. Above all, we should start in real earnest to lift from the colonial peoples the vast dead-weight of female ignorance and backwardness.

Most of this could be applied to other development and social service departments. Here we can show much effective work, but our new sense of the ramifying and remediable dangers of backwardness asks for new time-tables. Some ills from which colonial peoples and their soil are suffering demand to be tackled in a mood of emergency. The cost of accelerated programmes will be urged, but we may have something to learn even from our enemies about the management of capital and credit, while if the true balance-sheet between Britain and her colonies were worked out, the recent development grant of £10,000,000 a year might not appear the final figure of generosity.

II. *Capital, Labour and the Colour Bar*

In considering old principles which time may have turned from merits to defects, we must examine that of economic *laissez-faire*. British colonial administrators, reflecting and, indeed, prolonging the attitude of their kin in Britain, lavished their attention upon political develop-ment, while the more powerful economic forces were allowed their free and devastating impact upon native society. Today, behind the impres-sive set-up of chiefs, courts and councils, the economic welfare of the people often swings helplessly up and down in the tide of world markets, and may be controlled by strong and remote commercial companies responsible only to themselves.

In the days when competition was a reality and economic pioneering needed the utmost initiative and variety, there were advantages in free-dom. But a position has now been reached when great metropolitan organizations, acting at times in combination, and exercising consider-able control at once over export and import trade, can take private deci-sions in Britain which deeply affect the lives of colonial peoples. Already the West Africans have shown their resentment of this position, and if they perhaps exaggerate the degree of control thus exerted over their livelihood, the fault lies in the secrecy within which commercial policy is made and operated.

Metropolitan capital also calls from their tribal villages great masses of ignorant labourers. The Colonial Office has lately embarked upon labour legislation which may in time alleviate some of the evils of this abrupt industrialization. But we have not faced the larger issues raised by the creation of these tropical East Ends. What are the social conditions, especially in the families and the farms, of communities from which a large proportion of their young manhood is always absent? We do not know. As single, migrant labourers these men are used in some areas during their best years as low-paid and, by reason of the colour-bar, permanently unskilled workers. Meanwhile the maintenance and care of the community which provides them, and which in Britain, through wages, insurance, rates and taxation for social services, would be fully shared by industry with the state, is thrown upon distant and often impoverished tribal areas. Here is one among other colonial economic problems which calls, not for *laissez-faire*, but for urgent study and for action in which colonial authority may have to advance from its functions of providing first aid and arbitration from the side lines and play a much fuller part in the game.

We must, however, probe more deeply if we are to understand the limitations of our colonial methods and especially those fissures in the 'plural' or stratified societies which seem likely to prevent their developing into healthy communities. We must ask whether we can continue to indulge ourselves any longer in an attitude of mind which, at its worst, regards other races of men almost as if they were other species. Here, too, the war has shown us the dangers of this attitude and our last Secretary of State, Lord Moyne, thinking, doubtless, of the discrimination upon grounds of colour which we tolerate in our colonies, warned us against earning the reproach, while we blamed Hitler for his policy of *Herrenvolk*, that we were denying full equality within the empire.

The attitude, in greater or lesser degree, is deep-seated and will not easily be modified. It reinforces the caution of our constitutional policy, making us unwilling, in view of our traditional conception of the status and capacities of 'the natives', to risk experiments with more democratic and responsible forms of government.

Upon the other side the bitterness of many coloured leaders, men whom we should train and assist in every possible way, springs from incidents of personal humiliation or neglect. Governors or other officers are seldom long enough in one country or district to know or be known. Many an officer works and overworks with the utmost devotion for the peasants in his charge, while, in their clubs and in European residential quarters, he and his wife may live almost wholly insulated from the aspiring educated minority of the country. Why are the stimulating and friendly relations possible in this country between ourselves and coloured visitors and students almost wholly barred in some of our colonies? Is the answer, which has to do with official and racial prestige, sufficient to justify this numbing of personal relationships? No impossible alternative need be presented. Differences of race, colour, language and customs *are* barriers; backwardness *is* a dividing fact. But there is a level of education and of potential common interests upon which we are held back only by our prejudices from co-operation and friendship. Yet, without these, imperial rule cannot change into the working partnership which the coming age demands.

This question of racial attitudes has wider relevance. Japan's attack in the Pacific has produced a very practical revolution in race relationships. An Asiatic people has for the moment successfully challenged the ascendancy of three great white imperial Powers. Indian troops, towards whom a changed India may develop a more direct connexion, are fighting for our colonial empire; Chinese, Indonesian and Filipino soldiers, as well as American and Dutch, are all in the same battle. Will our colonies, saved from Japanese conquest by this alliance in arms, revert to the same status of imperial possessions with all their links gathered exclusively to Whitehall? Yet, if the alliance of arms is to develop into a Far Eastern co-operation for defence and development, what an energetic exercise in racial understanding with the Asiatic Powers, including Russia, must be built up almost from nothing in the next few years!

The shock of defeat and loss in the Far East has shaken our minds open to the use of an opportunity for adjustment which was denied to France. We must not seek relief from the painful stocktaking which our dangers demand by heaping blame upon local agents for immediate disasters. Our questioning should be wider and deeper than this. It need not, however, be carried out in a mood of humiliation. In the colonial as in other spheres of our national life our conservatism is the almost inevitable consequence of successful achievement in the conditions of the past. Much that is good can still be conserved.

Our colonial empire is too varied and gives too much play to initiative, native and British, to be a suitable subject for complete generalizations, and there is no statement in this article that could not be challenged from some part of the empire. In much of Africa our services have been vital and progressive. In the West Indies, after long blindness, we have lately made a new start. All over the empire there are exceptional officers who chafe at the obstacles in their way and sometimes break through them. A reforming spirit, to which Lord Hailey has done much to give substance, has lately appeared in this country and needs reinforcement from the new intolerance of official delay and privileged incompetence which the present crisis has aroused within Britain.

Nor should our stocktaking be made in a spirit of dissociation from our own colonial services. In their defects and their virtues they are extensions of our society. For all crown colonies, moreover, the final responsibility still remains in this country. The degree of interest and knowledge here will decide the quality of the men who devote themselves to the colonies, whether as Secretaries of State or as junior cadets in the Service. No bureaucracy can work effectively unless it is braced by interest, study and criticism. Until this comes more effectively from the governed, it must be supplied from Britain through a Parliament better informed than hitherto to carry out this responsibility, or else remote colonial administration must flag into a stale routine.

Nothing can make up for the misery and loss suffered in the territories Japan has conquered. It would, however, be some compensation if they stirred us to read those passages in the writing on the wall which refer to our colonial empire, and which warn us to infuse a new energy into its administration and to achieve a new and more intimate and generous relationship with its peoples.

The Times Leader 14 March 1942

THE COLONIAL FUTURE

The lessons of Malaya are many and are not all to be learned or understood in a period of weeks or months. But some of them are so conspicuous and so pressing that there is no excuse for ignoring them; and among these are its lessons in the sphere of colonial government, which are discussed by Miss Margery Perham in two articles appearing in these columns yesterday and today. By common consent the old order in colonial government has been exposed to a searching challenge. It has performed great services in the past, and has constituted a remarkable stage in the expansion of European civilization all over the world. Much in it was good and some still remains good. But new ideas have broken in rudely upon it, and have exposed the need for a radical revision of many traditional notions and practices. What has been destroyed will not be rebuilt in its former shape; what still stands will undergo profound and far-reaching changes. The future lines of colonial policy are being struck out now, in the furnace of war; and the form which they take will probably determine the future development of the colonial territories for many years to come.

Empire of the old pattern was founded and maintained by superiority of technical skill and monopoly of armed power vested in a colonizing and ruling race. These conditions are rapidly disappearing. Nothing can in the long run prevent the colonial peoples from acquiring the arts of their masters. They learn to use machinery in mine or farm; they learn

R

to understand and desire the new standards of living with which they are brought into contact; they are recruited and armed by their rulers with weapons requiring, as time goes on, more and more skill in the user, to fight in defence of their homeland and sometimes beyond it. They increasingly demand education as a means to economic proficiency and political advancement. It stands to the credit of British colonial government that it has long recognized the emancipation of the ruled as an ultimate goal, and responsibility for their welfare and development as an overriding obligation. But the application of these ideals has too often been piecemeal, intermittent and faltering; and their incompatibility with the survival of the old system and the old spirit, and with the interests for which that system and that spirit stood, has never been squarely faced.

The world pattern of economic organization which inspired the old colonial order is also changing. The exploitation of untapped sources of raw materials no longer provides easy and certain profits to the colonizing power. Except in a few special areas, the colonies are probably now more important as markets than as sources of supply. It is as markets that they will make their major contribution to the rebuilding of world trade. Colonial markets will automatically expand with a rising standard of living among native populations; and this in turn will be promoted by the development of better and more varied cultivation, by the organization on co-operative lines of the marketing of native crops, and by the establishment of simple industries, beginning perhaps with the processing of local products. Educational and administrative reforms will not go far unless they are given this sound economic basis. *Laissez-faire* rendered valuable service in its day and generation. But it has left behind it in colonial territories a legacy of monopoly exploitation, of whole communities disrupted by the demand for male labour, and of economic organization incompatible with native ways of life and society. To reconstruct the economic as well as the social and political life of colonial territories and to bring them into a healthy relation with the more advanced countries is a task which demands careful and deliberate planning.

The British colonial services, as Miss Perham observes in her second article, reflect the virtues and defects of the nation to which they belong; and some at least of the aspersions to which they have been subjected should perhaps have fallen on other heads. Still more trenchant criticism has been heard recently of the non-official British residents, business men and others, who do so much to determine the character of a colonial society. It is indeed notorious that life in tropical or sub-tropical lands, remote from the restraining discipline of an enlightened public opinion, has sometimes bred in the resident white community habits of self-indulgence and irresponsibility which militated against the development of a vigorous and progressive colonial policy. But it must in fairness be said that the 'stratified' societies which are the characteristic product of European tropical colonies reflect a corresponding stratification of society in Europe at the time when the foundations of the imperial system were laid. Even in detail, the marked differences discernible between, say, British, French, Dutch and German colonies before 1914 sprang from differences in the spirit, tradition and organization of government and society at home; it is certain that in this respect the integrity, humanity and progressiveness of British administration have nothing to fear from comparison.

The defect of the British colonial system, and the essence of the challenge which it has to meet, is that it has been too long and too deeply rooted in the traditions of a bygone age, and that it has retained too much of that 'stratified' spirit of inequality and discrimination, whose last strongholds are now being rapidly attacked and eliminated in our contemporary society. To break down the barriers – economic, political and psychological – which still sharply divide colonial communities is a task calling for both intense determination and infinite patience. Misguided conceptions of racial prestige and narrow and obsolete interpretations of economic interest are grave obstacles. But they must be surmounted if democracy is to have any meaning or appeal for the colonial peoples. The price of failure is the perpetuation of those 'plural' societies whose fissiparous tendencies and inherent weaknesses, luridly revealed by the Japanese assault, make them unfit for survival in the modern world.

America and the Empire

The Times 20 and 21 November 1942

1. Dangers of Misunderstanding

The debate with America about the future of imperialism continues. Mr Churchill – in fact if not in form – answered Mr Willkie's broadcast. Mr Willkie has found his answer shocking, and has asked whether the Pacific dependencies are to revert to their previous status 'under the governmental custody of some one nation', or become 'wards of the United Nations'. It is unlikely that any satisfactory reply can be given until we in this country understand the strength and character of American feeling on this subject. Mr Willkie's speech has had its critics in his own country. But it was no isolated explosion: it came as the climax to a large volume of American questioning and criticism, and as this arises from habits of thought long and deeply rooted in American minds the climax is not likely to be the finale.

It is unfortunate that Mr Willkie's original broadcast was hardly anywhere reported in full. Studied as a whole, his address was one of striking vigour and colour, keyed to the tune of the times as only the best American speeches seem to be. He came to the microphone fresh from a flight of 31,000 miles – 160 hours' flying, with 30 days on the ground. He spoke to 'hundreds and hundreds of people in the world', to 'residents of Belem or Brazil, to one toting his burden on his head in Nigeria, to the Prime Minister or King of Egypt, to the veiled woman of ancient Baghdad, to a Shah or the weaver of carpets in legendary Persia, to strong-limbed, resolute factory workers of Russia, or to the Chinese soldier at the front'. Bestriding the world like a philanthropic Colossus, he seemed to link the common man in the East to the common man of America in an immediate and exciting contact.

While Mr Willkie distinguished between the Empire and the Commonwealth and recognized unselfish British efforts to transform the first of these into the second, yet the general picture which the speech must leave on the mind of the world – and it will have had an exceptionally wide circulation – is of America drawing herself aside from the contamination of an imperialism of which Britain is the main exponent. It would be an injustice, as well as a delusion, to discount the speech as merely the latest form of the old act of twisting the lion's tail to win domestic applause. Whatever its original motives, once words like these have been spoken, the situation is no longer the same. Moreover, Mr Willkie was expressing, in no immoderate form, an attitude of the American mind which is part of America's political inheritance.

It was not to be expected that Americans whose ancestors broke away from the British empire in 1776 should march to its direct defence in 1942 without asking themselves and us uncomfortable questions. Nations shape their character by pressure against something external, and that something is often the character of another nation. America was born out of negation of the British empire; her democracy has been bred in the tradition of anti-imperialism. When Americans wake up to find their soldiers beside ours in India and Africa, and marshalled, it may be, for the recovery of Burma and Malaya, they have to put their minds suddenly into reverse; and this jarring process has been freely reflected in their Press during the last nine months.

Americans themselves can, for obvious reasons, put up the most effective reply to any ill-informed criticism of our empire. They have been doing so vigorously. But even the most friendly papers and journalists, though they combat extreme opinion and throw light on far places and complex problems, still speak from the common substratum of American anti-imperialism. At the time of the Japanese invasions almost the whole Press emphasized the liberal character of the Philippine Government, which Mr Roosevelt in a recent broadcast held up as the pattern for training for ultimate independence, and pointed to the strong contrast they found in Burma and Malaya. To quote a moderate comment:

This is the difference between even a benevolent overlordship which treats 'natives' kindly but as children, and our idealism which sought to enable them to grow adult and self-reliant.

The long-established distrust of British policy in India, shaken by the Cripps mission, began to form again when Americans, quick-witted and practical people as they are, had reason to suspect that the British were going to 'stand pat' on the 'right' policy even though it clearly would not work. They became increasingly uneasy at being involved, by the presence of their soldiers in India and in the apparently acquiescent silence of their government in a policy which they felt was alienating from them, not merely India, but – even more important in their eyes – the Asiatic giant of the future, China. Miss Pearl Buck pointed to the incalculable danger of the eastern world drawing together against Western imperialism and of America finding herself upon the wrong side.

As regards the British empire, American attention has passed somewhat lightly over the Caribbean – where co-operation is already a fact – and across Africa – though current events may change this – to fasten upon the immensely larger problems of the Far East. The magazine *Fortune*, one of Mr Henry Luce's group of journals, began a few months ago to issue a series of 'reports' on future American policy. The first of these deals with relations with Britain. It affirms that the British predominance of the past is now the heritage of America, but urges the absolute necessity of Anglo-American co-operation and American recognition of the great rôle Britain has played and should still play. The second deals with the Far East on the assumption that 'at the end of this war the function of British imperialism in the Orient will have been fulfilled', and works out in detail a system by which, after the Western powers have surrendered 'all their exclusive rights and preferential positions in Asia', they should co-operate with America and China in commissions which will promote the economic development and self-government of the reconquered territories.

Will America, we must ask, act upon these ideas? Or will she stay out in the world after the war? She came gradually to the realization that she is potentially the strongest Power in the world, but she has to decide rather suddenly whether she means to use that power – and how. The riddle of her recent elections is not easy reading: but we know what we want to read into them – an America which believes like Mr Willkie, 'that there are no distant points in the world'. If America stays out in the world she needs a world-policy and that policy is on the anvil now. It is being hammered out as much by military acts as by words, but words have their part, and to a question which presents, perhaps, the gravest of all dangers to Anglo-American friendship, a considered answer should be made.

II. *The Need for Definition*

The previous article will have failed in its purpose if it arouses only an attitude of protest and resentment towards American criticism. Its object was to point out the danger of America's moving into a position in which she not only draws away from us but also outflanks us in liberalism. In recent months there have been several signs of such outflanking, due as much to our own inaction as to American movement.

And now Mr Willkie has talked to the leading men in Turkey, Egypt, Iraq, Iran and China and found them 'in substantial agreement as to the necessity of abolishing imperialism'. He was left 'amazed to discover how keenly the world is aware of the fact that we do not seek anywhere in any region to impose our rule on others or to exact special privileges'.

No responsible quarter in America desires a rift with us on this question. Like us, Americans see the need for an alliance in which their solid continental strength will find its complement in our diffused power and influence. But public opinion there is active, and on this question, as we have seen, has a deep tradition which, latent though it generally is, no government could for long ignore when it finds expression. Mr Churchill's declaration of tenacity may represent a mood of justifiable self-confidence but it does not answer American doubts. Mr Morrison points to our self-restraint in Ethiopia. But Ethiopia, since the Emperor's return, has been allowed to fall into complete obscurity, and forms too slender a basis for generalization. An answer must be framed broad enough to meet the doubts and questions that are being raised.

This answer should touch the past, the present and the future. Study of the past would lead to the common admission that, though empires may develop varying margins of altruism, the energy of national self-interest is always the biggest factor in their making. The same imperial impetus which lay in part behind the establishment of the thirteen colonies continued to radiate all over the world from this congested island. It was inherent in the American colonists themselves, though they were able, by the munificent accident of geography, to satisfy their virile appetite within a single lightly peopled continent. Not until almost this century did Americans need to reach beyond, and American doubts of this necessity made their hold upon the far Philippines a light and so a liberal one.

In this expansion the rights and interests of Red Indians were considered as little as those of Australian aborigines. Force, bloodshed and insurrection marked the subjection of the Filipinos as it did that of the Maori or Matabele. In the heyday of nineteenth-century empire-making the most sustained moral protest against its abuses came from the British humanitarian movement which softened the rough business of subjugation and grafted trusteeship on to exploitation. If history can be used not to select points for a political brief but as truth which may correct the complacencies of nations and confirm their best traditions, then its study is the essential introduction to such a discussion as this.

When we turn to the British empire of the present we face a great difficulty. It is probable that the large majority of our people when they suddenly come across American criticism in their newspapers are genuinely puzzled, and ask themselves, 'What is the truth of this? Is there something in what the Americans say?' They could be told of the immense and beneficial task being carried out by some 40 governments among 65,000,000 people; of how deeply the colonies are interlocked with Great Britain in long-established cultural, political and economic relationships, and even, in many parts, by treaties and by mutual affections and loyalties. It could be said that the empire is not static, that every week here or there some forward movement happens, and that, stimulated from the centre, its pace has greatly quickened in the last few years.

It requires both intelligence and industry to master this long lesson; and if, as we have lately realized, we have failed to teach it to our own people, how in these war-crowded days can we hope to present it to America as well? Yet, for all its difficulties, the double task must be attempted. The Americans have, indeed, begun it. Upon the plane of scholarship, where all good teaching must find its source, they have done fine service. A very well-informed and appreciative analysis of our African administration has recently appeared entitled *The Atlantic Charter and Africa from an American standpoint*. On the popular plane, Negley Farson's African best-seller, *Behind God's Back*, is a vivid tribute to our Colonial Service.

The Americans are, however, forward-looking people and we must do more than explain that, as empires go, ours is doing meritorious work. While few of them expect us to walk out of the colonies tomorrow, many feel strongly, if somewhat vaguely, that the idea of 'colonial possessions' is obsolete and dangerous. They want us to convince them that we are liquidating this idea from above by a readiness for international co-operation and from below by strenuous education in self-government. It is not enough for those of us who move in government or colonial circles to convince ourselves in our own undertones that this is exactly what we are doing. Clarity and urgency are needed. For all the good work being done by the Colonial Services and the Colonial Office, a service and a department are not constituted to make, still less to proclaim, policy. Colonial policy is lost in its own complexity; in constitutional machinery admitted for years to be inadequate; in the indifference and delays of politicians; in fear to experiment; in distrust of the governed, and in an economy – to give a concrete example – which has chosen this time to suppress the one annual publication which could give the world a brief general picture of the colonial empire.

Is it too much to hope that a voice might be heard from this country with the ring of leadership proclaiming a clear plan of advance that would catch the imagination of the common man in Britain and in the colonies and give them the sense of working together to achieve it? There are difficulties and risks in proclaiming plans. But today there are greater difficulties and risks in not proclaiming them. This language would be understood in America and help to win that full co-operation without which it is difficult to foresee the re-establishment of the lost territories or the future well-being of Empire or Commonwealth. These words will be called defeatism by some. It is rather realism to recognize the relative reduction in our world position, which is something quite different from an absolute decline. Our position will be stronger if we shift our stance from unsound planks to firm ones.

The Americans, candid friends themselves, do not expect us to accept all their criticisms or to believe – we have evidence to the contrary here – that they have solved all their own difficult race problems. But, taken broadly and at best, the American challenge to us to hasten the work of de-imperializing the empire can lead only to good. The solution will be neither upon their ground nor ours, but on some common ground we must both reach. We have to continue in the colonial field the present process of 'mixing-up'. We bring our sense of political values, standards of humane and expert colonial administration, some beginnings in the control of commercial interests. Those who have been in America and seen her marvellous adaptability and economic vigour, have met the men who administer her world-wide philanthropic trusts, or have investigated her administration in the Pacific, will know how much America could contribute to the mixture.

The Times Leader 21 November 1942

A COLONIAL DEBATE

Reasons might easily be found to discount Mr Willkie's recent utterances on the British colonial empire. They were the sequel of a whirlwind world tour which offered little occasion for study of colonial questions on the spot; and they were made at a time when a forthright assertion of the speaker's standpoint as a leader of advanced American opinion may have seemed politically remunerative. But it would be a mistake to minimize on these or other grounds the importance of Mr Willkie's remarks. The fact that they have a popular appeal to an American audience is significant by itself. So cautious and friendly an observer as Mr Winant warned us some time ago that there was, between the two countries, 'a greater divergence of viewpoint on British colonial policy than on any other subject'. Moreover, Mr Willkie has stood out courageously in the ranks of the Republican Party as the champion of full American participation in the risks and responsibilities of the post-war world; and this alone would enhance his claim to a hearing on the shape of the world in which these responsibilities would be assumed. A certain correlation in this respect of right and obligation might profitably be observed on both sides of the Atlantic. People in Great Britain – and they are the vast majority – who look to a future in which the United States will be actively concerned to promote security and well-being beyond its own borders must recognize that Americans will in return claim full consideration for their opinions, however far these may diverge from our own, about the conditions in which this task is to be performed. Conversely it should be kept in mind in both countries that international policies, however attractive in principle, rarely work in practice unless those who advocate them accept a corresponding obligation to face the hazards and to shoulder some part of the burden of carrying them out.

Discussion across the Atlantic about the British colonial empire, carried on with mutual goodwill and an open mind on both sides, can do nothing but good; and two articles on this page by Miss Perham yesterday and today have dealt with some of the issues involved. Nobody should forget that the debate is charged with emotion as well as fortified by argument. It has, for example, puzzled some people in this country that Americans should proclaim without cavil their intention to re-establish the integrity of the French colonial empire, while apparently regarding the integrity of the British empire as an inadmissible war aim. In part, the issue is affected by the emotional colour of words. For American as well as for Russian and Chinese ears the words 'empire' and 'imperial' have distasteful historical associations which make them taboo. Nor do Americans share the British love of dignified, but obsolete, form and phrase. When the Prime Minister referred to Malta the other day as a 'jewel in the British Crown', he was indulging in a flight of traditional rhetoric which, though certainly devoid of any political connotation whatever, bewildered some American readers. This is not, however, the whole truth. The ceremonial language associated with the British monarchy does not grate on American ears because Americans have come to understand and appreciate the monarchy as an integral part of British democratic institutions. High-sounding phrases about the colonial empire have, on the other hand, caused suspicion and resentment because they appeared to reflect a survival, not merely of traditional forms, but of antiquated attitudes – an inclination to think of 'British possessions' in terms of property rights vested in a particular owner and denied to the rest of the world. Mr Willkie has dwelt on the need for Great Britain to understand the American point of view on this question. There is equal need that the British point of view should be understood by Americans; and this is the more difficult in that British Government circles are apt to speak in what Miss Perham calls 'our own undertones' and have been lamentably backward in formulating opinions and policies on this vital question.

The cardinal quality of the British empire in the past half-century has been its constantly changing and developing character. Americans may be forgiven the half-conscious assumption that the 'British Empire' of today is the same institution with which they parted company, in discouraging circumstances, in 1776. But it is less excusable when British spokesmen appear to nourish or encourage the same belief. To deprecate the 'liquidation' of the British empire is surely a false approach. The pride and achievement of the modern British empire are that it has become in a certain sense a self-liquidating concern, dissolving itself by an orderly process into a commonwealth of peoples united by a common ideal of partnership in freedom. British colonial policy, as conceived by the majority of British people today both in Great Britain and in the Dominions, can only be a continuation of this process. Its aims can be defined in terms not of 'have and hold', but of the Atlantic Charter and the 'four freedoms'. Its methods may sometimes have been mistaken. The difficulties and dangers of accelerating the process may sometimes have been exaggerated in Whitehall or Westminster as much as they have been underestimated elsewhere. But Great Britain has never lacked a devoted body of colonial administrators, of anthropologists and other specialists in the study of colonial conditions, and of ardent pioneers of colonial reform and of the welfare of native peoples. That the execution of policy has often lagged behind its highest aims, and that vested interests or racial prejudices have hampered the realization of professed ideals, are as true in this as in other fields of government. But the reinforcement of American interest in colonial problems, so freely displayed in the past through the generosity of American philanthropic foundations, will be an encouragement to all in this country who are seeking to grasp the opportunities that the war has offered for a fresh and rapid advance towards wider political freedom and enhanced economic well-being for the colonial peoples.

In his speech this week Mr Willkie referred to the 'specific and difficult example' of the Malayan peninsula and neighbouring islands. There is no reason whatever to shirk an issue which is bound to arise in concrete and urgent form as soon as the tide of battle turns in the Pacific. Two main facts govern the situation. In the first place it would be fanciful to believe that a mere restoration of the *status quo* of 1941 in the Pacific is practicable or even desirable. So great a cataclysm will not pass over the vast territories in the Far East formerly under British, French or Netherlands rule without leaving its mark. Apart from other considerations, the joint character of the military action by which the aggressor will be expelled from these regions determines that the future settlement must also be a matter of joint concern. Secondly, positive measures will be required. Abdication is not a policy. In none of these countries would the mere withdrawal, or non-restoration, of the former authority by itself provide a solution or guarantee the maintenance of security, political order and freedom, and economic well-being. Even in the Philippines, with their relatively high degree of internal unity and advanced civilization, Americans found themselves thwarted in their desire to hasten the moment when they could divest themselves of responsibility. Interest and responsibility go together; and the future organization and progress towards freedom of the colonial territories in the Far East depend in part on the nature of the interest which the American people take in this progress and the extent of the responsibilities which they are prepared to assume in order to further it.

Once agreement is reached on these two fundamental points – the recognition of joint concern in the settlement of these territories and the recognition of the need for a positive policy involving political responsibilities – then there is ample room for debate, initially perhaps between Great Britain and the United States, and eventually among all the United Nations principally concerned. This debate in its more detailed phases can hardly be conducted from political platforms or in the columns of the Press. But in the forms which it has already assumed it is a revelation of the keen and widespread public interest in these vital questions and a call for fresh and unconventional thinking by governments to meet problems which are both new and pressing.

From Power to Service

Talk in the B.B.C. Home Service reprinted in *The Listener* 22 April 1943

One day, just before the war, I found myself sitting on the side of a steep hill. I was in a very remote part of tropical Africa. I could see a village below me, with its little round huts of sticks and mud, with grass roofs, dark inside, full perhaps of smoke and vermin and stinking of goats. I could see a line of women. They were naked, except for some leaves round their waists; they were bringing great pitchers of water on their heads from a well about half a mile away. Some others were pounding grain in big wooden bowls, a most exhausting business. They had babies slung on their backs in goatskins, and the babies' eyes were all clotted with flies. Just underneath me a little boy stood on a platform, scaring birds off a little patch of grain. But he had not been able to scare the elephants who had come the night before and trampled down half the crop. Close to me some other boys were herding cattle, very skinny-looking beasts they were. The children sounded happy enough, yet they had the reedy limbs and football-stomachs that go with semi-starvation. And even from where I was sitting, I could see that some had chronic red sores on their legs. I had been seeing this sort of thing for years, but somehow that day it just hit me: the utter poverty of these people, their miserable tools for tackling life. Their productive capacity, their minds, their spiritual powers, all were half asleep. They had been like this, I suppose, for hundreds, perhaps thousands of years. And I wondered what would happen to them, how soon the influences, the new social services that are breaking into this backwardness in other and less isolated parts of Africa, would come to them. These people had not the least idea that their lives were now linked with those of another people living four thousand miles away, or that when and how they became members of the civilized world depended very largely on how far those other distant people had the knowledge and the will to help them.

Well, how much knowledge and will have we? I could answer that question better if I could look into your minds when I say 'British Colonial Empire'. For your automatic reaction to those three words deeply affects the future of millions of people. Probably most people do not get any very positive reaction at all. The most definite views, I think, come at the opposite extremes. In some of us, the words 'Empire' and 'Colonies' raise a vague sense of pride, and the picture of a map with a lot of very pleasing pink on it. In others at the other extreme the words make us feel ashamed; we see the whole story of the empire as one of bloodshed and oppression and capitalist exploitation. I think that people who hold either of these extreme views do not generally study the facts. After all the facts are people – 60,000,000 of them – and it always seems to me equally, shall I say, impertinent, to shout, 'We possess them and we're darned well going to go on possessing them' as to say 'We object to colonies on principle. Cut them adrift. Give them up'. And I must say, I think of the two, the anti-imperial critics are more useful. They do at least keep us on the alert. They remind us that there has been some exploitation and oppression, that there are mistakes being made even today. We have heard a good deal lately about the achievements of empire. There have been great achievements, and also many important reforms in the last few years. But that is not what I'm going to talk about now. I would rather ask: 'Isn't there something in what our American critics say – that empire is not something to take for granted, but something abnormal, terribly difficult to run? How could it be otherwise? Here are we, 45,000,000 busy, self-absorbed, rather ill-informed people, trying to settle their destiny for 60,000,000 other people scattered all over the world. I should sometimes like to hear a speech in which we were given a list not of our achievements but of our mistakes. And a list of our biggest problems – for example, the great conflict between the British principle of racial equality and the colour-bar, which is coming to a head, and very soon too I think, in Africa. And here's another: the circle of disease, poverty and ignorance, their own ancient circle, that we have got to help them to break, not slowly, not in three hundred years, but in the shortest time in which modern science and economics can break it.

But why do we have to go on doing the helping? Why not relinquish some of our lion's share? How? By internationalizing them? I'm all for co-operation, even supervision, applied to all empires, but – international administration? It's asking these people to take a pretty risky leap in the dark. And one that most of them, I think, would regard as a step back, not forward. Don't forget that the relationsip between a ruling nation and a colony is, or can be, a rich and intimate thing. Backward peoples need, and take, a great deal from their rulers: our social conventions, our laws, language, literature. Africans, those on the West Coast, quote

Shakespeare and Burke in their speeches; they talk of their historic right of habeas corpus and the freedom of the Press. Not easy to wrench all this away, replace it with a sort of Esperanto of culture as well as language. But co-operation is another matter: the more the better. There's much, I think, that we can learn, are learning indeed, from the Americans. The Dutch can teach us a lot about colonial economics, the French about liberal race-relations. Then there's that great empire of the Russians in Asia, a vast experiment in civilization; I wish we knew a little more about it. And there are things that we British can very confidently add to the pool.

But, you may say, there's another alternative to empire. One the Americans are pressing upon us: self-government. That is very true. We have never forgotten it since the Americans first brought it to our notice in 1776. It's deep, I think, in the whole instinct of all we do. Perhaps too deep. Perhaps we ought to bring it out much more into the open, discuss and plan and experiment. Of course, I know that governments are growing and changing all over the empire every year, every month even. Ceylon and Jamaica are not so far now from full self-government, and the rest are strung out at different points in the race. That's all right, but in these days it is not enough to *do* things. We have also to explain that we are doing them.

At the same time, we must not forget that political backwardness is a real thing. When you give a slice of the earth's surface a name, you don't make a nation. Take a motor-car in, shall we say, Nigeria, and drive straight north from Lagos, the capital. What would you see? First, a modern city. Among the crowds, African bank-clerks, mechanics, African doctors, town councillors, newspaper-editors, bishops. Then, farther north, country towns with a few more African clerks and merchants; then villages with intelligent but illiterate cocoa-farmers. Then very poor peasants, living on their own crops and earning perhaps a few pounds a year. People who don't know or care about Lagos, one tribe after another, each talking a different language, building a different sort of hut, wearing different clothes or skins or it may be a string of beads: pagan people living absolutely naked, on the hills, or in the forests. Then farther north – four hundred miles now – something quite different: another race, another religion and culture: Moslem people with mosques and walled cities and flowing robes. People who do not feel, never have felt, any common nationality with those naked pagans, they were raiding and enslaving them not so long ago, still less with the Christians in the schools and churches of Lagos. What sort of self-government is going to fit all these different people, this utterly uneven development?

We imposed unified government from above. A capital, government departments, the whole centralized European state system. Now we are having to work from the bottom up, turning clans into district councils and tribes into county councils, helping them to group and to federate. We are training their loyalties, not only upwards to us but outwards into a network of ties with neighbours that they were fighting yesterday, encouraging leaders with something more than a tribal patriotism. There are such leaders already, of course, and we need more of them. But leaders (especially the young men) want self-government tomorrow. They can't wait. They won't recognize the backwardness, the disunity, of the vast majority of their people. I have often argued with them. They listen to me with their heads, but I know that in their hearts they resent their dependence on foreign rulers, however well-intentioned we may be. That's human and young, but it's none the less a problem. It's an intensely difficult job we have taken on to transform our autocratic power gradually into self-government. We have learned much about that in India. Couldn't we, in the colonies at least, carry through this difficult change-over without friction and misunderstanding and even bloodshed? We could. But it will take all our – all your – sympathy and knowledge to do it.

Then there is something else; something it has taken us about a century to learn in Britain. Political freedom is a very hollow prize if alongside it you have economic chaos or economic subjection or economic oligarchy. I think we are mostly agreed here that after the war we have got to have more state control and more planning. How much more in the colonies! There people are much more helpless than ourselves, much less organized. I have seen how great European mining and plantation companies have sprung up in the bush almost overnight and sucked thousands of simple tribesmen into their labour lines. Of course we want this capital and development in the colonies; we want much more of it. But we have got to learn how to control it in the interests of people who cannot yet say, or cannot even know, what it is going to do to them.

What does all this add up to? I think that we have still got a job to do in the colonies. Whatever they become some day, for a good many years, they are going to need help and help that only we can give them. But help in a new spirit. I think we ought to face the fact that our power is not what it was. Great nations have lately come forward into world affairs: some of them are enemies who are covetous, some of them are friends who are critical. We have got to reckon with both as well as with the colonial peoples themselves because they are reaching forward for more political rights. I assure you it is no cant phrase but plain realism to say that we have to shift the basis of our empire still more from power to service, change it from a distant, half-forgotten affair that we leave to professionals, to officials. Make it much more a direct contact between them and us – between all the branches of their community life and ours. Do you realize that they want almost everything that we have to give, if we can give it in the right spirit? Parliamentary and local government, trade unions, universities, rural colleges, co-operative systems, penal reform, ideas about architecture, or midwifery, or football. They want to know what *we* have and use it for their own needs, in their own way. Now you cannot leave all this to officials, not even to the best officials, not even to ours, not to the Colonial Secretary himself, not to Parliament. You cannot, because unless we take an interest, unless we let the colonies share in that new life that we can feel running through this country under the iron surface of war, like a river under the ice, well – our colonial empire will go stale and dead.

And yet, how are ordinary men and women going to understand all about this widespread, ever-changing empire? It is a very real difficulty and I am not going to give you some easy answer. There are a dozen ways of tackling it. I am just going to suggest one. Don't think that people can be made interested in other people by lessons and books or by all the speeches in the world. They have got to see each other, speak, shake hands. Obviously in this case it is not easy. But is it impossible? Let us decide – and if we really wanted to we could do it – to have after the war a Colonial Fortnight, or a month if you like. We will invite delegations from all the colonies to visit us, chiefs and educated men and women; some who can talk English and some who cannot – our guests. They shall split up and visit the provinces, go into big towns, small towns and little country places. Don't you think that that might help us to realize that the empire is not a list of names of places or crops or statistics but that it is made up of persons? And that in the next ten or twenty years there is a constructive absorbing job that we can do for them or, better still, with them?

S

General Smuts on the Colonial Future

Letter to *The Times* 7 December 1943

On 25 November 1943 General Smuts addressed a gathering of Members of Parliament of both Houses arranged by the United Kingdom branch of the Empire Parliamentary Association. The title of this talk was 'Thoughts on the New World'.

Sir, – In his bold and impressive speech of 25 November General Smuts said many new and wise things about the empire. Yet, in these frank passages he seemed to leave one or two unanswered questions.

1. Why should the dualism between the decentralization of the Commonwealth and the centralization of the colonies cause 'grave thought' or be unsafe? It arises from the strongest of reasons, that the Dominions have reached political maturity and the colonies have not. Nor is it, as he seemed to suggest, a static division. The colonies are all moving towards the line of division; two, at least, are very near to it. But until the moment for crossing it comes, the imperial government is obliged by historic obligations, and qualified by long experience, to make up in varying measure for the immaturity or disunity of the dependent peoples. The representation of the Dominions upon regional advisory councils is so desirable as to be beyond discussion almost as soon as it is mentioned. But it cannot mean a division in the actual administrative responsibility of the British Government, and it is worth pointing out, when London centralization is under fire, that the connexion with the colonies is daily broadening out from a canal through which trickled a narrow stream of official and commercial communication to a wide stream of contact between the colonial people and our own, now reawakened to their imperial duties. Improvements in communications moreover, make this London centralization – which in practice means wide decentralization to officials and unofficials on the spot – increasingly rapid, full and reciprocal. A reformed Colonial Office and the promise of a more continuous Colonial Secretary contribute to a picture of imperial control which is being adapted to new and changing tasks.

2. General Smuts says that British people are restive under our

centralization. This must refer to those few thousands who in Kenya and Northern Rhodesia have settled among the African millions. The suggestion cannot be that the power of ruling those millions should be handed over to these minorities, important and enterprising though they are: this course has, indeed, been renounced, after thorough consideration, by this country. No regional grouping could mask this underlying racial situation: the addition of purely African to 'mixed' territories would only turn the white groups into still smaller minorities. If not the imperial government, then who is to fill the political vacuum?

3. The General urged that, upon grounds of efficiency and economy, the time has come 'to tidy up the show', 'to do away with units which have simply arisen as an accident by historic haphazard'. These reasons are good for grouping at the highest level of administration, but it must be hoped that this does not mean any suppression, as active parts of a large whole, of those states and tribes with which we have treaties or long-cherished understandings, and whose sense of community makes the only basis upon which to build modern local or provincial government. A premature ironing-out under a regional steamroller of the vitality and rich variety of native groups might fatally interrupt their education in self-government.

4. The speech does a great service by raising in the most serious terms the race and colour problem. These words will have been read eagerly in the vain hope that they were leading to some principle upon which we should seek to solve this problem. Few here would presume to advise South Africans how to deal with their formidable problems. We know that it has been relatively easy for us to proclaim the principle of racial equality as against the colour-bar. But we have not regarded it easy to apply as 'a general formula'. Equality is a fact for some of our colonial people, for others it is a test for present policy and a hope for the future and all the time, in spite of our many failures, an encouragement under which, in West Africa and other parts, some of them have risen to high leadership and to great economic skill and prosperity. This is the main reason why they cling to government from London. Does this mean there must be a clash of policies in Africa? Will not General Smuts, out of his unrivalled and authoritative experience of this complex colour problem, give us some positive lead that he would wish to see followed throughout Africa, however far ahead his goal may be?

Yours faithfully, MARGERY PERHAM

African Facts and American Criticisms

Foreign Affairs Vol. 22 No. 3. April 1944

I

People who live in a city get a wholly different impression of it from strangers who look at it from a neighbouring hill. The two parties would find difficulty, if they could conduct a discussion by telephone, in coming to any sound conclusions about its architecture or layout. Much the same is true of an institution. It seems desirable, therefore, before discussing any part of that most controversial of institutions, the British colonial empire (as distinct from the dominions), to consider frankly the American and British views of it, in the hope that the distance which separates them may at least be measured, and even, possibly, narrowed.

The American view which reaches us through war's interruptions and by way of our shrunken newspapers may be put in the following brief and therefore blunt terms: 'The British are guilty of a sin called Empire. They committed it against the American people until these broke clear of British control to become a nation. The Americans are innocent of any such a guilt. They thus are in a moral position to condemn Britain as they watch her continuing in her way of sin against other people. The situation is the more distressing to Americans as they are being asked, in this war, to defend and support the British empire.'

Now let us move over to the British angle of vision: 'The American colonists were, in the main, an extension of the British people. They enjoyed a liberty then unknown to colonists of other empires. When a British government foolishly tried to restrict this liberty, the Americans, having reached a situation in which they could dispense with British protection, very rightly asserted their independence. The same expansive energy continued to carry both peoples forward. The Americans, finding a large and undeveloped continent at their doors, drove across it, and, indeed, beyond it. The British, confined to a small island, burst out into large and undeveloped regions overseas. Neither nation allowed the rights or interests of foreign states or of the native inhabitants to stand in the way of their main purpose. The British do not admit, in this context, any fundamental moral difference in the records and character of the two peoples.'

All this has to do with past history. But Britain also makes a claim regarding the present and future of her empire. This, in so far as it refers to one continent, forms the subject of the present article.

II

Tropical Africa is appropriately chosen to illustrate Britain's position. Of the three main groups of Britain's colonial territories, it is, for obvious strategical and geographical reasons, the one which is likely to emerge from this transforming war with the least change, and to continue the longest thereafter with a minimum of change.

There is one internal reason for this which must be discussed at the start, as it takes us to the heart of the British misunderstanding with America. It is the backwardness of tropical Africa. Critics treat statements of the fact of backwardness with suspicion, on the ground that the British either exaggerate it in words or, still worse, prolong it by policy. Many of us in Britain have shared this view and consequent impatience in some measure. But the word 'measure' is all-important. When we in Britain hear it said that the African colonies should be emancipated today or tomorrow we realize that we are working with different conceptions of time and on the basis of utterly different estimates of African realities from those used by American critics. It is ungracious and may be politically embarrassing for Britain to enlarge upon the backwardness of colonial peoples. It is also discouraging to them. That is why the central answer to the demand for their speedy emancipation is seldom given, or given in such general terms that it conveys little meaning and causes much suspicion.

How, then, are the British and Americans to find the common criteria for making the necessary political assessment? It cannot be made in an idealistic vacuum. The only method seems to be to translate Britain's problem into terms of America's own experience. America might, for example, be invited – though in a spirit far removed from that of *tu quoque* – to consider some of her own difficulties in the assimilation of backward citizens. She has found the betterment and education of the American Negroes no easy task, even though these are only a minority, cut off for generations from their African roots and forming a mere fraction of the most active, efficient and prosperous society in the world. There are also the remnants of the American Indians who, as a study of the annual reports of the Office of Indian Affairs reveals, have presented most stubborn problems to those charged with fitting them into their changed environment. It is against such difficulties as these that the immeasurably greater problems of African backwardness should be set.

In British tropical Africa there are nearly 50 million tribesmen, who have broken little or at all with their past, and who, instead of finding themselves a small part of a vast new whole, are subjected to the relatively weak and uneven influence of a mere handful of white officials and missionaries. Add to this the fact that the period during which there has been anything like close and full administration is little more than a generation, even in favoured areas, and in others has hardly begun. By far the greater part of British tropical Africa was only being occupied in the early years of this century, and the preliminaries of establishing law and order, roughing out forms of administration, driving the first lines of communication into huge, inhospitable regions, and initiating social services, had hardly been completed by the outbreak of the first World War. Tropical Africa was involved in the hostilities and suffered also from the ensuing shortages of staff. Then followed a peace of boom and slump which struck the new unbalanced tropical economies with peculiarly damaging effect.

To deal with poverty, ignorance and inertia on the immense scale in which it exists in tropical Africa demands, ideally, a proportionately immense effort. This has to be generated in the metropolitan country, and to do so between the two world wars did not prove easy for the British, distracted by many internal problems, new and old, as well as external dangers. Since we live in a real world and not an ideal one, it may be asked what other country in those particular years would have had the knowledge and devotion to do better. Perhaps Britain might have learned more from Russia's experience in raising the standard of living of masses of people. The two cases are not, however, really comparable. The culture-bearers in Russia were some millions in number, if we count members of the Party and their assistants, and they had leaders who were fired by revolutionary ideas and were ruthless in method. Their task was to push their influence outward over a vast but continuous stretch of territory and to act upon peoples with many of whom they shared common languages and a long history, and who were not divided from them by any single clear racial gulf. In order to judge accurately the effort that has been made in British Africa we would not only have to be aware of the varying conditions of a dozen different territories, but to read the annual reports for each territory of almost a dozen departments of government over as many years, and also to survey the scientific researches that lie behind the activities of these departments. An understanding of the subject as a whole must be based on a knowledge of these details. Fortunately Lord Hailey has summarized much of this vast material in his great *African Survey*. Certainly no critic would be justified in judging the British record who had not studied at least that work.

The charge that all this African poverty and backwardness is due mainly to British exploitation is a blind sweeping blow that utterly fails to hit the really vulnerable spots. Africa is a poor continent in almost every way apart from some very localized mineral wealth. The whole of Africa south of the Sahara provided in 1929 only 2.8 per cent. of world exports. Even the proportion of primary products for 1935 was only 2.8 per cent. It must be remembered that these figures include the Union of South Africa, a self-governing member of the British Commonwealth, and all the non-British territories. British tropical Africa offered no essential product in important quantity except Northern Rhodesia's 12 per cent. (1934) of the world's copper. Among foodstuffs, the only striking figure is 57 per cent. of the world's cocoa. It contributes 43 per cent. (1933) of its palm-oil, which is, of course, only one of the world's nine main vegetable oils. To see the development of African production in terms of immense British profits is to disregard all the published figures, except in rare and generally short-lived instances; to connect it with monopoly is to ignore the outstanding problem of colonial economics, which, in many of the inter-war years, was to find markets at prices which would repay cost of production to European and and African farmers.

Discriminating criticism would probably find its best target in the practice of collecting large numbers of raw tribal labourers in certain mining areas. Since southern Africa is no longer an imperial responsibility, this criticism must in the present connexion be directed mainly to the copperbelt in Northern Rhodesia. Here British and American capital is permitted by the colonial government to maintain two complementary evils. One is the concentration of about 26,000 Africans (pre-war figures), some of them from distant areas, as so-called 'migrant labour'. These men, adults in their prime, leave their homes for a year or more at a time to work in the mines, thereby seriously disturbing tribal and family life. The men may gain physically from regular rations and labour, but they are unlikely to become good farmers, husbands, fathers or members of the tribe. Most of the women stay home and try to do all the heavy agricultural work; but some follow the men to the labour lines to become prostitutes. The complementary evil is that the men are for the most part treated and paid as temporary bachelor labour.

The influence of white labour from the south is working successfully to establish a colour-bar to prevent the blacks from improving their skill and pay; and government and industry are excused from the burden of providing the social services that established married labour would require. The native reserves are often very poor farming land. They provide cheap breeding-grounds for labour, inadequate maintenance for wives and children and a scrap-heap for discarded miners. In the last few years native labour riots have twice had to be put down with blood-shed. It is true that some doubts about the system are at last being expressed and some alleviations are under way. The factors in the problem have been summarized here in strong terms, however, to show that indefinite and generalized allegations about exploitation are far less effective than criticisms which go straight to a few real targets.

The same could be said of the frequent charges against the white settlers in Kenya. There are important inequities in the situation in that colony. But when American critics assert that the Kenya settlers have all the best land, while the natives are confined to the poorest, British critics of many specific conditions existing there are obliged to swing round and hammer in some facts on those who they had hoped were their allies. The truth is that though much of the 'white highlands' is good land, much is dry and suited only for ranching, while the two largest, continuous blocks of fertile, well-watered territory are, with very minor encroachments, still in the hands of their original African owners.

American criticism seldom seems to be very specific about economic exploitation. The strongest attacks on imperialism from an economic point of view, inspired by Communist doctrine, seem to come from Negro intellectuals who have grievances of their own against white capitalism. They quite understandably find an ideological safety-valve for these grievances in attacks on the British empire. It was the writer's impression when in America some years ago that this also was the case even then.

III

The main weight of American criticism falls squarely upon the political aspect of British imperialism. This part of the charge seems to us to be couched, as was indicated at the beginning of this article, in somewhat fundamentalist terms. These conjure up a picture of a strong power destroying the independence of the weak and keeping under subjection nations which (in the inappropriate words applied to the Sudan by Gladstone, who tended to be fundamentalist himself when in opposition) are 'rightly struggling to be free'.

Unfortunately the conditions which made it so easy to annex colonial territories at the start make it correspondingly difficult to free them. Once modern means of transport had brought Europeans armed with modern weapons to the fringes of primitive lands, annexation by European governments became an urgent necessity. Up to that moment primitive society, however static and simple, had been fitted through centuries to its environment, and had its own equilibrium and vitality. But now, with drink and rifles at their command, and new, dangerous ideas and ambitions, foreign and native adventurers had acquired terrible power. They could corrupt or destroy tribes which were unable to defend themselves or even to understand what was happening and what could happen to them. The worst of European governments – and the worst was very bad – was better than the alternative chaos. To understand this we have only to note what happened where pioneers outran government control on the moving frontiers of North America and South Africa, or when European and Egyptian slave-traders penetrated the innocent sanctuaries of the equatorial Nile or the first scum of traders reaching New Zealand exchanged guns, spirits and poison for tattooed heads and other native products. In the late nineteenth century Britain joined with a will in the process of African annexation. There was a time just after the middle of the century, however, when expansion there was contrary to her policy and her economic interest. Yet even in that period she found herself forced by the necessities of the situation in West Africa, and sometimes by the demands of the local tribes, to maintain or extend the power of her grudging settlements on the coast.

Since these annexations, Britain may perhaps be accused of lacking clarity of purpose and a sense of urgency in her task of educating tropical Africans for self-government. But there was never any possibility that self-government would be denied to them. Colonial officials from the first began shaping tribal institutions into local governments, even when they worked to no final design. They were acting upon a tradition which led to the development of dominion status for white colonies; there was no reason why it should cease to operate for brown or black ones.

The progress of some non-African colonies has already made this clear. Ceylon, the only colony comparable to the Philippines in its history and civilization, had before this war reached the threshold of responsible government. Twelve years ago it was given adult suffrage for men and women, by which 50 members of a State Council of 61 are elected. This Council is divided into seven committees which are in charge of the main branches of government and select seven out of the ten ministers. In the administration only the highest directing posts are still reserved for Englishmen. The island has been offered full responsible government after the war under a constitution drawn up by the peoples' representatives. A similar promise has been made to Malta. Jamaica has been offered a constitution, upon lines hammered out by its own leaders, somewhat on the Ceylon model, including adult suffrage.

Even in tropical Africa there has been some advance. Thus, in west Africa, elected African members were added to the Legislative Councils in the early 1920s, and anyone who cares to read the proceedings can judge how great an influence these outspoken men are able to exert, in spite of the official majority. Quite recently, African members have been added to the Governor's Executive Council, the all-important, confidential body in which policy is discussed and legislation planned, and steps have been taken to increase the number and status of Africans in the civil service. The administrative service has hitherto been regarded as the holy of holies, but last year, in the Gold Coast, two young Africans, one a graduate of Oxford and the other of Cambridge, received appointments. In Nigeria a committee upon which African chiefs and 'intelligentsia' sat with officials has just recommended the same step.

All this represents an advance in the central, foreign organization imposed over a large area which had never known any unity before. Hitherto the more important task has been that of 'indirect rule', the recognition and education of tribal communities as local governments. It is a highly flexible, illogical and empirical method, and it takes a hundred shapes according to the heterogeneous realities of tribal life to which it adapts itself. It has received its clearest form in Nigeria as a result first of the inspired expediency, and then of the wise rationalization, of Lord Lugard. Under 'indirect rule' the people themselves carry out the vast majority of their affairs – judicial, administrative and financial – under British guidance. It is true that there have been places and periods in which British officials have been too lethargic in acceptance of an only partially reformed native government. Let it be admitted, also, that indirect rule could, at its worst, offer a temptation to preserve old lordships in the common interests of conservative chiefs and alien imperialists. In Africa, however, in contrast with some of the Indian states, even where the traditional forms of tribal government appear unaffected, the content is deeply changed. In more advanced units, tribal government includes an audited local revenue, with a civil list; a police force; a public works department; reformed, supervised law courts; schools, hospitals and dispensaries; perhaps a forest department drawing its own royalties from foreign concessionaires or even exploiting its own timber. No more economical and penetrating expedient could have been devised for teaching peoples divided into small tribes the meaning of modern government and civic responsibility. We are now reaching a point where better ways of linking local and central government are required, and these are being developed. In the Gold Coast Colony the chiefs – extremely democratic potentates who rule by and through their peoples' will and are frequently 'destooled' – are grouped into three provincial councils which elect representatives to the central Legislative Councils, where they sit alongside, and co-operate fully with, the elected, urban members. In the Anglo-Egyptian Sudan which is administered by British officials, a central Advisory Council has been set up this year, composed of representatives from Province Councils which, in turn, are really federations of tribal governments.

To the doctrinaire emancipator these must seem small advances. In order to appreciate their importance it is necessary to leave the sophisticated-looking capitals and ports, with their African lawyers, clergy, civil servants and merchants, and go on to see – as in Nigeria – the millions living their almost untouched life in the roadless bush; to visit the naked pagans on hill and plateau; to listen to court cases of witchcraft and inter-tribal fights and occasionally of cannibalism and ritual murder and the pawning of children.

Disunity as well as backwardness adds to the political problem. The semi-civilized Moslem emirates of northern Nigeria represent a different race and culture from the true Negro south, and they always regarded it as a land of pagans whom it was a duty to conquer or enslave. The Sudan is similarly cut in two. Such regional differences, in addition to tribal divisions, are deeper than those that have cracked some eastern European states. To say this is not to argue for eternal tutelage, but to suggest the necessity for a period in which African peoples may develop a common education and a habit of co-operation. The Gold Coast is more homogeneous and the southern of its three sections more ready for further constitutional advance than any other part of British tropical Africa. (One of its African Executive Councillors has recently been expounding his very sensible views about this in a committee room of the House of Commons and at Chatham House.) But Sierra Leone has its rift, an accident of history which, as in Liberia, planted a handful of freed slaves generations ago on the coast. They hardly show the sense of beneficent responsibility defined as 'trusteeship' towards the primitive population of the large hinterland. And the Gambia, two river-banks cut off by another accident of history, is about as ready to stand alone as, shall we say, a Samoan island.

When we turn to East and Central Africa, we find another obstacle to self-government. It is a major difficulty which has common features with America's own great racial problem, although unwilling American opinion seldom seems to draw the parallel. The population figures for these countries, with those for the southern self-governing territories (Southern Rhodesia and the Union of South Africa) added for comparison, reveal the racial composition and suggest what the problem is:

Country	Africans	Europeans	Indians
South Africa	6,596,689	2,003,512	989,352[1]
Southern Rhodesia	1,319,000	60,720	2,460
Northern Rhodesia	1,366,425	13,155	1,174
Nyasaland	1,672,787	1,847	1,748
Tanganyika	5,217,345	9,165	33,900
Kenya	3,280,777	20,894	44,635[2]
Uganda	3,725,798	2,282	19,141

What of self-government under such conditions? The white minorities of the two southern territories have self-government and have used it to set up an economically and politically stratified society. The white minorities of the centre and east look to them for their model. Yet Britain, in an issue as deep if less wide than that which once split the United States, refuses to allow minority rule in the name of colonial self-government. Attempts of whites to construct eastern and central federations have hitherto broken against this British opinion, which supports the Africans of the territories next to Kenya and Southern Rhodesia in their fear of the dominant white settler influence.

If a regional council is established for Africa, or for this half of it, and the great conflict of principles noted above comes to an issue, what would be the opinion of an American representative? Would he ask for self-government? If so, self-government for whom? If he condemned the colour-bar of South Africa, he would condemn one of the main results of the grant of colonial self-government. (For just as, by the evidence of American historians, Britain strove to protect the Red Indians from the

[1] Including coloured.
[2] Arabs 14,077.

colonist and so added fuel to the revolutionary fire, so in South Africa, she struggled unsuccessfully to the last in the interests of the natives.) And Britain still maintains a refusal, which is most embarrassing to herself, to hand over her three remaining native protectorates within or alongside the Union.

Would the American representative be directed to oppose white groups, when, as in the Southern States, these refuse to tolerate the exercise of full rights of citizenship by Negroes? He would observe that the Negroes in Africa are immeasurably more numerous and backward than those in America, and whereas equal rights for one-tenth of the population, and that tenth largely assimilated, could never be a serious danger to the whole American nation, the colonists in Africa can claim with some justice that for them it might mean the utter submergence of their one per cent. or less under a vast flood of barbarism. Might he not in the end be inclined to agree that, in this dilemma, the arbitral power of the British Government must for the present be maintained?

If we turn back to the economic questions which were raised earlier, we see that here too an American regional representative will face some awkward problems. We in Britain have spent the last quarter of a century learning that a democratic polity is largely sterile unless wedded to a democratic economy. Most people here in Britain think the public interest requires that the huge powers of big business be brought under greater control by the state. Is not this control much more necessary where these business interests operate upon the weak and ignorant African peoples? There are many here, even in the right wing, who support the idea of a large infusion of socialization in the colonies. The Nigerian Governor who kept the coalfields as a state concern, and his successor who warned off Lord Leverhulme when he came there demanding big plantations, were no Socialists. But it is very probable that in order to hold the ring long enough for Africans to take their first feeble steps in retail and wholesale trade, in co-operative production and in industry, an increasing measure of government financial assistance, with control of outside capital, may be found necessary. Investment may not therefore be in the form of the 'private capital, free capital and competitive capital' which the president of the United States Chamber of Commerce advocated in England a few months ago.

British policy in this matter has not yet taken shape. A compromise has to be found between a policy which discourages the external equity capital which is so much needed, and one which exploits the natural and human resources of the colonies in ruthless ways which offend the rising standards of public morality and the emerging political and economic consciences of the colonial peoples themselves. The discussion, in which Lord Hailey has taken a lead, has covered the possibility of creating a general investment fund upon which enterprises sponsored or approved by colonial governments could draw; the possible creation of public utility companies in which the governments held a controlling proportion of the shares; and a stricter and more scientific control of the direction of investment and the conditions of its operation. Obviously the emphasis might vary according to which political party was in power in Britain, especially since policy on the periphery in such matters is bound to be a reflection of that in the metropolis. But there is no reason to fear that the Labour Party, which has recently issued the most moderate and well-informed of all its colonial statements, is likely to embark upon sudden and violent measures. Foreign investment has, indeed, always been welcomed in British colonies and is needed more than ever in the coming years. But it carries political as well as social dangers. Situations might arise in which a weak people might be politically independent and yet economically subject, or might be in the political empire of one power but in the economic empire of another. What nation, we may ask, will prevent its investors from despoiling a territory, will discourage colour-bars and will foster long-term loans, bearing little or even no interest, as investments in the people themselves? Only, perhaps, the nation that knows from long experience the need for this restraint, and has the imperial pride and sense of obligation that arise from intimate personal relationships with its wards. If we can achieve this restraint, will American investors and their representatives help us to maintain it?

Here it may be noted that Britain has recently – and this was in the grim days of 1940 – made a decisive break with her former financial policy towards the colonies. She had already, in the previous ten years, assisted colonies that were in difficulties to the tune of nearly £12,000,000. This was, however, in the nature of and subject to the restrictions of poor relief, and the grant in the same period of another £7,000,000 for development was on a scale, and under conditions, which did little to break away from the old principle that each colony must be financially self-contained. But in 1940 the need of generous external assistance for development was recognized and an annual grant of £5,500,000 was authorized for ten years. This sum was recognized from the first as being on a preliminary scale, and it is certain to be increased as soon as the end of the war makes it possible to spend even this amount. Already plans for development of all kinds, including research and higher education, are being vigorously worked out in the colonies and in Whitehall. But money is recognized not to be enough. The development must be of people rather than of things, and people are not passive instruments even for the most scientific and beneficent planning. They must be protected from dictation and educated into partnership.

Such, then, is the foundation upon which the post-war international or regional councils which are now being discussed will have to be built as far as Africa is concerned; and such are some of the problems which they will face. The form of these councils presents another problem, since they might be asked to fulfil at least four purposes, each of them requiring a different type of membership: (1) Co-operation in matters of common concern, such as health, tsetse fly control, communications, etc. (2) The allocation of development funds – if such can be raised – and the provision of technical advice. (3) The safeguarding of the interests of the rest of the world (which have still to be defined) with regard to access to raw materials and other economic and political desiderata. (4) The expression of the world conscience with regard to the rights and welfare of the native peoples.

The Mandates Commission did not attempt the first two tasks. It found the third the most practicable. The fourth was, and is, almost impossible for the reason that a common world conscience does not exist. Something has been achieved internationally in the field of native labour, thanks to the skill and persistence of the International Labour Office. But in the more complex issue which is of greatest interest to Americans, the development of self-government, little could – and can – be done in Africa, so long as Britain is the only imperial power there which is educating its subjects for self-government in anything like the sense in which Americans use this term. There has therefore been some bewilderment in England that Americans should have directed their criticism almost exclusively against Britain. Britain (alone, I believe, among imperial powers) has officially welcomed the idea of regional councils upon which non-imperial powers could sit. But if American opinion continues to concentrate all its attention and disapproval upon only one of the several empires, will this not provide somewhat incomplete instructions to the American members of such councils?

IV

I have now touched on the chief questions that American criticisms of the British colonial empire seem to raise. They are not rhetorical questions designed to wound or retaliate. America's armed partnership with Britain throughout the empire carries with it a right to criticize. Criticism is indeed the salt of empire, but to be constructive it needs the full savour of knowledge.

As, in this sphere, light succeeds to heat, so the possibilities of co-operation will grow between two nations which have some distinct and complementary qualities to bring to the common fund. In the interests of power for peace, the solid, detached, continental strength of the United States needs to be linked with Britain's heterogeneous dominions and dependencies scattered through every part of the world. If Britain can still rise to her changing tasks she will for a period remain the heart of this empire, a centre that must now express itself less in power than in service. This service will be of various kinds; but in the case of the colonies discussed in this article it will include political control for some time.

The world oscillates between the need for progress and the need for order. Europe is perhaps more conscious than the New World of the present need for order. Nationalism, whether old and crafty or young and headstrong, must bow to that necessity, either now or after another world war. This seems hardly the time to weaken or abandon a system which, even if it is called an empire, has yet shown its capacity to act as a setting and a training ground for weak and immature groups and also to fit itself into a peaceful and co-operative world system.

Education for Self-Government

Foreign Affairs October 1945

The core of the difference between the American and the British approach to British colonial problems lies in the American belief that the interests of the colonies require that they be given self-government either immediately or in the fairly near future in accordance with a stated schedule. The British answer is an invitation to look more closely at the colonies, to observe the obstacles in the way of their acquiring full nationhood, to estimate the various distances they have already advanced towards self-government, and to study the active processes of education for further responsibilities that are now being pursued. Thus, I tried in a former article[1] to state some of the reasons why complete self-government could not be given tomorrow to the African colonies. I also stressed the perplexing constitutional problems that arise where European colonies have been planted among primitive African tribes, and pointed out that some British colonial problems have analogies with the situation of the Negroes in the American South. I do not wish to repeat any of these points in this article but rather to carry a little further the attempt to bring about a meeting of minds, to ask what self-government for colonies means and to give some examples both of the achievements and of the difficulties of the British in the sphere of colonial government.

Let us first consider the misconceptions which, in British eyes, seem to lead some critics of British policy on to the wrong road from the very start. The great majority of human beings have two standards in such matters, one highly indulgent, by which they judge the acts of their own nation, and the other an exacting perfectionism by which they judge the deeds of other nations. Nor is even this perfectionism wholly rational; it is often coloured by subconscious prejudice and jealousy. The British are, of course, as prone to this dualism of judgement as other peoples, but criticism of America by Britain is small and intermittent in volume compared with the stream that flows in the opposite direction.

A thoughtful American writer has bidden us consider the contrast between moral man and immoral society, and it is well to ask ourselves at the outset of our discussion, 'What is national virtue in international

[1] See pp. 250–62 above.

T

affairs?' In the absence of a comprehensive and generally accepted law of nations and an effective machinery for its enforcement, each nation has pursued and will pursue its own interests according to its own point of view. Can any nation afford to take a purely unselfish action that damages its own position in order to forward the interests of another country? If not, then the relative virtue of nations must depend upon the degree of restraint with which each promotes its own objectives; and this in turn depends upon its own social and political character. A mature, educated and democratic nation is likely to take long views and, to the utmost extent that is consistent with its own interests, to understand and allow for the interests of other nations: the frankness, tolerance and habit of compromise practised within the borders of a nation will be reflected in dealings with a neighbour. By the same token, an ill-adjusted dictatorial state will perhaps take short views and use violent methods.

But this conception of degree of restraint, or of the difference between an enlightened and an unenlightened self-interest, is not sufficiently flattering to nationalist sentiment which, when passing judgement, demands that the particular line of self-interest which the accidents of history and geography have marked out for its own nation should be accepted as the universal ideal. It is scarcely a rational standard. Let us, for example, imagine that the Alleghenies were an impenetrable range and that the vast tribal hinterland upon which the American people expended their energy and built up their power had to be reached not by horse and wagon and railroad but by ship. Would this have changed their expansion into an act of questionable morality and rendered vulnerable their tenure of this territory? Was the overruning of the Matabele by British colonists in Central Africa in an entirely different category from the destruction of the tribes which stood in the path of American colonists? And when Americans reached their marine frontiers and overleaped them to seize colonies and strategic bases in the Pacific and Atlantic Oceans, was there then something more sacred in the idea of American security than in the idea of British security which dictated similar annexations? The main difference, suggested by British self-righteousness, is that a small trading island needed more overseas bases than a vast, almost self-sufficient continental nation. And when it comes to domination short of annexation, is there not a reasonably close parallel between the motives and methods by which one power gained control over the Suez Canal and the other over the Panama Canal?

One effective American reply to this might run as follows: 'Yes, we agree with this in the main as regards the past. But it so happens that American self-interest, unlike that of Britain, does not now prompt her to hold any large, populous, and civilized or semi-civilized countries against their will. She is, even in the uncertainties of war, carrying out her promise to give the Philippines independence, and it is possible that Puerto Rico may be allowed a referendum to decide between independence and some form of connexion with the United States.' It is true that the United States has shown the greatest political generosity towards her two main colonies. But she has not and could not give the same treatment to the Samoan or Virgin Islands. In other words the necessary complement to the liberalism of the imperial power is the strength and political maturity of the dependency.

In the British empire, of course, India stands alone in size and importance. The Indian question has been canvassed from both sides in this Journal and this article is not about India. We must consider the British colonies and ask whether any of them are ready for self-government and even full independence – in so far as any but the greatest powers can be independent today. Again, it is not easy to get the comparison between the United States and Britain on all fours. Outside the small strategic Mediterranean colonies, there are not any states in the British empire closely comparable with the Philippines and Puerto Rico, both of which knew centuries of European government and were endowed with Christianity, Spanish culture and a very large measure of European blood before the United States took possession. The Puerto Rican political leader, Muñoz Marín, recently stated before a Senate Committee that his country was 'part of Western civilization and of Christendom'. To visit Puerto Rico, to meet the Spanish professors and officials and to visit the farms and plantations is to realize that dependencies of this type are more comparable with South American states than with any British colonies of similar size, with the possible exception of Ceylon. And Ceylon has made very substantial progress towards self-government, with further extensions of self-rule in view.

From a constitutional point of view, perhaps the nearest rough approximations to the American dependencies – in spite of striking cultural dissimilarities – would be Iraq and Egypt; and, except for certain security privileges granted by treaty, both of these, after a period of protection, were recognized by Britain as independent some years before the war. The emancipation of these two nations, in regions of the highest strategic and political interest to the British Commonwealth, is too often forgotten.

It might be noted at this point that Ethiopia is another state which has a very strong physical and moral claim to independence. Her ancient culture and sovereignty and the intelligence and high spirit of her ruling class may be held to outweigh her great economic backwardness and the treatment which she accords some of her many subject peoples. Twice, in 1867 and again 74 years later, Britain had Ethiopia in her military power, and both times, though it would have been arguable that a period of sympathetic European protection and development might be in the interests of the mass of the people, the British armies marched away after a brief occupation. It thus appears that where the situation warrants it, Britain, like America, is capable of renouncing imperial rule.

These situations warranted such renunciation because, however possible and desirable the subordination of weak territories of this kind may seem to some great power, the territories themselves can gain only temporary and limited advantages from the status of protectorate or colony. If they have fallen into a state of disorder, or like Iraq and the Philippines had been freed from an unconstructive domination, a period during which order and economic development are supplied from outside may have a steadying and unifying effect. It did, for example, in Egypt. But in so far as such territories, in spite of many weaknesses, possess at least some of the elements upon which an ordered state can be built or rebuilt – a measure of unity in tradition or in constitution, an educated class, a historic culture and religion and a lingua franca – then their peoples will be able to absorb only a measure of direct help from alien rulers and will quickly develop a resentment against subordination that may seal their minds against further influence of this kind. Peoples in this category can best be helped through treaty relationships, through the services of an international organization, or through the formation of regional groups like that of the League of Arab States. The most suitable methods for this purpose must be developed by experiment in the next two or three decades.

II

But it does not seem to most of the British that this kind of independence is the only goal. There are peoples unready for anything approaching independence, and a tutelary power has much to give them: they need it and will accept it. In the course of a prolonged connexion, such a dependency partakes deeply of the culture of the ruling power, including its language and political traditions, and develops close ties of interest and sentiment. The two may thus become so fully integrated that as the dependency approaches maturity it may see that its best and most secure destiny lies in free partnership with its former rulers. Dominion status in the British Commonwealth offers a terminal point of equality and dignity which is not inferior to, but merely different from, independence. 'Commonwealth status,' as Mr Amery defined it, 'is not one of independence *minus* certain rights and privileges but of independence *plus* the rights and privileges and the practical advantages accruing from a world-wide free partnership. It is, in fact, the status of this country.'

The practical – and, admittedly, interested – British mind is not convinced that any good purpose would be served by wrenching even the more advanced colonies from their setting in an empire which in the last six years has proved its moral and physical value not only to its constituent parts but to the world. Were they thus cut loose, they would presumably be set up as very weak units under an experimental world organization. As colonies within the empire, or – as they make the grade – dominions, they can have all the certain advantages of the imperial connexion, without forfeiting any of the still uncertain benefits to be conferred by the international organization. It is worth remarking that, as Britain is never likely to continue to hold a territory by force, her hope and interest that colonies will wish to become dominions give her a far more positive impulse to serve them than could be imparted by the knowledge that her actions were being supervised by an international agency. The publicity and general stimulus such supervision could provide have, however, a marginal value even to a humane and liberal power.

But Americans who are still convinced that complete independence must be the ultimate destiny of colonies may be comforted by an investigation of British colonial policy as regards training in self-government, since this training will be equally valuable whether it eventuates in independence or dominion status. We may therefore now consider some of the achievements and discuss some of the problems of the widest, most variegated and most conscious experiment in political education that the world has known.

Britain's greatest achievement in this field has undoubtedly been her success in laying a strong foundation of local government, upon which central government can be built. This British method of teaching self-government – one might almost say this habit – sprang from many causes. The use of such political machinery as existed in dependencies was, first of all, an obvious convenience and economy, where staff and

revenue were short. But to the British, the harnessing of existing societies to the purposes of modern government became much more than
an initial convenience. It included the new respect for primitive institutions taught by anthropologists and the findings of modern psychology
on the superiority of evocative as against repressive influences. The policy
also drew upon the two main streams of British political thought. On the
conservative side was the surviving aristocratic tradition with its sense of
the necessity of organic growth, and, on the other, the liberal abhorrence
for arbitrary interference with, or intolerance towards, the rights of
groups or individuals. The result of this approach was that 'native
administrations', as they were called, were given real powers, with an
almost unbroken upward curve of increase in responsibility.

Let us take some concrete examples. The delegation of responsibility
has, perhaps, been most complete and successful in matters of justice.
The vast mass of litigation – and tribal people are highly litigious – is
settled by native judges in their own courts according to their own laws.
Only barbarous laws, procedure and punishments have been interfered
with. Powers of local courts vary according to the experience and advancement of the different communities. Some of the Moslem courts in
Nigeria have power of life and death, and from this summit the powers
range downwards through authority to imprison and fine to the petty
powers of a clan or village court. Appeals, generally through one or two
grades of native court, go to the British magistrate or administrator, but
the number of appeals is generally a minute fraction of the tens of
thousands of cases that pass through the native courts of any sizeable
colony. Inspection and review provide an additional check. I have myself
listened, with the help of interpreters, to scores of cases in native courts,
and have nearly everywhere been impressed by the independent bearing
of the accused and other principals in criminal cases, and also with the
way in which public opinion in these always-crowded court rooms plays
openly and often very vocally upon the process of adjudication.

The native administrations have executive, financial and legislative as
well as judicial powers. If authority is in the hands of a hereditary chief,
he exercises it nearly always in conjunction with ministers or assistants,
or with a council, though much still needs to be done to 'democratize'
some native governments. Councils are formed in various ways. In some
places they are partly elected and partly nominated; in others, constituent tribes or clans or even 'extended families' select their own representatives according to their own custom. Often, where custom tends to
create a gerontocracy, the government has persuaded the authorities to

add members of the younger, educated group, which is often organized into a 'progressive union'. The form of selection, the procedures and the powers of those in authority are everywhere in process of active development.

There cannot be any easy way of measuring the success of a policy which shows all the varieties of form both within and between dependencies which the indigenous realities demand. Finance, however, which, in British eyes, is the essential element in local government, offers a fairly solid yardstick. In nearly all colonies the figures show a rapid rise in the proportion of taxes levied by local authorities or in the amount retained by them as a rebate from the general tax. Thus in Nigeria, out of a total revenue in 1938–1939 of £5,811,000, £1,580,000 are retained and expended by native local governments, many of which have very wide powers. At the top of the list of Nigerian local government comes Kano, an ancient Moslem emirate with a highly organized system of ministers and district heads, and a revenue of more than £250,000. In the Sudan, where local governments were launched only a few years ago, nearly £500,000 are spent by the local governments, out of a total revenue of about £5,000,000 and out of the £1,000,000 spent on the provinces.

III

It might be illuminating to look a little more closely into the administration of one of the most politically backward and primitive groups. (To use such terms of description, incidentally, does not mean that the individuals composing the group are not highly educable and vigorous.) We shall take a district in the pagan bush country of the south-east of Nigeria. Here direct taxation was introduced only about 1930, because the political system – or lack of it – was so atomic, and because British officers found the tonal language almost impossible to learn. At that time, the fear that women might be taxed led to widespread and serious disorders, and the system of local government could be begun only about ten years ago. In 1944 a report upon one of these districts containing about 200,000 people showed that adult males paid the modest sum of 4s. 6d. a head in direct taxation. Of the total, 40 per cent. (£13,178) was retained by a council which represented a large number of small clans which had never co-operated for any purpose before. With this sum the local government maintained 207 miles of local roads (trunk roads are a central responsibility), 5 medical dispensaries with their native staffs, 5 leprosy inspectors and 19 leprosy clinics. It had built and maintained 124 buildings, courts, rest-houses, treasuries and staff quarters, and had on its payroll 146 salaried employees and an average of 167 employees paid by the day. Moreover, in its enthusiasm for progress it had refused to allow the African clan-heads to keep the 10 per cent. allowed them by the central government for their services in collecting the tax. Stimulated by the organized Christian and educated groups, the council insisted upon paying this money into a special fund to finance scholarships to the secondary schools.

In this district, especially among the 'progressives', resistance to taxation has given way to the desire for an increase in the present low rate, while the keenness to make the money go as far as possible caused many of the public works to be carried out at about a quarter the cost that the central government expected. So intense is the local patriotism that all posts under local government are kept for local men and are shared out in elaborate equity among every village and clan. When we note that the older generation can remember the days when almost every group of a few hundred families was ready to fight its neighbours, and that ritual murder and cannibalism are even yet not completely stamped out, it is proper to conclude that an astonishing apprenticeship to self-government is being served in this part of Nigeria.

The foregoing describes in barest outline the achievements of a federation of native local governments in a single district which represents only one-three-hundredth part of the total population of the British colonies. Many other widely differing instances could be given. Their common features are that government is moulded as far as possible upon the tribal institutions, but with progressively more modern procedure and functions. I think it may justly be said that the powers conferred, however limited in some cases, are real. Local government is probably weakest in the West Indies. Among other reasons, this is because most of the Islands were so small that central government tended to fill the whole stage, and partly because slavery was a far less promising foundation for local government than a vigorous tribalism.

Municipal developments in the colonies have not, on the whole, kept pace with progress in the rural areas. In most dependencies, towns are the mushroom results of European intrusion. Municipal administration demands high standards and a grasp of new techniques, yet the shifting and heterogeneous crowds attracted to the urban centres have least solidarity and political tradition. Even in this sphere, however, and even in Africa, there have been important recent advances as the educated and professional groups in the towns begin to show increasing interest and ambition. Those who charge Britain with following a dilatory policy may note that in some places the opportunities offered appear to have run beyond the capacity of the people to make use of them. The Governor of the Gold Coast, for example, recently chided the people of Accra and Kumasi for not making use of their franchise, pointing out that in the latter city at the recent municipal elections only 828 out of 14,000 voters came to the polls.

IV

The control of central government, which seems to raise a clear-cut issue between independence and subjection, inevitably attracts more attention from America than the essential, multiform foundations upon which central government must be built. Unfortunately a closer view shows that there is nothing clear-cut even about the central machinery. True, in every colony the ultimate control of affairs is reserved by Britain, and that control is expressed in the strong, formal and discretionary powers of the governor. But, as with local government, there are all degrees of delegation of authority, not only in the forms of the constitutions but still more in the spirit in which, under the varying conditions, they are worked.

The institution most relevant to our inquiry, the legislative council, comes down (with much metamorphosis) in direct descent from the first colonies in America. There is almost every conceivable variety of legislative council, from the type which is wholly an official body to the type which is almost wholly elected and unofficial. The composition of the councils is in a state of constant revision and, except in very rare cases, the development is in the direction of including a greater proportion of 'unofficial' members, and of electing rather than appointing them. In practice, the legislative council almost always operates more liberally than the form itself seems to imply. This is because, though the governor and his officials must have in reserve the power to put through the policy of His Majesty's Government even against opposition, the precondition for a happy and effective régime for a governor is the fullest harmony between himself and the community under his charge.

Only by reading the debates of these councils, which are published in full, is it possible to realize how completely all the business and finance of government pass under the public criticism of representatives of the people and how large a measure of influence and even of control they exert over the affairs of the colony. Wherever an active public opinion exists, it never ceases to play continuously upon the governor and his

staff through a dozen different channels. The House of Commons institution of questions has spread to the colonies; and all colonial governments are open, during sessions, to a rain of interrogations. There was,
for example, an African elected member in the Nigerian chamber whose
questions, arraigning the conduct of government departments, used to
run into hundreds during the brief sessions of council. And he got his
answers, which fill many pages of the records.

Most of the councils have finance committees with heavily unofficial
representation, and these examine every item of the budget and summon
heads of departments to defend their estimates. Select committees are
appointed, again with strong and sometimes predominant unofficial
representation, to work over all important bills put forward by the
government. These bills, in turn, are often the outcome of earlier
discussions with unofficial groups, such as chambers of commerce or
professional associations, which may originally have proposed them.
Nor is the committee system confined to the limited circle of legislative
councillors: there is an ever-increasing tendency to set up standing or
special boards and committees, some advisory and some with executive
powers, which are largely staffed by other unofficial members and which
do an immense amount of work. This development has been much
accelerated by the war; colonial governments could not have carried
through the heavy tasks of production of food and other supplies without
the unqualified support of the leaders of the peoples. No official staff
was available to administer all these tasks and the solution was to entrust
an important part of them to unofficial administrators. The plans for
post-war development, which are to be financed largely from imperial
funds, are being built up with the advice of central and provincial
planning boards with strong unofficial representation.

The true picture of a colonial government does not, therefore, show
an autocratic governor and his henchmen standing in lofty detachment
above his resentful subjects, but rather a wide diffusion of political
functions and an intricate dovetailing of official and unofficial activities.
Even when, from the far distance, the ear catches nothing but the
clamour of one of those constitutional clashes which inevitably break out
from time to time where complete self-government is withheld, the
actual situation may be very different from that evoked by the echo. The
same man, white or black, who makes a resounding speech that will
please his constituents and attract attention in Westminster, quoting, it
may be, fiery tags from the days of the American Revolution, may very
well be an influential member of the councils of the colony, working all

other days of the week in effective partnership with the official side. It would, of course, be a great mistake to assume that his speech has, therefore, no reason or significance: it may indeed be a kind of formal announcement, like a notice put up to prevent the formation of a legal right of way across private property, to make plain that a working partnership for the present does not mean renunciation of the demand for self-government in the future. However valuable the training given by membership in the legislative council, however large a measure of co-operation may be attained, there must be a point, so long as a territory remains a colony, at which full responsibility is denied, and since man is a political animal, that will always be a potential point of friction.

The existence of this point does not turn the legislative council into the 'farce' that at times angry colonial unofficials call it. I have had the opportunity of attending sessions of councils in a number of colonies and of discussing their affairs with councillors; and, during the last few years, as editor of a series of studies of the working of colonial councils, it has been my task to read many volumes of their debates. In all of these debates, and especially, of course, where there are politically apt and virile British groups, as in Kenya and Northern Rhodesia, there is a fairly constant pressure upon the government to advance the pace of constitutional development. Similar ambitions and pressures are found among the non-European groups, especially in Jamaica, Ceylon and the Gold Coast. It would indeed be a sad comment on the political vitality of the colonial peoples and of their constitutional training at the hands of Britain if this were not so. But to assume that because, *when a certain stage is reached*, good government is no alternative to self-government, is not – as I read the evidence – to say that until that stage is reached, there are not many effective and educational compromises on the way.

V

'On the way.' That is the keynote today in the empire. Colonial policy is being continuously woven from many strands: the warp is drawn from the ideas and experiences of the colonies overseas and the woof from the varied interests and opinions in Britain – commercial, strategic, humanitarian, religious. Who is to pronounce whether in each case these most difficult decisions which determine the pace of the journey and its direction are just? When the United States conquered the Philippine Islands was it right to refuse the Filipinos the independence for which they were then struggling, and to keep repeating that refusal until a few years ago? The United States refused because it thought that it had not yet trained the Filipino people sufficiently in self-government. Is it right to give them full self-government now, at the moment of liberation from the Japanese? Americans would reply, 'Who has the right, the knowledge or the power to decide these issues except ourselves?' So Britain has made her own decisions for her empire, delegating responsibility stage by stage. There are no precedents to guide; each dependency is a case by itself. Every large delegation is an act of faith, and to go too fast may be more harmful for the people and for Britain than to go too slowly, since it is almost impossible to retrace a step.

Much more could be said of this process of political training. I have considered here mainly the local government and the central legislative side. There is also the question of the infiltration of the colonial peoples into the executive ranks of the central government in replacement of metropolitan officials, a process which has gone very far in Ceylon and the West Indies. This in turn leads on to the question of higher education, which is closely bound up with training for self-government and upon which three important reports are now due from commissions of inquiry. But that is a subject which would demand an article to itself.

For all that could be written of Britain's colonial achievements, as much or more could be written, by those with first-hand knowledge, of mistakes due to lack of knowledge or sympathy, to bad timing by this governor or a repressive action by that. But these criticisms would be directed to the working of the system and would be made with the hope of improving it. There are now very few in Britain, even on the left wing, who do not recognize that the best way in which certain parts of the world can come to unity and civilization and release their latent powers is through a period of tutelage by a mature and democratic nation. When, for example, we in Britain contrast Liberia with the Gold Coast, or Haiti with Jamaica, we believe that the peoples of the two states which have been under steady tutelage are nearer the goal of a civilized and sound self-government than those who never knew such tutelage or who lost it too soon.

When attempts are made by Britishers like myself to answer American criticism of the colonial Empire it is because we so deeply regret a misunderstanding which impairs the co-operation essential to the interests of both powers, not because we feel that the existence of this colonial relationship needs any excuse. If Americans are to understand us they should ask themselves what it is in their own national life that calls up a sense at once of pride and energy. Is it that expansion across a great continent and the exploitation of its natural riches into the world's greatest industrial system? The British feel much the same about their own expansion and their founding of dominions and colonies all over the world. Do Americans feel proud of having drawn men from so many foreign and often unhappy countries, of having assimilated them and given them freedom and unity in their melting-pot? So do the British feel pride in having carried all over the world a flag that stands for the rule of law and constitutional government. Britain is proud that men of very diverse races have received these liberties, proud that they eagerly demand more; and she is proud that they have shown themselves ready to fight beside the mother country from which those ideas of freedom are derived. We do not know yet if these people will always wish to remain with us. We have made many mistakes and may make a good many more. But Britain is not in doubt or in retreat about this question. She is resolute to show that the imperial bond can be made of equal service to herself and to the dependent peoples.

Empire Child Migration

Letter to *The Times* 28 November 1945

Sir, – On 6 October it was announced that a Fairbridge Memorial College was to be set up in Rhodesia to take British child emigrants from the age of eight upwards. On 11 October you published a letter from the General Secretary of the Fairbridge Farm Schools pointing out that this venture was not in any way the work of his society. His society had decided, upon authoritative expert advice, that Southern Rhodesia was not a suitable country to which to send batches of young children, some of whom might be of 'undistinguished talent'. They would have to compete with African labour and run the risk of becoming 'poor whites'. His society offered its advice, but only with regard to older children.

The promoters of the scheme have ignored this experienced advice and in their prospectus actually offer preference to children of under 11 years. We in this country are full of admiration for the magnificent achievement of Southern Rhodesia in the war, and we can sympathize with her very natural desire to increase the proportion of her white population, but we are bound to question whether it is right to make this decision for very young children, and especially for those who need the most helpful and bracing social environment, such as that which they are certain to get in the white Dominions, where the old-established Fairbridge Farm Schools are well equipped to receive them. It might be said that the laws and conventions of Rhodesia guarantee a privileged position even for those who may prove unable to achieve the level of skill and stability demanded of those on the upper side of the colour line, but such privileges, though they may protect the weak, do not necessarily strengthen them. It seems likely that if opinion here could be directed to this question it would support the view of the General Secretary of the Fairbridge Farm Schools that only older children in their late teens, whose character and capabilities are at least partly matured and revealed, and who can have some opinion of their own, should be invited to go to Africa. It is true that Southern Rhodesia might not thus obtain child-immigrants in such large numbers, but this method, besides being more fair to the children, might in the end prove a better bargain for the Colony.

It might also be questioned whether it is suitable to make use of the name 'Fairbridge' which is associated with a long-tried and successful enterprise in the white Dominions, for a new venture of very different character, and one which has been rejected by the Fairbridge Farm Schools Society. It is a commentary upon these proposals that at this very time the Fairbridge Farm Schools in Canada are being asked to take in the children of poor whites from a West Indian island, because they are unable to hold their own against the competition of the majority of African race.

Yours faithfully, MARGERY PERHAM

Ethiopian Claims

Letter to *The Times* 12 March 1946

Sir, – There is a great sense here of friendship towards Ethiopia and of admiration for her Emperor, and it is regrettable that his Prime Minister should endanger them by claims that go far beyond any historical justification. Industrious research into Ethiopia's long and sometimes obscure history will yield material for almost any expansionist argument, but the weight of evidence is clearly against the two claims made to Eritrea as a whole and to Italian Somaliland as 'lost provinces'.

Modern Eritrea is a unit traced by the Italian sword on the map of Africa in the eighties. It has neither historical, racial nor cultural unity. Part of the southern highlands are indeed the northern shoulder of the old, and often very disaffected, Ethiopian province of Tigre: its people speak Tigrinya and not Amharic, but historically, racially and religiously they are part of Ethiopia. After some 50 years of European rule, opinion among them as to their future is reported, in spite of intense propaganda from the south, to be mixed; but the historical claim is very strong. As for the south Eritrean coast, Ethiopia once used it as her outlet to the world, but she lost control of it, including the port of Massawa, to the Muslims in their great mid-sixteenth century advance which overran her and cut her off from the world. Muslims ruled it until Italian days and still hold it culturally.

Clearly Massawa, which handles Ethiopia's northern trade, would be of great value to her, but historically she lost it when England lost Calais. The northern hills knew Ethiopia's influence, and the western plain at intervals up to the seventeenth century felt the tread of her armies, but they were not incorporated into the Ethiopian system, and for centuries before the Italian annexation they had been politically a Muslim no-man's-land. Thus, whatever may be true of some individual Tigrinya Copts, it is meaningless to apply touching conceptions such as 'loyalty' and 'homeland' to this arbitrary and unhomogeneous patch of Africa. Eritrean troops, after all, formed a large part of Italy's armies in the campaigns both of Adowa and of 1935–36.

For Italian Somaliland the claim is even less valid. There is evidence that Ethiopia from time to time sent raiding armies into Somalia in the

Dark and Middle Ages, and at periods used some of its ports. But here, again, after the Muslim onrush of the sixteenth century, she was cut off from Somalia, in which arose Muslim states that fought her on equal terms. It was not until 1887 that Menelik, who joined in the 'scramble for Africa' to conquer large non-Amharic regions to the south, seized Harar, and not until 1891 that he annexed, not Italian Somaliland, but the Somali Ogaden. Those who know this part of the world – and I once lived for the best part of a year on the Somaliland–Ethiopian border – know how little the Ethiopians did, and perhaps could do, with the desert they had annexed, and how deep is the gulf between the Christian highlanders and the sparse, fanatical Muslim nomads of the plains. The Prime Minister pleads for the rights of small nations: has the potential Somali nation no rights? The claim to Italian Somaliland as a 'lost province' – why not also to the nearer and more useful French and British Somalilands? – can be rejected on every ground.

It is, indeed, sad that Ethiopia, so recently herself the victim of imperialism at its most ruthless, and faced with such immense tasks at home and especially in the formerly misgoverned regions conquered by Menelik, should appear to be reviving his imperialist policy. Ethiopia would be wiser not to embarrass her friends by making inordinate and historically untenable demands, but to limit her claims to the very reasonable ones for part of Eritrea and for access to the sea; and to base them upon arguments that are likely to carry weight at the peace conference.

Yours faithfully, MARGERY PERHAM

U

Chief Tshekedi

Letter to *The Times* 10 August 1946

During 1946 there was alarm among the Africans of the Bechuanaland Protectorate that the South African Government intended to annex the neighbouring Mandated territory of South West Africa. Chief Tshekedi Khama asked to be allowed to come to England to discuss the matter with the Labour Government. This was refused.

Sir, – I should like to second Lord Faringdon's plea with regard to Chief Tshekedi. Nothing is more highly valued by colonial leaders than the opportunity, in matters of importance, to come to London and put their case before the highest authorities. The obvious administrative embarrassment at both ends of such a proceeding should not be allowed to outweigh its great political importance as a safety valve. Even if a decision adverse to the colonial claim has to be made, the complainants feel that they have had a full and fair chance to state their views.

Chief Tshekedi is a man who studies his Blue-books, and he knows that the Bechuanaland Protectorate itself might not exist today if his grandfather, the great Khama, had not insisted upon coming to London in 1895 to put his case against Rhodes and the British South Africa Company to Chamberlain. 'It is humiliating to be utterly beaten by these niggers,' was Rhodes's comment. 'They think more of one native at home than of the whole of South Africa.' The comment of Khama and his friends was to confer on Chamberlain a name meaning 'The Man who Rights Things.'

Yours, &c., MARGERY PERHAM

Relation of Home Universities to Colonial Universities

Address Delivered at a Conference of Home Universities on
27 September 1946

Universities Review November, 1946

Sir James Irvine, Ladies and Gentlemen, when those who organized this Conference asked anyone as inexperienced as I am in University administration to speak upon this subject, they cannot have expected that I would talk about the many technical questions that it presents to our universities. I therefore intend to take the implied permission to luxuriate in generalities and to leave it to those who have been especially associated with these questions, to translate these generalities into hard – very hard – administrative realities.

In trying to understand this subject, I think we need to ask ourselves four questions. One is, 'Why is it that this problem of the colonial universities has been put before us at this time?' The second: 'What is it that we are being asked to do?' The third: 'Why should we do it?' I want to try and answer those questions this afternoon. The fourth question is, 'How should we do it?' That we shall have to leave to the discussion: indeed we shall have to try to work out the answer to it in the immediately coming years.

In trying to answer this first question, 'Why has this problem been presented to us at this time?' may I remind you of one of two of the major facts and figures of this colonial empire. It contains, with the Sudan (which, with various qualifications, we may include in our problem), nearly 70,000,000 people, and for those 70,000,000 people there are at present four universities. The problem is all the more formidable when we remember that of those four universities two are in small islands, in Malta and in Hong Kong; one in a somewhat larger island, Ceylon; and the fourth is confined to the relatively small Jewish population of Palestine. Roughly, we may say, those four universities cater for less than 10,000,000 people. So we have still got nearly 60,000,000 on our hands without any universities at all. Those

60,000,000 people are served by five or six institutions in which there is
some kind of higher education; there are colleges in West Africa,
Nigeria, the Gold Coast and Sierra Leone. There is a college in Uganda
serving East Africa. There is one in Malaya; one in Khartoum. But these
institutions give only very limited facilities for advanced students and
they actually hold within their walls only a few hundred students out of
that 60,000,000.

There is, of course, a reason for this meagre educational provision; it
is the backwardness of the people as regards what we must call Western
education when we became responsible for them. Remember that the
majority of the 60,000,000 – about 45,000,000 of them – are in
tropical Africa, most of which we began to administer in the full sense
of the word only about thirty years ago. If you make a rapid visit to
Africa today and travel there by air or on the railway, you will hardly
realize how much of the continent which lies away from the main lines
of communication and the advanced urban centres is still almost the old
primitive Africa. I have spent a good many years wandering about
Africa and have seen the large areas where the people live half naked in
little mud-and-thatch huts, in great poverty and ignorance, scratching a
little patch of ground with their hoes. Only a minority of the children go
to any school at all and most of them never get beyond the little barn
where a native teacher-evangelist tries to communicate his own measure
of literacy to the children for the two or three years of their attendance.
This is painting the picture at its worst. There are the richer, more advanced areas; where schooling is slowly improving. Both in and outside
Africa – in Malaya, for example – there are small educated groups who
have for long been ready for full University education and have found
it outside their countries. In the West Indies there is, of course, a class,
white, coloured and Negro, which is highly educated and which has long
been making use of the British and North American universities. We
were beginning to consider this situation just before the war, but it is
since the war that a great change has come about, and we are being asked
now, most urgently, to try to meet the needs of this vast population for
more higher education.

There are several reasons for the rather sudden demand. Firstly, I
think, there is the natural maturing of the people under educational
systems which were only begun upon any effective scale and standard
some thirty years ago. We could hardly have expected before this to have
produced many students ready for higher education. They are just
beginning, in a little trickle which will soon be a steady stream to come

on from the secondary schools. Upon this unavoidably slow maturing of the peoples have come the effects of the war and they have speeded up the development that was taking place slowly. When you have a total war you have to take stock of your total assets in the way of people as well as of material assets: they suddenly attain a new value both as soldiers and citizens in the eyes of the government, and if this government does not wish to use coercive methods it has to appeal to them as persons with minds. So we took stock of our peoples in the empire as we never did before. They have produced the necessary goods: obeyed the necessary controls: they have also gone out to fight in large numbers and have come to new conceptions of life and of their own possibilities.

The war has had other effects. Very important criticisms of imperialism have been made by the two major powers in the world and these are finding now, particularly among the growing number of literate colonial groups, a very ready echo. I think also that our having been thrown together in such close association with them has made us feel a sense of gratitude and obligation towards them. All these things together have produced an atmosphere in which a very great and rapid advance towards self-government must be made possible, and, on the very edge of that advance which they desire with such passion the colonial people realize, more fully than they ever did before, their great backwardness and unreadiness. They know it is impossible to develop their countries any further until they have many more people with enlarged minds and professional qualifications who cannot be, and should not be, supplied from this country. They need them quickly, because they are held up in every single branch of their services. They also realize they cannot have their self-government until they understand better the rest of the world, and have people of their own capable of leading and ruling. For all these reasons this new need is being felt by them and they look to us to help them quickly.

Our second question is, 'What is it they want from us?' First of all, as you who are engaged on university administration know too well, they want a great many more places in our universities at home. That 60,000,000 have at present none of their own to which to send their people. About ten or fifteen years ago there were very few colonial students coming to our universities. The number rose, rather quickly, to about 400 just before the war. In the spring of this year it was calculated that there were 1,000 colonial students, not quite, but nearly all of them in universities, and I was told yesterday that the number has since gone up. The Sudan, which presented nobody before the

war, now has about forty-five students in this country. A friend who
the other day came back from the Gold Coast, told me there were
forty-five from the Gold Coast alone in his ship, all booked for our universities. There is no doubt that the pressure will increase rapidly, and it
would be even greater now if we had more room for these people, and
if there were better means of selection and other finance facilities for
them to get over here.

The second thing they are asking from us is staff for the new university colleges that are planned. The established universities also want
to have their staffs increased. Obviously, this is the key problem for the
future, to staff at the very earliest possible moment these new or existing
institutions so that they can give their own degrees or at least take
external degrees and save us from congestion and them from disappointment and frustration. What sort of staff do they want? It would be easy
enough if we could say to them, 'Well, it is difficult enough for us to
staff our own universities at present, but you can have what we don't
want, the people that we can spare.' That, of course, is just what they
don't want either. They are asking for principals and vice-principals,
and for men of some seniority, who have had a great deal of experience
in university administration. The reason for this is that the first men
and women appointed have to create these new institutions; to build
them up from the foundation in structure and in spirit and set the
standards of scholarship. They need men of strong and humane
character who would be able to adapt themselves to new and strange
situations; to deal with dark, different and sometimes difficult – but
always vital and demanding – students. So they would need to be fresh
in mind, firm and yet sensitive.

The colonies are asking us to try and give them this staff they are
wanting at once. It is estimated that they require about fifty in the very
immediate future and in the next three or four years they are going to
need at least two hundred and probably more. In order to provide this
staff, those of us who have been working on these questions have been
considering whether some plan could be found by which staff could be
seconded for a time to these new universities. You will find this discussed
in the Asquith report. We are getting now on to one of the technical
questions which I don't wish to pursue further in this introductory talk.
I only throw out that idea as a possible point for discussion. I realize
that it is a very difficult arrangement to make in practice and we shall
have to work it out very carefully. But we should not allow the colonial
universities to staff themselves at this vital early stage with unsuitable

people, and then, several years afterwards, when we have perhaps more first-class people to spare, they will have to start changing their staffs with unsettling results all round.

The third thing they want will come a little later, and it will not be such a difficult matter for us. They will want, as they get established, to send us a number of post-graduates. It will be especially important for them to send students for post-graduate work because, by coming here, they will get the whole atmosphere of an old civilization, and learn especially something of our traditions of academic freedom and professional conduct and take these back with them to their own universities and public life.

In addition to these three quite definite things which they are asking from us there is something more general without which we cannot do the rest. They want our interest and understanding. They want us to know them, to be aware of them; to study their problems much more in our researches; to welcome them when they come over here; to go over and visit them. There is, indeed, nothing they do not ask of us. They want advice on almost every aspect of the problems of building up a university, whether it is the layout of their building; how to run an extended extra-mural organization; to make and administer libraries. Very important in colonial conditions are the constitutions of these new universities; their relations with the governments; the grading of their staff; the terms of appointment; and, indeed, the whole range of problems with which we have to deal in our own universities. They want to know what a university is and how it can be developed. They cannot possibly do this without a great deal of advice and help. Even our people we send out cannot do it unless we and they are in close touch and we know what is going on out there and maintain a constant interest in their problems.

I have spoken mostly of the needs of the more junior institutions which are going to be built up into university colleges. But of course there are also the relations with the established universities. These are somewhat different and much simpler. Whereas we have to be in a really maternal relationship for a time with the new institutions, it is much more a fraternal relationship we have to form with the colonial universities. Although they are small, they are very proud, and they want to take from us in a spirit of equality, for they upon their side have something to show us and to give.

That then, is what the colonies want. To give it will mean a sacrifice. There could not be another hundred men in this country who understand better than you the exact practical meaning of the sacrifice they are asking of us at this very, very difficult moment in the life of our own universities. You might knock off on your fingers each one of these items which I have put before you, saying, 'Staff! An outrageous demand, asking for staff when we cannot man our own universities. Undergraduate entries! Crowding us out with colonial students when we ought to keep places for our own men, the children of taxpayers of this country. Asking for our interest, our attention, when we are all so over-worked! When we cannot find time even for taking a new idea into our minds!' I know very well that sympathy in this new direction, which sounds so easy, means in the crowded day more memoranda to read, more committees to attend, more people to interview. It seems as though they were asking us to do the impossible. Well, clearly we shall not attempt the impossible unless we can see some very good reasons for doing so. Therefore our next and last question is, *why* should we try to help the colonial universities? That can take us into the very wide question of our whole relationship with the colonies, which is at present in a very difficult and very transitional state. I won't, however, venture to say much about our obligations towards the colonies. But I would ask you to notice how deeply that relationship is changing and how that very change is one that brings us and our present subject right into the foreground of the picture.

There was a time when, apart from missionary and trading contacts, our control, our influence, reached the colonies through one narrow official line of communication. All control was from the Colonial Office through the Colonial Service which ran the colonies and supplied law and order and other minimum elements of government. Partly as a re-sult of the war, that relationship has changed. The colonies' needs are so great now and their development so rapid that we are coming into contact as entire communities. All the facets of our national life are now being turned one by one towards the affairs of the colonies. If you watch the colonies you will see, as many of you who are working on the scientific subjects will know, how very close and wide the relationship is be-coming. If you are interested in boy scouts or juvenile delinquency or women's institutes or editing newspapers you will find the same -- new contacts being developed directly with persons and groups in the colonies with similar contacts. But of all those contacts, I know that none is of greater importance than this direct contact of our universities with theirs. Their need is so great that we should require very strong reasons to refuse it or even give a half-hearted reply to it.

However, groups of men generally act upon groups of reasons, rather than upon one, and, therefore, I will try to summarize briefly some of the other reasons as they appear to me. I think we have undoubtedly a very great obligation to our colonies arising out of the history of our relationship with them. It was we, after all, who took the initiative; we took those colonies and in most cases by force. We used them for our own purposes. In some cases we enslaved them. True, we gave them benefits as well as doing them a great many injuries, but, whatever the final balance-sheet, the truth is that it was our initiative, it was our will, that they should come under our control. We are now coming – in many territories, if not quite all – to the climax of this relationship; they are on the verge of coming forward as communities fit to govern themselves and they are asking from us this one great essential, the training of their leaders and experts so that they may take back from us the control of their own affairs. I think it is our historical responsibility to them to assist them in this way. I would even suggest that as a result of this changed situation the British Universities have now got a more important task than any handled by the Colonial Office itself.

A further reason lies in the very great importance of the university in their life. We ourselves probably have an exalted view of the function of our universities. But, after all, they are part of the whole cultural pattern of this country, a concentration of the whole intellectual life of the people, who have many other ways at other levels and in other forms of expressing and renewing that life. But in the colonies the universities with the secondary schools which will be linked with them are the one possible medium through which the new knowledge they desire can be communicated to them. They are isolated from the mental life of the rest of the community, and their importance, their unique responsibility within it, is almost frightening, and as these institutions cannot at this stage live and grow unless we help them, this formidable responsibility comes indirectly to us.

They are very conscious at this moment of their need. That is one of the most remarkable things about the colonies – the sudden way in which they have wakened up to the vital importance of university influence and education. It is not only the rational calculation that they need so many chemists, doctors, agricultural experts, teachers of history in secondary schools and so on; it comes from that, but also from something much deeper than that, something with very great emotional content. In so far as in the past they have been politically subordinate and even – let us be frank – socially despised, so, in ratio to that is the passionate strength of their desire to prove their intellectual and social equality both as individuals and as communities. They can do this only by showing that they can come right on to the level with us in the intellectual tests. It is perhaps a paradoxical situation that while on the one hand – and sometimes with a very violent gesture – they are rejecting our political control, with the other hand they are reaching out for everything we can give them of our culture and our social advice. So that, however difficult our political relations may become, we can meet on the university plane in almost complete understanding. We can, through our work in the universities, build up a wholly new relationship of friendship and intimacy with them. It is their wish too; I do not feel any doubt about that. And I do not think there is any danger that we shall fall into complacency or prostitute our intellectual contact into a sort of propaganda for national purposes. We know that we are giving them something which is by no means wholly ours, even if it has been coloured by our national character and is presented through the medium of our own language. Nor is it only the content of knowledge which we can share with them; in this uneasy world we offer also our principle of intellectual freedom and our still largely Christian tradition.

How else could they get it? They have already taken so much from us and are so bound to us that they could hardly make a fresh start. Could UNESCO give them a sort of Esperanto of culture divorced from any national heritage? Could they develop it from their own inheritance? There is a school which believes that the best hope lies in cherishing and developing the indigenous culture, not only because of its inherent merits but because by this the self-respect of the people will be preserved. Of course there is much truth in this – there is value and vitality in what they possess; it need not and must not be erased. But do not let us be too clever about this. It is not for us to invent a specially adapted form or standard of intellectual life for their needs. Let us face the truth – which I am sure they have faced – that in the university sphere we have to offer almost everything. We must give what we ourselves value most highly and keep nothing back. They will do the adaptation. Learning, like the spirit, bloweth where it listeth and we cannot direct its movements or limit its force.

I have, indeed, often seen proofs of this. Sir James Irvine will remember when we were wandering about the campus of Puerto Rico University, we saw those dusky and beautiful young men and women, those students who have some Spanish blood, some Negro blood, very exotic-looking young women with roses and hibiscus in their hair, with young men who made one think of South American tango-dancers. When inspecting the library we asked what English literature they liked best and we found the books for which they had a passion were the novels of Miss Austen. Similarly, I remember that some young boys in a Gold Coast school appeared to shock and surprise a great many people because they got a tremendous satisfaction out of acting the plays of Euripides. Again, I remember how in Basutoland, I came across a very horrible murder in which a man had killed another and cut open his body in order to extract some parts for purposes of witchcraft. I went from there to the native University College at Fort Hare and in the library I was introduced to his brother. He was a post-graduate, doing research for an advanced degree, and when I asked him the subject, his eyes lit up as he told me – the poetry of Dryden and Pope. Here then, are some of the reasons why I think we should try to attempt the impossible and attempt it now.

What of the 'now'? I can well imagine that some of you are thinking, 'It is all very well, all very reasonable, but now isn't the time. Let them come back in three or four years when we have got over our difficulties and things are more normal.' It would take a long time to run through all the reasons why it is impossible to wait – the frustration, the bitterness, the closing-down of plans or of half-achieved improvements, the political situation. Sir James Irvine will take that up because he can make it clear to you much better than I. You may feel daunted because it may look, from all I have said, as though there is everything to do; that nothing has been done; that there is nothing yet to encourage us. But that is very far from being the case. There are most encouraging signs. We have already begun to attempt the impossible, and it might interest you if, for two minutes, I tell you something of what has been done already.

I must begin by giving you a little sketch of the genealogy of the institutions which have produced these first results. There is a Standing Colonial Office Committee called the Advisory Committee on Education in the Colonies: early in the war some of us raised the question there and a small sub-committee on higher education was set up. And here I should like very much to pay a tribute to Professor Channon, of Liverpool University, who was really the man who at this stage had the foresight and the vision and who got all of us working on this, and who tenaciously nagged and worried the authorities of the Colonial Office and told them and us to get on with it. I should also say he found a worthy partner in Christopher Cox, the Colonial Office Education Adviser.

This little group worked away and soon afterwards the West African Commission went out there. But the most direct issue to which the Sub-Committee gave birth was the Asquith Commission.[1] The Asquith Commission produced its report upon the whole problem and it also generated a little sub-committee which went out to the West Indies under Sir James Irvine. I won't say the West Indies Commission, or Committee, was not a legitimate birth, but at any rate, the main issue and legal heir of the Asquith Commission was the Inter-University Council for Higher Education in the Colonies upon which all your universities are represented, and of which Sir James Irvine is Chairman. It has already done an immense amount of work in its short life; it is quite astonishing to see what it has done. In addition to this Council the Asquith Commission also produced the Colonial University Grants Committee, the financial advisory body as a twin of the Inter-University Council. There was a good deal of delay and anxiety about that birth but I understand it has just been safely delivered. But perhaps I had better not carry the metaphor any further in case I get into difficulties.

I must add to this list of achievements the efforts of the university of which we are guests today. In spite of all they have suffered during the war with the dispersal of their work and damage from bombardment, it is impressive to see what London has done in the first few months in setting up a strong committee to direct all the colonial activities, sending delegations to the colonial centres and adapting their examination system to meet the special needs of the colonies. An achievement of this kind generally comes from the devotion of two or three people who have given their whole care to it, and it has been so in this instance. One or two of them are here now.

A further phenomenon – also I think an encouraging one – is that the sky has been darkened by a migration of Vice-Chancellors flying to warmer climes and it appears that these flights are to be seasonal. But seriously, it is most astonishing what has been done in a very short time. It is a beginning and the process will go on, because the problems themselves are so fascinating and what we are being asked to give is one of those things which does not make us poorer in giving. It will, I am sure, enrich us. I have for a long time been a specialist in this colonial field, and I sometimes think that I am tempted into over-enthusiasm, a quality so much reprobated in the eighteenth century, and which it is still unwise, if not to feel, at least to show, in public life. But I begin to think

[1] *Report of the Commission on Higher Education in the Colonies, 1945. Cmd. 6647.*

that it is not I who am to blame; it is the subject. I have sat round these committee-tables and have watched with delight while one by one these hard-headed administrators who handle your university affairs have been captivated by these colonial problems. They have opened some new windows with some very exotic and fascinating views of distant places and peoples and they have been drawn to give more and more of their minds and of their time to these affairs.

I think therefore that we can say that the work of helping the colonial universities has, at least, been well begun. But I do not think it can be carried further unless these beginnings lead on to a relationship at once wider and closer between all our own universities and those of the colonies. That can come only from a much wider knowledge among ourselves of their needs. It was for this reason I suppose that this subject was put down for the first meeting of your conference and why I have been given the great privilege of speaking to you upon it this afternoon.

Anglo-Egyptian Treaty

Letter to *The Times* 10 December 1946

Sir, – It is to be hoped that the announcement about the Anglo-Egyptian treaty in *The Times* of yesterday and the statement of the Governor-General will meet the grave situation that has been developing in the Sudan. But the government may need the strong support of British opinion.

While Britain and Egypt have been arguing about the interpretation of a still undisclosed agreement, the Sudanese have been kept in a state of feverish suspense about their fate. If Britain has signed away her share of sovereignty and given it solely to Egypt, how can it honestly be maintained that there will be no change in the administrative *status quo*? The heart of that *status quo* is the guidance of the Sudanese towards full self-government by British officials; this will not easily survive either the penetration of Egyptian influence or the loss of faith in the British by the Sudanese, both of which are likely to follow upon the concession which Britain is said to have made.

The British negotiators, admittedly, had a difficult task. The question of sovereignty over the Sudan has a long and complex history and it is said that, had the Egyptians taken it to international law, their case would have been strong. But is the best way to deal with a weak case to make it weaker? And was it so weak? Is it possible in 1946 that a people's future should be decided according to lawyers' interpretation of the legal terms in which other parties defined their status 50 years ago? Would their subsequent growth towards nationhood and their brave part in the second World War, in which the Egyptian sovereign stood aside, be irrelevant factors? It may be said that Egypt has quite literally vital interests in the Sudan. True, but she is more likely to secure them if her neighbour joins her as a Scotland rather than an Ireland and if the delicate modern mechanism of Nile water control in the Sudan is not jarred by discontent or disorder. Moreover, 'the unity of the Nile valley' is a slogan that has little support in history, race, politics, or, as those who have traced its immense course can see, in geography.

There are other complex problems, including that of the Southern Sudan, which cannot be dealt with here. But one issue is clear and urgent. The Sudanese accuse Britain of having broken the pledge made by Mr Bevin on 26 March and repeated to the Northern Sudan Advisory Council on 27 April. It was 'that no change should be made in the status of the Sudan as a result of treaty revision until the Sudanese have been consulted through constitutional channels'. It is now stated that this pledge is to be kept. This is a great gain, but what, at this stage, will it mean? It seems certain, in spite of their divisions upon the subject, that when the question of sole Egyptian sovereignty is put to the Advisory Council it will be rejected, and that this action will be supported by a majority of the Northern Sudanese. The British, who promised the Sudanese, as part of the same pledge, that 'they shall decide their political future for themselves', will not, it appears, override such a decision. If we do not, it will then appear that we have offered Egypt something which it was not ours to give.

Everything must be done to re-create the conditions in which the Sudan Government, as at present constituted, will be free to give, and the Sudanese willing to accept, the last 10 or 20 years' service that is needed to round off half a century of skilful and devoted administration that has brought the Northern Sudanese within sight of full self-government. It is the misfortune of the Sudan that, neither a colony nor a foreign country, but lying in the twilight of its embarrassing status, it has been kept almost deliberately out of the public eye. No comparable pressure of opinion in this country has supported our ministers against the pressure from Egypt. Those who know and care about the country should appeal for support for the government in its intention to safeguard the work and perhaps the security of a fine service, both British and Sudanese, which has been put by the events of the past few weeks into a position of acute difficulty. Let us remember that the Sudanese are a high-spirited and intelligent people – and also that they are not remarkable for patience or docility.

Yours faithfully, MARGERY PERHAM

Studies in Colonial Legislatures

Editorial Introduction to the series *Studies in Colonial Legislatures* and to the first volume *The Development of the Legislative Council 1606–1945* by Martin Wight.[1]

To students of politics history can offer no richer collection of constitutional situations and devices than are to be found in the British Empire. Yet the attention given by these students to the subject has been very selective. The development of the white colonies, whether towards independence or dominion status, has been fully studied both in Britain and in these former colonies, now grown to a nationhood which brings pride and devotion to the task of scholarship. For the greater white colonies the development of the imperial relationship may be regarded, so slight is the constitutional difference between dominion status and independence, as having reached a terminal point, but the climax of their development served to show the full extent and character of that other colonial empire which required, and still requires, the safeguards of dependency. It is the constitution of this empire, inhabited mainly by non-European peoples, which has been so strangely neglected by students, and this though it adds to its historical interest the importance of a major contemporary problem, or, rather, list of problems. It is, indeed, difficult to explain why the British, a people much interested in their own institutions and proud of them, should have directed so little attention to the prolonged and exacting attempts of their own agents to adapt these institutions to some forty remote and various dependencies. It must be that scholars have been embarrassed by the very riches of the subject and its wide diffusion through time and space.

The opportunity arose through a very generous grant for colonial research made in 1940 by the Trustees of the Higher Studies Fund of the University of Oxford. The grant was administered by Nuffield College. The task was appropriate to its Founder's purpose, which was the study of current political and economic problems through co-operation between those with academic and executive experience, a principle which,

[1] Faber & Faber 1946.

thanks to the unselfish help given by some of those most intimately concerned with colonial government, has been followed during these researches.

The choice of the main constitutional subject was not difficult. It was already apparent in 1940 that the circumstances of war were forcing the growth of political consciousness in many of the colonies and that this would very soon necessitate some adjustments in Crown Colony constitutions which had been expected, not induced to remain stationary, but to be developed very much more slowly than now appeared desirable. The clash of principles which accompanied the clash of armies was more profound in this war than in the last and had much greater significance for dependent peoples. The increasing numbers among them of the literate and the politically aware led to a wide understanding of the injurious new concepts of race and authority, and of the opposing principles asserted from the British side. In addition to this the collapse of three out of the four European imperial nations; the extreme danger of Britain; her own imperial losses and the disturbing economic effects of the crisis in communications forced upon her and upon the colonial peoples a sharpened sense of interdependence. Modern war, moreover, demands a solidarity in which every adult member of the population achieves a new value as a fighter or a producer and consequently, when the new techniques of coercion are not employed, as a citizen. In 1940, therefore, in the certainty that colonial governments must soon be made both more efficient and more representative, it seemed useful to take stock of some of our colonial constitutions, analysing their character and assessing, from an objective historical viewpoint, their efficacy. Developments in the colonial empire since that date have more than justified these expectations.

To avoid too wide an approach it was decided to select the legislative council as the central institution for study. This council in spite of the proposed limitations within which it works, represents that part of Crown Colony government which is most likely to be affected by the liberal impulses which have been reinforced by the war. It is the institution which, thanks to the full records kept of its proceedings, can most easily be studied in this country. The governor, still the keystone of the Crown Colony arch, sits in the council as president and in his character and policy and the activity of his leading officials the nature of imperial control can be examined. Since the council, in its many different degrees and forms, is designed to be representative of the main interests and racial groups in the colony, its proceedings reveal, often in very

x

lively and human fashion, the point of contact between colonial aspirations and imperial control. They reveal also the political capacities and character of the several groups of representatives and the relationships between them. Through the processes of legislation, debate, questions and financial appropriations, all the affairs of the colony pass across the table of the Council which thus mirrors the life of the colony.

It will, therefore, be the purpose of this series to describe in some detail the composition and conduct of the legislative councils of certain selected colonies. In so doing the evidence will be presented in such a way as to answer some of the main questions that any consideration of this institution must provoke. What, for instance, is the relationship of the council to the other elements of a colonial constitution, the superior executive authority of the governor upon the one side, and the organs of local government upon the other? Do the councils, when their year-to-year working is analysed, appear to serve effectively the needs of the colonial peoples and train them for the responsibilities of self-government? How far are they – and in the circumstances of some dependencies, how far can they be – representative? Do differences of racial composition as between dependencies result in very different uses being made of constitutions which are closely similar in form? Do the proceedings of the councils reveal the relative part played in the making of policy by the imperial agents on the one hand and the colonial representatives on the other?

These are some of the more immediate questions to which it is hoped this series will help to provide an answer. There are, however, larger questions, a little further in the background, the answers to which will hardly be found in these studies but which will condition the form and spirit of future constitutional development in the colonies. It is worth while to consider these questions for a moment at the introduction of this series.

The first of these questions relates to local government. This is especially important for the African colonies, from among which the first subjects for study will be chosen. Here the political backwardness and disunion of the millions of tribesmen prevented them from playing an effective part in the traditional central institutions Crown Colony government and led to the development, especially in West Africa, of the system known as indirect rule. By this an attempt was made to incorporate the tribal societies as working parts of the structure of government and to develop these into strong units of local government. *These* were the important and interesting institutions: the peoples' loyalties and interest was bound up with them rather than with the somewhat exotic central council, in which the natural leaders of the people could play no part. As, however, an English-speaking, educated minority came into being, especially in the coastal towns and in the service of the central government, they began to talk the language of nationalism and unity and to look to the legislative council as the future parliament. They quickly learned to see in the system of 'indirect' administration an obstacle to their pressing ambitions and even to the impartial observer it began to appear that some of the colonies had been endowed with two systems of government so different in character and in their probable rate of progress that their future development appeared to run upon lines that would never meet.

It is for this reason that the new proposals for the Nigerian Constitution are so important.[1] They represent, even allowing for some earlier development on the same lines in the Gold Coast, the first consciously and comprehensively planned framework within which the numerous native administrations, their regional groupings and the central organs of the imported state system can all work and develop as parts of a constitutional whole. We must not follow the subject further here: the third volume of this series, which will contain a study of the Nigerian Legislative Council, will be the proper place for a discussion of a plan which may by the date of this publication have gone beyond the stage of proposals. It has, indeed, been mentioned only as an example of the great influence that new developments in local government may have upon the structure of legislative councils. In other colonies, as in East Africa, the presence of immigrant races, presenting far more formidable constitutional problems than any known to West Africa, may demand very different forms of local government. In others, again, especially in older colonies such as the West Indies, the problem tends to be the reverse of that in West Africa in that local government has been much neglected and now needs to be built into the constitutional edifice to strengthen the foundation upon which the relatively advanced central institutions are resting, an operation of obvious difficulty. Wherever we look in the colonial empire it is clear that local government, which of course includes the very important sphere of municipal government, has an importance as an educational and unifying process far greater than in a mature democracy like that of Britain.

Even larger questions arise when we consider the political goal of the

---

[1] *Proposals for the Revision of the Constitution of Nigeria, 1945, Cmd. 6599.*

colonies. The end of self-government may have been implicit in all the constitutional means Britain used since she merely extended to the colonial dependencies, with limitations of representation and powers, the forms which had served for the white colonies. But, as this volume will show, with the emancipation of the dominions the full distinction between the two kinds of colonies became apparent. The reason for the distinction is clear; whereas the coloured dependencies shared with the white colonies certain weaknesses which for a period prevented the latter from achieving self-government, they had, and have, additional handicaps to overcome. British colonists may have been weak economically and strategically as communities but they were individually at least as capable of the functions of citizenship in a parliamentary democracy as their cousins in Britain, and, indeed, claimed to carry their civic rights with them across the seas. This is obviously not true of most of the coloured dependencies which, though they claim through their advanced minorities this same parliamentary democracy, show very few of the conditions under which it has hitherto been effectively conducted. Some of the colonies are accidental collections of independent and primitive tribes of different cultures and languages which happened to fall within an arbitrary zone of European annexation: in nearly all there is widespread lack of the Western education by which Western forms of government can best be understood. In most colonies there is great material and cultural poverty and often cleavages of race and religion so deep that it must be many years before they can be bridged by a sense of unity and the resultant faculty for political compromise which alone can make majority rule practicable. Whereas with the white colonies Britain had only to guard and to help nations that were making themselves, the colonies as nations have still to be made and Britain must herself join actively in this work of construction.

It is in the face of these difficulties that the imperial government has in the last few years turned the promise implicit in British forms and traditions into an explicit statement that self-government is the goal for the coloured dependencies. It is therefore the task of this country to think out very clearly what is meant by this promise and how it can be fulfilled. Consideration has recently been given to two aspects of the task. As this book goes to press, the reports of three bodies set up to investigate higher education in the colonies, on two of which the writer was privileged to serve, have drawn attention to the intimate connection of their subject with the development of colonial self-government and have made urgent proposals for the creation of new colonial universities.[1] A much wider aspect of the question was realized before the war and has been given increasing attention during its course, especially by Lord Hailey and Colonel Stanley. It is that political self-government cannot be built upon a basis of extreme economic poverty and dependence. Yet economic development, as envisaged today, raises in the colonies, as elsewhere in the world, its own constitutional problems. A heavy burden must be put upon their political institutions by the immense new economic tasks that have to be attempted in the next few years. There is no need here to do more than refer to problems and developments that are to some extent treated in the colonial economic studies which are being published simultaneously with the first volume of this series.[2] It is, however, important to realize that the complex and intimate regulation of economic and social life which taxes the intelligences and solidarity of the most mature communities will throw a very sudden and heavy strain upon the skeleton structure of colonial administration and upon legislators, representative of peoples whose backwardness and inexperience of modern conditions is most marked in economic matters.

The necessity for economic development raises, however, an external as well as an internal constitutional problem, and one which was not put to the young dominions in such difficult terms. It is recognized that colonial economic development must not only be financed largely from British capital but initiated by outright grants from British revenues. The voting of the Colonial Development and Welfare funds in 1940 and again, upon a larger scale in 1945, has been accompanied by the firmest official promises that these grants will not be the occasion for any increased intervention in the growing sphere of colonial self-government. There is no doubt that these promises are genuine, and that the first schemes of expenditure have been drawn up very largely within the colonies. But there can equally be no doubt that quite apart from the narrower implications of financial control, the colonies are in need of a great deal of expert advice and service from Britain and that the commercial and currency problems of the post-war world will add to the need for very close economic co-operation in which – since partnership is the current word – Britain must be the senior partner.

To these economic impulses towards greater imperial integration must be added those of the military dangers and obligations of the

---

[1] *Report of the Commission on Higher Education in the Colonies, 1945, Cmd. 6647.*

[2] *The Native Economies of Nigeria. Vol. I, 1946, Vol. II, 1948.*

British empire and the many other new international and regional responsibilities which for many years to come can best be performed by the dependencies grouped under British leadership. It certainly appears that the highly independent kind of self-government reached in a safer and more loosely knit world by the dominions is not so readily accessible to the present colonies. It has been a sign of these times that we have even had to see a small dominion, Newfoundland, take a constitutional step backwards.

These apparent contradictions can be harmonized if, in the Empire, as in the world in general, constitutional devices and habits are developed which allow at once of local initiatives and freedoms and of large-scale guidance and protection. Certainly it is most unlikely that any of these doubts and difficulties will cause Britain to change her policy with regard to colonial self-government. The pressure from her own political principles, and from within those colonies which have learned them from her, as well as from the world outside – where other nations, even the most illiberal, are liberal in their neighbours' affairs – will impel Britain forwards. Although there is as yet no example of an Asiatic or an African people having successfully operated the Anglo-Saxon model of parliamentary democracy, this is the model they demand and the only one, it seems, that our own faith and experience allow us to give. Even to make some adaptation of the model to local conditions will not be easy as the opposition of many of the political societies of Nigeria to the recently proposed constitution serves to show. There must always be an element of blind faith about constitutional advance since no political situation can ever have an exact precedent. Our faith need not, however, be so blind that it excuses us from any attention to the point of departure from which we are to go forward. We may have to expect much of our colonies but not that they should change all their institutions, political habits and personalities overnight. A study of colonial constitutions in their forms and in their working today and during the last ten years should therefore be a useful and, I venture to believe, an encouraging preliminary to the constitutional plans of the next five or ten years. In this hope the present series is being written. The first study which deals with the Legislative Council of the Gold Coast, and is the work of Mr Wight, is already in the press. The next volume which should appear a few months later, will deal with the Councils of Northern Rhodesia and Nigeria and it is hoped that the succeeding study will be devoted to Kenya. It is still too soon to make any definite promises about further volumes in this series.

It remains only to say a few words, as editor, about this introductory study. No excuse is needed for presenting at the outset an historical survey that traces the development of the Protean institution of the colonial council from its origins in seventeenth-century Virginia to its chief manifestations today in some forty colonial dependencies. It will be clear to those who have studied this subject how much labour was required to select from the mass of conquests, annexations, laws, constitutions, persons and places, the most significant factors and fit them into the clear and restricted design of this book. The result is to show once more the fascinating relevance of history. The problems of remote control, and of restricted delegation are fundamentally the same at all periods and the Englishman can study with interest, and perhaps, with some pride, the ways by which across three and a quarter centuries, through experiment and precedent, his fathers dealt with these same problems. The uninitiated may learn with some surprise how decorously conducted for the most part has been the potentially boisterous process of political advance in the colonies. The movements take place within a set constitutional pattern which might be compared to a stately quadrille if a quadrille were always, however imperceptibly, moving forwards. Even opposition and change has generally been governed by precedents and carried out with dignity. The main reason for this of course, has been that the dominant patterns have come from Westminster and Whitehall and have won the profound respect of colonial leaders. Critics, indeed, of the British empire, might learn much from this first attempt to trace in outline the long and complex story of colonial constitutional development. They would have to admit that it is only half the truth to say that colonial freedom was extorted in the teeth of imperial obstruction: the other half is that it was latent in the imperial forms because they in turn were derived from a constitution moving towards freedom and that in the rhythm of ideas and of men liberalism and beneficence, if not continuous, were at least constantly recurrent. As for the British reader who studies these records and pronouncements marshalled by Mr Wight, he may well hope, as he views the difficult yet vital years that lie before the colonial empire, that British ministers and imperial agents may in the future show as much wisdom and political art as, by the record of these pages, the best of their predecessors have shown in the past.

Christian Missions in Africa

Talk in a Programme to Africa for Christians in the Mission Field.

B.B.C. 16 October 1947

I feel that it is a great privilege to be allowed to talk for a few minutes to you who are serving Our Lord in Africa. These are difficult times for you out there, as they are for us at home. There must be moments when you must feel that as members of our nation you are in the position of advanced patrols operating far ahead of a base which is itself very hard pressed. It may be that the situation of this country looks worse from the distance than it really is. Many of our difficulties are mechanistic, they arise not from our mistakes, but from world maladjustments and these, if peace can be kept, may right themselves in a few years. And even though some of our problems cut deeper I believe – these are only the impressions of one mind – that the spiritual leadership needed to overcome our weaknesses is within our community. Above all there seems to be a growing realization that the main questions that face us are moral ones and must be answered in moral terms.

I can see this in the sphere of our colonial affairs in which you will be most interested and in which my own work lies. I have lately been at two Conferences – Summer Schools – organized by the Colonial Office. One was at Cambridge: it was attended by senior officers from Africa. It set itself to study the problems of local government and to report upon them. The other was at Oxford. It was attended by the more junior members of the colonial services and was intended as a kind of curtain-raiser to the second or refresher course of training for the colonial services. This will be held for the first time in the two coming University terms.

The first thing that is encouraging is that these schools should have been held at all. We organized two Colonial Service Summer schools at Oxford before the war, but they were university ventures. This time the Colonial Office itself organized the Schools. The second encouraging thing is the *way* in which they were run. There was none of that secrecy, that stuffy super-confidential atmosphere which has too often suffocated the frank discussion of colonial policy. To begin with all kinds of queer outsiders were invited to join the Schools – university people like myself, writers on colonial affairs – even critical ones – and observers from European countries, from America and from the Dominions. There were, of course, some coloured members of the colonial services and these often spoke in a racially representative, rather than a service, capacity. Discussion, whether in groups or in the main Conference, was absolutely free and frank, with senior members of the Colonial Office as well as the services answering questions and criticisms and facing problems as earnestly – I had almost said as humbly – as anyone there. It seemed so right, so sensible, that one marvelled that it had never happened before – but actually it represented a revolution in methods and in attitudes of mind. The windows of the Colonial Office seemed to have been opened and the air – even the gales – of new ideas and criticisms were blowing in.

Of course, a great deal of the discussion was specialized – forms of local government, agricultural betterment, social service problems and so on. But not only did fundamental issues often arise on these specialized questions, but they were deliberately and honestly faced.

At Cambridge, for example, the whole subject of race relations was fully discussed, without evasion, by one of the groups. Then its report, a very strong and frank report, was debated – and at more length than any other – by the whole School. At Oxford Bishop Furse gave one of the main speeches. His subject was 'The Challenge of Christianity to the Colonial Service'. It was a sermon, and a very noble one, and at night the hall was crowded for a debate in which the Bishop and other Christian speakers answered questions.

When we review these conferences and many other things that are happening at present, we can, I think, begin to see a new conception of our colonial task taking shape – and new difficulties, too. We are committed by solemn public promises to a policy of speedily developing self-government in the colonies. The colonial peoples are responding to this and to the great encouragement they get from the United Nations and the general world situation – including (let us face it!) the decline of our relative physical strength – and they are demanding immediate instalments of self-government. They see what is happening in India, Burma and Ceylon. The beginnings of nationalism can be seen in more than one African territory. Yet few who know tropical Africa can believe that the peoples living in these arbitrary pieces of the continent, with their separate tribes and languages, their poverty and ignorance, can be ready for many years to conduct their own governments. There is still much for us Europeans to do and many years in which we must go on doing it. But we – I am speaking of governments – shall have to do it in a very new spirit. The spell of our absolute authority is broken. Quite small groups can challenge our right to govern, and by their political leadership and journalism and the outside support they get, they can undermine the confidence of the people in our government. Remember that over here we see their newspapers and meet their students. With each advance in literacy their opportunity will be greater. Yet without the confidence of the majority of the people we cannot carry through our task. There is another problem – a new one which complicates the situation further. The vast new schemes of economic development by their very nature demand a high degree of European planning and control. They put matters deeply affecting the lives of every African family into the hands of the state or of large commercial corporations. And this, just as African leaders are claiming more political freedom! Here, indeed, are some circles to square!

This situation is going to demand a great deal from us in the next five – ten – fifteen years. We have got the science, the managerial skill and the constitutional expedients to meet it. It may be that we have the cultural help to give, for our universities are awakening to the needs of higher education in the colonies. But have we got the political art to handle this major problem of how and how fast to hand over power to the African peoples? More than this – have we got the moral qualities that the situation is going to demand of us – the power of sympathy of understanding to reach across racial divisions – the patience to bear the attacks of crude young nationalistic groups – the restraint to efface ourselves by degrees and to transfer real responsibility. Are we willing to trust – to take risks? Individuals can and will achieve these standards, but it is asking a great deal of a nation – of a service.

I think that more and more people over here realize that we shall not succeed in all this, or even approach success, unless many more of us who are concerned with this great enterprise find our purpose and our strength in Christ. You are working to give the Christian faith to Africa. But it seems to me that the policy of the state cannot be regarded as something wholly separate, wholly indifferent to your purposes. We have never been logical in this matter in Britain or seen the relations of Church and state as a choice between complete association or complete separation. After all, what Britain is trying to offer Africa is the liberal democratic system – call it what you will – which we have developed in our own nation. If, as I think we should agree, our form of government was largely moulded by the Christian elements in our civilization, it will lose much if not all of its confidence, its spirit and purpose, if it becomes far divorced from Christianity. Africa is being offered, or will soon be offered, a very clear-cut dynamic, and wholly non-Christian alternative from the other side of the world. What do we offer? No nation and no agency or service representing a nation has ever been wholly Christian in character or in action, and we need not expect to see this happen now. But the framework of the connexion between Britain and tropical Africa should be of a kind that will give Christians full opportunity to carry out their own special duties and also – and this of course matters most – to build up personal friendships with the people of the colonies, that one-ness we can find only in Christ. In this way they may not only help to humanize policy but construct something on a deeper level than policy or even the existing imperial connexion. The political framework will gradually be removed – we have watched it go in India and Burma. We must work so that it leaves behind – like some fine building emerging from the scaffolding – an enduring and fruitful relationship between the Africans and ourselves.

You know all this. What I am trying to state is my hope – my belief – that slowly, and perhaps still rather dimly, more and more people over here and in the colonial services are beginning to see our task in this new and spiritual light.

Foreword to *Path to Nigerian Freedom*[1]

I have never met Mr Awolowo. An editor, an English friend of his, sent me the script of this book and asked me if I would try to arrange for its publication and write a foreword. I did help to arrange for its publication. I do not, however, claim any credit for this, as I have no doubt that the book would have found a publisher upon its own merits without any intervention upon my part. With regard to the foreword, I wrote to Mr Awolowo saying that I considered some passages of his book were misleading and inaccurate and that he might, on second thoughts, wish to revise them. He replied in uncompromising terms that he would alter nothing that he had written. I thereupon told him that if I were to write the foreword he must on his side agree to accept whatever I should write. He accepted this condition.

I will explain the reasons why I commend this book to British readers. Firstly, because it is a good book. It is written in the forthright, almost sledge-hammer tradition of political pamphleteering, and it is full of hard thinking and strong feeling. I think the feeling has sometimes discoloured the thought and even led to some misinterpretation of the facts. But I am sure this results neither from malice nor from any dishonesty of mind and my disagreement does not change my respect for the writer.

In addition to its inherent merits the book has a great representative importance. We are at a stage in our relationship with the colonial peoples when it is absolutely necessary for us to know what is going on in their minds or at least in the minds of those who claim, because of their education in the knowledge of the modern world, to lead their people. The stage of their passive acceptance of colonial status, during which the British Government had to supply all the purposes and the initiatives and decide the form of government, has passed. Colonial constitutions will increasingly be shaped by the ideas of the people and moved by their wills.

We must, then, welcome any constructive contribution that comes from them. We should not be unduly distressed if it is coloured by resentment or even enlivened with abuse. There will be British readers who will be shocked and surprised by some of the remarks in this book;

[1] *Path to Nigerian Freedom* by Obafemi Awolowo, Faber & Faber 1947.

others who have knowledge of Nigeria and especially of the local Press during the last year or two will realize that the author, when compared with some others in the territory, is a relatively moderate and certainly a rational and constructive critic of British rule. His arguments, therefore, deserve serious attention and we can no longer sit back in the comfortable assurance that because our intentions are beneficent and our agents irreproachable, the well-being of Nigeria will be automatically secured and that we need not be unduly disturbed if the young nationalists are, according to their habit, somewhat noisy and tiresome as they march along their road to self-government. That attitude will not do. The Nigerian situation makes a call upon our intelligence rather than upon our indulgence and it demands what we find it so hard to give, our continuous attention.

I do not propose to anticipate the many points of criticism or of constructive advice in this book, even those with which I venture to disagree. I would rather take the opportunity to seek for the underlying causes of the tension and even the bitterness it reveals and which at present hinder the full co-operation between the British officials and the younger educated Nigerians. It must be said that I have not been in Nigeria in recent years: my knowledge is derived from reading the material which is available in Britain from that country, including the native Press, and from many contacts with Nigerian students and officials. It is clearly possible, from this restricted viewpoint, to see the sudden political intransigence of a few hundreds out of its proper proportion to the steady and quiet advance of the millions. But the situation in the empire and in the world today gives to the hundreds, whose voices reach across their boundaries, an irresistible opportunity.

What is it they are asking? This is not always clear and it is indeed one of the great merits of this book that its author is precise and offers detailed and reasoned amendments to the constitutional proposals put forward by the British Government. Generally speaking, the extremists are pressing for a much more rapid advance in self-government than the British authorities believe to be possible in the present state of Nigeria. It is the unfortunate condition of a debate of this kind that the British are in the difficult position of being obliged, with natural restraint and reluctance, to point out the present advantages of their own rule and the political unreadiness of Nigeria, while their critics, some of them without any restraint, condemn that rule and attempt to destroy the confidence and good faith in which alone it can be of service to Nigeria.

Readers will observe that Mr Awolowo, by spirited offensive tactics, tries to knock out of British hands at the very start the two main arguments in defence of their present position, the backwardness of the Africa they annexed, and the general beneficence of their rule. We cannot submit to these tactics. Indeed, Mr Awolowo himself, in spite of this and the denunciations in his earlier pages, admits, as his book proceeds, the disunity and political immaturity of Nigeria, while his frank analysis, both of achievements and problems, is in effect a justification of much, if not of the whole, of British policy. In other words, he himself is ready to recognize and to face truths which he resents hearing from us. This suggests the idea, which there is plenty of other evidence to support, that the main barriers between the British and the Nigerians – and by Nigerians I mean in this context the very small educated minority which Mr Awolowo measures as between 2 and 5 per cent – lie more in the sphere of psychology than of practical politics. Our author himself states as much.

The causes of this barrier are not far to seek. One of the strangest situations in history has resulted from the prolonged isolation and retardation of human culture in equatorial Africa followed by the sudden intrusion, little more than half a century ago, of the action and influence of the civilized world. The results were bound to be incalculably disruptive, but the depth of the disturbance was for a time masked by the difficulty, both for the European and for the African, of understanding and interpreting what was happening. It is only in quite recent years that a small but rapidly increasing number of Africans have acquired a clear knowledge both of the world in general and of their own people's position in it. For the first time they can measure the obstacles that lie between them and their acceptance as citizens of that world with the full and free national states which they so passionately desire. The realization brings with it a sense of shock and of distress. To achieve success and recognition as individuals in the universities of the West, as do so many Africans today, only strengthens their revulsion of mind from the inferior conditions and status of the African homeland to which they return. This state of mind finds its easiest relief in an explosion of angry blame, and it is easy and obvious to direct this entirely upon the British Government. It is right that Africans should hold the imperial power responsible for any faults or mistakes in her self-assumed trust but it is intellectually enervating for them to find relief in blaming 'imperialism' for the great facts of history and geography that have exposed isolated and tribal Africa to the sudden dislocating effects of twentieth-century civilization.

This must be stated. Indeed, to ignore or deny the complex conditions that are covered by the word 'backwardness', must weaken the case of the colonial critic and diminish respect for his honesty or his intelligence. But, once this self-evident fact which so largely creates their problems and must govern our policy is accepted, there is no need, least of all for the British, to insist upon it or to exaggerate it. It is, indeed, regrettable that some colonial nationalists and most 'foreign critics should be perpetually forcing these general arguments upon us at a time when all energies are needed for a vigorous partnership in building up united and self-supporting states.

In this practical work we have the whole situation to deal with and not just those elements in it which are congenial or easy. It is part of that situation, the psychological part which is so important, that educated Africans desire with a passionate intensity which history alone can explain, to prove their equality and to exercise it. It follows that many of them are in a highly sensitive and even emotional state of mind and it is part of the responsibility we have undertaken towards Africa to understand this and to put ourselves at their service in every way in our power. If we can convince them of this understanding and goodwill, the area of disagreement in the main practical question of the advance towards self-government will greatly diminish. Though it is dangerous to generalize about the character of a race – and Nigeria has a mixture of races – yet I will venture the opinion that most Africans have, to a very marked degree, the generous and responsive qualities of character: they can recognize and value highly, not indeed a generalized and self-righteous beneficence, but personal friendliness and appreciation at once of their achievements and their difficulties. They are not yet, and need never become, morose and embittered in their nationalism; they have a magnificent power of laughter which, like the English, but unlike most Indians I have met, they are prepared to turn even upon themselves. They have a great appreciation for British constitutional and legal traditions and for what their orators so often call 'British justice and fair play'. It is therefore just conceivable that even the most difficult process of the gradual transfer of power may be carried through as between Africans and British in a friendly and co-operative spirit.

It is not a vague, mutual goodwill that is required. The great value of this book seems to me that it defines from the African side the common purpose for which the British and the Nigerians have to work. It is the achievement of self-government as soon as possible within the British Commonwealth. This policy which has been defined only in the last few years – I think it was first stated by Mr Malcolm MacDonald not long before the outbreak of war – has been taken up by the African people themselves and reiterated at international councils. It marks a very great change, one from a long-term implicit purpose to one which is short-term and explicit. The theme of this book represents a question, or several questions, which we should also ask ourselves: 'Have we really accepted this change of purpose? Have we adjusted our hearts and wills to it, or do we enter upon it reluctantly and grudgingly as an unpleasant duty in which we have little faith? Can we not bring ourselves to share with the Nigerians their sense of the urgency and excitement of this political adventure?'

If the answer to all these questions is 'Yes', then we are obliged to bend all our energies and intelligence to the attainment of Nigerian self-government. Of course there are obstacles – they are faced in full measure in this book – but we must recognize them only to attack them. We must consult Africans on all points and at all times in what must be, in daily action, a joint enterprise. If we fail to pursue in this spirit a policy which we have ourselves declared, we shall forfeit the confidence of the African leaders. The British officials should be instructed to carry out this policy, and should be judged not by their success in administration, but in administrative education. If there are, perhaps, some older British members of the Colonial Service, who cannot make the very great and difficult adjustment of mind required by this newly-defined policy, then they should be enabled to retire at once, and to do so without any loss even of the respect due to the valuable and necessary services of another kind which they have rendered in the past.

If there are great obligations upon the British in the years of co-operation that lie in front of us, there are also obligations upon the Africans. Hitherto I have believed that in a relationship which we forced upon a once ignorant and helpless Africa, we were responsible for all that *they* did, even for any apparent crimes and follies in their reaction to our intrusion. But educated Africans would claim now to have come to an age of discretion and to have attained full political consciousness and would no longer ask indulgence for irrational, childish or reckless words or actions. I believe in common with Mr Awolowo that the Nigerians and the British are now inevitably in this business together and, whatever the ultimate solution, it is their interest as well as – perhaps even more than – ours to make the very best of our association in the immediately coming years. There is at present – and this is a grave thought, as the author himself shows – no Nigeria but the one traced on the map by Britain and held together in a state-system maintained by this country. If Mr Awolowo is right, as I believe he is, that in face of the deep divisions of race, culture and religion in Nigeria, political advance through natural groups and regions is the only way to a wider unity, then Britain may for long be required to provide the framework which holds these groups together until they are able to fuse into unity or federation. She will not do this successfully if journalists and others use the immense powers of influence now in their hands to destroy the goodwill and confidence between the British and Nigerian communities.

The Nigerian people, while still largely ignorant of the political and economic realities of the world, are strained and bewildered by the rapid changes in their societies and nothing is easier than to direct their vague uneasiness against the government. These propagandists may succeed in weakening the government; they will certainly weaken the will of the Nigerians to face and deal with the difficulties inherent in their present position. They might make the already difficult task of helping Nigeria towards nationhood so uncongenial that the best men of both races would hesitate to enter the public service. Further, they will undermine the respect and confidence of their British friends in this country. Already in circles friendly towards Nigeria there is disappointment at the tone and standards of some of the Nigerian newspapers. I could support this by quoting some of the intemperate, unworthy and childish generalizations that sometimes appear in editorials, but since this may be a passing phase, I hesitate to perpetuate in a book statements which, like the absurdity quoted by the author about Wilberforce, will depress those in this country who claim that Africans are ready for political progress.

I hope that when I do meet him, Mr Awolowo will forgive me for having strayed a little away from the immediate subject of his book. I have tried to sketch in for English readers, what seemed to me, its essential background. I have no doubt that his book will be carefully considered in Nigeria as well as England, and I fully expect that he will continue to contribute, in act as well as in word, to the constitutional development of his people. Nigeria's neighbour, the Gold Coast, has just made a most auspicious start with a new and advanced constitution and now the leading groups within the wide frontiers of Nigeria have a similar opportunity of showing their political capacities. They can be sure that any serious difficulties they meet will be inherent in Nigerian

Y

conditions: they will not be barriers to their advance set up by this country.

I do not mean by this that the British Government will or should in the immediate future hand over the final responsibility for this vast region with its still unintegrated groups of peoples to the first small group of African officials and professional men who emerge at the centre. The advice and help of these men – and I include women of course – should, however, be used to the full, both in central and regional affairs. It rests largely with this group to make use of the new constitution to hasten the political education of their people. It is not, as this book shows, by manifestoes and editorials, that the power to govern Nigeria will be gained, but by hard political and administrative work, whether at central, regional, provincial or municipal levels. The evident readiness of at least a substantial core of each regional group to conduct the business of modern administration will be the unanswerable argument for further advance. No British government would have the wish or power to meet this practical argument with a negative.

Nigerians, building on their old foundations, have a fine administrative structure to show for the half-century during which they have drawn upon European forms and ideas. Each of the three main groups should now be able to develop further its special capacities. The Hausa have their large and historic city-states and their Islamic traditions of law and discipline. The Yoruba have their happy and fertile marriage of aristocratic and democratic principles and of urban and rural societies. The Ibo, lacking in social cohesion, supply their equalitarian outlook and intense individual vitality. If the new Nigerian constitution can express and develop the special virtues of the main groups, each of these might well make, out of its many component societies, a unit sufficient in size, numbers and in its unified culture, to rank some day as a nation. If, however, the main groups can come together at the centre to pool and share their traditions and resources, whether through a federal or a unitary system, then there may some day be a Nigeria which will be a leading power on the African continent and might make Africa's main contribution in the international sphere.

The day when Nigeria from being a name written on a map by Sir George Goldie and an administrative framework put together by Lord Lugard, becomes a true federation, still more a nation, is still far away. Yet there lies before us here as large, as interesting and honourable an aim to pursue as we achieved in the building up of the great white dominions. This book gives us the opportunity to enter into the mind of a Nigerian nationalist and, perhaps, to sympathize with his ambitions. If Nigerians could be made, in these first stages of the construction, to feel that we shared with them both the ultimate vision and some of the ardour and urgency they are trying to put into its realization, trusteeship would in fact as well as in current theory give way to partnership.

Sir Donald Cameron

OBITUARY

16 January 1948

As I had the privilege of studying the administration of Tanganyika when Sir Donald Cameron was Governor, and had the same experience shortly afterwards in Nigeria, I should like to offer my testimony to his work as Governor in these territories.

I think that his most individual and creative work was in Tanganyika. His predecessor had got the country into something like normal condition after the prolonged fighting and dislocation of the 1914–18 war, but there was still a largely blank sheet upon which the new Governor could design the form of administration which Britain would give to the ex-German colony. Cameron worked boldly and quickly. He took the principles his old chief, Lugard, had developed in Nigeria but, being no slave to forms, he adapted them freely and intelligently to the scores of chieftainships, large and small, which covered most of the area, and put them firmly aside where they did not suit detribalized conditions. The result was a system at once flexible in form, realistic in execution, and very consciously aimed at developing political experience even in the smallest units.

In Nigeria his task was less clear-cut and he felt the contrast after the freedom Tanganyika had given to his masterful initiative. He was very critical of much that he found, especially in the north, and was determined that no misguided respect for the forms of indirect rule or illusory ideas of building up princely states should be allowed to interfere with Britain's duty to promote just and progressive administration in the interests of the common people. I do not think he was wholly satisfied with what he achieved in this governorship but the sum of his influence and of his judicial and other reforms was surely to head the country into a direction more in line with modern developments and the awakening consciousness of the people.

Cameron will certainly stand out as one of the greater governors. He had unlimited confidence and courage and no fears of the new forces which he recognized. Close up, he had his blemishes. Though a most kindly and generous host and quickly sensitive to selfishness and injustice, his humour could be too mordant, his dislikes too violent while, in later years, as great personal sorrows and increasing blindness shadowed his life, he sometimes seemed to lose his old sense of proportion. But when we look at the administration as a whole, or at the man in the prime of achievement, he stands as an impressive figure in the colonial record, a man of power, almost ruthlessly decisive, and of original and humane mind. The key to his success is to be found in the humanity. Without it his strength and efficiency would have been overbearing: with it he never forgot that the material upon which he was working was composed of people and of people whom he meant to serve and in whom he had faith.

Destiny of the Sudan

The Times 3 May 1948

The most striking change in the Sudan in the last 10 years has been in the political climate. In the towns it is politics all day long, over every meal and drink, in the clubs and schools and coffee-shops. Yet it was only 12 years ago, at the signing of the Anglo-Egyptian Treaty, that the educated element was stung into political consciousness by the fear that Britain and Egypt were settling their political destiny over their heads. The war drew attention away from politics. The Sudanese suffered little, but played their part in the great campaigns of North Africa. When these ended their pent-up political energies burst out with fresh vigour and the recent deadlock between Britain and Egypt has fallen upon them with bitterly frustrating effects.

If this political restlessness portended the birth of a true Sudanese nationalism the British task would be simple. Once again, in endeavouring to transfer her powers, she is faced by disunity among the recipients. In the Sudan the disunity is complex: beneath the superficial political cleavages there are deeper causes, both economic and social. The most immediate cleavage is that between rulers. The Egyptian Government is right in asking that Britain should not drive a wedge between two natural and necessary allies, but it is grossly overplaying a good hand. Long-term Egyptian interests lie in orderly and efficient government, not in undermining civil discipline and hindering the smooth and gradual transfer of power. Below this disunity, and partly conforming to it, are the divisions among the Sudanese. The main parties are the Ashigga, who hope for self-government in co-operation with Egypt, and the Umma, who desire complete independence but are prepared to work for a time with Britain to attain it.

The party leaders, in search for a wider support than that of the urban and official Graduates Congress, turned to the great sectarian divisions of the northern Sudan, grouped round the two Sayeds, Sir Ali Mirghani, and Sir Abdel Rahman el Mahdi. These historic religious divisions conform to the still deeper division between the sophisticated urban riverain peoples with their commercial and racial links with Egypt, and the tribes of the sandy plains reaching west to Darfur and east to the Red

Sea. The first group profited on the whole from nineteenth-century Egyptian rule; the second had their revenge in the Mahdia. Behind lies the oldest social conflict in the world, that between the nomad and the sedentary, between the desert and the sown.

This picture is, in fact, over-simplified; Mirghanist sections exist among the tribes, while some of the ablest officials belong to the Umma. Nor is the Mahdi's son the figure his name and leadership suggest. As a great cotton producer he has a vested interest in security and efficiency. As a progressive educationist, with many British friends, he protests that his father never intended Gordon's death, and asks why the Mahdi should be made responsible for the oppressions committed after his death by the Khalifa.

Cutting across the political and religious divisions is the opposition between age and youth. Western knowledge without western social discipline isolates young men above the illiterate masses in a kind of moral vacuum. They are all government officials, junior or potential, and the gradualism of the plans for Sudanization baulks their natural impatience for promotion. Those attracted to Egyptian universities reach new heights of antagonism to Britain, and even absorb (a new development this) some undergraduate Communism. Those literate only in Arabic are enclosed within the mental sphere of the Egyptian extremist Press or of the dozen local papers, mostly begun since 1945, which denounce the 'colonizers' week after week. To the division of youth and age must be added, for the educated, that deep and tragic inequality between themselves and their wives which is driving some of the men to give eager support to female education which will at least benefit their sons-in-law.

All this refers to the northern, the Arab, Sudan. The largest cleavage of all is between this and the Negro south. The Arabs have been deeply suspicious of the government's intentions here. The difficult decision has now been made not to give constitutional endorsement to this division, but to trust that the southern peoples will develop their own characteristics and interests while gaining the economic advantages of union with the north.

In the new proposed constitution the British are endeavouring belatedly, and therefore hastily, to introduce parliamentary social democracy in these unreceptive conditions. The constitution can do little but paper over the cracks of the country's complex divisions. These were vividly illustrated at the recent meeting of the Northern Advisory Council. The British character of the government was represented at a central table where sat the three Secretaries, Civil, Financial and Legal.

The 28 nominated and elected representatives of northern Sudan faced them in a half-circle. In the middle were the 13 sophisticated members representing social and economic interests and the Khartoum province. The most active of these were the senior officials in European dress. Right and left sat the tribal representatives, Nazirs and Sheikhs in spotless white turbans and flowing robes. The division between the two groups emerged when the urban members showed some consternation at the electoral clauses of the draft constitution which, on the population basis, gave a large majority to the indirectly elected tribal members as against the directly elected townsmen. They pressed for more democratization, for the immediate appointment of Sudanese ministers, and a 50 per cent. Sudanese Executive Council. The Nazirs, not much interested in democracy, firmly claimed their right to stand for election and to retain their tribal offices if elected.

What hope can there be of a successful semi-parliamentary system which is in advance of the desires and capacities of the vast majority while it is rejected by Egypt and by the young Sudanese as hopelessly illiberal? To political difficulties could be added economic in a country which, however poor and simple its economy, has achieved its present rising standard of life under an elaborate system of state control which would quickly break down in inexperienced hands. The revenue depends largely upon the great Gezira scheme, which supplies four-fifths of the cotton and represents 80 per cent. of the exports. This scheme will be taken over by the government from the companies in 1950. It will present most difficult problems of state-trading and of the relation of agricultural control and local government among a population of 500,000 tenants and their families, who are just beginning to wake up to their corporate interests and to organize themselves. Meanwhile the Sudan is running into labour problems illustrated by the railway strike last March.

Such a list of difficulties leaves out the human factor which may well turn the scale against them. First among these is the quality of the British service. Its past record, probably the most beneficent in the history of any empire, is well known. But it may not be realized that in the last few years its members have carried out one of the most difficult of all adjustments, that from an authoritarian tradition towards a new relationship of co-operation. In most departments progressive reforms are being enacted. Tribal government is changing from the old system of indirect rule into local government on British principles. In spite of the political excitement, the British have retained the confidence and even the friendship of most of the Sudanese officials and notables. With little support and understanding from British opinion, in a bewildering diplomatic situation under a fusillade of abuse from Egypt, taken up by sections of the Sudanese, they have maintained a steady and sympathetic administration.

If intense political consciousness is the first thing that strikes the observer, the second is the astonishing way in which the Sudanese, especially in the upper and middle official ranks, have accepted British standards and principles, grafting them upon their own dignified and virile characters. The visitor to the Sudan who makes contact with these generous and hospitable people feels charged with a message from them to his own country. It is that, behind all the ferment and extravagances of youth, there is, at least in the north, a fine nation in the making, eager to emerge from the status under which they have so long remained, and be recognized and appreciated by the world and especially by Britain. The leading Sudanese with experience of administration have shown themselves to be men of high intelligence, integrity and ability. Britain has an opportunity in the Sudan to transform imperial rule by stages into friendly cultural and economic co-operation. The task will be difficult, but the visitor travels the Sudan today convinced as much by the evidence of the heart as of the head that it is not beyond achievement.

Former Italian Colonies

Letter to *The Times* 7 July 1948

In the summer of 1948 the future of Italy's three lost African colonies was the subject of international discussions in which Russia and Poland favoured their return to Italy.

Sir, – There appears to be some movement of opinion favouring the return to Italy of her former East African colonies.

The reasons are obvious: this solution seems the most likely to obtain four-power agreement and to prevent any form of Russian intrusion into Africa, while Western support of it will strengthen the present Italian Government against Communism. These reasons, however immediately weighty, have nothing to do with the African merits of the case. Decisions taken thus have more than once landed us later in political and moral difficulties. Let us summarize the arguments on the other side.

While it is difficult to find agreed standards by which to judge an empire, I submit that Italy's record in East Africa makes a poor case for her re-establishment there. In road-building her work was magnificent; her artisans, able and industrious, are still in demand in Africa; her medical services, especially for her own people, were excellent. But she did little to develop the native peoples, and the excessive numbers of petty Italian officials and tradesmen barred their advancement. Economically, her monopolistic egoism and corruption were destructive: in spite of immense capital outlay the colonies remained unproductive and burdensome.

Among other records, turn to the objective, almost incidental, evidence of our soldiers and administrators, especially in the recent *British Military Administration in East Africa 1941–7*. We learn that in Cyrenaica the human and animal population in 1939 was less than before Italian occupation: of Somalia we read of 'savage repression and punishments backed by large military and police establishments which were the rule under the Italian régime'; of 'brutality' in prisons which were 'deplorable in every way'. The agricultural experiments there were based on 'a labour policy of considerable severity in theory and actual brutality in practice. It was, in fact, indistinguishable from slavery.'

British support of retrocession would lay us open to a charge of betrayal. The promises made explicitly in Cyrenaica were surely implicit in the anti-Italian propaganda and the appeals to the peoples in East Africa to rise and help us to expel their rulers. A reversal would have wide effects among coloured peoples, especially in our colonies.

Ethiopia's interests deserve respect. Italy's aggression against her is generally regarded as one of the most brutal and lawless in modern history. It was followed by further brutality, including the deliberate massacre of the intelligentsia. After liberating and supporting Ethiopia would it, to say the least, be logical for Britain to replace the aggressor in one or both of her invasion bases? Admittedly Eritrea was, before Fascism, the best administered Italian colony. But Mr Bevin (*Hansard*, 4 June 1946) and Mr Jebb (Peace Conference, 29 July 1946) both accepted the justice of Ethiopia's claim to the greater part of Eritrea, presumably referring, though in too large a term, to the plateau which from ancient days has been culturally and racially Ethiopian.

The old strong reasons against putting Somalia, inhabited by one nomadic and high-spirited people, under divided control become stronger with the realization of the increase of this people, their resultant disturbing drift south-westwards, and their belated but intense infection with the germ of nationalism.

While the colonies offer a powerful diplomatic weapon for immediate use, they have been more a matter of prestige and party politics in Italian history than of sustained national interest or necessity. With Ethiopia lost, the semi-arid colonies could not, even with the virtual displacement of their peoples from the best lands, solve Italy's economic or population problems.

The Western powers are committed to a tutelage in democratic self-government in the colonies. Would Italy be a good tutor even in the local government sphere? After a series of rapid and complete defeats, publicly staged before her native subjects, could she regain the prestige and moral authority to rule and lead them?

Retrocession might prove a boomerang. Should Italy, against all our hopes, turn Communist, then the alternative version of 'democracy' would find a local headquarters in Africa.

I have been obliged to restrict myself to the negative aspect of the question. If the international inquiry commission fails to offer a unanimous, just, or viable solution, Britain, as conqueror and caretaker of these colonies, will have to offer her own positive proposals.

Yours faithfully, MARGERY PERHAM

Rome in Africa

On 10 January The Times *published an article upon excavations of the splendid Roman remains in north Spain, with comment in a leading article. This inspired Mrs Huxley to write a letter in further comment. She noted the success of the Romans in developing agriculture even in the dry lands of the Mediterranean coast. She also remarked upon the Roman success in binding peoples to her 'civilized glories' and incorporating them in her imperial structure. This letter provoked me in turn to further disagreement with my old antagonist in this letter published on 17 January 1949.*

Sir, – I would suggest that Roman analogies applied to the British empire in 1949 are as misleading as at first sight they are fascinating. In so far as Rome won the loyalty of her subject peoples, it was surely when she alone could offer them security and civilization.

Today Britain is one, and not the most powerful, among several imperial nations, while one of these offers alternative leadership and a seductive, anti-imperial philosophy to colonial peoples. In addition, the nations are trying to build up super-national agencies, more and less inclusive, which compete with the colonial powers in offering civilizing services and security to backward peoples. Even if a Roman policy were possible in such an un-Roman world, it is a policy which Britain deliberately rejected many years ago. She has already emancipated her white Dominions and has extended this freedom to Ceylon, India and Pakistan, leaving Burma and Eire to prove the character of the new Commonwealth by leaving it. Whether this policy has been right or wrong, a sudden attempt to reverse or revise it with regard to the present colonies is less likely, in the present world situation, to hold them in the Commonwealth than to precipitate a complete separation which need never occur.

Mrs Huxley has a gift for putting dramatic questions, but we need not be dejected if we cannot find in this large and complex empire and world the material for a dramatic answer. But if we dismiss the possibility she raises of reconsidering the policy of self-government, we should admit that her letter calls us to face the very great difficulties of carrying it out. It has so happened that the colonial peoples least qualified by their past degree of civilization and unity to conduct a modern state are likely to have the shortest apprenticeship in that art. We have to find ways of giving their leaders responsibilities that satisfy their need for self-expression and status without ourselves abandoning the tasks, including, as Mrs Huxley is so well qualified to insist, the scientific management of their imperilled natural resources, which the realities of the situation impose upon us. These are moments when this dualism seems impossible, but I have confidence in the power of the realities to assert themselves and in the capacity of the educated – the fully educated – African leaders to recognize them.

We did, after all, give centralization and repression a short trial in America and a long trial in Ireland, and learned that it was largely by our readiness to lose the white colonies as dependencies that we won them as Dominions. There are not, of course, the same ties of blood and culture with non-Europeans, but Africans, to fill the voids with which history left them, are taking as much from us as the Gauls took from Rome. There is, as Mrs Huxley suggests, much to be gained by greater expression, both imaginative and practical, of the Commonwealth idea. But, if there is anything to be learned from Rome's experience, it is surely that we shall hold the colonies as long as we serve their needs and as long as the imperial nation is sound enough at home to command respect and imitation.

To pursue Mrs Huxley to the ruins at the end of her letter, I see no reason why the council chambers and law courts, with the university colleges now being built out of taxes collected in this country, should not attest centuries hence, whether as ruins or as institutions with a life of their own, that with even more generosity, if with less art, than the Romans, we took to remote and primitive lands the best things we had to give.

Yours faithfully, MARGERY PERHAM

Native Policy in South Africa

Letter to *The Times* 11 March 1949

This letter was evoked by the movement on the part of Dr Malan's govern-
ment towards the policy of apartheid *based, in the first place, upon the*
removal of remaining rights of Africans to the vote and to their Native
Representative Council.

Sir, – Measures are being taken in the Union of South Africa today
which threaten the few remaining political rights of Africans. The constitution and conventions of the Commonwealth forbid any official
intervention by our government; unofficial opinion also is silenced by
this knowledge and by fear of appearing to claim a moral superiority by
sitting in judgement upon those who are dealing with a profoundly
difficult situation of which we in this country have no experience.

These are strong arguments for silence, but there are some strong
ones for speech. Our government has, of course, no status to interfere
directly with the racial policies of the Union. But the new solidarities of
the world oblige it to have a policy and deploy its influence in these
matters. On the plane of the United Nations, British representatives
have to speak, to vote, or to abstain from voting about the future of
South-West Africa and of Indians in Natal, and on these occasions our
nation is under severe public observation. On the narrower plane of
relations with the United States and the Western Union there is a great
range of consultation in which, even upon economic and defence issues,
our government cannot wholly ignore the dangers and uncertainties of
the new Union policy. These problems occur again in most embarrassing
form in the councils of the Commonwealth. On the plane of Africa, a
continent which is being quickly drawn together, the decision of South
Africa to turn back on the road of native policy just when Britain is
increasing her forward pace in a dozen African colonies raises most
serious future possibilities. Our plans for orderly political progress in
tropical Africa may be ruined if the south becomes a breeding ground
for racial hatred expressed in Communism or worse. Even if we narrow
the picture to southern Africa our government must shortly decide upon

the future of territories on the very borders of the Union, while, for all practical purposes, within the Union, lie the three Protectorates clinging desperately to our rule. At all these levels British ministers are obliged to take decisions which must directly or indirectly affect the Union's native policy. It is surely preferable that they should be assisted in these questions by expression of British opinion rather than that they should be negotiated in the weakness of an embarrassed secrecy.

There can be little doubt as to where the weight of informed British opinion lies in these questions. It might, however, be retorted that if, in the hundred odd years in which we had the power, we tried and failed to impose our own native policy upon South Africa, we can hardly expect to do so now. But it may be that since we lost our old power to impose, we have gained a new power to influence. Then we could draw only upon our own strivings towards a Christian and equalitarian policy and this tended to be doctrinaire and inconstant. Now it has been strengthened by democratic advances at home and by bold enfranchisements in many parts of the empire. Then the world was unorganized and indifferent to native interests; now, for reasons good and less good, it supports them and has organs for expression and action. Then South Africa could go her own way in the isolation of its sub-continent: now no nation can do without strong friends and supporters. Then Africans were politically impotent: now about 130 million people of African Negro blood, some half of them our fellow-subjects in the Commonwealth, have leaders who are beginning to be conscious of their race, both in the whole and in its parts, and who are voicing today demands for political and social equality which will yearly become more difficult to refuse. We have indeed accepted them, and our future position in Africa depends upon the constancy with which we act upon that decision.

In the face of this changed situation I suggest that we should use all our influence with the Union, and use it with greater hope than ever before that it will be effective. But our approach should be one of respect and restraint. We should remember not only the gravity of her many internal problems, not only the great services which in spite of them she gave to the allied cause in the last war, but also that, however mistaken we must regard her recently proposed native policy, in some of its educational and social achievements she still gives the lead to Africa. But we should be encouraged most of all by the knowledge that a very large section of both elements of her European population themselves disapprove of the proposed measures and that among them are men and women of great courage and humanity who, while they may welcome our moral support, have nothing to learn from us upon this subject, and everything that hard experience and personal self-sacrifice can teach.

Yours, &c., MARGERY PERHAM

Native Policy in South Africa and the High Commission Territories

Letter to *The Times* 16 December 1949

Sir, – May I take up the question at the end of your leading article today upon *apartheid* and express the hope, which I believe is generally held in this country, that Dr Malan will not ask for the transfer of the three High Commission territories in the New Year? The question, embarrassingly entangled as it is with that of Union native policy, was fully debated in 1909 and 1934: in 1949, in so far as conditions, internal and external to South Africa, have changed, they unfortunately strengthen the case for refusal.

On the internal side there is no need to repeat the strong historic claims of the tribes upon Britain. But their original unwillingness to enter the Union because of its failure to extend the liberal system of the Cape to the other provinces is stronger now when Dr Malan proposes – and his plans are only postponed – to destroy the last remaining civic rights of the African majority. The consultations to which we are pledged could lead only to the full expression and consolidation of the tribes' rejection of transfer and, at least among the high-spirited mountain people of Basutoland, a British colony and not a protectorate, its enforcement might well lead to prolonged resistance and bloodshed. Even if Britain could conceivably agree to coercion, would South Africans really wish to add an embittered million to their native population just when its affairs are entering a critical stage? Externally, the difficulties would be greater. If both sides shrank from enforced transfer when it would have been a domestic matter, how much more when it would cause a world-wide scandal? Support expressed at the United Nations and offered by Communism would sharpen and prolong the discontent of the transferred. Within the Commonwealth, especially among its newest members, the effects would be most unhappy, while, for herself, Britain would seriously weaken the confidence she is asking from all her colonial peoples during the difficult advance towards self-government.

It is in Africa, however, that the results would be gravest. The Commonwealth states there are being developed upon principles utterly

z

opposed to those of South Africa, a position which, history suggests, too often leads ultimately to physical conflict. Britain's wide responsibilities in the continent impose upon her the duty of mediating between these two extremes, while in the east and centre she faces other versions of what is fundamentally the same problem as in South Africa. In dealing with this situation she will need all her moral and political authority, and both will be endangered if, while she treats Africans as men in the Gold Coast and in Kenya, she agrees to treat them as something less south of the Zambesi. Does not the question of these territories, itself a microcosm of the race-relations problem of Africa as a whole, force all those concerned with the continent to face the dangerous drift of its affairs and to look for a way in which, at whatever cost, the security of the white communities and their great contributions to Africa can be preserved without refusing the surrounding Africans any share of the rights inherent in our civilization? So long as South Africans see the transfer of the territories as an isolated, bilateral question they will condemn our lack of understanding for their peculiar difficulties and regard our 'not now' as an officious and unthinking 'never'. If they could see the question in its continental, indeed, in its world perspective, they might realize that Britain has both the right and the power to help in the solution of one of the widest and deepest problems of our century.

The development of larger views and counsels would take time. On the immediate issue the only way to avoid blank irreconcilability and persuade the Union Government not to use the pressures which geography and economics have put into its hands, is to treat this question with the utmost restraint and endeavour to bring moderate opinion on both sides into touch. We know that South Africans are divided both upon native policy and upon the demand for immediate transfer of the territories. Even among the adherents of *apartheid* there are some who give the word its genuine meaning and support it, not as a device for hardening the present stratification of society, but as a real and maybe costly opportunity for native development. We upon our side should guard against allowing our wards to crystallize, under our protection, a jealous and archaic tribalism: we should rather deliberately train leaders who, with knowledge wider than their own diminutive nationalisms, may eventually guide their people towards a willing and intelligent acceptance of their South African environment.

Yours faithfully, MARGERY PERHAM

Parliamentary Government in the Sudan

The Times 20 June 1949

During the last few months the new Constitution of the Sudan has been in action. An Executive Council of 12 – six British members and six Sudanese Ministers and Under-Secretaries – have worked under the presidency of the Governor-General. In British cabinet fashion the 12 have sat, with eight other Sudanese Under-Secretaries, in the Legislative Assembly. This also includes 10 members elected in the six major towns on a low property franchise, 52 northern rural members indirectly elected; 13 elected at provincial councils for the Negro south, and 10 nominated by the Governor-General.

The constitution has started well. The Council meets in private, but it is no secret that its proceedings have been wholly constructive. Abdalla Bey Khalil, an ex-Army officer with a distinguished record and the secretary of the Umma, or Independence Party, was elected almost unanimously by the Assembly as its leader and helped to choose his Sudanese colleagues. These, in the dearth of experienced politicans, are all senior officials who have resigned or been seconded and whose moderate and realistic conduct in both the administrative and legislative sides of their work has won the confidence of the Assembly, which has steadily voted down extreme motions. The members have brought their natural dignity and courtesy into their Parliament and have conscientiously learned House of Commons procedure under the Sudanese ex-judge who is their Speaker.

There have been two surprises. One was the spate of questions, obviously inspired by constituents who have taken immediate advantage of their new representation to press local needs for education, medical services, roads, but, above all, in this thirsty land, for water supplies. The other surprise came from the southerners. These, after much British heart-searching, have been brought into the Assembly, and the northerners have now the chance to win these people, once regarded as potential slaves, as their fellow-citizens. All wondered what would be both the competence and the attitude of the first dozen educated Christian tribesmen. The 'Black Bloc' has shown ability, dignity and restraint. The writer heard an impressive speech from one of them deprecating a demand for speedy self-government and pointing out the danger of an unready people passing under a government which – here he quoted Mr Churchill – would own the people instead of being owned by them. In general, the proceedings of Council and Assembly, the experience of free and full debates on legislation and finance, the questions and answers, the crowded galleries, and the radio and Press reports of proceedings, have all constituted an effective apprenticeship in the art of parliamentary government.

The Sudan Government, including their new Sudanese element, may be congratulated upon this initial success. The atmosphere in Khartoum and Omdurman today is far different from that of a year ago. Yet the success is limited and precarious. For the new constitution has been enacted in the face of its repudiation by Egypt. Moreover, the parties which, in their fear of a revived Mahdism, favour some degree of 'unity of the Nile Valley' boycotted the elections, encouraged protest demonstrations, and still, with Egyptian encouragement, refuse all co-operation. As they include many of the educated and urban elements their absence weakens the effectiveness of the new institutions. The 'unity' groups do, however, appear to have been impressed by the moderate conduct of the Assembly and agreeably disappointed to find that it has not become an instrument of the opposing extremists. Some of them regret their non-co-operation, but their demands for changes in the electoral law, such as would restrict the influence of the tribal leaders – here they share in one of the main problems of tropical Africa – would be difficult to accept, at least in full, in the present social stage of the country.

In face of these problems, the difficult decision as to the pace of political advance rests mainly upon a few senior British officials. Placed between a hostile Egyptian Government and a British Foreign Office neither constituted nor qualified to direct the internal administration of the Sudan, their chief loyalty is to the Sudanese, whose interests they must interpret as best they can. After a belated start – an Advisory Council for the Northern Sudan was set up only in 1944 – the Sudan Government have now taken a large step forward and the arguments for a compensating pause seem strong. The 7 million people, spread thinly over 1 million square miles, are poor and, away from the towns and rivers, educationally backward; many are semi-nomadic. They suffer from multiple divisions – between the two main parties; between tribes, races and languages; between nomad and sedentary; between Muslim, pagan and Christian.

Half the revenues, prosperous at the moment, are drawn from cotton and mostly from schemes which depend upon expert and steady government control and upon irrigation services and research. The great Gezira scheme, with its 20,000 tenants and its 1 million acres watered from the Sennar dam, will pass entirely into the hands of the government in 1950 and all the difficult questions of the relations between state and public corporations and the maintenance of labour efficiency will arise. It would not, therefore, be surprising if a government of officials, whose whole training prompts them to aim first at efficiency and purity of administration, should be tempted to hold back, after their recent great act of faith, from further devolution of power.

Among the arguments for advance are the recent clear promises to the Sudanese. The test for self-government can no longer be a politically mature majority but a sufficient minority of capable leaders and experts to take over control from Europeans who will continue to help and advise. This human material is not a fixed element; in Khartoum today the leaders are growing in political stature as they brace themselves to shoulder true responsibility. As for the test of unity, we must be content with an adequate nucleus which will grow with the gathering together of representatives of all groups in the absorbing task of building up their own government. As reinsurance against failure there could be, as in Nigeria, regional institutions to allow of an orderly retreat upon federation or even partition. The world tendency against the old imperialism and in favour of equality gives strength to the weakest national cause; to bar or unduly check its momentum is to betray the experienced and co-operative group to the extremists and make impossible a gradual and friendly transfer of power. Nor will the emancipation of Cyrenaica be unobserved in the Sudan.

The problem has its Egyptian aspect. The political immoderation of Egypt and her Palestine distractions have allowed the Sudan Government to advance the Sudanese to a position from which there can now be no retreat. Only last year there was serious discussion as to how Egyptians could be introduced into the new councils; today, with these in being, it is difficult to imagine their presence. Nor, with the new proposals for Nile control, can Egypt any longer claim the need to rule the lands from which she draws her water. But the problem must be viewed even more widely against the great political and strategic division of the present world. If, in this context, Britain defines her interest and her interests in the Sudan – for she has both – she might find that her exclusive imperial needs have decreased with the widening of the general west versus Slav cleavage, but that this cleavage finds social and political reflection in the Near East. Communism has reached Egypt and will find fertile soil in her gross contrasts between privilege and poverty. From Egypt it has just reached the Sudan. In this country of poor but independent and equal peasantry pashadom hardly exists. But political frustrations and divisions and student intransigence offer some nourishment to a creed of discontent. Further, a new workers' movement, independent so far of all parties, has recently shown its power to call a token general strike.

This situation demands from Britain a policy which both resists the temptation to take undue advantage of Egypt's mistakes and embarrassments – since the Sudan has got to live always with her more powerful neighbours – and also avoids slipping into an alliance with Egyptian reaction out of fear of Communism. She has to make Egypt realize the emergence of the Sudan and make the Sudanese realize it themselves by trusting them with increasing responsibility.

If the 1936 atmosphere of reason and confidence between Britain and Egypt could be revived it might be possible to repeat the British offer of an Anglo-Egyptian–Sudanese joint council to review and assist Sudanese evolution. In the Sudan we should show the moderates of both parties – who are not really divided on domestic issues – and the workers that the new constitution offers a really constructive and unifying society where members of all parties, sects and classes can work together.

This is what the British officials and their new Sudanese colleagues are beginning to do. If they succeed they will create a new nation, at least in the north – for nationhood is far distant for the backward tribal south – which will be free to join Egypt in fusion or alliance. And Britain will retain that widespread trust and friendship which our fellow-countrymen have won in the Sudan by fifty years of good administration.

The Colonial Dilemma

The Listener 15 July 1949

The idea, I think I might say the anxiety, behind our title, 'The Colonial Dilemma', is this. There is today a widespread expectation, even a demand, for large and quick results, economic and political, from the colonies. We feel that many of these hopes may not be fulfilled unless the great obstacles in their way can be understood and, as far as possible, overcome. It is these obstacles which we want to try to explain.

First, let us see how these expectations have been built up. Almost every time the colonies are mentioned – and that is often these days – you may notice as a constant refrain the two words 'colonial development'. In this country we hear about our Colonial Development and Welfare Fund, our Colonial Development Corporation, our Overseas Food Corporation. Some of the plans under them – that for ground-nut development, for example – come excitingly near our own kitchens and dinner tables. Then, dovetailing into our own efforts, are all the ten-year development plans drawn up in the colonies.

The colonial leaders are using these same two words, 'colonial development', in very different tones. They say they want much more rapid development, generally political or, it may be, industrial. But they have behind them, in asking for this, a strong urge towards equality, not only material equality but what is called 'parity of esteem', which affects, not only individuals and classes, but nations and races which feel that they are regarded as inferior. Then there are the critics at the United Nations taking up this idea and addressing denunciations to us in even stronger tones for the way we are developing – or rather *not* developing – the colonies, especially in the political and social field. They demand results, revolutionary results, not in ten years but in five years or one year. Again, we have recently heard that the colonial powers of the western group have set up an 'Overseas Territories Working Group' through which to direct European Recovery Programme funds towards colonial development. And now we hear of Mr Truman's Fourth Point and of the first appropriation of 45,000,000 dollars to help the rapid development of the colonies. And in the last three or four days ideas have been thrown out of solving the dollar crisis by turning the colonies – and especially Africa – into a kind of economic extension or buttress of western Europe. Altogether a pretty formidable concentration of what might be called developmental urge upon the colonies!

Yet the conditions and the difficulties in the countries from which these results are expected are still little known, even to many people who belong to them and certainly to most of our critics at the United Nations. This is not at all surprising. After all, there are so many colonies. And they are so different from anything our experience of Britain or Europe can help us to imagine. And they are so different from each other. Each group of colonies and often each colony within a group has its own character – its own climate, crops, history, people – which need their own special plan, not some generalized 'colonial' plan. To take only one example – the West Indian group is unique in its history and in many of its conditions. Yet even within the group how different is Barbados from, say, British Guiana. Barbados is a compact, crowded, highly cultivated little island with a large, relatively solid population of African ancestry and a historical beginning as a British settlement. British Guiana has half its population East Indian; it is not an island but an edge of the Latin-American continent and it began as a Dutch colony. It has great rivers, a vast undeveloped hinterland and the special problems set by its dangerously low coast.

But the main obstacle to the rapid development of the colonies lies in their general backwardness. When we talk about development we are looking ahead to a point of destination. But do we sufficiently remember the point of departure? Do we realize the conditions of poverty, ignorance and isolation in which most of the colonial peoples lived when we began anything that can be called development? Think of the utter isolation of the Pacific islands – their static human conditions in all that physical loveliness. Think of the slave-population of the West Indies at the time of the emancipation – deprived of country, community, language, family, freedom and self-respect. Think, above all, of Africa, as seen by the explorers or described in the earliest official reports. There were areas of higher culture, especially in West Africa, but for the most part tropical Africa was inhabited by many hundreds of independent tribes, often at war with one another, speaking different languages, each following different customs and pagan religions. They had for centuries or, indeed, millenia, been adapting themselves to a tropical environment that in most parts made life easy up to a low standard but very difficult to improve beyond that. Then, for the most part only about fifty years ago, modern Europe broke with great suddenness upon this continent. For the first ten years after annexation the

British governments were finding their way about these regions, making their first full contact with the many tribes, and building up a rough and ready system of administration. Serious attempts at education and economic development could only come later as knowledge, funds and staff allowed. And remember that two world wars cut across the attempts of this fifty years and between them came the great slump which hit primary producing countries – and their revenues – hard. Even so, much has been accomplished.

Anyone who knew what Africa was and what it is today – and I have been visiting Africa at intervals for twenty-five years – anyone looking at the roads and railways, the schools and ploughs, and bicycles and clothes, at African journalists, lawyers, doctors, African political leaders making resounding English speeches in the legislatures, might exclaim 'What amazing changes! What wonderful development in the time.' But all this is a mere start. A lot of the changes that catch the eye are changes only on the surface. You do not have to go very far away from the main roads and railways or the areas that have felt the chief impact of economic development, to find the old Africa lying almost untouched, immense areas of it. And we need also to face the superficial or even the damaging nature of many of the changes that at first sight seem so impressive. For you cannot change people as quickly as you can change conditions. One of the great questions today, in face of the terrific conditioning influence of the modern state, is how fast you can change people without spiritual injury. Often the new influences we have brought break up the close-knit families and tribes too quickly and the people have not been able in time to absorb a new religion, or build up new bonds and loyalties, new incentives to work. Hence, alongside the successful adaptation, you find restlessness, disruption, even demoralization such as you see among the raw tribesmen-turned-proletariat and the runaway tribal girls who make the prostitutes or the temporary wives of the new African slums.

How can a society in this condition become very productive in a very short time? Some people seem to think that colonial development is rather like using an automatic machine – you put your capital in at one end, and you pull out cotton, cocoa, sisal, sugar, rubber, oils and minerals at the other. And the more capital you put in the more of these desirable colonial goods you pull out. They may base their hopes on the quick upward curve of colonial exports and revenues which – with interruptions – we have seen in the last thirty years. But this was mainly due to two things. Firstly, to peasant farmers in areas favoured by climate and transport all planting out on their little farms an extra patch of cotton, cocoa, rubber, or ground-nuts. Secondly, to the building of roads and railways to transport the produce. (But the curve flattens out when the limits of the land or of the family labour are reached.) Thirdly, the increase was due to European capital coming in and starting large-scale enterprises – plantations or mines. These might expand more quickly, but in Africa – though not in the West Indies – the curve again flattens out in face of a growing shortage of the man-power that can be taken from the native areas. And do not let us forget that even if we do succeed in stimulating the production of a great deal more food, a lot of it ought to be eaten by the population themselves if malnutrition and all its attendant diseases are to be overcome.

In all this, you will observe, I am looking at the purely internal difficulties of economic development. Once you have solved all these you have still to consider the external problem of finding remunerative, and above all steady, prices for colonial products in all the dislocation of trade and currency which affect the world today. But that problem I can do no more than raise and leave to your consideration.

There, then, you have some of the difficulties in the way of the economic side of colonial development. What of the political aspect? And how does it tie-up with the economic? At first sight the way forward seems easier here. The colonial peoples are pressing for self-government and it appears from all our official statements, and especially those of our present Secretary of State, that that is exactly what we want to give them. Here, indeed, except for the United States, our policy as compared with that of other colonial powers has long been uniquely favourable to the colonies. It is only in very recent years that the other European empires began to think about any kind of autonomy for their colonies, even as an ultimate goal – and some of them have still got quite a different end in view. But with us this goal was implicit in our history. Following our experience of emancipating the white colonies, we went on to grant self-government to the relatively large, advanced and civilized dependencies which I hope I shall not cause offence by calling 'brown'. Now, logically, we have begun – I think as concerns the near future we only began about ten years ago – to think of extending this liberal policy to the black colonies – those mainly of the Negro race. Again – I hope there is no offence in my using the word 'black'.

What are the prospects for this policy? Put into political terms there are four chief obstacles to the achievement of early and effective self-government. Firstly there are those primitive or retarded conditions –

it is almost impossible to state this inescapable fact in words that do not offend – which mean that the mass of the people are still too ignorant, too unaware of the purposes and practice of modern or even large-scale government to be able to play their part as full citizens, while the educated minority – which *is* there – is still too small to carry all the responsibilities entailed or to leaven the lump politically at least in the immediate future though they will do it eventually.

Secondly, there is not sufficient unity upon which to build a democratic government. This lack of unity is of two kinds. There is the fact that these small tribes and groups never had any unity in the past, and have to build it up. And there is the much more difficult kind of disunity made by deep cleavages of race, religion or culture – or all three together. Such cleavages divide some of the West Indies, and several colonies, for example, Kenya and Northern Rhodesia, Nigeria, Malaya and Fiji. Some of these colonies have attained more rapid economic development through the immigration of economically more competent people – British, Chinese or Indians – at the cost of losing their homogeneity. The third obstacle is that there are a number of colonies which are so inconsiderable in size, numbers and resources that it is impossible to imagine their attaining anything more than a limited internal self-government, and even in that sphere they may remain very heavily dependent upon financial and other help. Fourthly, there is that immense task of economic development, which we have been talking about, without which most of the colonies cannot become reasonably self-supporting communities.

It is here that the themes of our discussion, the economic and the political, come together. The so-called welfare state of today, even in a social democracy like Britain, now controls almost the whole life of society; it runs the major utilities and industries; it manages and allocates the entire national income and it applies science and the art of administration to the betterment of the standard of living – the golden calf of the modern world. And in order to do all this it employs a vast army of general administrative officials and another army of highly trained experts. And do not think that all these expensive services are simply luxuries for advanced nations. Most colonial societies need them as much or even more, because there is much more to be done and done quickly if they are even to start to catch up with the rest of the world. Indeed the vanguard of all these expert services is already in the colonies, overwhelmed by the vast size of the jobs which face them and clamouring for more recruits.

This leads us to another point. We know all too well in this country what the new welfare state costs in productive effort. And self-government means also an economy which can produce a reasonable and steady revenue, and – if self-government is not to be a mere façade – the people themselves must be able to produce leaders and experts who, with some outside help, perhaps, can run that economy and manage that revenue, and the people ought to be able in some measure to hold those leaders to account for their national housekeeping.

Colonial peoples become very suspicious when anyone belonging to the imperial country lists obstacles in this way because the object so often seems to be to postpone the possibility of self-government to the Greek Kalends. That is certainly not my conclusion. I realize that, here again, the colonies are not uniform. Some of them – two or three of the West Indies, for example, and the Gold Coast – have less of the handicaps in the race for self-government than others; in some, while the majority is backward, racial groups are fully ready to play their part, though this in itself creates new problems. Nor is it possible to wait for some ideal of perfect readiness to be achieved, for complete unity, for universal literacy, but only for the necessary minimum of these conditions. It may certainly be regretted for their own sake that whereas the most initially advanced dependencies had the largest period of apprenticeship to self-government the most backward colonies look like having the shortest. This is because they are reaching it, not as with the older dependencies because of internal growth, but mainly as a result of external influences and pressures which accelerate the movement to self-government.

This brings us to the heart of our dilemma. Political development is in danger of outrunning economic development. There is a moment when the release of energies, the incentives of community pride and self-expression, may outweigh the dangers and difficulties of the plunge into the deep waters of self-government. I do not think that we are arguing this essentially political – even moral – issue: we are doing no more than point out the obstacles which impede development. And both the planners and the colonial leaders should try to assess the effect of early self-government in the colonies upon their needs – the capital, the science and all the skilled services which they so desperately need. Judging by some backward countries which have retained or gained independence, they would find it hard to attract capital or high-grade staff.

We thus reach the conclusion that rapid economic development and rapid political development are to some extent incompatible – to accelerate the one is to slow down the other. A choice has to be made. The circle could be squared only if Britain or the world in general were willing to go on pouring capital into the colonies for very long-term investments, for such objects as public utilities for which there might be a very low return after many years. Or if they were willing to invest heavily in education and other social services for which there would be no return except that of moral satisfaction. But is this immense and patient generosity likely in the present state of the world? If not, can the colonies build up domestic capital, without some discipline or some degree of tutelage?

Britain built up her capital not only by invention and initiative but by the long hours of hard skilled work by the labouring classes and – it must be faced – a low consumption enforced upon the majority of the population by the social system. Russia, abandoning that system and proclaiming equality, is building up her capital by an almost brutal self-denial imposed upon the people by what is probably the most effective autocracy the world has seen. And this autocracy is also used for forcing the rapid education, including the industrial and agricultural training, of a backward peasant population. If this kind of regimen could be extended to deal with the not wholly dissimilar situation in the colonies then, indeed, we might see quick results – of a kind! But this is not our method. Nations must act out of their own experience. Ours has been one of slow growth in civilization for some 2,000 years, with democracy coming only when unity and education were all but complete. It is this slowly-matured democratic system we are offering to the people of the colonies.

We must therefore face the problems that this supremely difficult experiment brings with it. Perhaps, in the context of these talks, the most important and grave is that our policy seems to produce, at least for a period, the maximum of political discontent and, above all, of distrust. The example of our free institutions excites among the first educated minority demands which our civil liberties give them almost complete freedom to express. Then comes the bitter discontent that follows upon the refusal of these first demands. So we get widespread suspicion and distrust which in some places is strangling our efforts to save the people from the ruin which threatens them from eroded land or diseased crops. We get not only the bitter distrust of many – by no means all – the educated leaders who demand self-government, but also of the semi-sophisticated groups. This distrust is, in part, spread by the

AA

more extreme leaders; it is partly due to grievances they cannot rationalize, and it is in part the natural suspicion of the peasant for all that is new and strange. We find this distrust also among the most primitive groups where it may lead to such extreme results as the murder by tribesmen of a British scientist sent to help them because of a belief that he will eat their children. I have myself come upon a forest officer in a remote tribe who was isolated and helpless because the people believed that it was he who was turning himself into the man-eating crocodile which was terrorizing them.

Here, again, regrets are useless: and worse than useless is any sense of grievance. We have to do our best with the situation as it is. And we might remember that it is of our making. We are dealing with societies and individuals in an abnormal condition. But it is we who took the initiative in going into their countries and producing these abnormalities by the sudden imposition of our kind of government and economy. Only, therefore, by the most wise and patient handling of our problem of political development shall we be able to make possible the economic development we have been discussing.

One last word. I have set myself the task of explaining in general terms our obstacles and difficulties. But they do not cover the whole picture, which has many brighter parts in it. The considerations I have talked about do not fill me with despair or even gloom. They are a call to effort since they show that we shall not succeed in this enterprise called 'colonial development' to which we have committed ourselves without much more understanding – not only by officials and experts but by much wider circles – of what this means in the lives of some 70,000,000 people in forty different colonies. It is not simply a matter of altruism – though there is unlimited opportunity for that. This country has solid interests in the colonies – economic and strategic – and it would improve and not embarrass our relationship with them if we defined these frankly and did not talk as if we had all to give and nothing to get. We have other less concrete interests. We want to turn wards into friends who will stay with us when they are free to go away. We want enrichment of our life by contact with them and with their strange and beautiful lands. We want to spread in the world the values which we believe make not only for individual happiness, but for freedom and peace. I believe that our success in colonial development depends upon our ability to make the colonial people believe that these interests are not only ours but are also theirs and that they can best be secured in friendly partnership with us.

Index